SUMMA PUBLICATIONS, INC.

Thomas M. Hines
Publisher

Norris J. Lacy
Editor-in-Chief

EDITORIAL BOARD

Benjamin F. Bart
University of Pittsburgh

William Berg
University of Wisconsin

Germaine Brée
Wake Forest College

Michael Cartwright
McGill University

Hugh M. Davidson
University of Virginia

John D. Erickson
Louisiana State University

Wallace Fowlie
Duke University

James Hamilton
University of Cincinnati

Freeman G. Henry
University of South Carolina

Edouard Morot-Sir
*University of North Carolina
Chapel Hill*

Jerry C. Nash
University of New Orleans

Albert Sonnenfeld
Princeton University

Ronald W. Tobin
*University of California
Santa Barbara*

Philip A. Wadsworth
University of South Carolina

ORDERS:
  Box 20725
  Birmingham, AL 35216

EDITORIAL ADDRESS:
  1904 Countryside
  Lawrence, KS 66044

The Literary Vision of Gabrielle Roy

The Literary Vision of Gabrielle Roy:

An Analysis of Her Works

Paula Gilbert Lewis

Summa Publications
Birmingham, Alabama
1984

To Meredith and Richard

ACKNOWLEDGMENT

I would like to express my appreciation to the Canadian Government, Department of External Affairs, that through its Embassy in Washington, D.C., awarded me a Canadian Studies Faculty and Institutional Research Grant for partial support of the publication of this book.

P.G.L.

Table of Contents

INTRODUCTION

After a brief correspondence with Gabrielle Roy during the spring of 1980, I was invited to visit her on Sunday 29 June 1980 at her summer residence in Petite-Rivière-Saint-François (Charlevoix), about sixty-five miles north of Quebec City. After having passed through this town that consists of one five-mile long street, running along the banks of the Saint Lawrence River, I arrived at her modest home, situated at the top of a hill, surrounded by a large lawn, and overlooking the river. Gabrielle Roy came to greet me and immediately exhibited the sense of warm and open friendship that was to characterize her attitude during my entire visit.

After about fifteen minutes of general conversation, we decided to begin what we both viewed as an informal interview. I then asked her permission to use a tape recorder. Mme Roy stated that in order for her to act naturally, we could not use a machine that would have, in her opinion, created a formal, stilted situation. I had already memorized a long list of questions, although in the normal progression of our ensuing dialogue, Gabrielle Roy herself approached many of these same questions, without my having to introduce a particular subject.

Our conversation included discussions of a multitude of topics, although those dealing with her fiction did predominate. Many of these related statements made by Mme Roy are now incorporated throughout this study.[1] She did, moreover, frequently speak of other writers and their works. Her knowledge of world literature appeared to be extensive, and she often referred to authors and quoted from their works. She stated that she especially loved and had been influenced by numerous Scandinavian writers, as well as by francophone authors. When I asked her which French writers she preferred, read, or viewed as influential upon her own professional growth, she mentioned Pascal, Rousseau, Proust, Colette, Montherlant, Mauriac, and Camus. She also greatly admired Françoise Mallet-Joris and Marguerite Yourcenar.

As for the writers and literature of Quebec, Gabrielle Roy was totally open and articulate in her opinions. Not surprisingly, she spoke highly of Germaine Guèvremont, Félix-Antoine Savard, Ringuet, Alain Grandbois, and Rina Lasnier. She considered herself to be part of a female triumvirate or trio with Anne Hébert and Marie-Claire Blais, both of whose writings she admired. Since Hébert was then—as at present—living in France, Mme Roy saw a more recent trio as consisting of Blais, Antonine Maillet, and herself.

Gabrielle Roy seemed displeased, however, with much of the current literature being published in Quebec. She felt that many modern-day works—and particularly those of the *nouveau roman* style—were no longer a pleasure to read, given their cryptic nature and their lack of a good story. Similarly, Gabrielle Roy viewed much contemporary feminist literature as hermetic and tedious. She felt that many such writers were wasting their talents on their obsessive feminist concerns. Quebec theater was also, in her opinion, in a precarious situation, for plays written in *joual* reached only a small, provincial audience and, not translating well, did not relate to a public outside Quebec. Finally, and most ardently expressed, were Gabrielle Roy's views on current Quebec literature that was oriented toward political matters. Hopeful that this literature, like other contemporary trends, was merely passing through a necessary stage, Mme Roy deeply felt that those authors who were so intensely involved in politics were allowing their political concerns to supersede their literary talents. They should, more traditionally, remain faithful to their original calling.

It was evident that Gabrielle Roy's opinion of the politically involved writers of Quebec stemmed directly from her own firm political views that differed from those of the majority of *Québécois* authors. She was strongly in favor of maintaining the Canadian federation and, therefore, was supportive of the Parti Libéral du Québec, then headed by Claude Ryan. She was vehemently opposed to René Lévesque's Parti Québécois and its stand on sovereignty-association for Quebec. Since our meeting occurred soon after the 20 May 1980 referendum on the issue of sovereignty-association, much of our time was understandably spent in discussing the political events in Quebec, as of the November 1976 victory of the Parti Québécois.

It was clear that Gabrielle Roy was deeply and painfully distressed about these events, for she frequently reiterated her political position and apparently desired to discuss in depth what she continued to see as a stage, as in literature, toward mature self-awareness and confidence on the part of the people of Quebec. Fully cognizant of the fact that her political views were probably causing embarrassment to the majority of Quebec writers who supported the Parti Québécois, Mme Roy still maintained that French-speaking Quebecers did enjoy a good life and were, therefore, being incited by what she called the games both of the government and of the writers in the forefront of this political movement. Whatever the outcome of these events, Gabrielle Roy ironically insisted that Quebec would remain where it was; one could not tow it to France. She would, of course, abide by the will of the majority of the Quebec people. She simply hoped that their wishes would continue to coincide with a strongly unified Canada, along with necessary reforms in the rapports between Ottawa and all the provinces.

The formation of Gabrielle Roy's political views had obviously been marked by her background as a French-speaking Manitoban and by her situation as a writer, greatly removed from the mainstream of Quebec literary circles. She defined her chosen profession, however—as is true for every author—as one predestined to loneliness and solitude. She herself needed this total peace and isolation in order to compose her fiction. In describing her procedure for writing, Mme Roy indicated that she always wrote her first draft quickly, sometimes even with fragmented sentences. She was constantly running after the common threads of her proposed idea. She then spent much time revising a given work. At its completion, however, her job was not yet done, since given the lack of literary agents in Montreal, she often had to fulfill this role herself. More recently, Gabrielle Roy had been aided in this task by François Ricard, the critic and writer who had become one of her close friends.

Despite her desires for solitude in order to pursue her literary projects, Mme Roy was a woman who intensely required the presence of others near her. A proud individual who, as a writer, understandably needed to hear words of praise, she clearly enjoyed talking—extending her love for telling stories from the written to the spoken word. She exuded an extraordinary sense of vibrancy and life, often speaking with gestures and intonations, as if she were on stage.

Yet there was a persistent air of sadness and melancholy, as Gabrielle Roy reflected upon her own words and, at times,

stared out of the window as she conversed. She spoke of all
that she still desired to write and, because of her illnesses, of her
fears of not being able to continue much longer, in particular
during the winter months. She agreed with her gentle literary
creation, M. Saint-Hilaire, that there was never enough time to
finish everything that one desired to do. She was, of course,
pleased with what she had been able to accomplish during her
life, but she would never be entirely satisfied. Gabrielle Roy
appeared to be at the source of her own characters.

Since the late 1930s Gabrielle Roy had been creating these
characters and the world in which they lived with a literary
vision that was distinctly *Québécois* and Canadian but that
was also international in scope. It is, therefore, an analysis
of the diverse and disparate themes, images, and concerns of
Mme Roy's numerous works of fiction that is the goal of this
study. With a descriptive exploration into the writer's world
of children, women, men, couples, and the aging, followed by
a synthesis of Gabrielle Roy's treatment of nature, travel, the
home, memories, dreams, aesthetics, and religion, this book
attempts to present the works and vision of one of French-
speaking Canada's most important authors.

Postscript

As this book was being revised for publication, I learned of the death
of Gabrielle Roy on 13 July 1983 in Quebec City at the age of seventy-four.
It is, therefore, with the deepest admiration of this writer and woman that
I dedicate the following pages to her memory.

NOTES

[1]A more complete and concise account of this interview can now be found in Paula Gilbert Lewis, "The Last of the Great Storytellers: A Visit with Gabrielle Roy," *The French Review*, 55, No. 2 (December 1981), 207-215.   Throughout the following pages, therefore, note references to the personal interview with Gabrielle Roy, 29 June 1980 can now be located in the aforementioned article.

CHAPTER I

Quebec Literature and the Fiction of Gabrielle Roy

In his concise introduction to the literature of Quebec, Laurent Mailhot discusses the origins of this literature first in the writings of New France, that is, from 1534, the date of Jacques Cartier's written account of his first voyage to North America, to 1760, the date of the British conquest of what is now Canada. Mailhot then treats what he considers to be the second phase of these origins in the writings spanning the years 1760 to 1837, the year of the Patriots' Rebellion led by Louis-Joseph Papineau. It was in that same year that Philippe Aubert de Gaspé (fils) published *L'Influence d'un livre,* later entitled *Le Chercheur de trésors,* considered to be the first novel of French-speaking Canada. The subsequent literary period, from 1837 to 1918, is viewed by Mailhot essentially as that of an attempt to define one's history and ideology and to reflect a North American continuation of French Romanticism.[1] The nineteenth century in Quebec, however, did see the birth and development of four types of novels: the historical novel, the novel of adventure, and, especially, *le roman de la terre,* as well as, in 1884, the first psychological novel, *Angéline de Montbrun,* by Laure Conan.

The ties between France and Quebec remained strong, however, especially when, in 1914, a Frenchman, Louis Hémon, published the novel with which most people begin their study of Quebec literature, *Maria Chapdelaine.* This work was to be followed four years later by Quebec's first naturalistic novel, Albert Laberge's *La Scouine.* The 1930s saw the publication of three very popular novels: Claude-Henri Grignon's *Un Homme et son péché* in 1933, the 1937 *Menaud, Maître draveur* by Félix-Antoine Savard, and Ringuet's *Trente Arpents* in 1938. After a tradition of rural novels, the literary depiction of urban life finally appeared in 1944 with *Au pied de la pente douce* by Roger Lemelin. The force of the true urban novel would strike the Quebec public one year later in Gabrielle Roy's *Bonheur d'occasion.*

In 1950, five years after the publication of *Bonheur d'occasion,* Gabrielle Roy published her first collection of short stories, *La Petite Poule d'eau.* It was in that same year that Anne Hébert's powerful collection of short stories, *Le Torrent,* appeared. Prior to the 1950s, Quebec had not had a strong tradition of this literary genre. Laberge, Ringuet, and Lemelin had written some novellas, but these works were certainly not as well known as the previously mentioned novels. The publication in 1944 of Yves Thériault's *Contes pour un homme seul* heralded the first major collection of this genre. With Roy and Hébert in 1950 and, especially, with Roy's 1955 *Rue Deschambault,* the short story had finally made its mark on *Québécois* literature.

Even from this briefest of introductions to the origins of the novel and short story in Quebec, it is evident that Gabrielle Roy has had a major impact on the literature of French-speaking Canada. Although she had been publishing journalistic articles since 1938 and short stories since 1939, her important role in the field of *Québécois* literature dates from 1945 and the publication of *Bonheur d'occasion.* Winner of France's coveted Prix Fémina in 1947, translated as a selection of the Literary Guild of America, planned, but with unsuccessful results, to be filmed by Universal Studios with Joan Fontaine in the starring role, and, finally, translated into at least eight languages, this work is often described as Quebec's first "modern" novel. It is certainly considered to be a classic of *Québécois* literature.[2]

Since the publication of *Bonheur d'occasion,* Gabrielle Roy has continued to dominate the literary scene in Quebec. She has written three additional novels, one of which, *La Rivière sans repos,* was published along with three short stories.[3] Six collections of short stories have also appeared, as well as a recent compilation of some of her earlier journalistic writings and essays. She has, in addition, published two stories for children, the second one in honor of the International Year of the Child in 1979. Despite her determination to maintain a distance from the literary circles of Quebec and, in particular, despite her lack of an overt role in the contemporary political issues facing her province and country, Gabrielle Roy has remained one of the best known authors of francophone Canada. Her reputation both in French and English-speaking Canada, as well as her increasing international renown, have offered her a well-deserved, although still modest, place in the annals of world literature.

It was, perhaps, Roy's shying away from any direct involvement in the fervent literary activities of Quebec that caused the wide appeal of her fiction. D. G. Jones, in his study of themes and images in Canadian literature, predominantly English but, at times, French, describes the latter as exhibiting a sense of exile, a "garrison mentality" that reflects a reaction to a hostile North American environment. According to Jones, many writers of francophone Canada have reinforced this mentality by the use of spiritual weapons such as detachment, mortification, and renunciation. They have tended to be "haunted by the sterility of an overly ascetic order resulting from a complete withdrawal from life." This withdrawal from present reality into the ideal has taken the form of a world of the past, in the French Régime or in childhood, of a world of memory and dream, or of a world of religious and aesthetic ideals. Such ideals, however, have often been sterile. Only more recently, believes Jones, has a generation of younger writers in Quebec rejected this "garrison mentality" and moved toward action and the outside world, toward a true voice of the land.[4]

Jones then states in his critique that Gabrielle Roy, although of francophone Canada, arrived at this healthier point of view early in her career and "without having to go through the same painful disengagement from an oppressive garrison mentality that typifies so many writers in Quebec." Such an unusual attitude for a French-speaking Canadian author stems from the fact that Roy was born in Manitoba and not in Quebec. For this reason, plus her literary talent, her works have all been translated into English and have been highly regarded in English-speaking Canada. She has taken her place in Canadian literature, states Jones, because "the problems she explores, the way in which she resolves them and her over-all vision of life place her within the same imaginative world as that inhabited by the English-speaking writers. . . . She speaks for Canadians, both English and French."[5]

Gabrielle Roy was, in fact, more French-Canadian than *Québécois.* Born and raised in Saint-Boniface, Manitoba, she chose to live in Quebec for more than thirty years, but she retained her character of a French-speaking Canadian rather than of a Quebecer. Several critics of her works have recognized this important aspect of her fiction and have seen her both as a

Manitoban, that is, as an *étrangère*, and as a *Québécoise*. But rather than analyzing Roy's works as a Canadian, these same critics have preferred to label them as internationalist, universal, and humanistic. Roy has been seen as speaking for the human condition, as being involved in truth rather than in politics.[6] Once again, the works of Gabrielle Roy belong to world literature.

But despite these accurate assessments of Roy by the aforementioned critics, she must still be viewed as a writer of French-speaking Canada. She had to have been influenced by her stay in Quebec, and the human nature that she describes in her works has been particularized by the character of those around her, the *Québécois*. Many of the traditional themes of the literature of Quebec have been treated by Roy in her fiction: the myth of the large family, of maternity as duty, of Christian charity, goodness, and sacrifice, of a love for the land, of a call to the North. In many instances, Roy's characters have painfully demonstrated the failure of these myths. They have, in the final analysis, portrayed the great solitude of the French-speaking Canadian, of the inadapted *Québécois*. If D. G. Jones can state that, unlike the typical writer of francophone Canada, Gabrielle Roy disengaged herself from an oppressive "garrison mentality" and, therefore, avoided the pitfalls of barren ideals in the past or in visions of the future, one can also argue that Roy's characters do often resort to a past world of memories and dreams or to an ideal aesthetic future. They do not reject the present world of reality, but they do often seek escape from it. The fictional world of Gabrielle Roy is universal, but it is also that inhabited by the French-speaking Canadian. It is, in short, diverse.

It is, indeed, important and significant for critics to try to classify a given author and her works and, in this particular instance, to attempt to analyze Gabrielle Roy's fictional world in its rapports with *Québécois* and Canadian literature. Equally revealing, however, is the writer's own opinion of and attitude toward such matters. In a long interview in June 1980, Roy fully discussed both her actual and desired place within the realms of provincial, national, and international literatures. Her remarks were not at all surprising. It was the increasing intensity of her feelings that was the most noteworthy.

Almost as a leitmotif throughout this six-hour interview, Roy's deep desire to reach as large a reading public as possible and as diverse an audience in as many countries as possible was frequently expressed. She proudly felt that both she and her fiction were difficult to classify, for her works were usually included in anthologies of *Québécois,* Western Canadian, and Canadian literature. The appeal of her fiction thus coincided with her literary goals, as she moved toward her dream first of rising above any appellation of being a *Québécois,* French-Canadian, or Canadian writer, names that she viewed as unimportant, and then of gaining a reputation as an author of world literature.[7]

In order to achieve this primary goal of recognition both inside and outside Canada, Roy realized that her works had to be made available and comprehensible to varied publics. It was for this reason that she was especially pleased about the translations of her fiction. She herself worked closely with her English translator, and the positive result of this association was an English-language edition faithful to the original French version. Her works were, in addition, usually published in English within a year of their initial publication date, thereby successfully maintaining her popularity in anglophone Canada. It was precisely because of this immediacy of a dual language publication, and in one instance a simultaneous publication, that Roy sensed some resentment on the part of francophone Canadians who desired to claim her for their own. Roy's reaction to such an attitude was one of bitterness.[8]

Deep feelings of bitterness, mixed with cynical but painful detachment, also characterized Gabrielle Roy's attitude toward the treatment of her by other *Québécois,* especially by writers and critics. In an interview with Mireille Dansereau, published in an issue of *The French Review* devoted to Quebec, the film maker referred to Gabrielle Roy as "une Québécoise du Manitoba qui regarde le Québec," as one who projects "le regard des autres sur nous." When Roy was informed of this statement, she appeared to be annoyed but not surprised. She stated that she had usually been labelled as "une Manitobaine qui parle français," as "un Canadienne-française du Manitoba," or as "une Manitobaine qui habite au Québec." She insisted however, upon the fact that her family roots were in Quebec, since her mother had been born there, and that she had voluntarily chosen to live in the province for over thirty years. Despite all of this, Roy felt that she had never been fully accepted by the *Québécois,* never considered as one of them. Somewhat reluctantly, she had relinquished all attempts at belonging.[9]

It was, however, an underlying tone of bitterness that revealed the complexity of Gabrielle Roy's attitude toward her situation both as an inhabitant and as a writer of Quebec. On two occasions during this 1980 interview, she repeated these words about *Québécois* literary circles: "They don't know what to do with me; they can't deny me or ignore me; and yet I am not a part of them." Roy viewed herself as being different from other Quebec authors for several previously mentioned reasons. She was Manitoban and not *Québécoise* by birth. She not only refused to be a political writer or to become involved in the current political situation in Quebec, but she firmly supported the Parti Libéral du Québec, was against the government of the Parti Québécois, and believed in the unity of Canada, rather than in the status of sovereignty-association for Quebec. In addition, despite the fact that she saw herself as part of a female triumvirate, originally with Anne Hébert and Marie-Claire Blais, and now with Blais and Antonine Maillet, Roy felt that her fiction represented a tendency that was counter to that of current literary trends. She preferred to write what she saw as traditional novels and short stories and scorned all "new" tendencies in literature. Finally, she did not espouse in her works what she labelled as extreme feminist causes and preferred to remain "liberated" but more traditional in her views on and depiction of female characters.[10]

Roy's statement quoted above concerning her literary status in Quebec, therefore, did suggest, as her tone clearly indicated, a mixture of bitterness, amusement, sarcasm, and nostalgia. Its irony can be found, however, in the fact that precisely because she did not become too closely associated with any of the typically *Québécois* concerns in literature, she managed to rise above a simple national, or rather provincial, classification. Roy's increasing obsession with her international reputation as a writer and her intense desire to reach as wide and as diverse a public as possible corresponded, in addition, to her own creation of a fictional world that represents all of humanity.

This diversity inherent in Roy's fiction or, more specifically, the author's sensitive awareness of the diversity of people and of the world around her, stems directly from her years as a journalist. In 1938 during a lengthy stay in Europe, first in London and then in France, Gabrielle Roy began to write articles about her travel experiences for *La Liberté et Le Patriote* of Winnipeg and for *Le Devoir* of Montreal. In the same year she published her first article about Canada in the Parisian journal, *Je suis partout.* In 1939 *Le Jour* of Montreal began publishing numerous articles by Roy concerning aspects of life in London, Paris, and Montreal. But it is especially as of 1940, after her return to Quebec and as of her association with the journal, *Le Bulletin des Agriculteurs,* that Roy began writing the articles that most deeply influenced her maturing ability as a writer and that can be seen as the most important journalistic precursors to her later fiction.[11]

From November 1940 to November 1945 Gabrielle Roy travelled throughout the Province of Quebec, as well as throughout Canada, researching and writing articles about the varied facets of life in Quebec and, most importantly, about the diverse immigrant groups that had settled in Canada. This growing interest in the struggles and determination of Canadian immigrants profoundly affected Roy's humanitarian consciousness and remained a constant theme in her later writings. Secondly, four articles were published in *Le Bulletin des Agriculteurs* in 1941 in which the future author of *Bonheur d'occasion* sensitively and accurately described the city of Montreal. In 1942 there appeared a journalistic article that, as a third important category of her reporting, pointed toward a continued concern of Roy in her fiction: the dedication and plight of the schoolteacher in rural Canada, a profession that Roy herself had practiced from 1929 to 1937.[12]

Despite the numerous studies that have been written on the works of Gabrielle Roy, only three critics, all of them major, have recognized the importance of these journalistic writings. All three also appear to agree on their fundamental tone. The only sign of disillusionment in these otherwise realistic but optimistic articles occurs in Roy's depiction of the city as a place where material wealth has become too important and where as sense of uneasiness reigns. Her assessment of industrialization, however, remains positive, since she views industrial progress as a necessity and as a promise for a better future. Although she openly accepts this inevitable industrial world, Roy also underscores the need of a return, if only temporary, to the land. Throughout these early articles, pro-rural values are emphasized, a love of and tenderness for the land are evident, and a desired balance, therefore, between industry and agriculture is expressed. The country, and that of Quebec in particular, is seen as the promised land where communication among different peoples can thrive.[13]

On this land diverse ethnic groups, in the movement of colonization, maintain their distinct cultures but work together toward a collective society of participation and equality. During this period in her life, Gabrielle Roy leaned toward a form of Communism or, rather, Christian Socialism in which she envisioned the workers of the land in harmony both with the rhythm of the universe and with a universal collectivity. Her concerns already extended both to human relationships and to the natural world. She consistently expressed her faith in people, her belief in a society working toward self-construction, and her optimistic hope for the betterment of the world.[14] In her future fiction, Roy would retain these same hopes, but some of her optimism would wane.

If Gabrielle Roy's journalistic writings reflect her early views of society and the world, some of them also prefigure the later development of her fictional characters. In "De turbulents chercheurs de paix," for example, Roy writes about the Russian immigrants, the Doukhobors, who appear later in "Le Puits de Dunrea" and "La Vallée Houdou." In this same article can be seen Masha who spends her life planting flowers. She is the fore-runner of Martha of "Un Jardin au bout du monde." Martha's Ukraine, transplanted to the Canadian plains, also appears in the early "Petite Ukraine" where, in addition, one meets "celui que l'on retrouve dans tous les hameaux, dans tous les bourgs de l'Ouest, celui qui paraît toujours s'ennuyer et ne jamais se décourager, celui que partout on nomme Charlie: le restauranteur chinois." One meets, in effect, in 1943, Sam Lee Wong of the 1975 "Où iras-tu Sam Lee Wong?"[15]

Prior to 1945, however, Gabrielle Roy did not practice her chosen vocation merely by working as a journalist. In 1939 appeared her first short story, "La Conversion des O'Connor," the first of a group of early short stories published essentially in *La Revue Moderne* and in *Le Bulletin des Agriculteurs* until 1948. Even more than in her articles, many of Roy's early short stories can be viewed as precursors of her major works of fiction. Her four articles on Montreal had clearly described the physical aspects of that city, but "Le Joli Miracle" depicts the problems of poverty in the urban metropolis, while "La Sonate à l'Aurore" concerns the love and marriage that can be destroyed by war. Both short stories prefigure *Bonheur d'occasion.* Three early short stories, "Feuilles mortes," "La

Justice en Danaca et ailleurs," and "Sécurité," all appear to be forerunners of the 1954 *Alexandre Chenevert* and its atmosphere of emprisonment and absurdity. These same three stories also offer an additional response to the conclusion of *Bonheur d'occasion:* that it is useless to go to war, for world conflicts only feed upon exploitation, alienation, and, once again, absurdity.[16]

Other early short stories can be interpreted in a similar manner. In "Le Joli Miracle" the musician, Loubka, understands the duty of a writer to create, while she jealously views this profession alone as offering independence. One immediately thinks of Roy's "La Voix des étangs" of *Rue Deschambault.* Similarly, the difficulty of writing and the agony of the writer before a creative void are expressed in "La Source au désert," as they will be later in *La Montagne secrète.* This same short story also prefigures the 1972 *Cet Eté qui chantait,* with an early emphasis on nature and the portrayal of the 1946 heroine, Anne, as sensitively communing with the natural world. Gabrielle Roy's increasing interest in the world of children does culminate in the 1977 *Ces Enfants de ma vie* but originated in the 1940 "Gérard le pirate." And finally, if Bédette of "La Grande Voyageuse" is a precursor of Roy's later obsessive nomads, the hero of "Un Noël en route" is the brother of Gustave of "Un Vagabond frappe à notre porte."[17]

Gabrielle Roy's early short stories, therefore, are essential to a complete understanding of her major works of fiction, but it is these later works that do deserve the greatest amount of critical attention. Analyzing four novels, six collections of short stories, six additional short stories, and two childrens' tales can be a difficult task, and, as a result, critics have attempted to divide Roy's major works into chronological periods, categories based upon literary genres, or groups stimulated by either a semi-autobiographical or purely fictional idea. All such divisions are valid but usually imcomplete.

François Ricard elects to divide Roy's works into three chronological periods. The first period, including *Bonheur d'occasion, La Petite Poule d'eau,* and *Alexandre Chenevert,* essentially expresses a feeling of exile and pessimism, or, more precisely, a triptych with suffering and dispossession in the two outer panels and peace at the center. Roy's second period encompasses *Rue Deschambault, La Montagne secrète,* and *La Route d'Altamont,* seen by Ricard as a return, a development and deepening of consciousness and need for meditation, and a feeling of harmony and repose. It, too, is a triptych, with outer panels of reconciliation and an inner panel of exile and separation. *La Rivière sans repos* and *Cet Eté qui chantait* comprise the third period, subsequent to 1966, and reflect a more serene and peaceful compassion by the mature writer toward humanity.[18] Although this profound sensitivity toward the world and a sincere love for all people do continue with poignancy in *Un Jardin au bout du monde* and in *Ces Enfants de ma vie,* the peace and serenity that Ricard discovers in what he defines as Roy's third period are subtly accompanied by an underlying sense of sadness and solitude. Here there are no distinct panels of joy and sorrow.

In addition to his chronological divisions, Ricard also discerns differences in Roy's works dependent upon their structure as novels or short stories. Novels depict the chaos of reality in its anxiety and uneasiness, while short stories usually portray the tranquility of utopia with its inner sense of sweetness and repose. This general definition does appear to be more valid for Gabrielle Roy's novels than for her short stories, for the latter are certainly not always utopian nor especially tranquil. More importantly, however, is the fact that Roy herself saw little distinction between the novel and the short story, an opinion that will be consistently confirmed below in the brief discussion of the structure of her varied works. Since her greatest literary desire was simply to tell stories, she felt that some tales merely took longer to recount. In her opinion, all her works were, therefore, novelistic in nature because in all of them, one finds common threads throughout: themes, characters, and concerns. Some publishers, critics, and readers have had difficulty with this concept of the structure of her works. It was for this reason, in fact, that the English-language edition of *La Rivière sans repos* was published without the "Nouvelles esquimaudes."[19]

A third type of convenient divison for Roy's major works is based upon distinctions between semi-autobiography and fiction. Réjean Robidoux sees *Rue Deschambault, La Route d'Altamont,* and *Cet Eté qui chantait* as "mémoires romancées," to which one must add *Ces Enfants de ma vie.* He views *La Montagne secrète* and *La Rivière sans repos* as allegories. André Brochu, however, treats *La Montagne secrète* as semi-autobiographical, a continuation of *Rue Deschambault.* In addition,

Alexandre Chenevert and "La Voix des étangs" of *Rue Deschambault* lead to *La Montagne secrète* and its queries on the roles
of art and the artist.[20]   Arguments can also be made that Roy's
works should be divided according to ther domination by female
or male characters or according to their geographic location
in an urban or rural setting.   All such divisions are plausible,
and all are inherently limited.

Whether or not one prefers to place Gabrielle Roy's major
works into distinct categories, one can still approach her individual works in reference first to their structure and then to their
predominant nature or tone, both as an introduction into Roy's
fictional world.   Conceived initially as a short story, the 1945
Bonheur d'occasion still retains a concentration of space and
time that is characteristic of the shorter literary genre.   Its thirty-
three chapters, each as a unity or the whole as a series of individual theatrical vignettes, can be chronologically divided into eight
groups or into four larger sections.   These larger parts appear
to follow a curve, rising and falling, or disintegrating, as the
action progresses toward the typically Royan open conclusion
of the novel.   The general tone of the work is one of a struggle
against poverty, a struggle in which the reader tends to take
part.[21]

Marc Gagné uses the same symbol of the curve, as mentioned above for the novel, to describe the consistent structure
of Gabrielle Roy's collections of short stories.   François Ricard,
however, sees the 1950 *La Petite Poule d'eau*, Roy's first such
collection, more as the opposite of *Bonheur d'occasion:* three
stories novelistically linked by one character, Luzina, and continuously ascending, once again, toward an open conclusion.
Its overall optimistic and utopian nature can be seen to describe
the three dimensions of one being, with Luzina's "vacation"
as the physical, the school as the intellectual, and the priest as
the spiritual, each facet's corresponding to one story.[22]

If *Bonheur d'occasion* retains certain characteristics of
the short story in its concentration and curve-like structure,
the 1954 novel, *Alexandre Chenevert*, can also be described, in
one sense, as a long novella, centered around one main character.   Like Roy's previous work, this novel is divided into three
distinct parts.   Part I, relating essentially the physical aspect
of the hero's life in an urban setting, corresponds to *Bonheur
d'occasion.*   Part II, with Alexandre's attempts to communicate
in writing, can, in part, describe the intellectual and, therefore,

correspond to the central story of *La Petite Poule d'eau* and, with its utopian rural setting, to the entire previous work. In its spiritual overtones, this section also leads to Part III. This concluding section returns to the city, deals with both the physical and the spiritual, resolves the crisis in death, but, as always, remains open at the end, with a sense of hope for the future.[23]

As with the two previous works, the structure of the 1955 collection of short stories, *Rue Deschambault,* is characterized by a novelistic unity of action, revolving around one central character or, more precisely, of one conscience, that of Christine. The work is presented almost as a journal, a series of recollections that document the spiritual biography of the narrator, on the road toward self-discovery and self-acceptance.[24] This same need for introspection continues in the 1961 novel, *La Montagne secrète,* Roy's most symbolic, although often too didactic work. It, too, is divided into three parts, all of which are linked by one male character, Pierre, and the second of which, the discovery of one's ideal in the form of a resplendent mountain, corresponds to the second part of *Alexandre Chenevert* and its ideal at Lac Vert. *La Montagne secrète* is also similar to *Rue Deschambault* in that it relates an inner quest, a search for one's own identity, here equated with the realm of aesthetics.[25] Unlike the collection of short stories, however, Pierre's journey is marked by constant dissatisfaction, solitude, and sense of failure. His moments of heightened joy are usually counteracted by total disillusionment.

The four stories comprising the 1966 *La Route d'Altamont* continue both the semi-autobiographical tales of *Rue Deschambault* and the introspective searches of the latter work and of *La Montagne secrète.* Unified, once again, by the sole consciousness of the narrator-character, Christine, this collection recounts a journey not only toward self-understanding but also toward a fuller and more poignant comprehension of the links in time, especially of the links among generations.[26] Poignancy turns to *malaise* and anxiety in the 1970 *La Rivière sans repos,* both in the three preparatory short stories or prologue and in the novel that follows. It is the constant antagonism between White and Eskimo cultures that creates an atmosphere of tension and fear throughout the work. But the tone of *La Rivière sans repos* is equally characterized by an extreme sensitivity toward the natural world, by a feeling of a close rapport with an often hostile but fragile nature.[27]

The dream-like qualities of utopia already created in *La Petite Poule d'eau* and at Lac Vert in *Alexandre Chenevert* and the closeness with nature fully explored in *La Rivière sans repos* culminate in the 1972 collection of short stories, *Cet Eté qui chantait.* With a structure unified both by a sensitive narrator and by an awakened nature in summer, these tales also suggest a lingering sense of sadness at the realization of the temporary status of such a beautiful world. This increasing feeling of sorrow, rather than the more vivid and absurd tragedies evident in some of Roy's earlier works, becomes even more touching in the 1975 short stories of *Un Jardin au bout du monde.* The four stories of this collection are quite distinct, perhaps because two of them were written in the 1940s, but all of them seem to express a similar concern and, therefore, tone: the almost desperate need to create bonds either with other people or, especially, with nature.[28]

Such bonds are initially formed during childhood but often suffer in light of possible destruction when, in adolescence, one is on the solitary threshold of adulthood. This is the message of *Ces Enfants de ma vie,* the collection of six short stories published in 1977. With the unity that is typical of all of Roy's collections of short stories, this work actually recounts six stages in the lives of two beings: a young schoolteacher and a composite young boy who passes from childhood through adolescence. *Ces Enfants de ma vie* returns Gabrielle Roy to her deep love for children, evidenced, as well, in the publication of the two stories for children, the previously composed *Ma Vache Bossie* in 1976 and *Courte-Queue* in 1979, and continues the author's need to relate semi-fictional events from her past.[29]

It is apparent that the reader can sense the presence of Roy as the author in her semi-autobiographical works. But this presence can also be felt in her purely fictional creations. It has been noted that Gabrielle Roy intervenes in most of her creative works essentially because of her sincere affection and compassion for her own characters. Such an intervention, however, has also been labelled an interference or an intrusion, for, as an all-knowing author, Roy sometimes too carefully directs the outcome of events and the development of her characters. If this omniscience can even be considered a flaw in her technique, however, it occurs primarily in her earlier works. Gabrielle Roy is often, in addition, a realistic or even a naturalistic writer. Like the great writers of these schools in nineteenth-century France, she remains a realistic observer but, with her sense of creative imagination, cannot resist the opportunity to interject her opinion and, especially, her emotions. She often analyzes or reflects upon what has just occurred in her works, and, with a sometimes ironic but always sympathetic tone, she presents her readers with her vision of the world.[30]

It is precisely Roy's vision of that world around her, as well as the creation of her own literary universe, that form the focus of this study. Before delving into the individual texts that comprise that universe and in which that vision is reflected, however, it would be useful to identify some of the major themes that appear throughout Roy's fiction or, more specifically, some of the common threads that connect all of her works. There have been obvious modifications in the author's view of the outside world and a distinct progression in the development of her fictional world, but certain concerns and goals have remained constant, providing a continuous link from 1939 to the present day.

Several critics have noted that underlying all of Gabrielle Roy's works and, especially, the lives of all of her characters is the search for happiness. Like Stendhal's "chasse au bonheur," the Royan quest assumes many forms as it tries to attain satisfaction. Characters look for happiness in love, human recognition, and, even, the absolute. Solutions are sought in youth, escapism, women, and artistic creation. And, increasingly, the search for happiness is oriented toward oneself, toward self-understanding and self-acceptance prior to an understanding and an acceptance of others.[31]

Inherent in such an obsessive search are numerous conflicts that cause anxiety. Royan characters inevitably experience, for example, suffering as they try to discover and then maintain a relationship based upon love. Human interaction is of the utmost importance, but a persistent and often desired solitude accompanies these driven individuals. They will also create intimate rapports with nature and will then discover that this tender or harsh nature is, at times, hostile and, at best, fragile. But they will continue their search.

The characters of Gabrielle Roy will begin their quest in childhood and will continue throughout adulthood and old age, until death. They will search in their environment; they will travel, both in actuality and in memories and dreams. They will long for an ideal aesthetic world and will seek a more natural form of spiritualism. And throughout this "chasse au bonheur," they, as their creator, will maintain both a realistic and a tragic vision of their world and their future. But underlying any sense of sorrow will always shine a profound hope and a desire to "s'ouvrir le plus possible et comprendre toujours davantage les êtres les plus cosmopolites, les plus solitaires et relater chaleureusement chaque étape de leur marche à travers le vaste monde."[3][2]

If each of Roy's texts remains open at its conclusion, inviting the next work to commence, her literary universe as a whole stands equally open, inviting its readers to hope and dream optimistically about the future of humanity and the world and beckoning them to work toward common, humanistic goals. It is a universe that has, in this sense, disengaged itself from an oppressive "garrison mentality." Like an increasing number of works of the current literature of Quebec, the fiction of Gabrielle Roy is universal.

NOTES

[1] Laurent Mailhot, *La Littérature québécoise,* Que Sais-Je? No. 1579 (Paris: Presses Universitaires de France, 1974), pp. 9-42.

[2] Gabrielle Roy remained somewhat distressed about the fact that *Bonheur d'occasion* was not filmed and that so much money was wasted upon the preparation for the movie. As for the translations of this novel, Roy was never pleased with the first English-language version. A new translation of *Bonheur d'occasion* appeared in 1980. Personal interview with Gabrielle Roy, 29 June 1980. In March 1982 production began on a new filming of *Bonheur d'occasion,* as a movie directed by Claude Fournier and as a five-part bilingual television series co-produced by the Office National du Film and Radio-Canada. The film received its world premiere at the Moscow Film Festival on 14 July 1983, one day after Gabrielle Roy's death. It was also viewed at the close of the Montreal International Film Festival in August 1983.

[3] These short stories, entitled "Nouvelles esquimaudes," do not

appear in the English edition of *La Rivière sans repos*. The novel, in addition, was also to be filmed in the United States but, once again, without any success. Personal interview with Gabrielle Roy, 29 June 1980.

[4]D. G. Jones, *Butterfly on Rock: A Study of Themes and Images in Canadian Literature* (Toronto: University of Toronto Press, 1971), pp. 9-10.

[5]Jones, p. 10.

[6]John J. Murphy, "Visit with Gabrielle Roy," *Thought: Review of Culture and Idea*, 38, No. 150 (Autumn 1963), 454; Donald Cameron, "Gabrielle Roy: A Bird in the Prison Window," in *Conversations with Canadian Novelists* (Toronto: Macmillan of Canada, 1973), pp. 134-136; François Ricard, *Gabrielle Roy*, Ecrivains canadiens d'aujourd'hui, No. 11 (Montréal: Editions Fides, 1975), pp. 10, 12-15; John Hind-Smith, *Three Voices: The Lives of Margaret Laurence, Gabrielle Roy, and Frederick Philip Groves* (Toronto: Clarke Irwin, 1975), p. 123.

[7]Personal interview with Gabrielle Roy, 29 June 1980.

[8]Personal interview with Gabrielle Roy, 29 June 1980. *La Rivière sans repos* was the work published simultaneously in French and in English. Roy was also frustrated that the literature of Quebec did not sell well in France. As for the United States, her former association with Harcourt Brace ended when the New York publishing firm rejected *La Rivière sans repos*, as not realistically depicting Eskimo life.

[9]Arthur Greenspan, "A propos de *L'Arrache-coeur*: Interview avec Mireille Dansereau," *The French Review*, 53, No. 6 (May 1980), 871; Personal interview with Gabrielle Roy, 29 June 1980.

[10]Personal interview with Gabrielle Roy, 29 June 1980. Given the fact that the above-mentioned issue of *The French Review* was devoted to the culture, language, and literature of Quebec, Gabrielle Roy's picture was originally to be placed on the cover of the journal. Because of a technical error, this picture did not appear. When Roy learned of this, she was delighted about the intention and disappointed at its lack of success. She stated that it would have been wonderful to have seen her picture in the journal, as if as a victory for her, in defiance of the literary circles of Quebec. Personal interview with Gabrielle Roy, 29 June 1980. Her picture did finally appear on the cover of the December 1981 issue of *The French Review*, an issue that contained an account of this interview/visit.

[11]Roy fully recognized the importance of these years of journalism on her formation as a writer. Personal interview with Gabrielle Roy, 29 June 1980.

[12]For a complete listing of these articles, as well as of all of Roy's journalistic articles, see the bibliography in Marc Gagné, *Visages de Gabri-*

elle Roy (Montréal: Librairie Beauchemin Limitée, 1973), pp. 291-297. Some of Roy's articles about the immigrants of Canada were published as a series, "Peuples du Canada," in *Le Bulletin des Agriculteurs* and have been republished as part of Gabrielle Roy, *Fragiles Lumières de la terre: Ecrits divers, 1942-1970,* Collection Prose Entière (Montréal: Les Editions Quinze, 1978). It was François Ricard who convinced Roy to republish these articles. Personal interview with Gabrielle Roy, 29 June 1980. The articles on Montreal are: Gabrielle Roy, "Les Deux Saint-Laurent," *Le Bulletin des Agriculteurs,* 37, No. 6 (juin 1941), 8, 9, 37, 40; "Est-Ouest," *Le Bulletin des Agriculteurs,* 37, No. 7 (juillet 1941), 9, 25-28; "Du port aux banques," *Le Bulletin des Agriculteurs,* 37, No. 8 (août 1941), 11, 32-33; "Après trois cents ans," *Le Bulletin des Agriculteurs,* 37, No. 9 (septembre 1941), 9, 37-39. The article concerning school teachers is: Gabrielle Roy, "Pitié pour les institutrices," *Le Bulletin des Agriculteurs,* 38, No. 3 (mars 1942), 7, 45-46.

[13] Gagné, pp. 27-42; Ricard, pp. 46-47; Paul Socken, "Gabrielle Roy as a Journalist," *Canadian Modern Language Review,* 30, No. 2 (January 1974), 96-100.

[14] Roy's sister, Marie-Anna, also mentions this adherence to Communism in *Le Miroir du passé,* Collection Littérature d'Amérique (Montréal: Editions Québec/Amérique, 1979), p. 142.

[15] Gabrielle Roy, "De turbulents chercheurs de paix," in *Fragiles Lumières de la terre,* pp. 33-43. This article originally appeared in *Le Bulletin des Agriculteurs,* 38, No. 12 (décembre 1942), 10, 39-40. See also Gabrielle Roy, "Le Puits de Dunrea," in *Rue Deschambault* (1955; rpt. Montréal: Librairie Beauchemin Limitée, 1974), pp. 141-161; Gabrielle Roy, "La Vallée Houdou," in *Un Jardin au bout du monde* (Montréal: Librairie Beauchemin Limitée, 1975), pp. 133-149; "Un Jardin au bout du monde," in *Un Jardin au bout du monde,* pp. 153-217. "La Vallée Houdou" was originally published in *Amérique Française* (février 1945), pp. 4-10. Gabrielle Roy, "Petite Ukraine," in *Fragiles Lumières de la terre,* pp. 77-86 and especially p. 84. This article originally appeared as "Ukraine" in *Le Bulletin des Agriculteurs,* 39, No. 4 (avril 1943), 8, 43-45. See also Roy, "Où iras-tu Sam Lee Wong?," in *Un Jardin au bout du monde,* pp. 61-130.

[16] Gabrielle Roy, "La Conversion des O'Connor," *La Revue Moderne,* 21, No. 5 (septembre 1939), 4-5, 32-33; "Le Joli Miracle," *Le Bulletin des Agriculteurs,* 26, No. 12 (décembre 1940), 8, 29-30; "La Sonate à l'aurore," *La Revue Moderne,* 22, No, 11 (mars 1941), 9, 10, 35-37. Gabrielle Roy, "Feuilles mortes," *La Revue de Paris,* 56e année, No. 1 (janvier 1948), pp. 46-55; "La Justice en Danaca et ailleurs," in *Les Oeuvres libres* (Paris: Librairie Arthène Fayard, N.S. No. 23, 1948), pp. 163-180;

"Sécurité," *La Revue Moderne,* 29, No. 11 (mars 1948), 12, 13, 66, 68, 69; Ricard, pp. 76-78. "Sécurité" was first published in English as "Security," *Maclean's,* 15 September 1947, pp. 20-21, 36, 39. Roy herself had a very low opinion of her early short stories and would have liked someone, in fact, to collect and burn them. She did admit, however, that some of them did contain future literary concerns and themes and could be seen as precursors, in particular, of *Alexandre Chenevert.* Personal interview with Gabrielle Roy, 29 June 1980.

[17] Roy, "Le Joli Miracle," p. 30; Gabrielle Roy, "La Source au désert," *Le Bulletin des Agriculteurs,* 42, No. 10 (octobre 1946), 42, 32, 35, 36; "Gerard le pirate," *La Revue Moderne,* 22, No. 1 (mai 1940), 5, 37-39; "La Grande Voyageuse," *La Revue Moderne,* 24, No. 1 (mai 1942), 12, 13, 27-30; "Un Noël en route," *La Revue Moderne,* 22, No. 8 (décembre 1940), 8, 32-34. "Un Vagabond frappe à notre porte," published in 1975 as part of *Un Jardin au bout du monde,* originally appeared in *Amérique Française* (janvier 1946), pp. 29-51.

[18] Ricard, pp. 51, 88-90, 125, 128, 152-153. Ricard does not specifically use the image of a triptych.

[19] Ricard, pp. 117-119; Personal interview with Gabrielle Roy, 29 June 1980.

[20] Réjean Robidoux, "Le Roman et la recherche du sens de la vie: Vocation: Ecrivain," in *Mélanges de civilisation canadienne-française offerts au professeur Paul Wyczynski,* ed. Pierre Savard, Cahiers du Centre de Recherche en civilisation canadienne-française, No. 10 (Ottawa: Editions de l'Université d'Ottawa, 1977), p. 232; André Brochu, "Gabrielle Roy," Notes from course on author, Université de Montréal, Printemps 1978, taken by one of his students.

[21] Gabrielle Roy, *Bonheur d'occasion* (1945; rpt. Montréal: Librairie Beauchemin Limitée, 1973); Ricard, pp. 58-62. Brochu, in "Gabrielle Roy," describes the novel as an ellipse. Monique Genuist sees *Bonheur d'occasion* as classical theater, obeying the three unities, and with the secondary characters as the Greek chorus. See *La Création romanesque chez Gabrielle Roy* (Montréal: Le Cercle du Livre de France, 1966), pp. 111-112.

[22] Gabrielle Roy, *La Petite Poule d'eau* (1950; rpt. Montréal: Librairie Beauchemin Limitée, 1970); Marc Gagné, *"La Rivière sans repos* de Gabrielle Roy: Etude mythocritique incluant 'Voyage en Ungava' (extraits) par Gabrielle Roy," *Revue de l'Université d'Ottawa,* 46, No. 1 (janvier-mars 1976), 98; Ricard, pp. 69-74; Annette Saint-Pierre, *Gabrielle Roy: Sous le signe du rêve* (Saint-Boniface, Manitoba: Editions du Blé, 1975), p. 40.

[23] Gabrielle Roy, *Alexandre Chenevert* (1954; rpt. Montréal: Beau-

chemin, 1973); Saint-Pierre, p. 67. Genuist sees *Alexandre Chenevert* as a classical tragedy in five acts. See Genuist, pp. 113-115.

[24]Roy, *Rue Deschambault;* Ricard, pp. 95-97; Genuist, p. 108. It is precisely this focus on self-discovery and self-acceptance that produces a serious and, at times, melancholy tone to this work. For this reason, Roy decided not to include the happier *Ma Vache Bossie,* originally written for *Rue Deschambault* and later published separately. Personal interview with Gabrielle Roy, 29 June 1980.

[25]Gabrielle Roy, *La Montagne secrète* (1961; rpt. Montréal: Librairie Beauchemin, 1974); Ricard, pp. 101-106. Genuist describes this novel as a prose poem. See Genuist, p. 115.

[26]Gabrielle Roy, *La Route d'Altamont,* Collection L'Arbre, No. 10 (Montréal: Editions HMH, 1966). "Le Vieillard et l'enfant" of this collection was also made into a scenario for Radio Canada but never produced. Personal interview with Gabrielle Roy, 29 June 1980.

[27]Gabrielle Roy, *La Rivière sans repos* (Montréal: Librairie Beauchemin Limitée, 1971); Ricard, pp. 132-133, 138.

[28]Gabrielle Roy, *Cet Eté qui chantait* (Québec-Montéal: Les Editions Françaises, 1972); Roy, *Un Jardin au bout du monde.*

[29]Gabrielle Roy, *Ces Enfants de ma vie* (Montréal: Editions Internationales Alain Stanké Ltée, 1977); Gabrielle Roy, *Ma Vache Bossie* (Montréal: Les Editions Leméac, Inc., 1976); Gabrielle Roy, *Courte-Queue* (Montréal: Editions Internationales Alain Stanké Ltée, 1979). Roy's various essays, memoirs, speeches, and interviews will be treated throughout the critical study.

[30]Phyllis Grosskurth, *Gabrielle Roy,* Canadian Writers and Their Works (Toronto: Forum House, 1972), pp. 20-21, 25; Gérard Bessette, *Une Littérature en ébullition* (Montréal: Editions du Jour, 1968), pp. 236, 249-251, 274-277. It is Bessette who objects to this intervention of Roy. The aspect of irony in Roy's works will be more fully treated in Chapter VIII in a discussion of the role of the narrator. As for the label of a Realist or a Naturalist, Roy acknowledged the direct influence of the former school but only the indirect influence of the latter. She is a Naturalist only in that the elements of determinism effect all literature. Personal interview with Gabrielle Roy, 29 June 1980.

[31]Jean-Paul Desrochers, "La Famille dans l'oeuvre de Gabrielle Roy," Thesis Université Laval 1965, pp. 14-19; Michel-Lucien Gaulin, "Le Thème du bonheur dans l'oeuvre de Gabrielle Roy," Thesis Université de Montréal 1961, pp. 11, 29-30; Michel-Lucien Gaulin, "Le Monde romanesque de Roger Lemelin et Gabrielle Roy," in *Le Roman canadien-français :* *Evolution—témoignages—bibliographie,* eds. Paul Wyczynski, Bernard Julien, Jean Ménard, et Réjean Robidoux, Archives des lettres canadiennes, Tome

III (Montréal: Fides, 1977), pp. 143-150.

[32]Thuong Vuong-Riddick, "Aspects du monde de Gabrielle Roy: *La Rivière sans repos* (1970), *Cet Eté qui chantait* (1972), *Un Jardin au bout du monde* (1975)," *Les Lettres Québécoises*, No. 7 (août-septembre 1977), p. 49. See also Gagné, *Visages de Gabrielle Roy*, p. 260.

CHAPTER II

The Fragility of Childhood and Adolescence

In a 1970 essay in which she discusses her memories of
Manitoba, Gabrielle Roy speaks of "le pouvoir enchanteur de
l'enfance."[1]   Although referring in this essay specifically to her
own childhood, as related to the composition of *Rue Deschambault,* Roy has, in effect, underscored an essential facet of all
her writings: the importance and the power of childhood to her,
to all her characters, to her entire literary universe, and, hopefully, to her readers.   Throughout her fiction she has treated
this period of time as what she finally describes in 1977 as "le
séjour naturel," those marvelous years when one can be oneself, looking forward to the possibilities of the future, while
nurturing the adult individual that one will become.[2]   That
adult being will, in turn, attempt to retain this lasting sense
of childhood.

If Gaston Bachelard is accurate in his assessments of childhood, assessments that correspond closely to the views of Gabrielle Roy, the attempt to cling to a sense of childhood in oneself will not be futile.   Bachelard, like Roy, sees childhood as
cosmic, a communicable marvel greater than reality and remaining within us throughout our lives.   There exists, therefore, a
"permanence, dans l'âme humaine, d'un noyau d'enfance."
Those who cultivate these seeds of childhood will discover that
"un excès d'enfance est un germe de poème."[3]

In the Royan fictional world one cannot escape one's past,
especially one's youth, even if one desires to do so. Most characters in fact, like Florentine of *Bonheur d'occasion,* wish to be
understood as adults through their childhood, as they were in
years past.   They, as their creator, recognize the fact that, like
the world itself, we are "nous tous, les enfants de la Terre," in
effect, "des enfants perdus qui aspirent à un commun rivage,"
in one sense, the common shore of our childhood.[4]

Since we are all a little Proustian, jealously guarding our

past within our present selves, Gabrielle Roy can easily treat us, her readers, as children. We are certainly treated as such in *La Petite Poule d'eau,* specifically in order to bring us closer to that child-like world. In 1955, interestingly enough the same year in which *Rue Deschambault* appeared, fully exploring Roy's semi-autobiographical world of the child, the author herself stated that "c'est à l'enfant en nous, au cher enfant amoureux de songes, que s'adressent ces livres. . . ." And in 1972 she dedicated her sensitive stories on nature "aux enfants de toutes saisons," to all of us.[5]

It is possible to view all of Roy's characters as children, or at least as retaining child-like qualities, but it is the children themselves in Roy's universe who truly stimulate an atmosphere of purity, innocence, and simplicity in that world. Beginning in 1940 with the imaginative games of children in "Gérard le pirate," Gabrielle Roy has increasingly oriented her vision toward the world of youth. In her novels, children are some-what pessimistically painted: The Lacasse children of *Bonheur d'occasion,* Paul of *Alexandre Chenevert,* and Jimmy of "La Rivière sans repos." They are either overburdened by the firm-ness of reality, or they are egotistical and selfish. Roy's short stories, however, portray children in a more tender and sensitive light, although even young ones are never too distant from adult reality. With *Rue Deschambault* and *La Route d'Altamont,* in particular, a child, Christine, becomes the focal point of the collections, as the world is seen and interpreted through her eyes. *Ces Enfants de ma vie* exclusively concerns the lives of children, for even the schoolteacher is not much older than an adolescent. And finally, *Ma Vache Bossie* and *Court-Queue* were written for a public of children, those actually in their youth and those adults who can relate to the world.[6]

Not only are children important as predominant characters in, especially, *Rue Deschambault, La Route d'Altamont,* and *Ces Enfants de ma vie,* Roy's three semi-autobiographic collec-tions of short stories, but the actual composition of these works also indicates a need and a desire, on the part of the author, to remember, to return to the past, and to recapture her childhood, her *temps perdu,* through literature. If such needs and desires are true for Roy, they are overwhelming for most of her adult characters. Either by reflecting upon their own past or by remaining in contact with children, these characters often des-perately try to remain young.

In Gabrielle Roy's imaginative world, this desire to retain a sense of youth is often associated with what the author calls *recommencement,* a new beginning. Although all of her characters experience this desire, since all people are "toujours prêts à recommencer," it is especially her female characters who cling to this notion and are capable of affecting this fresh start.[7] Their fervor for life, their contact with children, and their fear of growing old perhaps account for this determination.

Ironically, therefore, it is one of Roy's male characters, Azarius Lacasse of *Bonheur d'occasion,* who retains the most youthfulness about him, without any conscious determination to do so. His attempts to begin anew inevitably fail, but, as a child, he maintains his outlook of optimism and hope. Around him are women, in particular, his wife, Rose-Anna, and his daughter, Florentine, who both yearn to recapture a sense of innocent and simple childhood within themselves. Florentine is often described as a child but has been forced into the harsh reality of adulthood. Rose-Anna appears old, much older than her husband. In her one attempt to return to her youth, to her maternal home in Richelieu, an aura of childhood does at first surround her, but the trip soon becomes a disaster, and her true age quickly returns.[8]

Many of Gabrielle Roy's characters make trips, frequently in similar attempts to rediscover their youth. When Alexandre Chenevert travels outside of Montreal to Lac Vert, he returns to the warmth and security of maternal paradise: "Une impression d'enfance enveloppa Alexandre." Similarly, Maman of *Rue Deschambault* travels back to Quebec from Manitoba in order to renew ties with her youth and that of her husband. She appears to change as she travels: "Et je m'aperçus combien maman rajeunissait en voyage. . . . C'est vraiment joli de voir une vieille femme reprendre un air de jeune fille." In fact, youth returns to Maman even when she discusses the trip after it has ended. Later, this same woman, as Eveline in *La Route d'Altamont,* accidentally travels to the sole chain of hills in Manitoba. In linking these hills to those of her youth in Quebec, now in her memory, the elderly woman appears young once again.[9]

Trips into nature and, in particular, nature itself often stimulate a renewed sense of youth for Royan characters. Like Eveline, Sam Lee Wong searches throughout Western Canada in an attempt to rediscover the hills of his childhood in China. Pierre Cordorai of *La Montagne secrète* senses his youth when he feels the warmth of the sun upon him. Martha of "Un Jardin au bout du monde" returns to her youth and to hope in this youth when she is surrounded by her flowers. She begins to feel that the young being within her is her true self: "Pourtant c'était bien moi. C'est maintenant que je ne suis plus moi." And finally Martine of *Cet Eté qui chantait* is envelopped in a sensation of youth as soon as she places her feet in the water of a stream, while both the narrator of that work and Christine of *Rue Deschambault* travel back to their childhoods when they are rocked by the wind.[10]

This rocking motion, in effect, can clearly stimulate a sense of childhood in an individual. As Roy's characters are rocked in a hammock, a swing, or a horse-drawn carriage, their memories involuntarily return to the maternal security of childhood. Their imaginations become active, lost in day dreams, as they rediscover the comfort of the cradle.[11] Related to this importance of movement is the power of dance. When Hippolyte and Luzina Tousignant dance together at the Métis celebration, they both seem to regain their youth. In a similar fashion, music, and in particular the Ukrainian songs sung by Nil of *Ces Enfants de ma vie,* inspire a sense of youth in the elderly. The latter recall their happy childhood but realize that it exists no longer. Aging adults remain alone, like the elderly father of "Un Vagabond frappe à notre porte," "seul avec les ombres de son enfance."[12]

It is not, however, merely Nil's music that creates a nostalgia for childhood in the minds of adults. The actual presence of this talented boy, bringing "le pouvoir enchanteur de l'enfance," serves as an equally effective catalyst. Nil represents "l'enfant parmi nous. En ce jour, à cette heure, est-ce qu'il ne rapportait pas un peu de l'enfance de ses enfants devenus vieux, malades ou disparus dans la mort?" Older people desperately need this contact with youth, just as Nil's eighteen-year old schoolteacher longs to remain in touch with her pupils in order to retain some vestige of the childhood that she has only recently and painfully relinquished.[13]

Throughout Gabrielle Roy's fictional world, therefore, the image of a child symbolizes a life-giving force, especially when he or she is first born. When Rose-Anna Lacasse gives birth to her twelfth child, she experiences the same cleansing of all sadness and sorrow, the same sense of courage that she felt after the birth of her first child, "comme si elle venait de puiser

encore à la source mystérieuse, intarissable de sa jeunesse."
She is fully aware of the fact that "l'enfant, c'était l'avenir, mais
l'enfant c'était vraiment leur jeunesse retrouvée, c'était le grand
appel à leur courage." This new hope in the future and this
refound youth will, therefore, disappear as one's children mature
and eventually depart from the maternal home.[14] Once they
do depart, they will often travel as if in place of or for their
parents, especially for their mothers who, in effect, will live
their lives through their children, now adults. It is this inevitability of the cycle of life that reminds one of the temporary
nature of the world of childhood. It may be permanent, but
only in one's mind.

As a result, however, of the pre-eminence of childhood in
the fiction of Gabrielle Roy, some critics have classified her
works as "littérature d'innocence," defined by Marc Gagné
as "une littérature qui . . . se fixe comme but le retour vers la
perfection édénique." Roy's characters, desiring an innocence
that will bring both happiness and salvation, will search, in
part, in what Gagné calls "l'enfance-Paradis terrestre." François
Ricard views this aspect of Roy's writings rather as "la faculté
d'émerveillement et une certaine innocence du regard" on the
part of the author, while her characters possess "une pureté
de vision et une sorte de naïveté de coeur qui leur font juger et
éprouver le monde d'une façon toujours quelque peu enfan-
tine. . . ." Precisely because of this often naive and pure innocence of Royan characters, Phyllis Grosskurth believes that
the author treats them as simple children, or rather as lost
children "stumbling blindly through life." They have been
banished from the Garden of Eden, but they "have never tasted
the forbidden fruit of the Knowledge of Good and Evil. They
are bewildered, innocent exiles banished by a capricious God."[15]

This third interpretation is not fully accurate either in
reference to Roy's universe or to her characters. Both radiate,
rather, a duality of innocence and experience. Royan characters have been expelled from Eden, from childhood; they do
retain a sense of remembrance and, therefore, of regret; and
they do tend to view their present, real world with an aura of
wonder and child-like innocence. But despite their interminable
quest for innocent happiness, they are "aware of the constant
presence of tragedy, the possibilities of failure, and, above all,
the fleeting nature of this dream-like state," this temporary state
of innocent life in an inescapable present.[16] Ricard speaks specif-

ically of *Cet Eté qui chantait* in these terms:

> Car l'innocence et bonheur reposent ici sur un fond de détresse. . . .
> Une détresse vaincue, certes, dépassée par l'espérance, mais jamais
> au point de se taire complètement ni de se cesser de menacer,
> conférant ainsi à la vision heureuse un accent de gravité. . . .[17]

Considering the increasing presence of sadness in Gabrielle Roy's
fiction, the realistic awareness by her characters of life and the
world, and their pathetic acceptance of the fragility of childhood, one must extend this interpretation of an individual work
to her entire literary production. Her "littérature d'innocence"
is more a goal or a dream than an affirmation.

Despite the presence of reality in the world of the child
and in the desire of adults to recapture that world, one can
still not underestimate the importance of childhood in the
Royan universe and its role as adding hope, joy, and peace
to the adult world. If childhood is poetic, then Roy is certainly justified in her use of literary symbols to represent that
stage of life during which one is innocent and free. Children
are, in addition, seen as being close to nature, and, therefore,
it is symbols of nature that essentially depict their world. Childhood, in general, is filled with "des parfums de la tere . . . des
joies qui avaient le goût sain et profond des choses de la terre."[18]

More specifically, Gabrielle Roy identifies childhood with
spring: "La jeunesse, c'est le printemps, c'est le renouveau,
c'est l'espoir." It is also summertime, with the light, color, and
warmth of the sun. To the elderly Martha Yaramko, everything
in creation makes her think of youth: "Pour elle étaient vieux
l'hiver, la colère, l'ennui, mais d'une inaltérable jeunesse l'été
et la tendresse." Even as summer becomes autumn, a sense
of belated youth is, at times, retained in the Indian Summer
so loved by Roy and by her characters.[19]

Related to the rebirth of nature in spring and summer is
one of the author's preferred symbols of childhood: flowers
and bouquets. Throughout "Un Jardin au bout du monde"
and *Ces Enfants de ma vie,* in particular, flowers represent
the health, energy, beauty, and *naïveté* of childhood: "une
sorte d'enfance éternelle de la création." In the latter work,
flowers are also seen to be fragile, like the young summer soon
to die and the young child soon to grow up. André Pasquier,
the almost eleven-year-old boy, "n'avait plus l'air d'un enfant

fragile. . . . il me [the teacher] fit penser à une fleur ployant sur sa tige trop délicate."[20]

Trees, with the wind rocking their branches and leaves, birds, and the sky, either blue or with clouds, are also identified with childhood in the Royan literary universe. Jimmy's birth to Elsa Kumachuk is associated, for example, with clouds, the gentle wind, and the return flight of birds. In giving birth to Jimmy, Elsa has given herself a new life.[21]   Water also offers this same sense of renewal, in addition to a feeling of freedom. Even the animals that live in water are seen by Roy as symbols of youth. The trout that allow themselves to be picked up and caressed by human hands in *Ces Enfants de ma vie* are compared with Médéric, the adolescent soon to lose his child-like freedom. Médéric also often needs to travel from the Manitoban plains to the nearby hills, as if to cling to his last days of freedom and youth. Hills and mountains do symbolize childhood in Gabrielle Roy's fiction, although, in contrast, so do the open plains.[22]

Throughout her creative world, Roy views childhood as the dawning of a new day, as "cette clarté du matin." Morning is also associated with laughter, making Sally, for example, of "La Fuite de Sally" seem young once again: "Soudain, un rire frais, jeune, comme le printemps, bruyant comme un pépiement d'oiseaux, éclata dans la chambre obscure."[23]   Dawn, laughter, spring, birds, and childhood, all bring a renewed sense of joy to people. So do, finally, music and art. The flute desired by Daniel Lacasse is seen by his mother "comme un éclat de soleil . . . une flûte joyeuse qui exhalera des sons de bonheur. . . ."[24] Only in this instance the joy of music will not be powerful enough to preserve the childhood of Daniel. He will die, as must all phases of life and nature.

In addition to these sorrows of reality that inevitably touch the lives of children, it is interesting to note that Gabrielle Roy has, at times, endowed her literary children with negative characteristics, especially in some of her early short stories. Her initial venture into the domain of fiction depicted the O'Connor children as egocentric and spoiled, refusing to help in the home, and showing no respect for their parents. The children of the pitiful old woman in "La Pension de vieillesse" also act cruelly toward their mother, but Roy defends at least one of them, stating that he is "pas méchant, pas sans-coeur vraiment." He merely appears as such to the reader. No defense is offered on behalf of the son and daughter of "La Lune des moissons," the first of whom stands by while his father and then his mother are beaten by their spouse and the second of whom helps in this cruelty.[25]

The most wicked children in Roy's early short stories are to be found in "La Grande Berthe." The four daughters are portrayed by the author as jealous of their father's wealth and hostile, if not curel, toward Berthe, their father's second wife. They, with their brother, unite against the poor woman in the hope that she will die and that they will inherit the family fortune. They do not succeed.[26] At first glance, it seems unusual that Roy, who so deeply loved children and who would create such endearing creatures in her subsequent works, would have peopled her earlier works with these wicked youth. It must be noted, however, that, although treated as children at home or in relation to their parents, these characters are, in effect, quite mature, old enough to begin their own independent lives. Gabrielle Roy is, perhaps, telling us more about adolescents and young adults, or pessimistically, the types of individuals that children can become.

She remains fully within the realm of childhood, however, when she creates Paul, Alexandre Chenevert's grandson, not a very likeable child. But Paul is not wicked; he has merely inherited the suffering passed on to him from his grandfather and mother. Similarly, some of the blame for Jimmy Kumachuk's negative characteristics can be placed upon his destiny of having been caught between two cultures, Eskimo and White, and his having been spoiled both by his mother and by practically the entire community of Eskimo women. Despite this presence of determinism, however, Jimmy is a problem child, difficult to raise, and too materialistic. He incessantly demands more from his mother whom he treats cruelly and, increasingly, as a stranger precisely because she is a full-blooded Eskimo: "Un peu plus tard il en vint à lui [Elsa] demander qui était sa vraie mère; n'y avait-il pas eu substitution d'enfant à l'hôpital, lors de sa naissance?"[27] Although it is often unintentional, the curelty of children toward their parents can cause profound anguish to the latter.

Usually, however, the initial bonds that are formed between a parent and child are tenderly but realistically painted in Roy's fiction. The importance of the home and of one's parents, the devotion to, especially, the mother, and the feeling of maternal protection experienced during childhood, and long after regretted, are consistently emphasized. Roy also treats a child's natural fear of separation, of losing one's mother, as well as those typical moments in a child's life when he or she feels unloved or unwanted, as a mere "enfant de devoir."[28]

Throughout the Royan literary world, there are at work the forces of an almost Zola-like determinism, whether they are to be found in one's environment or in the qualities that an individual inherits from parents and family. Christine, at the center of both *Rue Deschambault* and *La Route d'Altamont,* and, perhaps, Roy's most delightful child, clearly exhibits the power of inheritance. She recognizes the fact that from her mother she has inherited her love for adventure and freedom, for daytime, and for the logic of words. From her father she has gained her love for maps and for night-time with its atmosphere conducive to thought. It is Christine's mother who explains this phenomenon, here in reference both to her daughter and to her own mother:

> "Ah, c'est bien là l'une des expériences les plus surprenantes de la vie. A celle qui nous a donné le jour, on donne naissance à notre tour quand, tôt ou tard, nous l'accueillons enfin dans notre moi. Dès lors, elle habite en nous autant que nous avons habité en elle avant de venir au monde."[29]

In addition to the actual inheritance of personal qualities, the influence of the parent on a child, and once again especially of the mother, is powerful in Roy's fiction. The Tousignant children learn their love for education from Luzina; Christine learns to mistrust men, love, and marriage because of the words of her mother. Children not only listen to all that is said around them, but also benefit from the experience of their elders. The young can be greatly aided on their road toward adulthood.

Although they can not negate inherited qualities, children can, after having observed their parents, either imitate them or refuse to be like them. Several of Roy's characters, as they mature, make a conscious vow never to become similar to their parents. Florentine Lacasse, for example, rejects for herself the destiny to which her mother has become resigned: " 'C'est pas vrai,' songeait Florentine. 'Moi, je ferai comme je voudrai. Moi, j'aurai pas de misère comme sa mère.' " She sees Rose-Anna's life as a long, gray voyage "que jamais, elle, Florentine n'accomplirait." Similarly, Eugène Lacasse will not allow himself to resemble his father, and Christine will reject in herself the misery that she observes in her father. She will also refuse to remain at home, with the painfully unfulfilled desires for travel of her mother. And finally, Pierre Cordorai will attempt to forget his father entirely.[30]

When children do emulate their parents, this limitation is often seen as a desire to act as an adult, with the corresponding wish to be treated as a mature person. Christine, in particular, wants to act seriously, especially during such a grown-up day as that of her trip to Lake Winnipeg with her elderly friend, M. Saint-Hilaire. She is proud when the man speaks to her as if to an adult. The young girl, in fact, does sometimes actually view the world of childhood in a negative light: "Est-ce l'enfance: à force de mensonges, être tenue dans un monde à l'écart?"[31] She does not like this aspect of youth, blocked from the adult world, for she is anxious to become a part of the latter.

But before entering into that world, Christine first has to learn to understand it. Throughout *Rue Deschambault*, Christine's apprenticeship before adulthood, she will earnestly try to understand the older world, but she will often find it difficult to do so. When her sister, Alicia, becomes insane, for example, Christine can only see the adult world as "the other": "C'est alors qu'*ils* ont décidé d'envoyer Alicia au loin. *Ils* ne me disaient pas la vérité; *ils* l'arrangeaient; *ils* la changeaient du tout au tout. A mes questions acharnées: 'Où est Alicia' *ils* répondaient qu'elle était bien soignée. . . ." But the young girl is determined: "Mais *ils* ne pouvaient pas m'empêcher de chercher [the truth]; et de chercher seule, sans appui, me ramenait quand même dans leur monde à eux."[32]

At other times, Christine's understanding of the world of adults will be fully mature. Ironically, however, during those moments when Christine does sympathize in particular with her mother, desirous of freedom and yet voluntarily tied to her home and family, the young girl regrets having entered into the adult world: "C'est la première fois de ma vie, je pense, où je n'ai plus souhaité être une grande personne; être une grande personne, c'est avoir trop d'explications à donner. . . ."[33]

Whether or not there is understanding by the Royan child of the parent, the intimate rapports that do develop between parents and children, and especially between mothers and daughters, in Gabrielle Roy's fiction are always realistically described.

Even when true communication is lacking, as between Rose-Anna and her children, relationships are profoundly affectionate and sincere: Florentine desires to help her mother financially; the Tousignant children recognize their mother's sacrifices for them; Agnès and her father show a deep and mutual love; and even Jimmy and Elsa, during their Sunday walks into the countryside, experience a peaceful sense of mutual confidence.[34]

In this last relationship, however, the reciprocal love will become one-sided as the young boy grows up. He had always been the center of Elsa's life, and when he departs, rejecting his mother and the Eskimo way of life, he will take with him this life-giving force. In the Royan universe, mothers do have a tendency for their lives to revolve around their children, often around an only child, as with Jimmy, or around the youngest child, as with Claire-Armelle Tousignant and Christine. For Gabrielle Roy herself, at least five years prior to the composition of "La Rivière sans repos," that which "justifie l'existence d'un couple, c'est une oeuvre. Un enfant. . . ." She further states: "Le plus grand mystère du monde . . . c'est le rapport humain entre la mère et l'enfant."[35]

Roy then, in 1971, creates Jimmy Kumachuk, the curly blond-haired, blue-eyed son, "le cadeau rare, 'unbelievable,' " born to Elsa after she had been raped by an American G.I. This child-god becomes the center of attraction for most of the Eskimo women who are enthralled by the daily ritual of his bath, followed by the combing of his hair. It is the pastor who warns Elsa that her child has become too important, the unique purpose to her life. She is, thus, indirectly forewarned that she will eventually lose her overly protected offspring, soon overpowered by his attraction to White culture in the South. When Jimmy does return, it is briefly and almost miraculously in an airplane: "Le fait merveilleux ne l'étonnait nullement. Son enfant, venu pour ainsi dire du ciel, ravi un beau jour par le ciel, était repassé par le ciel; tout se tenait."[36]

It is important to note that Jimmy does return, if only briefly, to his mother. Gérard Bessette aptly states that all of the children in Roy's work possess a sense of guilt because they have left the maternal home. They all need to return, therefore, essentially in order to prove themselves in their mothers' eyes. Even after having become adults, most of Roy's characters still see themselves as children before the maternal figure: Rose-Anna before Mme Laplante, Eugène before Rose-

Anna, Eveline before Mémère, and Christine before Eveline.[37]
Once again, the germ of childhood never dies within us.

Many of the general characteristics that an individual
exhibits as a child at home are obviously retained in adulthood,
although usually in a tempered state. During one's youth,
such qualities are often greatly heightened. In the Royan world
of children, as in the real world, young characters are, at times,
depicted as being more sensitive, tender, and loving, more astute
and intuitive than the adults around them. They can be, in
addition, just as responsible: the young narrator of *Ma Vache
Bossie* takes care of the animal, sells Bossie's milk, carefully
calculates the amount of money obtained from these sales,
and dutifully shares this money with her mother.[38] These children are also seen as talented, especially in *Ces Enfants de ma vie*,
and as capable of communicating beautifully and sometimes
silently, especially with the elderly as in *La Route d'Altamont*.

These elderly characters tend to thrive upon their close
relationships with young children who joyfully radiate the
qualities of freshness, honesty, and spontaneity. Most of these
positive characteristics that Gabrielle Roy identifies with children
are reflected in her prototype of youth, Christine. The young
girl is seen as extremely curious and, therefore, easily frustrated
and bored if her curiosity is not satisfied. She also thirsts for
freedom and adventure, like Jimmy and Médéric, like almost
all Roy's creations, young and old. She is typically excitable,
at times to such an extent that she has difficulty in expressing
herself, as when she tries to convince her mother to allow her
to travel to Lake Winnipeg. This excitement also leads to impatience, a desire to hurry and to experience everything: "Je
ne le savais pas. Tout ce que je savais, c'était que j'avais envie
de me dépêcher. . . . Si on ne se dépêche pas terriblement, me
disais-je, bien des choses nous échappent. . . ."[39]

When Christine's excitement and impatience reach an
intensely heightened state, and the young girl begins to fear
that her desires may be thwarted, she becomes obsessive. After
having decided, for example, that she has to have a yellow
ribbon belonging to her sister, Odette, who is soon to depart
for the convent, Christine can think of nothing else. Her desire
is more important than the object itself, for she can later recall
only the obsessive wish and not what became of the ribbon.
Similarly, when the youth makes up her mind to spend a day
with a local furniture mover in order to experience what she

envisions as a great adventure, her desire becomes a painful obsession:

> Maintenant le désir qui me poussait si fort, et jusqu'à la révolte [against her mother's wishes], n'avait plus rien d'heureux, ni même de tentant, si j'ose dire. C'était bien plutôt comme un ordre. Une angoisse pesait sur mon coeur. Je n'étais même plus libre de me dire: "Dors, oublie tout ça."[40]

Obsessions inevitably lead to a determination to fulfill one's desire, even if one must resort to exaggeration and theatrics, as in Christine's case. Her histrionic talents shine as she tries to convince her mother that she simply has to leave with M. Saint-Hilaire in order to see Lake Winnipeg. Her mother first smiles at her daughter's "effroyable pessimisme" before the possibility of not receiving permission to go, but then she appears to be touched by the child's desire that has developped into torture. The older woman can not be surprised, however, at Christine's emotional state because it easily coincides with the young girl's nature, that of profound imaginativeness. She, like most of Roy's children, is a child who needs, for example, to be alone, in her hammock or in her attic hideaway, precisely in order to daydream: "Je sommeillais d'un rêve à l'autre. . . . Le bercement de mon hamac aidait la trame de mes contes. N'est-ce pas curieux: un mouvement lent et doux, et l'imagination est comme en branle!"[41]

At times, however, the combination of an extremely imaginative child and total solitude can create a melodramatic, if not macabre, situation. When Christine's father cries out that he regrets having had any children, the sensitive young girl flees to her *grenier:* "face par terre, je grattai le plancher rugueux de mes ongles, je cherchai à y entrer pour mourir. Le visage collé au plancer, j'ai essayé de m'empêcher de respirer." She ignores her mother's call for dinner. her brother's invitation to go fishing, and her friends' equally macabre offer to comme "jouer aux enterrements." Christine wants to play the role of a martyr. She does, however, truly feel abandoned by everyone, and "sans plus en connaître la cause, je pleurai davantage le chagrin lui-même qui n'est peut-être qu'un enfant seul."[42] Solitude is conducive to creativity, but it can also result in deep sorrow for the child.

Gabrielle Roy's literary children are not ideal creatures,

therefore, living in a world divorced from adult reality. If Christine's desires to die are, in part, melodramatic, her sadness is, indeed, real. She, as most of the children in Roy's fiction, is not immune to the sorrow and suffering of the world. Christine, her sisters, Odette and Alicia, Florentine Lacasse, and Irène Chenevert, all possess an "âme révoltée": they pity the wretched of the earth and rebel against any predisposition, of others or of their own, for suffering.[43]

Suffering does exist, however, in Roy's world. Children observe it in others, and they endure it themselves, both emotionally and physically. From their earliest years they must learn, with difficulty, to fulfill the dreams of adults: "c'est pourtant sur ces frêles épaules [of fragile youth] que nous faisons porter le poids de nos espoirs déçus et de nos éternels recommencements." Children also suffer from the heavy responsibilities that are sometimes placed upon them: the 5½ year-old Emile and the eleven-year-old André Pasquier must both work at home in place of an absent father and to aid a bed-ridden mother. The children of large families, especially those urban families living in poverty, daily witness suffering. Attesting to these problems are the Lacasse children and Jean Lévesque, of whom the latter simply but unsuccessfully attempts to forget his unhappy youth.[44]

An additional common occurrence in poor, large families is malnutrition, although this is the least serious of the illnesses afflicting both children and adults in the Royan world. A far more grave sickness is the leukemia contracted by the young Daniel Lacasse. In his hospital bed, the child experiences solitude, alienation, fear, and physical pain. Equally poignant are the scences describing both the insanity of Alicia and Christine's juvenile attempts to understand what is occurring. The younger girl wants to help her sister, is, at time, fearful of her, and, ultimately will be marked for life by this traumatic event. Both Daniel and Alicia will die, as will the young Yolande Chartrand of *Cet Eté qui chantait.* Once again, Royan children are not exempt from the tragedies of life. They must, in addition, witness and try to comprehend the death of those around them, especially of old people dear to their hearts. This is a difficult lesson to learn, but it is a necessary part of maturing.[45]

It is, however, this actual process of maturing that Gabrielle Roy views as the most tragic aspect of childhood. Youth is fresh and spontaneous, but it is also fragile and vulnerable precisely because it is temporary. When the young school-teacher-narrator of *Ces Enfants de ma vie* leaves her rural school for another position, she is deeply aware of the fact that a stage of life, both for her and for her young pupils, has been completed:

> Je me penchai hors du train qui s'ébranlait. Je vis ces petites silhouettes fragiles, si menues contre le ciel de là-bas, m'adresser de grands signes, plus grands qu'eux, comme à quelqu'un qui s'éloigne du rivage, et eux, sur le quai de l'infini, les frêles enfants, s'amenuisaient à vue d'oeil. Il me semble les abandonner.[46]

In effect, both the schoolteacher and her pupils are departing—she further into structured adulthood and they from childhood into adolescence, those final years before the inevitable world of adults. The children are, in addition, waving good-bye to a young adult who has profoundly affected them. These young Royan characters first learned about the real world while remaining at home, but they themselves still had to venture out into that world in order to complete their training. Their first such venture was into the school.

Most of the aforementioned characteristics of children at home are retained when they attend school. They bring their smiles with them, as the most beautiful gift of all to their teacher. They are touched by tragedy when a young schoolmate dies. But in addition and most importantly, they are faced with a new experience at five years of age and with "les nerfs délicats des enfants subissant mal la tension atmosphérique," they are forced to depart from the home into the usually more structured world of the school.[47]

This departure from the enclosed circle of the protective home places the youth in a world where everything seems unknown. When, for example, the schoolteacher of *Ces Enfants de ma vie* must lock the door of the classroom on the first day of school in order to keep her young pupils inside, the five-year-old Vincento is seen as the sad image of "une petite créature brisée, sans soutien ni ami dans un monde étranger." Even to an older child, especially after a long vacation, school can be seen as a trap or a prison and the student as a prisoner of the adult world.[48]

This first day of school, therefore, is of vital importance to a young child. A sensitive teacher will understand the difficulties that the pupils are experiencing and will attempt to create links, in the children's minds, between home and the school. Vincento and his classmates are asked to draw pictures of their homes on the board. The teacher then traces a road connecting the houses with the school. What the pupils are drawing upon the board is the traumatic departure from the parent to the teacher. Since it is usually the mother who is responsible for a child's education in the early years, youngsters can experience painful separation anxieties when they first go to school: they cry and scream; Vincento kicks his teacher; and Demetrioff remains hostile. But this physical and emotional separation is necessary: "Non, quand il faut couper la branche, rien ne donne d'attendre." Even the mother must accept this inevitable departure of her child. Elsa would like to continue Jimmy's education at home but is forced to send him to school. Luzina, symbolically, sits at the teacher's desk immediately prior to the arrival of her children's first instructor.[49]

Once they accept school, children do not forget their parents, but they often grow extremely attached to their teacher who becomes a temporary replacement for, usually, the mother. When the Tousignant children first meet Mlle Côté, they stand before her with both fear and confidence, awaiting her first reaction. When she opens her arms to them, they are immediately "tamed," as Roy described it. They begin to follow her around, with a collective fascination and love for the young woman.[50]

Similarly, the natural tenderness of the teacher in *Ces Enfants de ma vie* eventually draws even the most resentful children toward her. The younger pupils exhibit a need to please her, as Demetrioff's desire to trace his letters perfectly on the board. Other children want to prove their love by giving something material to the teacher, by offering her, for example, a special gift for Christmas. In all of these instances, it is the child's powerful love for the teacher that is being expressed:

> Mes tout petits élèves me dévoraient de leurs yeux brillants d'amour. . . . Telle était la passion qui m'a tenue au cours de ces années-là, et je sais aujourd'hui que de toutes celles qui nous prennent entiers, pour nous broyer ou façonner, celle-là autant que les autres est exigeante et dominatrice.[51]

Precisely because of the demanding nature of this love of a student for a teacher, younger children often become possessive about this adult figure. The Badiou children, for example, are so proud of being allowed to take their teacher to their home that they treat her as if she belonged to them. They pull her along toward the house, crying out: " 'Maman! Maman! On amène notre mamzelle!' Sur le ton, me sembla-t-il, qu'ils eussent pu annoncer: 'On l'a capturée!' "[52]   These young pupils openly and eagerly accept this grownup into the world of their home. They need to be understood by their teacher as they are within the protective and parental domain, and they desire to reconcile any existing conflict between home and school and between parent and teacher.

The formerly enclosed circle of the home, therefore, has opened in order to make room for the school. At the same time, the school has taken on certain characteristics of the home. At the beginning of the relationship between the teacher and pupils, the latter often serves as a guide for the adult, especially if he or she is relatively young and inexperienced: "Il s'en trouva cinq ou six parmi les plus petits à finir par me prendre par la main ou le bras, et ils me tiraient légèrement en avant comme pour guider une aveugle. Ils ne parlaient pas, ne faisaient que me tenir enfermée dans leur cercle." In this instance, the children, actually guiding their teacher toward the home of a deceased schoolmate, are symbolically leading her into their world. In other instances, the pupil serves as a guide by silently and visually informing the adult of success or failure in the classroom.[53] In both cases, like the circle of the home, once the circle of childhood has opened, bringing the teacher into its realm, the school becomes "une sorte de famille, un monde en soi, on dirait aujourd'hui une commune." The teacher has become a parental figure with many children, as if, for the young woman of *Ces Enfants de ma vie,* they were hers:

> Mais qu'est-ce que je dis là! Ils étaient à moi et le seraient même quand j'aurais oublié leur nom et leur visage, part de moi-même autant que je le serais d'eux-mêmes, en vertu de la plus mystérieuse force de possession qui existe et dépasse parfois le lien du sang.[54]

In addition to the emotional development that occurs when a child enters school, the importance of the role of intellectual education cannot be minimized. In 1966 Gabrielle Roy referred to the school, especially that destined for the very young of isolated rural areas, as a temple. Elsewhere she speaks of the importance of schools on the Western Canadian plains and as the pride of Saint-Boniface. Throughout her fiction, to attend school means to be the honor of one's family, to be admired, and to be the proud guardian of knowledge. Royan children are generally excited about school, want to learn, make sure, as Josephine Tousignant, that the teacher fulfills the designated role, and, as Daniel Lacasse, are saddened if they are forced to abandon their studies.[55]

Their eagerness to learn, the orientation of what they learn, and the general effect of the educational process upon them are all, of course, dependent upon their teacher and the type of education that they receive. The Tousignant children thirst for knowledge, as a result of the inspiration of Mlle Côté who teaches them, in particular, the nationalism and patriotism of French-speaking Canada. Fear is instilled in them from the strictness of Miss O'Rorke who insists upon their studies of English-speaking Canada. Armand Dubreuil, the only male teacher in Roy's fiction, does not really teach. Under his tutelage, the children learn only indirectly, as they listen to the stories that he reads to the entire family. Gabrielle Roy also appears to pass judgement upon severe and liberal forms of education for children. Irène Chenevert rejects the former:

> Et elle donna comme excuse que, dans les livres modernes sur l'éducation des enfants, il était recommandé de ne pas exercer sur eux une contrainte constante. Les temps changeaient. "On s'apercevait maintenant," dit-elle, "que la sévère éducation d'autrefois, où tout était défendu, était responsable de bien des névroses, de complexes qui marquaient la vie entière." Et elle ne voulait pas faire de son enfant un être craintif . . . comme elle-même. . . .

Roy obviously advocates an education based upon tenderness and understanding, but she clearly points out the fact that the truly liberal education given to Paul has produced a wild and difficult boy.[56]

As a result of the educational process, the children of Roy's fiction learn to understand themselves and others better, one of their creator's major goals for everyone, as they discover their future role in life. A child's initial departure to school is only one of the first stages of maturity, a growth that will soon include exposure to the outside world. This exposure will be further enlarged when the child begins to read. Armand Dubreuil does, in fact, inspire both Luzina and her children when he reads to them at night, just as Miss Evans of "Gérard le pirate" stimulates her students when she reads *Treasure Island* aloud in class, and as Elsa brings joy to Jimmy when she reads *Ivanhoe* to him. But the ability to read by oneself offers an even greater pleasure:

> Un soir qu'elle [Elsa] avait suspendu un instant sa lecture pour en suivre en elle le prolongement, elle saisit, au rayon de la lampe, le regard exalté de Jimmy. Sa réaction était celle de tout enfant qui se plaît à entendre des histoires. Il en voulait plus, toujours plus. Elsa décida de lui apprendre à lire, afin qu'il connaisse lui aussi ces carrefours et chemins passants que sont les livres et sache en tirer profit.[57]

What reading brings to the child, especially with books such as *Treasure Island* and *Ivanhoe,* is a sense of adventure and a new awareness of the world. A similar exposure is stressed in the Royan educational world in the geography class and its use of maps. One often sees Roy's literary children in such classes and, as a result, later dreaming of their own departure to the outside world.[58]

Education, therefore, with its books and maps, is the final cause of separation between the parent and a young child. The latter must inevitably depart, from the protective home and from protective parents, from the school and teacher, and, ultimately, from childhood. The now intertwined circles of home and school, and of parents and teachers, have both been forced open in order to send the child into the world. Before that final venture into the adult world, however, children must pass through one more stage, in this case, a transitional stage between childhood and adulthood: adolescence.

Many of the qualities inherent in childhood are still present during adolescence, but there often appears to be a deeper sensitivity and sense of sadness in these older youth, on the threshold of adulthood. Adolescents exhibit, in addition, a greater propensity for exaggeration, obsessiveness, melodrama, and romanticism. The few adolescents who people Gabrielle Roy's fiction possess all these characteristics, while they cling to the spontaneity and freedom of their passing youth.

Roy created her first adolescent in 1940, in the character of Lucile, the romantic, daydreaming, and exaggerating heroine of "Avantage pour." Fifteen years later, both Odette and her friend, Gisèle Guibert, behave like curious and romantic adolescents in their relationship with the two "exotic" black boarders in their homes and in their love for revolutionary-sounding music. It is, however, Christine who typifies adolescence in the Royan world. In "Wilhem" the girl experiences her first "crush" on a boy whom she describes as much older than she. Wilhem is, in addition, different because he is Dutch, a pensive foreigner trying to earn a living in Canada. Christine's first passion is humorously described as romantically melodramatic, ending only when the adolescent becomes aware of the ridiculous nature of this "bien grave aventure" that has become banal.[59]

In "Les Bijoux" the tendency toward obsessiveness that was evident in the young Christine turns into an adolescent mania, here in the form of an exaggerated love for costume jewelry and the related admiration for the saleswoman who sells this merchandise. The comically pitiful image of Christine, wearing all her jewelry, as well as cosmetics, sitting in her room before a buddha, and burning incense, is effectively described and creates the caricature of an egotistical adult woman. Christine's mother sees this obsession as a sickness from which her daughter will, hopefully, soon be cured, only to contract a new illness: the desire for adventure, to travel to Africa and take care of lepers.[60]

Médéric Eymard, Roy's most successfully created young male character, also demonstrates a penchant for melodrama. His first arrival at school is described as though it were a scene from a cowboy movie, carefully staged by the adolescent who, wearing a large cowboy hat, belt, pants, and boots, rides up to school on his horse and struts into the classroom as if into a saloon. Except for this one scene, however, Médéric is not a humorous adolescent, not comically depicted as was Christine in her adolescence. He is equally romantic, equally prone to daydreaming, but an aura of poignant sadness emanates from this youth who desperately desires to retain the freedom of his childhood, freedom that he knows will be, in part, lost once he enters adulthood: " 'Alors, la liberté . . . ' et il trembla de la prémonition que rien dans la vie n'est peut-être, à la fin, à la hauteur de ce qu'on en souhaite, à treize ans." For this reason, Médéric needs to ride Gaspard, needs to return to the nearby hills, and needs to be close to the free creatures of nature.[61]

This recognition of the inevitable destruction of the freedom of one's childhood, along with a growing determination to express one's new sense of independence as an adolescent-young adult, account for a frequent attitude of rebellion during these years. Florentine defiantly smokes in front of her mother, while Jean's character is totally transformed:

> Il passait violemment d'une soumission apparente à la rebellion ouverte. Il affichait le dédain, le sarcasme. A tout venant, il exprimait des opinions bien personnelles, teintées d'humour caustique. Il faisait naître des discussions pour le seul plaisir de contredire ses adversaires.

Christine's adolescent actions are also seen as being in defiance of her family's wishes and create antagonism, especially with her mother. The difficult adolescent years of Jimmy will similarly teach bitterness and revolt to his mother, as the boy tries twice to run away from home. Finally, Médéric's insolent attitude toward his teacher, pushing her as far as he can go, and consistently causing trouble in class, must be interpreted as a childish attempt to rebel against society and the adult world.[62]

The adolescent child also confronts adult society when he or she experiences the birth of sensuality, especially when that first love is directed toward an adult who already has a designated role to play in that grown-up world. Christine's feelings for Wilhelm were merely those of infatuation and totally devoid of sensuality, although the attraction that her cousin, Philippe, feels toward her is unmistakably physical.[63]   It is only with the composition of *Ces Enfants de ma vie* that Roy explores the domain of adolescent love, both sensual and painfully real, deeply affecting not only the maturing child but also the teacher, object of this love.

One can already detect a subtle trace of mutual sensuality in the warm and special relationship between the eighteen-year old schoolteacher and the ten, almost eleven, year-old André Pasquier: "Et je tendis la main pour lui caresser la joue, le front, que sais-je! Lui ne se recula pas, en faisant l'homme comme les autres fois où j'avais tenté ce geste, mais se laissa remonter une mèche tombée sur sa tempe." An analogous scene later occurs between the teacher and the thirteen, almost fourteen, year-old Médéric, only in this instance, the roles are reversed: "Une mèche de cheveux, envolée de mon bonnet, gonflée d'air, s'éleva, lui frôle la joue. . . . Je le vis ôter son gant et chercher à capter la mèche folle. Il fut près de la saisir au vol, mais s'arrêta, la main en suspens, surpris de lui-même et de son geste."[64] The feelings that André has for his teacher are only in their initial stages of development; he does not understand them, and simply, wants to act like a man. Likewise, the young woman can "safely" touch the boy's face and brush away a lock of his hair, for he is still a boy in her eyes. With Médéric, it is different. He, too, feels the birth of sensuality and love within him but at his age, is already fearful of these emotions that have brought him pain. He stops himself from acting freely. The teacher reacts in a similar manner, well aware of these mutual feelings: she moves away from him, and she herself pushes the lock of hair back into her hat.

Feelings of sensuality between the young teacher and Médéric are clearly suggested throughout the short story, from the first moment that their knees accidently touch under the youth's desk. The scene of their carriage ride to Médéric's home radiates a sensual atmosphere, while, despite the fact that they are both disturbed by the sexual insinuations made by the boy's father about their close friendship, their return trip in the wedding carriage of Médéric's parents is described as a surrealistic, romantic, and deeply sensual dream.[65]

They have reason to be upset by M. Eymard's words for, despite the increasing sensuality in their relationship, their love is pure and innocent. Gabrielle Roy beautifully describes this birth of adolescent love in Médéric: his exalted desire to share with his teacher his love for nature by taking her into the hills to see the trout that allow themselves to be caressed by human hands; and the inevitable pain, "la souffrance du premier amour qui . . . ne sait encore qui il est et frémit de peur, de joie et de désir incompris." All that the boy can do is to try to express his anguish:

> Et j'eus de chagrin à constater que sa solitude infinie l'amenait à rechercher de l'aide de moi qui me devais de l'éloigner pour lui éviter plus de mal encore. . . . Il poussa un gémissement faible: "Ah, mamzelle! Qu'est-ce donc qui m'arrive? C'est comme si je vous. . . ." Il étouffait de confusion: "Ce n'est pas de ma faute. Je ne l'ai pas fait exprès.[66]

Médéric is even further confused because, without fully understanding his own emotions, he, along with his teacher, is being malevolently discussed by the adult society of the village in which they live. His father had at least made insinuations, but other adults spy upon the "couple," while gossiping behind their backs. The teacher reproaches herself; Médéric is embarrassed; and adult society, dictating the roles that people must play, ruins a pure and beautiful relationship.[67]

Although structured society usually demands that individuals remain in their prescribed roles—the teacher as an authoritarian adult figure and the child-adolescent as a student—circumstances are such that sometimes the young are forced into adult roles. When Elsa is raped, her transformation into adulthood is sudden and complete: "de rieuse qu'elle avait été, elle devenait morose et renfermée." André Pasquier appears to have accepted more readily his adult role at home and to have become resigned to the constant fatigue of a man-child. He does, at least, experience pride in having helped his mother and having cared for his younger brother. As long as he continues to attend school, he can also retain his role as a child. When he is forced to abandon the classroom because of overwhelming responsibilities at home, however, his child-like face, free of worries and anguish, returns only when the boy is asleep.[68]

In addition to being forced into adult roles, children undergo the normal process of physical and emotional development that can, at times, produce a composite being: part child, part adolescent, and part adult, playing all three roles simultaneously. For example, Odette acts much older than she is and prefers the company of adults, while Christine is often treated as a half-child, half-adult. Since adolescence is that special and difficult period of time when one tries to discover one's true self before entering into adulthood, however, this transitional being can cause confusion, both to the adolescent and to others. When Médéric first arrives at school, the teacher is not sure if he is a man or a boy. She finally decides "qu'il n'était après tout qu'un enfant, la nuque fragile, le corps élancé, mais délicat," but still needs to convince herself: " 'Ce Médéric a beau avoir la taille d'un homme, il est enfant à ne pas le croire.' " During her visit to Médéric's home, the adolescent "disguises" himself in grown-up clothes but is later humiliated at his ridiculous attempt to appear much older in his teacher's eyes. He is also embarrassed when his voice changes. Médéric eventually flees from the school, his teacher, his painful love, and the onset of adulthood, but when he returns it is as "un long jeune homme-enfant," as if he had gone away to complete this transformation alone: "Jamais encore je n'avais vu pareillement enchaînés jusqu'à ce que l'un l'emporte sur l'autre, l'homme et l'enfant, et je pense avoir éprouvé de la peine pour tous deux qui paraissaient si mal faits pour marcher de compagnie." The teacher feels sad to see the boy become a man, to see "un enfant mourant sous la poussée impitoyablement de l'homme qui va en naître." She wants to save the child-like part of Médéric but does not know how to do so.[69]

There is further confusion before these characteristics of a child-adolescent-adult when, as a result, there occurs a reversal of roles between the adolescent and the adult figure. The teacher realizes, for example, that André is more knowledgeable than she is in certain practical matters, "comme si les rôles étaient renversés et que c'était moi l'enfant à qui on avait à ouvrir les yeux sur les dures réalités." With Médéric, this role reversal occurs for several reasons: "J'avais dix-huit ans, et lui s'en allait sur quatorze. Il me dépassait aisément d'une tête et sans doute davantage dans bien des choses de la vie."[70] In both relationships, however, this confusion in roles will eventually end. The teacher will depart in order to continue her adult profession elsewhere, and both André and Médéric, like all adolescents, will themselves soon depart from the world of childhood and into their designated roles as matured adults.

It is evident that Gabrielle Roy considers this loss of childhood as one of the saddest aspects of the life cycle, and she, therefore, imbues her characters with this same poignant sense of loss. Florentine, for example, shudders at the thought that with the death of her childhood, has come the inevitable death of her dreams. The young teacher of *Ces Enfants de ma vie* is pained to see the disappearance of youth in her pupils, for any such child loses, as well, "une part vive de son âme avec sa spontanéité en partie détruite." Cut off from one's "séjour naturel, au bord de la vie adulte," the individual experiences this separation from childhood as "un mal dont on ne guérissait peut-être jamais tout à fait." In addition, Royan characters feel deep sorrow when they realize that the loss of their youth brings the necessary departure from the protective home into the outside adult world. When they later reflect upon their past childhood, as do the Tousignant children, they feel as though it is scolding them for having grown up, for having become educated, and, therefore, for having bettered themselves to such an extent that they had to depart.[71]

Roy's adolescents not only feel sadness at the termination of their youth, but they also often experience "une solitude comme il ne peut y en avoir d'aussi profonde qu'aux derniers jours presque de l'enfance." They feel isolated on the threshold of adulthood, as they endure this inevitable pain alone, but they also seek out this solitude as a final refuge against "l'essentielle souffrance de la vie" that will soon arrive. The shelter of solitude, therefore, will ultimately be forced open, like the circles of the home and school, as the adolescent accepts the inevitable and becomes resigned to adult life.[72]

Underlying *Ces Enfants de ma vie,* therefore, Gabrielle Roy's final tribute to childhood and adolescence, is the poignant and persistent reminder that these delicate years are vulnerable and fragile. Médéric is, for example, compared to the trout that lose their freedom when they are picked up by human hands:

> Je voyais passer sur son visage [Médéric's] le frémissement joyeux que lui avait procuré la sensation de tenir, tout consentant entre ses mains, le poisson le plus méfiant du monde, et me disais que ce serait bientôt son tour d'être pris, vulnérable comme je le découvrais. . . .

Médéric is about to be captured by adulthood. Childhood and adolescence are also fragile, as are flowers, summer, all of nature, and all of the world. When the young teacher leaves for her new position, she desperately looks for Médéric in order to say farewell. Aboard the departing train, she finally sees him, riding Gaspard alongside the quickly moving train. The adolescent throws to her a bouquet of wild flowers: "Je le [the bouquet] mis contre ma joue. Il embaumait délicatement. Il disait le jeune été fragile, à peine est-il né qu'il commence à en mourir."[73]   Like the bouquet, the years of childhood and adolescence are sweet, delicate, and fleeting, but also like wild summer flowers that are reborn each year, the germ of childhood will remain preserved within Gabrielle Roy's characters and will continuously reappear throughout their lives.

NOTES

[1] Gabrielle Roy, "Mon Héritage du Manitoba," *Mosaic,* 3iii (1970), 74.

[2] Gabrielle Roy, *Ces Enfants de ma vie* (Montréal: Editions Internationales Alain Stanké Ltée, 1977), p. 179. See also Marc Gagné, *Visages de Gabrielle Roy* (Montréal: Librairie Beauchemin Limitée, 1973), pp. 151-152; John J. Murphy, "Visit with Gabrielle Roy," *Thought: Review of Culture and Idea,* 38, No. 150 (Autumn 1963), 448. Interestingly, Roy felt that her continued interest in and love for children culminated in 1977 with the publication of *Ces Enfants de ma vie.* Her former desire to write about them with such an intense focus was finished. Personal interview with Gabrielle Roy, 29 June 1980.

[3] Gaston Bachelard, *La Poétique de la rêverie,* Bibliothèque de philosophie contemporaine (Paris: Presses Universitaires de France, 1974), p. 85. See also pp. 18, 106-109; Gaston Bachelard, *La Poétique de l'espace,* Bibliothèque de philosophie contemporaine (Paris: Presses Universitaires de France, 1978), p. 33.

[4] Gabrielle Roy, *Cet Eté qui chantait* (Québec-Montréal: Les Editions Françaises, 1972), pp. 76, 198; Gabrielle Roy, *Bonheur d'occasion* (1945; rpt. Montréal: Librairie Beauchemin Limitée, 1973), pp. 296, 183; Gabrielle Roy, *Rue Deschambault* (1955; rpt. Montréal: Librairie Beauchemin Limitée, 1974), p. 293; Phyllis Grosskurth, *Gabrielle Roy,* Canadian Writers and Their Works (Toronto: Forum House, 1972), p. 44.

[5] Gabrielle Roy, "Jeux du romancier et des lecteurs," l'Alliance Française, Montréal, 1er décembre 1955, as quoted in Gagné, p. 264; Roy, *Cet Eté qui chantait,* p. 7; André Brochu, "Gabrielle Roy," Notes from course on author, Université de Montréal, Printemps 1978, taken by one of his students.

[6] Roy herself, however, was somewhat concerned that *Ma Vache Bossie* and *Courte-Queue* were not truly books for children. She recognized the fact that there were two levels, for two distinct publics, to both stories. Personal interview with Gabrielle Roy, 29 June 1980. According to her sister, Gabrielle Roy was interested in writing children's stories as early as her twenties. See Marie-Anna A. Roy, *Le Miroir du passé,* Collection Littérature d'Amérique (Montréal: Editions Québec/Amérique, 1979),

p. 118.

[7] Gabrielle Roy, *Ces Enfants de ma vie*, p. 34; Gagné, pp. 73, 152-153, 168; Bachelard, *La Poétique de la rêverie*, pp. 85-88, 90-93, 106-109. A complete discussion of the concept of *recommencement* in Roy's works, especially in reference to female characters, will be found in Chapter III.

[8] Roy, *Bonheur d'occasion*, pp. 38, 79, 139, 151-159, 168-170, 296, 301. André Brochu, "Thèmes et structures de *Bonheur d'occasion*," in *L'Instance critique* (Montréal: Leméac, 1974), pp. 244-245. It is also Florentine who reflects upon the fact that "certaines attitudes qui nous ont impressionnés pendant l'enfance nous poursuivent toute la vie, inchangeables, et figées pour toujours." Roy, *Bonheur d'occasion*, p. 124. Once again, childhood contains the germ of what one will become.

[9] Gabrielle Roy, *Alexandre Chenevert* (1954; rpt. Montréal: Beauchemin, 1973), p. 212. See also pp. 181-182, 218-222; Roy, *Rue Deschambault*, p. 113. See also pp. 100-101, 126, 130-131, 136-138. Roy speaks of her mother's desire, as well as of her own, to return to childhood in Quebec in "Mon Héritage du Manitoba," pp. 72-73. See also Gabrielle Roy, *La Route d'Altamont*, Collection L'Arbre, No. 10 (Montréal: Editions HMH, 1966), pp. 205-207, 229.

[10] Gabrielle Roy, *Un Jardin au bout du monde* (Montréal: Librairie Beauchemin Limitée, 1975), p. 212. See also pp. 170, 211, and, for Sam Lee Wong, pp. 62-63. Gabrielle Roy, *La Montagne secrète* (1961; rpt. Montréal: Librairie Beauchemin Limitée, 1974), pp. 55-59; Roy, *Cet Eté qui chantait*, pp. 49-51, 95, 146-147, 156-160; Roy, *Rue Deschambault*, pp. 82-86.

[11] The two most prominent examples of this *nostalgie du berceau* while being rocked, first in a hammock and secondly in a *berline,* occur in Roy, "Ma Coqueluche," *Rue Deschambault*, pp. 82-86, and Roy, "De la truite dans l'eau glacée," *Ces Enfants de ma vie*, pp. 177-186. See also Paula Gilbert Lewis, "The Fragility of Childhood: Gabrielle Roy's *Ces Enfants de ma vie*," *The American Review of Canadian Studies*, 9, No. 2 (Autumn 1979), 151.

[12] Gabrielle Roy, *La Petite Poule d'eau* (1950; rpt. Montréal: Librairie Beauchemin Limitée, 1970), p. 270; Roy, *Ces Enfants de ma vie*, pp. 49-50, 53-54; Roy, "Un Vagabond frappe à notre porte," *Un Jardin au bout du monde*, p. 22.

[13] Roy, *Ces Enfants de ma vie*, p. 35. See also pp. 28-29, 49-50, 53-54, 147, 151. There is one group of adult individuals in Roy's fiction that does not appear to require contact with children in order to remain young. Presumably because of their innocence, happiness, and closeness to nature, Eskimos are treated by Roy as *hommes-enfants,* as "les enfants de l'Arctique," at least prior to the encroachment of White culture upon

them. Gabrielle Roy, "Voyage en Ungava," in Marc Gagné, "*La Rivière sans repos* de Gabrielle Roy: Etude mythocritique," *Revue de l'Université d'Ottawa*, 46, No. 3 (juillet-septembre 1976), 375, 376, 380; Gabrielle Roy, *La Rivière sans repos* (Montréal: Librairie Beauchemin Limitée, 1971), pp. 23-24, 84.

[14] Roy, *Bonheur d'occasion*, pp. 327, 330. See also Roy, *La Petite Poule d'eau*, p. 147; Roy, *Rue Deschambualt*, p. 160.

[15] Gagné, *Visages de Gabrielle Roy*, pp. 238, 242; François Ricard, *Gabrielle Roy*, Ecrivains canadiens d'aujourd'hui, No. 11 (Montréal: Editions Fides, 1975), pp. 114-115; Grosskurth, pp. 37, 62. See also Phyllis Grosskurth, "Gabrielle Roy and the Silken Noose," *Canadian Literature*, 42 (1969), 7.

[16] Lewis, p. 148; Alain Brown, "Gabrielle Roy and the Temporary Provincial," *The Tamarack Review*, No. 1 (Autumn 1956), pp. 61, 62, 63, 69, 70.

[17] Ricard, p. 145.

[18] Roy, *Bonheur d'occasion*, p. 311. See also Roy, *Alexandre Chenevert*, pp. 209-213.

[19] Alice Parizeau, "Gabrielle Roy, grande romancière canadienne," *Châtelaine*, 7, No. 4 (avril 1966), 122; Roy *Un Jardin au bout du monde*, p. 178. In the second work, see also pp. 179, 211-212, 215; Roy, *Ces Enfants de ma vie*, p. 100; Roy, *La Montagne secrète*, pp. 55-59; Roy, *Bonheur d'occasion*, pp. 239-240.

[20] Roy, "Un Jardin au bout du monde," p. 170; Roy, *Ces Enfants de ma vie*, p. 122. In the second work, see also pp. 198-199, 210-212; Gagné, *Visages de Gabrielle Roy*, pp. 154-158; Jean Chevalier et Alain Gheerbrant, *Dictionnaire des symboles* (Paris: Robert Laffont/Editions Jupiter, 1982), pp. 447-449.

[21] Roy, "La Rivière sans repos," p. 137. See also Roy, *Rue Deschambault*, p. 168; Roy, "Un Jardin au bout du monde," pp. 178-179; Roy, "Voyage en Ungava," p. 372; Gagné, *Visages de Gabrielle Roy*, pp. 166-168.

[22] Roy, *Ces Enfants de ma vie*, pp. 149-150. See also pp. 148, 151, 202; Roy, *La Route d'Altamont*, pp. 164, 191-192, 198; Gagné, *Visages de Gabrielle Roy*, pp. 158-161, 220. Médéric's horse, Gaspard, also symbolizes the freedom of youth.

[23] Roy, *Ces Enfants de ma vie*, p. 53. Gabrielle Roy, "La Fuite de Sally," *Le Bulletin des Agriculteurs*, 27, No. 1 (janvier 1941), 40. See also Gabrielle Roy, "La Source au désert," *Le Bulletin des Agriculteurs*, 42, No. 10 (octobre 1946), 32; Gagné, *Visages de Gabrielle Roy*, p. 237.

[24] Roy, *Bonheur d'occasion*, p. 109. See also Roy, *Un Jardin au bout du monde*, p. 215; Roy, *Ces Enfants de ma vie*, pp. 41-59. For the rela-

tionships between childhood and art see: Roy, "La Source au désert," p. 11; Roy, *La Montagne secrète*, pp. 55-59.

[25]Gabrielle Roy, "La Conversion des O'Connor," *La Revue Moderne*, 21, No. 5 (septembre 1939), 4-5, 32-33; Gabrielle Roy, "La Pension de vieillesse," *Le Bulletin des Agriculteurs*, 39, No. 11 (novembre 1943), 8; Gabrielle Roy, "La Lune des moissons," *La Revue Moderne*, 29, No. 5 (septembre 1947), 13, 80.

[26]Roy, "La Grande Berthe," *Le Bulletin des Agriculteurs*, 39, No. 6 (juin 1943), 4-9, 39-49.

[27]Roy, "La Rivière sans repos," p. 278. See also pp. 245-246, 262-266, 278-280; Roy, *Alexandre Chenevert*, pp. 137-138.

[28]Roy, "Petite Misère," *Rue Deschambault*, p. 39. See also pp. 102-103, 133-134, 176; Roy, *La Petite Poule d'eau*, pp. 14-15, 19. Gabrielle Roy herself is said to have felt that she was *de trop* in her family. See Marie-Anna A. Roy, p. 30. Images of the protective home will be analyzed in Chapter VI.

[29]Roy, *La Route d'Altamont*, pp. 226-227. See also pp. 164-165, 212; Roy, *Rue Deschambault*, pp. 246, 268-270; Roy, *Ces Enfants de ma vie*, pp. 9, 24-28; Brochu, "Gabrielle Roy."

[30]Roy, *Bonheur d'occasion*, pp. 78, 104. See also p. 64; Roy, *Rue Deschambault*, p. 37; Roy, *La Route d'Altamont*, p. 148; Roy, *La Montagne secrète*, pp. 58-59.

[31]Roy, *Rue Deschambault*, p. 166. See also p. 160; Roy, *La Route d'Altamont*, pp. 105-106, 118-119, 122; Grosskurth, *Gabrielle Roy*, pp. 38-40.

[32]Roy, *Rue Deschambault*, pp. 172, 166. See also p. 180. These failures to understand the adult world can be found on pp. 74-75, 99, 100-101, 123-124, 185, 217. See also Paula Gilbert Lewis, "*Street of Riches* and *The Road Past Altamont*: The Feminine World of Gabrielle Roy," *Journal of Women's Studies in Literature*, 1, No. 2 (Spring 1979), 134.

[33]Roy, *Rue Deschambault*, p. 111. See also pp. 102-103, 108, 113, 127, 205. The explanations are those given by her mother to Christine's father concerning the older woman's secret trip to Quebec.

[34]Roy, *Bonheur d'occasion*, pp. 106-109, 146; Roy, *La Petite Poule d'eau*, p. 162; Roy, *Rue Deschambault*, p. 141; Roy, "La Rivière sans repos," pp. 166-171. Jean Paul Desrochers, "La Famille dans l'oeuvre de Gabrielle Roy," Thesis Université Laval 1965, pp. 63-72, 75-78. There will be further development of the relationships between mothers and daughters in Chapter III.

[35]Parizeau, pp. 120, 121.

[36]Roy, "La Rivière sans repos," pp. 197, 312. See also pp. 138-141,

143-147, 173-178, 313.

[37] Gérard Bessette, *Trois Romanciers québécois* (Montréal: Editions du Jour, 1973), p. 226; Roy, *Bonheur d'occasion,* pp. 172-177, 217; Roy, *La Route d'Altamont,* pp. 51-52, 248-249, 254-255.

[38] Gabrielle Roy, *Ma Vache Bossie* (Montréal: Les Editions Leméac, Inc., 1976), pp. 14, 15, 18, 19, 30-31, 38-40.

[39] Roy, *La Route d'Altamont,* p. 104. See also pp. 15-16, 93-94, 96, 101-103, 107-109, 141, 156-159, 163-164. Médéric's desires for freedom, in *Ces Enfants de ma vie,* are even more urgent and powerful since they occur later in life, during adolescence.

[40] Roy, *La Route d'Altamont,* p. 165. See also pp. 89, 159; Roy, *Rue Deschambault,* pp. 70, 71, 74-78.

[41] Roy, *Rue Deschambault,* p. 85. See also pp. 51, 72, 94-95; Roy, *La Route d'Altamont,* pp. 62, 64-69, 80-81, 96, 98, 149, 174; Bachelard, *La Poétique de la rêverie,* pp. 86-88, 92, 101-102.

[42] Roy, *Rue Deschambault,* pp. 38, 41, 42.

[43] Roy, *Rue Deschambault,* pp. 26-27, 169; Brochu, "Gabrielle Roy"; Antonine Maillet (Soeur Marie-Grégoire), "La Femme et l'enfant dans l'oeuvre de Gabrielle Roy," Thesis Université Saint-Joseph de Memramcook 1959, pp. 26-34.

[44] Roy, *Ces Enfants de ma vie,* p. 95. See also pp. 119-121; Roy, *Bonheur d'occasion,* pp. 179-181.

[45] Roy, *Bonheur d'occasion,* pp. 170-171, 192-203; Roy, *Rue Deschambault,* pp. 165-180. A full analysis of sickness and death will be found in Chapter IV.

[46] Roy, *Ces Enfants de ma vie,* p. 208. See also pp. 94-95, 122, 212; Lewis, "The Fragility of Childhood," pp. 148-153.

[47] Roy, *Ces Enfants de ma vie,* p. 43; See also pp. 32-33; Roy, *Cet Eté qui chantait,* pp. 180-181.

[48] Roy, *Ces Enfants de ma vie,* p. 12. See also pp. 139-140, 142-143, 162, 201, 203; Brochu, "Gabrielle Roy"; François Ricard, "Le Cercle enfin uni des hommes: Hommage à Gabrielle Roy pour sa trentième année de création littéraire," *Liberté,* 18, No. 1, année 1976, numéro 103 (janvier-février 1976), 73-74. The initial idea for *Ces Enfants de ma vie* came, in fact, from the remembrance of Vincento, one of Roy's former pupils. Personal interview with Gabrielle Roy, 29 June 1980.

[49] Roy, *Ces Enfants de ma vie,* p. 11. See also pp. 7-8, 12-16, 63-70, 75-78; Roy, "La Rivière sans repos," pp. 231-234; Roy, *La Petite Poule d'eau,* p. 68; Lewis, "The Fragility of Childhood," pp. 148-149.

[50] Roy, *La Petite Poule d'eau,* pp. 74-75, 85-89.

[51] Roy, *Ces Enfants de ma vie,* p. 197. See also pp. 16, 22-31, 79-83. Roy felt that the strongest and deepest love was that first love of a pupil

for a teacher. Personal interview with Gabrielle Roy, 29 June 1980.

[52]Roy, *Ces Enfants de ma vie*, p. 107. See also pp. 101, 104, 125.

[53]Roy, *Cet Eté qui chantait*, p. 183; Roy, *Ces Enfants de ma vie*, p. 21.

[54]Roy, *Ces Enfants de ma vie*, pp. 94, 207.

[55]Parizeau, p. 118. Gabrielle Roy, "Souvenirs du Manitoba," *La Revue de Paris*, 62e année, No. 2 (février 1955), p. 78; Gabrielle Roy, "Le Manitoba," *Le Magazine Maclean*, 2, No. 7 (juillet 1962), 107; Roy, "La Grande Berthe," pp. 47-48; Roy, *Bonheur d'occasion*, pp. 195-198, 318-319; Roy, *La Petite Poule d'eau*, pp. 42, 46-48, 53, 112-113, 118, 128, 133, 135-140; Roy, *Ces Enfants de ma vie*, pp. 102, 127.

[56]Roy, *Alexandre Chenevert*, p. 139; Roy, *La Petite Poule d'eau*, pp. 80-81, 99-101, 119-120.

[57]Roy, "La Rivière sans repos," p. 216; Roy, "Gérard le pirate," pp. 38-39.

[58]Roy, "Gérard le pirate," p. 37; Gabrielle Roy, "Pitié pour les institutrices," *Le Bulletin des Agriculteurs*, 38, No. 3 (mars 1942), 46; Roy, *La Petite Poule d'eau*, pp. 129-132; Maillet, pp. 18-24.

[59]Gabrielle Roy, "Avantage pour," *La Revue Moderne*, 20, No. 6 (octobre 1940), 6; Roy, "Les Deux Nègres," *Rue Deschambault*, pp. 26-27, 30-31; Roy, "Wilhelm," *Rue Deschambault*, pp. 226, 228, 230-232. This serious and romantic attitude toward love that is typical in most adolescents does not appear in the four adolescent Eskimo girls of "La Rivière sans repos." When these girls, including Elsa, see love scenes on the movie screen, they laugh, imitate the movie stars, and treat the entire notion as amusing. Such a reaction stems from a difference in cultures, as well as, most likely, Roy's opinion of the Eskimo as an innocent child-adult before being corrupted by White civilization. See Roy, "La Rivière sans repos," pp. 119-120.

[60]Roy, "Les Bijoux," *Rue Deschambault*, pp. 235-240. See also Lewis, "The Feminine World of Gabrielle Roy," p. 136.

[61]Roy, "De la truite dans l'eau glacée," *Ces Enfants de ma vie*, p. 147. See also pp. 132-133, 139-144, 148, 149, 170, 177-186, 202, 210-222; Lewis, "The Fragility of Childhood," p. 150.

[62]Roy, *Bonheur d'occasion*, pp. 180, 149, 240; Roy, *Rue Deschambault*, pp. 227, 228, 231; Roy, "La Rivière sans repos," pp. 281-282, 284-291; Roy, *Ces Enfants de ma vie*, pp. 133-134; Lewis, "The Feminine World of Gabrielle Roy," p. 136; Lewis, "The Fragility of Childhood," p. 150. This rebellion actually begins during early childhood and is seen even then, as having no chance of success. See Roy, *Ces Enfants de ma vie*, p. 43.

[63]Roy, *Rue Deschambault*, p. 257. Gabrielle Roy writes specifically of the sexual act only twice, and both times involving adolescents, or,

more precisely, young adults: the seduction-rape scene between Florentine and Jean in *Bonheur d'occasion* and the rape of Elsa by the American G.I. in "La Rivière sans repos." Because of the consequences of these events that deeply affect the adult lives of these women, sex and the attitude toward it by Royan characters will be treated in Chapter III.

[64] Roy, "La Maison gardée," "De la truite dans l'eau glacée," *Ces Enfants de ma vie*, pp. 97, 183-184.

[65] Roy, *Ces Enfants de ma vie*, pp. 141, 146, 149, 168, 171-175, 177-186, 197, 198, 200-203, 210-212; Lewis, "The Fragility of Childhood," p. 151.

[66] Roy, *Ces Enfants de ma vie*, p. 200. See also pp. 149, 152, 157, 190-192, 201-203; Lewis, "The Fragility of Childhood," pp. 150-151.

[67] Roy, *Ces Enfants de ma vie*, pp. 162, 172, 185-189, 200-201.

[68] Roy, "La Rivière sans repos," p. 130; Roy, "La Maison gardée," *Ces Enfants de ma vie*, pp. 96-99, 110-113, 119-121, 125-126, 128; Lewis, "The Fragility of Childhood," pp. 149-150.

[69] Roy, *Ces Enfants de ma vie*, pp. 135, 163, 197, 198, 201. See also pp. 169, 179, 188, 199; Roy, *Rue Deschambault*, pp. 27, 41-42, 65, 73, 74, 238, 243; Lewis, "The Fragility of Childhood," pp. 150-152.

[70] Roy, *Ces Enfants de ma vie*, pp. 111, 134. See also pp. 98, 121, 135, 141, 144, 146, 151, 160, 192. In earlier works, Yvonne treats Rose-Anna as if the older woman were her child, and Christine assumes her mother's role when she treats her father like a young boy. See Roy, *Bonheur d'occasion*, p. 315; Roy, *Rue Deschambault*, pp. 274-275.

[71] Roy, *Ces Enfants de ma vie*, pp. 177, 179-180. See also pp. 188, 199; Roy, *Bonheur d'occasion*, p. 240; Roy, *La Petite Poule d'eau*, pp. 143-147, 165.

[72] Roy, *Ces Enfants de ma vie*, pp. 137, 151. See also pp. 140, 153, 200-203; Marie du Rédempteur, Soeur (Pierrette Seers), "Le Thème de la solitude dans l'oeuvre de Gabrielle Roy," Thesis, Université de Montréal 1963, pp. 21-25, 35-40. This thesis analyzes the solitude of Florentine, Emmanuel, Jean, Eugène, and Marguerite of *Bonheur d'occasion*, Alicia, Odette, and Christine of *Rue Deschambault*, and Nina of *La Montagne secrète*.

[73] Roy, *Ces Enfants de ma vie*, pp. 149, 212. See also pp. 94-95, 122, 140, 159-160, 169-170, 200-203; Lewis, "The Fragility of Childhood," p. 152.

CHAPTER III

The Reality of Adulthood: Female Predominance, Male Presence, and Unsuccessful Couples

"Voyons, Médéric, bien sûr que je t'aime comme avant. Aucun élève ne me tient autant à coeur, si tu veux le savoir. . . ."

"Mais," dit-il, en reproche douloureux, "vous ne viendriez plus jamais avec moi dans les collines ou même sur la route dans la berline."

"Non, Médéric, ces choses sont finies pour moi. Du reste, je n'en ai plus le temps. A partir de maintenant, j'entends me donner entièrement à ma classe. Fais en autant si tu veux me faire plaisir."[1]

With these words, the eighteen-year-old schoolteacher of *Ces Enfants de ma vie* accepts the inevitable: that the free and spontaneous years of childhood and adolescence are finished; and that as a young adult, she must now resign herself to her chosen role in adult society.

All of the young adults in Gabrielle Roy's works are in similar situations. Some of them may still retain a sense of optimism about their future goals, but they are all fully aware both of the hardships that they will have to endure and, most importantly, of the decisions that they will have to make as they pass into mature adulthood. At times, however, exterior forces will impose a limitation upon their choices. The war-time society of *Bonheur d'occasion*, for example, affects the lives of the entire younger generation: Jean's ambition flourishes; Emmanuel chooses both marriage and the army; Boisvert, Alphonse, and Pitou are faced with a decision between unemployment and the life of a soldier; and Florentine, pregnant by Jean, becomes Emmanuel's wife immediately prior to his being shipped to Europe. In *Rue Deschambault*, Roy's young women appear to possess more freedom of choice, as Odette becomes a nun, and Georgianna marries, against her parents' wishes. Christine, on the other hand, insisting that she has received the calling to become a writer, satisfies her mother's desire and temporarily chooses teaching as her profession. In *La Route d'Altamont,* however, her decision to write will lead to her determination to leave Manitoba and to travel in Europe. With this independent decision to depart, Christine affirms her new role as an adult.[2]

If Christine typifies the Royan child and adolescent, she is also the epitome of the Royan adult: strong, imaginative, sensitive, and, especially, female. The world of children in Gabrielle Roy's fiction is peopled equally by male and female characters. Except for the prominant roles of Alexandre Chenevert, Pierre Cordorai, and Sam Lee Wong, however, Roy's adult world is dominated by women, while most male characters fulfill secondary roles and are portrayed as weaker individuals.

The author obviously felt that her strength as a writer was in this domain: "En outre, on ne parle bien que de ce que l'on connaît le mieux. Parmi les écrivains, il n'a toujours semblé que les hommes en général parlent mieux des hommes, et les femmes des femmes, que le contraire."[3] Many critics, in fact, have seen Gabrielle Roy primarily as a "feminine" writer, that is, excelling in the creation of women characters, continuously underscoring the important role of the mother, concerning herself with the problems facing her literary women, and, finally, viewing all of her characters and their world "with the loving and protective concern of a mother." Whether or not Roy and her literary creations are obsessed with the image of the mother, as believe Phyllis Grosskurth and Gérard Bessette, or whether or not that image is merely a literary theme among others, as states François Ricard, it must be agreed that the predominance of the Royan female character closely resembles the *Québécois* myth of the powerful and protective maternal figure.[4]

One must note, in addition, that although Roy has often been treated as a "feminine" writer, she has always been viewed as a traditionalist rather than as a feminist. When one becomes familiar with all of Roy's fiction, however, from her early short stories to her most recently published novels and collections of short stories, one sees an interesting development in her creation of female characters. Although neither feminist nor liberated in the 1970s and 1980s sense of these terms, Gabrielle Roy seems to have been more concerned with independent, "revolutionary" female characters in her 1939-1946 short stories than in her later works. Her deep preoccupation with women and their struggles, as well as her preference for female characters, has continued in her major fiction, but more of a general humanism, a deep sensitivity for women, men, children, and all of nature prevails. Gabrielle Roy seems to have evolved from an early feminist to what one can call a "feminine humanist."

Almost all of Roy's early fiction revolves around some aspect of a woman's life. In two of her short stories, in fact, the households consist entirely of women. In a third novella, one meets a mother and her ten daughters, while in two additional tales, all but one of the characters are female.[5] Throughout these and other early short stories, Roy treats every stage in a woman's life, from late adolescence or young adulthood to old age. Influenced by the society of the 1940s, her younger characters are often traditionally concerned with finding a husband. Even the honest and natural Sophie of "Cendrillon '40" refocuses her attention toward a man when she realizes that he is attracted to her rather than to her more superficial, "made-up," modern sisters. In "Avantage pour," Lucile, likewise, professes that she will pursue a career rather than marriage, that men prefer independent women, and that she will run after a man, but she quickly uses the ruse of tears to her advantage in order to gain the affection of Jean-Paul.[6]

This depiction of traditional women and of what can be called a marriage mania continues in other early short stories. The all-female household of "Le Roi de coeur," for example, is seen as a world of total disorder, in need of a man to straighten out this dizziness. The four women, anxious to marry well, become dominated by a male but, ironically, soon draw him into their confused world. Similarly, the importance of marriage is ironically treated in "Bonne à marier," as the younger women, almost ridiculously traditional, refuse to marry an older, wealthy widower who eventually is forced to choose their mother.[7] Roy seems to be directing her irony both toward women who are obsessed with getting married and toward men who, in their attempt to dominate these women, are soon overpowered by them.

Once a woman does marry, her life can be extremely harsh and difficult, as for "La Grande Berthe" and for the Mennonite women so greatly admired by Roy. The life of a housewife can also be boring. Sally, of "La Fuite de Sally," can not occupy her days alone at home and flees, for one day only, in order to rediscover herself as she was prior to her marriage. Lizzie, the heroine of "La Conversion des O'Connor," is a faithful wife and mother but decides that she needs to leave: " 'J'en ai assez

des O'Connor, de toute la bande. A moi la liberté!' " As a
1939 *Québécois* woman, however, she adds that there is sufficient food left in the kitchen, and she soon returns from
her little escapade to her traditional role in a family that still
does not respect her but needs her.[8] Roy, once again, portrays
ironically both the woman and her family.

     She is totally serious, however, when she describes the
embarrassment of "La Grande Berthe" at being pregnant and
her subsequent terrified stoicism during childbirth. Roy similarly treats with poignant gravity the situation of Juliette of "Sécurité" who desperately loves children, desires to adopt a child,
but finally resigns herself to her husband's wishes to remain
financially secure and, thus, childless. One must remember that,
for Gabrielle Roy, a child was the justification of a couple in
love.[9]

     Precisely because of her almost reverent attitude toward
children, Roy treats in a totally negative light Nathalie of "La
Source au désert." When this woman becomes pregnant, she
experiences "cette peur de souffrir, d'enlaidir, cette peur a-
troce. . . ." With an "accidental" fall down the stairs, everything
is conveniently arranged, and Nathalie loses the baby. To the
husband of this, in effect, self-abortionist, "en tout ceci, n'avait-
elle été guidée que par le souci odieux de sa beauté?" One has
the distinct impression that Gabrielle Roy is seconding these
words, for throughout this two-part short story, Nathalie is
portrayed as a perverted, evil, and maliciously voluptuous female
in the eyes of her husband, Dr. Raymond. She is constantly
compared to Anne, her husband's true love, who represents
purity, joy, and spring-like youth. But Anne is also the first
Royan female martyr, since she refuses to rebel against her
tragic destiny without Raymond and is not convinced of her
ability to begin anew. It is in this particular short story, in fact,
that Roy first clearly expresses this need, especially on the part
of women, for *recommencement*. It is the doctor who recognizes this essential difference between men and women: "En
vérité, elles [women in general] étaient capables d'une chose
que les hommes réussissent rarement: recommencer leur vie. . . .
Refaire leur vie! L'instinct de durer, de se terrer. Une plus ab-
jecte soumission à la vie que celle même de l'homme." Throughout Roy's early short stories, prefiguring her major fiction,
there is a common element linking the strong female characters:
precisely that of a determination to live and, if necessary, to

begin a new life. Ironically, Anne, the symbol of pure love, is the one woman in these novellas who refuses this possibility, prefers to die slowly rather than to compromise her desired life with Raymond, and, thus, ultimately becomes the symbol of his sorrow and death. Roy certainly does not advocate a life such as that of Nathalie in this story, but she also does not, nor will she ever, recommend female martyrdom.[10]

In fact, several of these early female characters are quite the opposite of Anne and present the image of the independent, working woman. Mariette not only works but is the boss; Bobinette also works and lives alone; and Loubka used to work but has left her job because of sexual advances made toward her by her boss. Loubka also does not particularly like men, despite the fact that, ironically, her name means love.[11] She is the literary sister of Judith, the militant, feminist, man hater of the 1940 "Les Petits Pas de Caroline." This heroine considers herself to be a true feminist: thirty-years old, unmarried, with no need for men. She meets Alain, an obnoxious chauvinist whom she treats with sarcasm and disdain:

> Ses narines [of Judith] se dilatèrent dans l'anticipation du combat.
> "Ecoutez, jeune homme. On a trop longtemps répandu dans ce monde la légende qu'une femme ne peut ouvrir une porte, allumer sa cigarette ou nouer ses lacets de souliers. Moi je suis venue ici [to the Gaspé Peninsula] pour prouver le contraire, et vous pensez que vous allez contrecarrer mes projets de réforme sociale. . . ."

Alain can not understand Judith, for he has learned about the "weaker sex" from the sentimental, romantic books written by a traditional female author, Caroline. In a desperate attempt to win Judith's affection, however, Alain promises to allow her to burn the fictional garbage that has so warped his mind. But Judith cannot do this, for she is, in fact, Caroline. She is the feminist with a penchant for what she calls "ces fantômes de l'imagination," romantic and chivalrous lovers who no longer exist but continue to enthrall adolescents who still believe in love. Judith will eventually destroy Caroline, will no longer write such novels, but one also has the impression that she will remain with Alain.[12] Once again, Gabrielle Roy has ironically placed in her heroine both feminist and traditional characteristics, the latter of which triumph in the name of love.

This same strain of female independence, however, does

continue into middle age, as witnessed by Mlle Lajeunesse, the humorously depicted, self-sufficient heroine of both "Six Pilules par jour" and "Embobeliné." This woman, as her name comically indicates, truly believes in *le recommencement,* for she is, in 1941, the modern nutritionist, exerciser, health food and vitamin pill maniac. She may be humorous, but she is youthful and happy. Much of this humor and irony is abandoned, however, when Roy creates women in their older age. "La Grande Berthe," for example, becomes resigned to the onset of menopause, and the pitiful old woman of "La Pension de vieillesse" dreams of her pension, receives it, and then dies. But although total independence is lost for these older women, Berthe does also ultimately triumph: she inherits her husband's money and keeps the family together with herself at the helm. And Bédette, "La Grande Voyageuse," although dependent upon the hospitality of her sisters, does learn to enjoy her, at times, humorously depected nomadic life, travelling from one home to another. In the end, she also cleverly convinces the railroad company to pay her an indemnity in her old age.[13] Most of Roy's early female characters valiantly succeed.

It is evident that throughout these early short stories, a constant and frequently ironic duality is present in almost all of Roy's female creations: they are both feminist and traditional. It must also be noted that the latter quality does usually appear to dominate. The fact both that the independent nature of these fictionalized women does often make itself known and that Roy is deeply preoccupied with the concerns of women, however, does indicate a feminist consciousness, on the part of the author, that was quite unusual for a woman in Quebec forty years ago.

This same awareness, divided between a liberated and a traditional viewpoint, apparently continued in Gabrielle Roy's personal beliefs. In a 1966 interview with Alice Parizeau, the author discussed her opinions on the status of women: that given the equality between men and women, the emancipation of the latter signified the attainment of their identity and the definition of their goals in life. For Roy, since women were "les esclaves des temps modernes," and worse in Quebec than in Europe, the "révolte de la jeune Canadienne est pleinement justifiée. Le fait que l'émancipation de la femme soit un phénomène très récent démontre, au fond, que notre société est encore très peu civilisée. Que l'attitude de l'Eglise à l'égard de la femme a été méprisante." She advocated taking advantage of "la liberté de choisir une carrière avant de créer une famille," before, in fact, getting married, for then the union between a man and a woman would truly be based upon understanding, mutual respect, and freedom. In such a marriage, therefore, the woman would also be able to make her own important decisions: "Tenez, il est inconcevable pour moi d'imposer à une femme des grossesses. C'est à elle de decider si elle veut, ou non, avoir un enfant."[14]

Closely linked to these feminist statements, however, were more traditional ones. Although Roy advocated a career for a woman, she felt that the search for freedom through work could merely lead to another form of slavery. She, therefore, advised young women not first to envision this career after marriage simply to prove that they were free. As a matter of fact, as of 1970 in another interview, Roy goes even further in stating that a chosen profession was more important for a man than for a woman, "parce que la femme a quand même comme compensation sa maison, ses enfants, sa famille, la cuisine. . . ."[15]

Once again it was predominantly in the domain of children where Gabrielle Roy became the most traditional, especially given her firm belief in the need of a marriage not based solely upon sexual attraction but upon love: "Ce qui justifie l'existence d'un couple, c'est une oeuvre. Un enfant. . . . C'est l'amour surtout! Ce n'est pas un travail qu'on accepte pour échapper à l'ennui." Although she was not herself a mother, or precisely because she had not had this experience of motherhood, Roy saw the birth of a child, despite inevitable pain, as the most wonderful joy in life and the rapport between a mother and child as the greatest mystery in the world. She also defended the role of mothers:

> Les mères sont aujourd'hui dépréciées et on les rend souvent re-
> sponsables des défauts, des lacunes, et des complexes de notre société.
> Tout le monde les accuse et les malmène. Il est presque indécent
> d'avouer en public qu'on s'occupe tout simplement de ses enfants
> et qu'on en est heureux. Que cela puisse suffire à une femme. Qu'elle
> puisse trouver là toute la satisfaction et tout le bonheur personnels.
> Et pourtant une mère qui réussit son enfant, c'est encore la plus
> belle réalisation humaine.

Although Gabrielle Roy never abandoned her deep preoccupation with women and with their concerns, it was this more traditional side of the author's beliefs that dominated her major fiction as of 1945 and shaped the lives of her female characters, essentially representing martyrdom, while extolling the virtues of motherhood.[16]

In that year appeared Roy's still best known character, Rose-Anna Lacasse of *Bonheur d'occasion*. This strong and energetic "femme du peuple" is the head of a large household living in the poor, working-class section of Saint-Henri in Montreal. Rose-Anna is portrayed as rational, practical, and lucid about the daily miseries that she and her family must face. It is precisely these confrontations with misery, however, along with her protective instinct toward her family, that also create in this woman the corresponding image of an old, tired, worried, and, at times, pitiful mother figure. She is seen as the traditional "Mère des Douleurs," as well as a source of strength for survival in the harsh world.[17]

Rose-Anna's awareness of the reality of this misery stems from many years of deceptions and hardships. She sees marriage, and her marriage in particular, as a serious situation, filled equally with joys and pain. She recognizes and accepts the boredom of her life, symbolized by the continual and monotonous whirring of her sewing machine, with its wheel infatigably turning around: "La roue de la machine se reprit à tourner; . . . elle tournait comme les années avaient tourné, comme la terre tournait. . . . Ainsi la maison semblait prise dans ce mouvement inlassable de la roue." Often seated by herself at this machine, Rose-Anna, at times, becomes fearful of this solitude that has been accompanying her throughout her life; however, at other times, she needs "justement d'être seule encore quelque temps avec sa peine et de la goûter, de la goûter, de la savourer jusqu'au bout."[18]

Rose-Anna Lacasse is, in effect, alone, almost alienated because of her tragic destiny, specifically being annually pregnant. Already deformed by these numerous pregnancies, she is, in the novel, carrying her eleventh child. Roy's description of the birth of this child clearly underscores the author's pride and pity for this woman, fearful of death and of her children's fate if she were to die. In her deep solitude, "comme une femme l'est toujours à ces moments-là," Rose-Anna proudly resists as long as possible without giving in to the pain. She eventually,

however, must abandon herself "à la souffrance et à l'humiliation du corps," as she descends "dans un abîme infini": "Elle
avait entendu bien des femmes prétendre que le premier ac-
couchement seul était dur. Mais elle savait le contraire. Elle
savait que le corps redoutait un peu plus, chaque fois, la honte
de cette nouvelle soumission à la douleur. . . ." Always desirous,
at the last minute, of a boy who will suffer less than she, Rose-
Anna gives birth to a son. Her courage is renewed, as it is after
each childbirth, and she returns to her daily routine.[19]

It is necessary to recommence her chores immediately,
for without Rose-Anna, the Lacasse family would not be able
to function. This woman is totally responsible for the manage-
ment of her home, including the annual spring-time house moves
in order to locate less expensive living quarters. Rose-Anna is,
therefore, constantly worried, constantly concerned about
financial matters, caught in "cette prison de soucis, de tour-
ments, de chiffres. . . ."[20]

Imprisoned within this circle of misery, Rose-Anna again
encounters isolation, for she can expect neither financial nor
emotional support from her husband, Azarius. She is, in fact,
the victim of her tragic destiny precisely because of her husband's inaction and daydreams. Before her mother, she may
defend Azarius' business schemes, failures, and perpetual unemployment, but she is well aware of his true nature. She
excuses him because, like all men in her opinion, he is less
capable than women of enduring hardships. In effect, she
treats him more as her child than as her spouse. Rose-Anna
would of course, prefer Azarius to work and to support his
family, and she is extremely proud when he does work temporarily—at a job that she has obtained for him—but maintaining
her love for her husband, she accepts the inevitable. Even on
the one day during which Rose-Anna is overpowered by Azarius'
youthful joy and optimism, and the two of them, with their
children, return to her childhood home, this *mater dolorosa*
resigns herself to the subsequent disasters: the loss of Azarius'
job, Daniel's illness, and Florentine's pregnancy. Rose-Anna
faces these events as all other occurences in her life: with
strength, pride, and solitude.[21]

When Rose-Anna visits her mother, Mme Laplante, one
realizes that solitude and independence have been forced upon
the younger woman since childhood. Like a shameful child,
Rose-Anna sits before her elderly mother and awaits her aid

and counsel.   What she receives, as usual, is a sermon, cold "comme le visage blanc et anguleux de la vielle femme":

> Qu'était-elle [Rose-Anna] venue chercher exactement?   Elle ne le savait plus. . . .   Car de la vieille femme, il n'y avait à espérer aucun aveu de tendresse. . . . jamais elle ne s'était penchée sur aucun d'eux avec une flamme claire et joyeuse, au fond de ses durs yeux gris fer. Jamais elle ne les avait pris sur ses genoux. . . . Jamais elle ne les avait embrassés. . . .

Mme Laplante did always care for the physical needs of her children, but " 'est-ce rien que ça qu'une mère doit donner à ses enfants?' "[22]

Rose-Anna would like to give more of herself to her own children, but tenderness "s'abritait presque toujours chez elle sous des regards discrets et des mots d'un usage familier. Elle eût éprouvé de la gêne à l'exprimer autrement." So Rose-Anna and her family have established, instead, a language of "tendresse silencieuse et d'amicale gronderie plutôt que de véritable conversation."   In addition, this traditional mother does not understand her offspring: Eugène who enlists; Yvonne who wants to become a nun; Daniel who, on his death bed, appears to prefer the anglophone nurse, Jenny, of whom Rose-Anna becomes maternally jealous; and, especially, Florentine who, in her rebellion and desires for a better life, has become pregnant.   When Rose-Anna realizes what has happened to her oldest daughter, for example, she remains silent "et les deux femmes se regardaient comme deux ennemies. . . . Florentine, la première, abaissa la vue. Une fois encore elle chercha les yeux de sa mère. . . . Mais Rose-Anna avait détourné la tête." With the avoidance of this look, Rose-Anna, increasingly ashamed of her daughter's condition, will cut off any possible communication.[23] Both women will remain alone.

Precisely because of the constant recurrence of such personal problems, Rose-Anna has always tried not to think about the misfortunes of others. She is not indifferent to universal unhappiness, but she feels that she must reserve her pity and tenderness for her own family. Only once does she allow herself to commiserate with others, specifically with other women who have been forced to see their husbands and sons depart for war:

> Il lui sembla qu'elle marchait par cette claire fin d'après-midi, non pas seule, mais dans les rangs, parmi des milliers de femmes, et que leurs soupirs frappaient son oreille, que les soupirs las des besogneuses, des femmes du peuple, du fond des siècles montaient jusqu'à elle. Elle était de celles qui n'ont rien d'autre à défendre que leurs hommes et leurs fils. . . . Une foule innombrable l'avait rejointe, venant mystérieusement du passé, de tous les côtés, de très loin et aussi de très près, semblait-il, car des visages nouveaux surgissaient à chaque pas, et ils lui ressemblaient. Pourtant, c'étaient des malheurs plus grands que les siens qu'elles supportaient, ces femmes d'ailleurs. Elles pleuraient leur foyer dévasté; elles arrivaient vers Rose-Anna, les mains vides et, en la reconnaissant, esquissaient vers elle un geste de prière. Car, de tout temps, les femmes se sont reconnues dans le deuil. . . . Rose-Anna allait d'un pas pressé. Et chez cette femme simple se livrait un grand combat. Elle vit le désespoir de ses soeurs, elle le vit bien, sans faiblesse, elle le regarda en face et en comprit toute l'horreur. . . .

But then she remembers her own children, her own personal problems and with "son instinct de gardienne," renews her strength in order to pursue her sole purpose in life: to protect her family.[24]   Rose-Anna Lacasse is united with all mothers of the world and throughout the centuries, and she does specifically symbolize the myth of the *Québécois* mother, but she is also a powerfully created figure who, in her own fictional world, has learned not only to accept reality but also to fight against it.

She has inherited this attitude of acceptance from her mother who, as a fatalist, does not believe in happiness and has simply learned to endure "son purgatoire sur terre." All of her life Mme Laplante "avait parlé de supporter ses croix, ses épreuves, ses fardeaux. Elle avait parlé toute sa vie de résignation chrétienne et de douleurs à endurer." She, therefore, reminds her daughter: " 'Tu vois à c'te heure que la vie, ma fille, on arrange pas ça comme on veut.' " Rose-Anna, in effect, will echo her mother's words to her own daughter: " 'Qu'est-ce que tu veux, Florentine, on fait pas comme on veut dans la vie; on fait comme on peut.' "   Rose-Anna's words, almost as an apology for her life, sound like those of a woman resigned to her destiny, but somehow she always manages to continue her struggle against misery, to refuse the type of life that society has imposed upon her and her family. Roy hoped, in fact, that the example of this character would inspire us all to hope for and envision a better world for everyone. In this way, there would be some sense to the sacrifices made by her heroine.[25]

The example of such martyrdom in one's mother does not go unheeded by a daughter. If Rose-Anna has been negatively, but unmistakably, influenced by her mother, Florentine has, likewise, observed her mother's life and has vowed not to follow along the same path. Florentine does love Rose-Anna, desires to aid her financially, and, at times, even sees the older woman's courage as a guiding light, but she also maintains that her future life will inevitably be separate from that of her mother. She is, however, fearful of the similar destiny of any woman entrapped both in the poverty of Saint-Henri and within her female body, constantly subject to pregnancy. Florentine expresses her "mépris pour sa condition de femme" and yet, ironically, finds no solace in any relationship with another woman, neither with her mother, nor with a friend: "Les femmes! pensait-elle avec mépris. Et d'ailleurs, est-ce qu'une femme peut aider une autre femme? . . ."[26]

Florentine has always avoided forming friendships with other young women, for she imagines that they are envious of her. Although egotistical, however, she is not a true loner. To the contrary, Florentine is terrified of being alone. She needs others in order to exist. In her eyes, solitude is that which haunts certain people: "Et pour elle, la solitude, cet horrible état qu'elle découvrait, prenait un goût de pauvreté, car elle s'imaginait encore que dans le luxe, dans l'aisance même, il n'y a point de pareille découverte."[27] By using chosen individuals in order to escape from her poverty, therefore, Florentine hopes to destroy this feared sense of isolation.

It is precisely this ambitious dream to flee from her present life of poverty in Saint-Henri that preoccupies Florentine throughout the novel. She is caught in the economic, social, and hereditary *tourbillon* of urban misery, and she desperately clings to the hope that "ses frêles efforts de recommencement" will succeed. Ashamed of her poverty and, thus, insecure about herself, she will defy society and prove that, despite her background, she is different, better than those around her. She is determined to be identified with her first, rather than her family, name:

> Florentine . . . était une appellation jeune, joyeuse, comme un mot de printemps, mais le nom [Lacasse], après ce prénom, avait une

> tournure peuple, de misère, qui détruisait tout son charme. Et
> c'était probablement ainsi qu'elle était elle-même, la petite serveuse
> du *Quinze-Cents:* moitié peuple, moitié printemps gracieux. . . .[28]

In order to demonstrate that she is superior to others and
in order to attract men who could possibly help her escape from
her poverty, Florentine pitifully and symbolically disguises
her true, insecure, and child-like nature in ostentatious clothing,
jewelry, and cosmetics. When, for example, her dream comes
true, and Jean Lévesque invites her to a restaurant, she is distressed that she is not wearing her best dress and her costume
jewelry:

> Une inquiétude s'ajouta soudainement à sa grande déception.
> Avait-elle au moins son bâton de rouge? Frénétiquement, avec
> des mains qui tremblaient, elle ouvrait son sac de faux cuir. . . .
> Ses doigts glissèrent sur le peigne, la petite boîte de fard. . . . A
> la fin, ses doigts rencontrèrent le tube de métal; elle le serra avec
> joie et elle fut soulagée, elle fut très soulagée.[29]

But despite her lipstick and her almost vulgar perfume. Florentine is pathetic in the restaurant. She is the caricature of a
woman outside her realm of misery and placed in a totally
unknown world.

Florentine, however, is blind to this parody because she
is with Jean. From the moment she first saw Jean, she had
been attracted to him because, in her eyes, he was elegant,
different from the other young men of Saint-Henri. Almost
immediately, Jean becomes a symbol for Florentine, something
for which she has been searching since childhood: her salvation,
her escape from sordid reality. Although she realizes that he can
destroy her life, or, perhaps, because she is attracted to someone
who has this power to hurt her, Florentine needs Jean: "Mais
Jean, c'était quand même sa fuite longtemps combattue en
elle-même, Jean c'était celui qu'il fallait suivre, jusqu'au bout,
pour toujours. Jamais elle ne le laisserait s'échapper."[30]

Despite her fascination for Jean, Florentine is childishly
anxious to make him suffer, just as she has been suffering because of his constant sarcasm and apparent desire to avoid her
after their romantic kiss during a snowstorm. She first tries
to make him jealous by flirting with his friend, Emmanuel;
she then pitifully confesses her love to him; and finally she

boldly invites Jean to her house.   During the seduction-rape scene at her home, Florentine remains a pitiful figure, as she will be subsequently, with her confused thoughts, her shame before Rose-Anna, and the hatred of her own image in the mirror.[31]

Florentine Lacasse, however, is Rose-Anna's true daughter, whether or not the young woman has inherited her mother's determination and strength, or is vowing not to become resigned to her fate, as she believes that her mother has done. When Florentine realizes that she is pregnant, she decides to avenge herself against Jean, as her initial resignation is transformed into defiance.   She knows that Emmanuel is quite entranced by her, so in a coldly sensual and calculating manner, she formulates and carries out her plan to persuade him to marry her before he leaves to war.   Emmanuel Létourneau has become Florentine's new source of security, her new salvation, and her new possibility for *recommencement.* She is especially proud to have succeeded in altering her destiny by "ses forces à elle de femme faible, ses forces irrésistibles," as well as "par la force seule de sa volonté. . . . Déjà elle se voyait renaître, aimée, plus jolie que jamais, sauvée."   Florentine can now envision a peaceful life ahead of her: "Il n'y aurait plus d'extase, plus d'abîmes dans sa vie, rien qu'une route plane, tranquille, où, s'y voyant sauvée, elle ne s'étonnait plus de se trouver engagée."[32]   Her peaceful road of marriage will lead to salvation in boredom.

On her wedding day, Florentine begins to fear that, with her marriage and pregnancy, she will merely be following the same fate as that of her mother:

> Et ce mot de "mariage" qu'elle avait allié autrefois à une sensation de bonheur éperdu, de réussite, lui parut austère, affligeant, plein d'embûches et de tristes découvertes.   Elle aperçut sa mère, lourde, qui allait et venait avec peine; et une vision d'elle-même ainsi déformée s'implanta dans son esprit.   Elle s'étira, sentit un frisson parcourir ses membres délicats; la pensée de l'épreuve qu'elle aurait à subir la remplit d'une atroce indignation.   Oh qu'elle haïssait le piège dans lequel elle était tombée!

Florentine accepts the fact that she is marrying someone whom she does not love but to whom she feels deep gratitude.   She will finally have her vengeance against Jean.   Only after she is

married, and after Emmanuel has left with his regiment, however, does she first think of her unborn child and how she will
never love this person who will undoubtedly make her suffer.
But as a traditional woman, at least she is married, and as an
independent female, at least she feels fully responsible both
for what has happened and for her future. Without the presence
of men who have gone to war, she and the other women around
her will now begin their lives anew, profitting from the money
sent home to them by their spouses.[33]   Florentine, like her
mother, has become resigned to her life, still in Saint-Henri,
but more financially secure and more socially accepted. And
once again like Rose-Anna, she will face the future bravely and
alone. Florentine Lacasse has only partially fulfilled her dreams.

The female characters of Gabrielle Roy's first novel, therefore, manifest the complimentary and yet diverse qualities of
independence, strength, and traditionalism, all subject to a
destiny of solitude. These same characteristics are evident
in Eugénie, wife of the hero of Roy's second novel, *Alexandre
Chenevert,* although one's image of her is shaped by the fact
that she is depicted essentially through her husband's eyes.
Eugénie is described by Alexandre as being indifferent and
stupid, almost disgusting because apparently healthy and well-
adjusted, she sleeps peacefully while her husband copes with
his insomnia. It is only when Eugénie becomes ill that one
begins to catch a glimpse of her mediocre and monotonous
life with Alexandre, a man who has never paid much attention
to her and who, to Eugénie's consternation, does not even treat
her illness seriously. Even her male doctor, with a typically
condescending tone, tells her that her problems are simply
related to menopause and will soon disappear.[34]

Eugénie's sickness becomes worse, and with this condition
comes a change in attitude in the aging woman: "A l'époque où
elle commença à sentir l'approche de la vieillesse, Eugénie Chenevert éprouve un désir accru de bonheur." She begins to desire
what she has never had: overt tenderness, understanding, and
joy. She also wants to be treated with patience by Alexandre
whom she has begun to resent: "Comme pour punir Alexandre,
elle retardait d'obéir à son médecin. Il est vrai qu'elle redoutait
beaucoup le traitement; elle y voyait une sorte de lien, la pauvre
femme, avec le mariage, l'injuste condition féminine qui vague-
ment lui paraissait imputable à l'égoïsme des hommes."[35]

Eugénie, however, is a middle-aged woman living in Montreal in the mid-1950s and as such, retains many of the attitudes prevalent in her times and to her particular social situation. Her anger, therefore, is only a temporary aberration. When she is hospitalized for her "female problems," for example, problems that Alexandre suddenly sees as "les misères particulières à leur sexe," she begs her husband never to discuss these personal concerns "qu'elle jugeait de nature à lui attirer la malveillance." She is embarrassed and fearful of additional medical complications. When she recovers and is faced with the necessity of returning home to her household chores, however, she does not want to leave the hospital where, for the first time in her life, she has been able to rest and to enjoy the company of other women. At home her only possibility of communication occurs during the brief and infrequent visits of her daughter, Irène, who herself with an unhappy marriage that has forced her to work full time outside the home, can confide in her mother, as the two women complain about their husbands. It is during these whispered sessions that Eugénie advises the same attitude of resignation that was counselled in *Bonheur d'occasion:* " 'Mieux vaut endurer, ma fille, prends ma parole.' " It is preferable to accept an unhappy marriage than not to be married at all.[36]

Roy does, in fact, delve further into this situation of an unmarried woman, and in particular an unmarried mother, when she creates the powerful and yet poignant figure of Elsa Kumachuk, the heroine of Roy's fourth novel, "La Rivière sans repos." If the heroines of Roy's prior novels can be seen as victims of their social status, of their men, and of their bodies, continually subject to pregnancies, Elsa is the ultimate victim, raped by an unknown American G.I. stationed near her Eskimo town of Fort-Chimo. As the typical Royan female of a novel, she accepts what has happened to her as perfectly natural and, in fact, would have forgotten the entire incident had she not become pregnant. The formerly happy young woman is, instead, transformed into a sad and morose individual, although predictably, she appears to be resigned and even indifferent to or apathetic about her destiny. She does care for herself as a white woman would do during pregnancy, with monthly visits to a nurse and frequent medical tests, but she does not treat the situation seriously. With the courage and resignation of her people, she ultimately "accoucha sans une plainte, le visage à peine défait, tout le temps occupée à regarder au plafond."[37]

With the birth of Jimmy, a sense of life returns to Elsa: "Son âme, si longtemps absente, y revint briller, mais plus grande qu'avant, plus aimante et plus émerveilleée." Looking at this marvelous child who appears to be entirely white rather than Eskimo, Elsa experiences deep pride and a sense of vengeance against those who had made fun of her during pregnancy and in whom she would now like to instill jealousy. She, a bit unbelievably, suddenly becomes fully versed in the art of child rearing, as she continues to follow the White norm and ritualistically, as well as humorously, daily bathes her son and combs his hair while surrounded by the other Eskimo women.[38]

Although Elsa is sensitively and compassionately portrayed, she becomes an exaggeration of the traditional, self-sacrificing mother who must continuously work in order to satisfy her desire of giving her son everything. As a result, she comes into conflict with her mother, Winnie, who takes care of Jimmy while Elsa is working and of whom, therefore, Elsa is envious. Winnie is seen by her daughter as lazy and unambitious, the epitome of the Eskimo nature that Elsa is trying to deny: "Winnie en venait à se demander si c'était bien toujours à sa fille qu'elle avait affaire. Or justement il arrivait à Elsa, en examinant sans bonté la pauvre Winnie toute édentée, peu soigneuse de sa personne, de se dire que ce ne pouvait être là sa mère." But Elsa continues in her chosen ways, purchasing "white" objects such as a playpen for Jimmy, and increasingly frustrated with her mother who has become "sa pire ennemie, en tout cas un obstacle dans la marche qu'elle poursuivait vers un but d'ailleurs sans cesse se dérobant."[39]

Elsa resents Winnie for two reasons: the older woman poses a threat to Elsa's possessive devotion to Jimmy; and she contradicts her daughter's chosen method of raising her son. When Elsa's pastor, Reverend Paterson, likewise points out to her that the rare happiness caused by Jimmy's birth has been totally exhausting and has placed her on a dangerous path where "son âme était occupée de lui à ne pouvoir accepter aucune autre entreprise," Elsa is still not convinced. The pastor continues, therefore, his sermonizing and explains that by raising Jimmy entirely according to White customs she may be instilling in him a sense of shame for his own people. It is only then that Elsa decides to "save" her son and to flee with him to old Fort-Chimo and the simple Eskimo way of life. Once again the pattern of her life is dictated by her sole desire to live through her son, as she moves in with her eccentric uncle, Ian, follows him even further North to Baffin Island in order to avoid having to send Jimmy to school, and returns only when the boy becomes gravely ill.[40]

The sacrifices for her child do not cease upon their return to new Fort-Chimo and, once again, to White culture. Elsa works hard in order to buy whatever Jimmy desires and is totally satisfied if the boy simply smiles at her. This maternal martyrdom reaches its culmination when Elsa experiences her first and only true attraction to a man, an Eskimo, and realizes that Jimmy, with his intense jealousy, will never permit such a relationship to continue. The man regretfully leaves, and Elsa "pendant quelques jours, parut en ressentir et se montra distraite et rêveuse. Mais c'est vraiment tout ce qu'elle devait jamais connaître dans sa vie qui se rapprochait de l'amour." The love of which Roy is speaking is that between a woman and a man. It is totally incompatible with this obsessive maternal love that leaves no room for the presence of a spouse.[41] Elsa Kumachuk is an independent female who is determined to provide for herself and for her son, but her exalted devotion to him will create inevitable solitude and distress for both of them.

Predictably, soon after Elsa's loss of the only possible mutual love in her life, she begins to lose Jimmy. In order to protect him, she even fabricates a pitiful story about her thwarted love for his father—a story that she wants to believe herself—but although she will continue to do anything to keep her son, she knows that he has become a stranger to her, as unknown as the American G.I. She painfully realizes that he will soon leave her:

> Ils ne prononcèrent aucune parole. . . .
>
> Pour cette nuit, elle alla se coucher à l'autre bout de la hutte, sur une peau d'ours étendue par terre. Parce qu'elle eut froid peut-être, ou se sentit trop seule, elle se recroquevilla, les genoux au menton, dans la posture craintive de la créature humaine avant la naissance.
>
> Elle entendit Jimmy pleurer au cours de la nuit. Elle tendait à aller vers lui pour le consoler et lui dire que tout chagrin passe, mais ne l'osait pas et sentait que peut-être jamais plus elle ne l'oserait.[42]

All maternal-filial communication has been destroyed.

Jimmy does depart, to the United States and then to Vietnam, and Elsa's life crumbles, as she returns to the indifference and resignation of her earlier years before her son's birth. She becomes fascinated with Vietnam and, pathetically, begins to confuse in her mind Jimmy and his father. She even studies the faces of Vietnamese women who appear in the newspapers:

> Elle finissait par en choisir une lui plaisant particulièrement pour se faire accroire que c'était elle que Jimmy un soir avait aimée. Pour ce qu'elle en savait, un petit-fils lui était peut-être né au bout du monde, qu'elle n'avait pas la moindre chance de voir jamais; en fin de compte la vie se révélait encore plus saugrenue et surprenante que ne l'avait naguère montrée le cinéma.

Everything in Elsa's life, in fact, seems to occur as if in a dream. To add to this sense of unreality, the poor woman also begins to drink beer and to smoke until "l'air hagard, les yeux ternes, elle se sentait pourtant délivrée et d'une certaine manière heureuse."[43]

At forty years old, Elsa already looks like an old woman. Always alone, she walks endlessly by the Koksoak river, "le visage dénué d'expression." Only when Jimmy briefly returns, speaking from his airplane by radio to the people of Fort-Chimo, does Elsa discover a new purpose to her life: the continual recounting of this miraculous event. She worries about her son, however, not possibly fit for the life of a soldier and, like a true martyr, "se sentait accablée par le sentiment de l'avoir mis au monde pour y être malheureux." Pitifully, she prepares for the imagined return of her son, but Jimmy has departed forever. Elsa is left in total solitude, with nothing remaining in her life but the river, the mountains, and the simple pleasures of nature.[44]

In *Bonheur d'occasion* the suffering of both Rose-Anna and Florentine was endured alone, for neither woman seemed able to confide in another female. Eugénie Chenevert could speak openly to Irène, but there were few times when the women were together alone. Similarly, Elsa suffers and does not know anyone with whom she can share her feelings. When Jimmy is first born, she is befriended by Mme Beaulieu, her employer, but although Elsa considers this white woman as her friend for life, as her companion in suffering, the relationship between

these two women is not entirely reciprocal.   Mme Beaulieu
confides in Elsa, but the young Eskimo woman's concerns
are not discussed.   By the time that she begins to encounter
serious problems with Jimmy, Mme Beaulieu has moved.   In
addition, Elsa tries but cannot understand her friend's boredom and melancholy: "La créature la plus choyée, la plus aimée
de Fort-Chimo, n'en était pas moins souffrante et triste."   Victim of her husband's chosen career, Mme Beaulieu has been
forced to live in an isolated, cold region.   She has a beautiful
home, is loved by her husband, and is surrounded by her children, and yet this woman does not particularly love these children, nor her role as a mother.   She sees herself as a prisoner
in her own home.[45]   In Gabrielle Roy's novels, even the secondary female characters are pathetically alone.

Throughout these novels, a sense of both pride and pity
toward female characters is evident.   They are all traditional
mother figures, the embodiment of the *Québécois* female, and a
sensitive, "feminine humanism" toward them is clearly felt.
But these women, especially Rose-Anna and Elsa, also represent
an attack against this maternal myth.   A raised feminist consciousness underscores in the lives of these characters both the
struggles, hardships, and pain that they are destined to endure,
caught in an enclosed circle of their biological and social fate,
and the dangers that are inherent in an obsessive maternal instinct.   Despite their common desire for *recommencement,*
Royan women are, in addition, forced to suffer alone, in the
virtual absence of men who are usually on scene solely to im-
pregnate these females.   Gabrielle Roy may have adored
children and may have considered them to be the culmination
of a woman's life, but after studying her novels, the reader
wonders if such a maternal life is worthwhile when so much
suffering and solitude seem to be the inevitable results.

Solitude can also be a fundamental part of the lives of a
particular group of women treated with great respect in Roy's
collections of short stories: "la figure de l'institutrice.   Cet être
fragile dans l'atmosphère rude des pays de colonisation apparaît
comme une incarnation de ce bien précieux mais parfois sous-
estimé qu'est l'instruction.   Elle fait figure tout à la fois de
pionnière, de professionnelle, de sacrifice."   As early as 1942,
Roy wrote about the distinguished career of these independent
women, practicing an almost sacred mission.   They are seen
as totally devoted individuals, since they must endure a life of

solitude and boredom, with little financial reward, and the likelihood of a future with no substantial change.[46]

It is interesting to note that the figure of a schoolteacher does not appear in the Royan novel, for the role of the educator, when it is even mentioned, is essentially assumed by the mother. It is, however, precisely the transfer of this power over education from the mother to the teacher that is one of the primary themes in Roy's first collection of short stories, *La Petite Poule d'eau* and, in particular, in the second and longest story, "L'Ecole de la Petite Poule d'eau." It is the ideal, traditional mother, Luzina Tousignant, who initiates her children's instruction by setting a good example for them and by using, essentially, a Rousseau-like nature as educator. Luzina herself, however, feels that her children need a more formal method of learning and decides to request from the Manitoban government a trained teacher, with the promise that her husband construct the school building. Given the official requirement of six pupils in order to employ a teacher, Luzina feels relieved that she has given birth to so many children, all of whom will become future students in this school.[47]

Mlle Côté, the first instructor, arrives in this isolated, northern region, and with her arrive exterior reality, culture, and the refined and elegant influence of an educated civilization. This young French-speaking woman is at first confused, shocked at being in so desolate an area, but with her natural tenderness and desire to inspire intellectual curiosity in her pupils, she soon begins to replace Luzina as the center of the children's lives. Despite Luzina's own "timide goût d'apprendre," this maternal figure tries to convince herself that such a transfer of authority is beneficial: " 'A l'école' avait prononcé Luzina, 'vous obéirez aveuglément à votre maîtresse.' Elle ne serait pas de ces femmes qui tiennent pour leurs enfants contre la maîtresse. . . ." After all, to "chacun sa tâche dans la vie: à la maîtresse d'expliquer, aux enfants d'apprendre; et à elle, Luzina, de les servir." But Luzina is jealous of Mlle Côté who makes her children laugh, is treated by them with deep love, and has caused an "autorité humiliée" of the self-sacrificing mother.[48]

The entire Tousignant family, however, is basically delighted with the first teacher, especially when they later compare her to their second instructor,   the English-Canadian, Miss O'Rorke, "une créature stupéfiante, prude à l'excès, férue d'hygiène, qui avait des principes sur tout, une vieille fille de l'Ontario, qui ne parlait pas un mot de français, protestante par surcroît." A vegetarian and an insomniac, this stereotype of an old maid schoolteacher spends most of her time complaining and attempting to instill in her pupils a sense of honor and duty, especially toward the British Commonwealth. But ironically, she is sad to leave this family once her job has ended, for this lonely woman has been deeply marked by their natural goodness, especially that of Luzina who has made Miss O'Rorke "une véritable amie de coeur, la seule femme au monde peut-être à comprendre parfaitement la solitude."[49]

After one summer under the tutelage of their only male teacher, Armand Dubreuil, who essentially teaches them to be themselves, the Tousignant children are left on their own, still remembering their teachers, especially Mlle Côté, and still desirous of continuing their education. It is Josephine who has been the most profoundly affected and who is now determined to become a teacher herself. Fearful of this inevitable departure of her child as the result of the educational process that she herself has initiated, Luzina tries to dissuade her daughter: " 'Il n'y a pas de pire misère qu'être maîtresse d'école,' " she counsels. But Josephine, anxious to help those less fortunate than she, feels the call of "la mission d'éduquer" and leaves the maternal home for this honorable career.[50]

Christine, as a young adult in *Rue Deschambault,* has received a different calling, that of becoming a writer. Unlike Luzina, Christine's mother advises her to become a teacher in order to be able to earn a living:

> "Si tu voulais, Christine, devenir institutrice! . . . Il n'y a pas d'occupation plus belle, plus digne, il me semble, pour une femme. . . ."
>
> Maman avait souhaité faire de toutes ses filles des maîtresses d'école—peut-être parce qu'elle portait en elle-même, parmi tant de rêves sacrifiés, cette vocation manquée.

Christine does follow her mother's traditional advice and does choose this career, essentially one of the few accessible to women at that time. She begins to teach in a small prairie school where she is immediately warned that, although very popular at the outset, " 'si vous faites tant l'indépendante [by not marrying a man from the town], cela ne durera pas. . . .' "[51] The life of a schoolteacher in a rural community is difficult indeed.

Mlle Côté, Josephine, Christine, and later the schoolteacher in "L'Enfant morte" of *Cet Eté qui chantait* are all young adult women, sensitive to their surroundings, and faced with the new problems of having to make choices and of accepting responsibilities. These three women are, in effect, precursors of the young schoolteacher in *Ces Enfants de ma vie*. Often described as a child herself, this woman, one of Roy's favorite characters, is emotional, at times naïve, and deeply idealistic about her career: "Telle était alors ma fièvre, impérieuse comme l'amour, en fait c'était de l'amour, ce passionné besoin que j'eus toute ma vie, que j'ai encore de lutter pour obtenir le meilleur en chacun." Like an intense adolescent, she also experiences extreme moods and reactions to situations—one day totally exalted by her new role, and the next day feeling imprisoned in its daily routine that will carry her into old age: "Je me voyais dans vingt ans, dans trente ans, à la même place toujours, usée par la tâche, l'image même de mes compagnes les plus 'vieilles' que je trouvais tellement à plaindre, si bien qu'à travers elles je me trouvai aussi à plaindre."[52]

But this woman is now only eighteen years old, only at the very beginning of her adult life and, therefore, finding it sometimes difficult to maintain her authoritarian role:

> J'en étais à peine moi-même guérie, à peine sortie des rêves de l'adolescence, si mal encore résignée à la vie adulte que, de ma classe, tôt le matin, lorsque je voyais apparaître mes petits élèves sur la plaine fraîche comme l'aube du monde, j'avais parfois l'impression que j'aurais dû courir vers eux, me mettre à jamais de leur côté et non les attendre au piège de l'école.

It is precisely her youth, however, the arrival of this "jeunette" in their classroom, that so deeply influences her pupils and leaves so profound a remembrance of her in their minds. In addition, either despite her youth and lack of experience or because of them, this teacher, again like Mlle Côté, radiates total sensitivity toward and understanding of both her younger and adolescent students. It is, therefore, quite natural for them to develop a special rapport with her, to the point where she becomes "Mrs. Mother teacher!" for some of the children, and for others, the object of their first love.[53]

This birth of love and sensuality has already been seen as

causing confusion and pain in the adolescent boy, Médéric Eymard, but it creates similar feelings in the young teacher, divided between her own maturing sensuality and the prescribed role that she must play in adult society. When she first meets Médéric, she is fascinated by him, but having been warned in advance about his disruptive ways, she plays her role as school-teacher well and treats the adolescent cynically, most likely as an innate method of defense. As their relationship develops, as true communication flourishes, and as they finallly spend one pure and ideal day together in the nearby hills, the rules of society weigh more heavily upon the teacher, and she begins to feel ashamed of her familiarity with this boy. Her fears are, in fact, confirmed when Médéric's father sarcastically and bit-terly insinuates that the relationship between his son and the teacher is not purely intellectual:

> "Or, dans nos pauvres campagnes où les femmes sont ignorantes et abruties, qui donc en vaut la peine sinon la petite demoiselle de l'école, qui nous descend, autant dire, quelque beau jour, du ciel. . . . elle n'est pas venue dans mon temps pour sauver de mon ignorance, guider ma vie. . . .
> Mon garçon lui a de la chance," poursuivit-il. "Aussi bien je lui dis: ne manque pas ton coup avec la petite demoiselle de l'école. C'est ton salut, mon enfant."[54]

The relationship between Médéric and his teacher is deeply sensual, especially during their return trip from the boy's home in his parents' wedding carriage. In this beautifully written scene, the carriage becomes a frail ship, struggling in a snow-storm, but also rocking its passengers and inviting them to day-dream romantically. It is the teacher who is the most inspired: "Je nous imaginai, Médéric et moi, tels qu'on nous retrouverait, la tourmente passée, deux pures statues . . . intacts et beaux. Tout juste aurions-nous peut-être incliné la tête l'un vers l'autre." She also imagines that they will travel extensively while growing old together. But after Médéric stops himself from brushing aside a lock of her hair, and after the teacher initially treats this sensual moment as an unreal game, she realizes that what she is truly experiencing are deeply felt desires, condemned by the adult society to which they must return. As if in fear and shame, she moves as far away from Médéric as possible, and the carriage arrives in the village.[55]

This adult society continues to dictate the young teacher's actions, for fearful of her reputation, she reproaches herself for having been imprudent and defensively reverts to the dignity of her authoritarian role. She realizes, however, that Médéric is dear to her and that the thought of losing him is frightening. Struggling between her emotions and her adult role as teacher or, more precisely, divided among her desires to present the figure of a teacher, mother, lover, spouse, and, finally, adolescent, this young woman needs to prove to herself that she has had, at least, a permanent influence on the boy, a greater power over him than his parents. But this influence, causing Médéric's love for her, must be expressed in her terms:

> Et quoiqu'il n'eût sans doute jamais été dans mon intention d'encourager l'amour naissant de Médéric, je saisis à cet instant que j'aurais grand chagrin de le savoir tout à fait mort. Mais qu'est-ce donc à la fin que je désirais sinon d'être adorée à distance comme une bonne étoile qui guide à travers la vie—enfant que j'étais moi-même.

The object of, in effect, a courtly love, the teacher can then safely but sensually speak of her pupil: "Mes lèvres formèrent silencieusement, à son intention, le seul mot qui me venait à l'âme: Ah! Médéric! Médéric!"[56]   The teacher departs from the small town; Médéric grows up; and the mutual influence born in the classroom permanently marks them both. With *Ces Enfants de ma vie,* the Royan schoolteacher has become a mature female character.

If the traditional women of Roy's novels are painted with pride and pity, and if the author creates portraits of independent and sensitive women as schoolteachers in some of her major novellas, the other female characters who people her collections of short stories also appear to be traditional mother figures, at least overtly satisfied with their role in life. There are, however, even deeper inner conflicts, deeper desires for *recommencement,* in some of these women, more so than in the novelistic characters. With these desires having been thwarted by a determined destiny, the effect of these mothers on their children, especially on their daughters, is more profoundly felt, as the older women realize their dreams through the lives of their offspring.

Luzina Tousignant, the central and unifying force throughout the stories of *La Petite Poule d'eau,* has been seen as a strong but tender maternal figure, initially responsible for her children's education and somewhat disturbed when she sees her authority transferred to the schoolteacher. She is the warmest, most open, friendliest, and most maternal of Roy's female characters, since she superficially symbolizes the joy and plenitude of a woman in the home. Living in an isolated region and without frequent contact with the outside world, Luzina possesses a natural attraction to other people, loves to talk to them, finds goodness in everyone, and inevitably wins the affection of anyone whom she meets: "La bonté maternelle de la grasse Luzina, ses prunelles chaudes et curieuses, son avide intérêt envers autrui, tout en elle invitait à la confiance. . . . Elle inclinait les gens à s'apercevoir qu'ils avaient des raisons d'être heureux." Luzina's materialsm extends to everything and to everyone around her: to her own family, to strangers, to the wild nature of the Water Hen district where she lives, to the fictional characters of books. She is "maman Tousignant" even to the local priest who, before this woman, experiences "la vieille faim de l'homme d'être dorloté, choyé, protégé par l'affection toute maternelle de la femme."[57]

As the traditional mother figure, Luzina also manifests the characteristics of self-sacrifice and martyrdom. She is always working in her home, even when everyone else is asleep, forever mending, cooking, and serving. This aspect of her life appears to upset her, for one senses her annoyance on a few occasions, although she only once actually expresses her feelings: "Elle se fâcha. Est-ce qu'elle pouvait toute faire: élever onze enfants indociles, leur servir à manger, ravauder leur linge, s'occuper du père à peine plus raisonnable et, en plus de tout cela, connaître encore la grammaire. Doux Jésus! Personne n'y aurait suffi." Luzina is, in addition, fearful that all of these domestic responsibilities will prevent her from being closer to God. She admits that she has a good life, but not a perfect one:

> Luzina n'était pas une femme malheureuse. Elle ne croyait pas avoir sujet de se plaindre. Sa vie lui paraissait aussi bonne qu'elle le méritait, et, pourtant, quelquefois, elle avait éprouvé un bref pincement au coeur, la tristesse commune à tous ceux qui vivent sur terre de n'être pas totalement compris.[58]

Luzina needs to be appreciated.

Even with these misgivings, it is evident throughout the novellas that Luzina accepts her role in life, especially that of being a proud mother. With a sense of Catholic and familial obligation, she feels that it is her responsibility to have children, to populate her desolate region of Manitoba. She can, in fact, respect even the Protestant, anglophone Queen Victoria precisely because of her nine children. But even in this most essential aspect of her life, there are problems, problems that first become apparent when Luzina expresses embarrassment at being pregnant when she meets Armand Dubreuil. It is possible that this sense of shame stems from the association of pregnancy with sexuality that, in turn, is allied, in Luzina's mind, with marital duties that she does not fully accept. After having born eleven children, Luzina's yearly confession to *le capucin* remains the same:

> Chaque année, au même endroit, Luzina confiait au capucin en rougissant qu'elle ne se pliait pas avec une entière soumission aux exigeances du mariage. . . . Elle aurait voulu espacer un peu plus les naissances. Elle était d'abord de mauvaise humeur, portée à se décourager, disait-elle, lorsqu'elle se découvrait "encore une fois partie pour la famille." Elle résumait la situation: "Comprenez-moi, mon Père; les enfants que j'ai déjà, je n'en donnerais pas un pour tout l'or du monde, mais j'aimerais quasiment mieux ne pas en avoir autant. C'est mal de penser comme ça, hein mon Père?"[59]

With a sense of guilt, Luzina would prefer to modify her destiny. In her words she resembles Florentine, fearful of what she will have to endure in marriage; Eugénie, resentful of the egotism of men; and, especially, Rose-Anna, proudly resigned to her lot but not fully satisfied with it.

Luzina also resembles Elsa, a woman so preoccupied with or, as Rose-Anna, so overpowered by her maternal responsibilities that she has little room left in her life for a true relationship with a man. In the role of a sovereign female, she is the one who dominates in the household, gives orders, makes decisions, and is able to travel outside the home. With an innate sense of practicality, it is Luzina who represents strength and what can be called a tender authority. Finally as in the relationship between Rose-Anna and Azarius, although she loves her husband, Hippolyte, she is so blinded by her maternal-

ism that she treats him merely as her eldest child.[60] There is
a subtle irony that is suggested in the depiction of these female
characters, victims of wifely duties and male passion and yet
totally dominating over their spouses.

To a woman whose life revolves around her children,
their inevitable departure must cause great anguish. After
having given birth almost annually by making the difficult
trip to the nearest hospital, Luzina sees this process reversed:

> Presque tous les ans elle partait, et elle faisait vite afin de revenir
> avec un enfant de plus contre le désert à peupler. Maintenant
> elle restait, et c'étaient les enfants qui partaient. Luzina voyait
> en quelque sorte la vie. Et elle n'en croyait pas son bon coeur:
> la vie qu'elle avait tant aidée, déjà, petit à petit, l'abandonnait.

But given the lack of total satisfaction with her own life, the
self-sacrificing Luzina has learned to live through her children.
She feels that she has succeeded if her offspring succeed, and,
especially, if they recognize and appreciate her devotion to them:

> Luzina avait dans sa vie lu autant de romans qu'elle avait pu s'en
> procurer. Presque tous l'avaient fait pleurer, que le dénouement
> fût triste ou consolant. Simplement c'était la fin en soi de toute
> histoire qui la portait à un inconsolable regret. Plus l'histoire
> avait été belle, et plus elle était chagrinée de la voir achevée. Mais
> dans quel roman, raconté par main d'auteur, avait-elle assisté
> à un dénouement mieux conduit, plus satisfaisant que celui de sa
> propre vie et qui eût pu la faire pleurer davantage![61]

It is noteworthy that Luzina compares her life to the most
beautifully written novels, for her life, or rather all of *La Petite
Poule d'eau,* is pure fiction, life as it could have been at the
beginning of time, and not as it actually is. Luzina is, therefore,
an ideal and, as such, represents the author's preference for
the traditional maternal woman, content with her role in life.[62]
There are, however, problems even within this dream-like,
idyllic world, as Luzina expresses certain doubts about her
given situation and suffers when her children leave. Life in
La Petite Poule d'eau radiates a female quality that is, once
again, filled with both pride and poignancy. It is also a life
that is, at best, temporary and, fundamentally, neither real nor
possible.

In part because it is a semi-autobiographical work, *Rue Deschambault* does not have any of the idealistic qualities of the previous collection of short stories. Its characters are portrayed as totally realistic, as they encounter varied events and interract with others throughout their lives. The central figure of the novellas is, of course, Christine, especially since everything that occurs is seen and interpreted through her eyes, those both of a child on stage with the other characters and of the adult narrator recalling these events. But given the particular importance of a mother during one's childhood, it is not at all surprising that Christine's mother, simply called "maman," assumes a major and equally realistic role in most of the stories. With Maman, Roy has created a complex female character. She is an intelligent, creative, and curious woman, capable of jealousy, anger, and frustrations, and faithful to her time and situation in a small Western Canadian town, extremely concerned about outward appearances.[63]

Maman is also a typical Royan traditional mother, devoted to, protective of, and worried about her family. Her own adult, married life has not been very joyous, for she is the wife of a much older man whom she respects but does not seem to love and who is frequently absent from home. As a result, she is, as in the normal Royan household, the dominant figure, although untypically she is somewhat fearful of her husband and becomes less demonstrative and less natural whenever he is home. Her children receive, therefore, the focus of most of her attention. If something happens to one of them and Maman feels separated from their fate, she is distraught, so much so that she cannot even relate to her other offspring. Usually she tries to hide these emotions in order to avoid upsetting her children: "Souvent je m'approchais d'elle, lui demandant ce qu'elle avait, elle me répondait: Rien! Mais en me regardant avec une curieuse intensité, comme si j'allais disparaître sous ses yeux." When Alicia becomes insane and does not recognize Maman, the woman is so heartbroken that she is unable even to perceive Christine's emotions: "*Ils* disent que le chagrin rapproche les gens; ce n'est pas toujours vrai; ce jour-là, autour de maman assise sur une chaise droite, le chagrin faisait un petit cercle bien fermé." This lack of awareness of her younger daughter's feelings is not typical of Maman's nature, however, for despite certain instances during Christine's childhood—particularly, her adolescence, when this child may complain that her mother does not understand her—the older woman consistently and honestly tries to be sympathetic and sensitive to all of her children's needs.[64]

Within this household Maman symbolizes for her children positive maternal qualities, related to the cycle of nature. Called "maman" by everyone, including her husband, this woman is identified with daytime, summer, sun, flowers, health, fire, warmth, religion, light, activity, morning, logic, and the beginning of life. The antithesis of her husband, she is hopeful that her children, especially Christine, will follow her example and become, therefore, more successful and happier during their adult lives, more so than both their parents.[65]

Maman's children will indeed by affected by her, both by her own model of mother, spouse, and woman and by her unconscious attempt to influence them through her words of advice during their childhood and adolescence. Christine, the youngest in the family, remains at home with her mother after her siblings have departed and as her mother's companion, is especially subject to this counsel. When she is still a young child, for example, on at least three occasions her mother warns her about men: "Après, quand nous nous sommes trouvées seules dans le village, Maman m'a mise en garde contre les hommes. 'Tu vois,' dit maman, 'comme il faut avec eux garder sa distance. . . .' " Similarly she tries to place a fear and mistrust of marriage in her older daughter, Georgianna, and indirectly in Christine who overhears this advice, as the woman insists that what one feels as love in the beginning of a relationship will not last. Maman, however, expresses this opinion with regret, for, a true romantic, she does sincerely cling to the notion of the power of love: " 'La plus belle couronne d'une femme c'est d'être aimée. Il n'y a rien, ni topaze, ni diamant, ni améthyste, ni émeraude, ni rubis, pour mieux embellir une femme!' " It is simply that she has not been blessed with such adoration and believes that, realistically, it is a rare woman who is. Her words must inevitably mark her daughter.[66]

The adolescent Christine is equally influenced by her mother, as the relationship between the two females becomes strained, and the older woman pits her will against her maturing daughter, obsessive first about a boyfriend and then about jewelry. Determined to put an end to Christine's fascination for Whilhelm, "Maman devenait comme une espionne. . . . Et où étaient nos belles relations franches, entre maman et moi!

Vient-il toujours une mauvaise époque entre une mère et sa fille? Est-ce l'amour qui l'amène?" It is, however, the adolescent's mania for jewelry that elicits Maman's understanding of her daughter, as well as a reaction that not only indicates a new aspect of the older woman's nature but also, in turn, affects Christine:

> "Toute femme," disait maman, "a dans le fond d'elle-même une pauvre petite âme paienne, et il me semble que vous autres, les hommes [and here, specifically, her son], c'est bien souvent cette paienne que vous adorez. . . . Au fond, il n'y a pas d'égalité entre les hommes et les femmes. Les belles vertus: la loyauté, la franchise, la droiture, l'admirable simplicté, vous les revendiquez pour vous, alors que vous prisez les femmes pour leurs détours, leurs caprices. C'est très mal, d'abord pour vous-mêmes qui êtes les premiers à en souffrir, et pour les femmes que vous vous plaisez, on dirait, à maintenir dans un état d'enfance rusée. Oh! quand donc," fit maman, "les mêmes qualités seront-elles bonnes pour tous! . . . ."

With this outburst of anger against men, Maman, the traditional mother figure, has become a modern, bitter woman.[67]

It must be stressed that this is the sole occasion on which Maman so vehemently expresses her anger ånd frustration. Throughout most of her life, she remains the typical Royan image of the self-sacrificing mother who tries to influence her children so that they might pursue goals in their lives that the older woman has not been destined to fulfill in hers. She urges Christine to be a teacher but also accepts her preference to become a writer, especially since it is she who taught the young woman a deep love and respect for words. In either choice, however, Maman will have to realize her own dreams through Christine. She will, therefore, as all Royan mothers, inevitably experience intense solitude when this child departs.[68]

Such a departure will cause an even greater sense of anguish for Maman than for the other mothers of Roy's fictional world because this woman is a totally divided creature, torn between her longings to be free, to travel and her need, desire, and duty to remain at home: "Maman me dit qu'elle avait encore envie d'être libre; elle me dit que ce qui mourait en dernier lieu dans le coeur humain ce devait être le goût de la liberté; que même la peine et les malheurs n'usaient pas en elle cette disposition pour la liberté. . . ." She admits that, if circumstances had been different in her life, she would have spent most of her years as a true nomad. Although she does not appear to fault her children for their greater opportunities for freedom, she does reserve some envy and bitterness for her husband who, constantly travelling in his work, does not understand his wife's unfulfilled desires: "Maman, un peu piquée, répondit que c'était bien d'un homme de parler ainsi; qu'un homme parce qu'il avait la chance de sortir de la maison, s'imaginait que la maison, c'était le paradis. . . ."[69]

It is precisely this home that has created the chains to keep Maman captive and to prevent her from following a nomadic life. Such a life, however, would have caused her misfortune—or so she believes—for despite her desires for freedom, Maman maintains that she would never want to relinquish her present, domestic life. During her one adventure when she does leave home without informing her husband in order to travel to Quebec, she feels that she has made the correct decision and enjoys her freedom, but continuously expresses guilt at having departed, at having, perhaps, exceeded her prescribed role in life. Of course before leaving on her trip, she had made arrangements for the care of her older children and actually takes her youngest daughter, Christine, with her on this voyage that, in addition, returns Maman first and foremost to her husband's past.[70]

Interestingly enough, Christine expresses fear at the change in her more liberated mother and affirms her preference for the former, more traditional woman. Paradoxically however, it is this newly independent mother who, during their trip, teaches her child about the importance of being married. With a sense of pride and, most likely guilt as well, Maman spends much time while she travels discussing her husband. Christine, therefore, sees "combien une femme qui se réclame d'un mari est mieux vue dans la société qu'une femme toute seule. Cela me parut injuste; je n'avais jamais remarqué qu'un homme eût besoin de parler de sa femme pour avoir l'air important." In other words, as Maman becomes more independent, she unconsciously exposes her daughter to traditional views. Christine, ironically, reacts to this lesson in the manner of a future feminist.[71]

Maman does, of course, return home to her husband and family. She is content and, especially, desirous of making amends, as she thoroughly manipulates her husband by inspiring in him, as well as in her other children, the same interest in their past that she had experienced while in Quebec. As a powerful storyteller, she becomes the dominant center of the household once again.   Although Gabrielle Roy herself has categorized Maman's flight as a revolt, it is more of a determined but short-lived manifestation of independence, just enough to make the woman happy to return to her home and family.[72]

The development of Maman as a complex female character in *Rue Deschambault* is continued in *La Route d'Altamont* where both she, now as Eveline, and her mother, Mémère, along with Christine, affected by both older women, are cele-brated in this intense orbit of maternity and womanhood. These three females are seen, in addition, as attempting what Gagné calls "le jeu de la rencontre," that is, the linking among three generations of women, all leading toward the inevitably desired *recommencement.* The first story of the collection, "Ma Grand-mère toute-puissante," introduces the reader to Mémère, the proud and powerful woman who, as a traditionally devoted wife and mother, had always desired some time for herself but who now, as a solitary old woman, feels as though she has too much.   Mémère is, in fact, likened to an old oak tree, incapable of moving, but from which are born young trees, singing happily through all of their leaves.   She is proud of her family, of what she has accomplished during her life:

> "J'ai peut-être fait tout ce que peut faire une créature humaine. J'ai deux fois construit le foyer. . . . C'est de l'ouvrage," me confia-t-elle.   "Oui, une maison, une famille, c'est tant d'ouvrage que si on le voyait une bonne fois en un tas, on se sentirait comme devant une haute montagne, on se dirait: mais c'est infranchis-sable!"[73]

Although anxious to exalt what she sees as a maternal adventure in life, Mémère does still harbor some resentment and bitterness toward her late husband, the "trotteur," the "bel aventurier," the Bohemian whom she followed from Quebec to Manitoba in order to rebuild her domestic mountain.   Stand-ing firm against the wanderlust of her entire family, she contin-ued to represent maternal stability, while, against her own in-clinations and wishes, she dutifully went with her spouse.[74] Mémère is truly the traditional Royan mother figure.

As such, she has deeply affected her offspring, both her daughter, Eveline, and her granddaughter, Christine. Eveline becomes fully aware of this influence of her mother on her only when she herself begins to age. She then tries to remember and to understand Mémère, as she ultimately sees many of the characteristics of the older woman in her own elderly self. During what is probably middle age, however, when Mémère is still living, Eveline's attitude is somewhat different. Suddenly cognizant of her mother's old age and fearful of her own encroaching years, she begins to feel guilty about her treatment of Mémère, is worried about the old woman's life alone, and convinces her mother to move and live with her. It is at this point that the young Christine begins to perceive that strange and complex rapport that exists between a mother and daughter, the reversal of roles that occurs especially when the parent becomes old. Eveline remains a child before Mémère whom she continues to call "maman," while she treats this increasingly infirm woman as if she were a young child, a baby to whom she asks " 'Votre conscience est tranquille, n'est-ce pas? Tout votre devoir vous l'avez fait. Soyez sans crainte.' "[75] As she matures, Christine will better understand such a relationship.

Throughout *La Route d'Altamont,* Eveline will continue to be depicted as the proud and powerful mother of *Rue Deschambault.* Like her own mother, she is compared to an isolated tree, almost an earth mother, maternally rocking and protecting her children. She also maintains her traditional views of life, particularly those on the importance of love and marriage as " 'le seul chemin . . . pour avancer un peu hors de soi. . . .' " Eveline represents, in Christine's eyes, the stability of the home, the link to a sense of permanence.[76]

The tensions that have already been seen as evident in Eveline's nature, however, become increasingly pronounced in this work. Despite her desires for stability, this woman can never seem to silence within her "son instinct migrateur" which sadly remains merely a passion for departure, never an action. This passion, therefore, locks her in as a "prisonnier toute sa vie dans une petite rue." As she grows older, Eveline more freely admits her former desires, both for travel and for a more independent life:

> "Jeune, sais-tu que j'ai ardemment désiré étudier, apprendre, voyager, me hausser du mieux possible. . . . Mais je me suis mariée

à dix-huit ans et mes enfants sont venus rapidement. Je n'ai pas
eu beaucoup de temps pour moi-même. Quelquefois encore je
rêve à quelqu'un d'infiniment mieux que moi que j'aurais pu
être. . . . Une musicienne, par exemple, n'est-ce pas assez fou?"
—Puis elle se hâte d'ajouter, comme pour me dépister, se cacher
de s'être à moi découverte: "Tout le monde fait pareil rêve, tout
le monde, te dis-je."[77]

Eveline cannot hide the fact, however, that unfulfilled dreams
can continue to be painful.

It is natural that Eveline's longings for freedom influence
her children who, in addition, have inherited these traits. The
mother can, therefore, easily transform her passion into reality
first by obtaining for her offspring what she herself was never
able to accomplish, that is, by allowing them to travel and to
better themselves, and secondly by experiencing such adventures
through their lives. Eveline, for example, will truly live through
her daughter when, as a young child, Christine makes the momentous voyage to Lake Winnipeg, never visited by her mother.
Later in her life, the older woman can honestly state that she
has no regrets about her married life, for "je [Eveline] te [Chris-
tine] regarde et me dis que rien n'est perdu, que tu feras à ma
place et mieux que moi ce que j'aurais désiré accomplir." Eveline
remains, throughout her life, a martyred mother.[78]

By encouraging such freedom, however, Eveline will have
to accept the eventual loss of her children. Instinctively she
reacts against this inevitability. When Christine announces to
her mother that she has decided to travel to France in order to
study and to write, Eveline immediately assumes the role of the
traditional mother and, like Mémère, defends the home. She is
deeply hurt and opposes her daughter with a hostility that
radiates intense jealousy, for she knows that Christine will
soon experience what she, Eveline, was never able to accomplish
during her youth and what it is now too late to do. The mother
tries to discourage her daughter but is too proud to beg her to
stay.[79]

The effect on Christine both of her mother's reaction to
this decision and of having been raised by such a self-sacrificing
woman is typical. She does leave for Europe, but anxious to
give her mother joy, she constantly reflects upon what she
will do for her if only the older woman will allow her more
time: "Mais toujours, toujours, je n'en étais qu'au commence-

ment. . . . je me hâtais, je me pensais toujours au bord de ce que je voulais devenir à ses yeux avant de lui revenir." And yet Christine does realize that Maman is growing older: " 'Peut-elle seulement attendre que je sois prête à lui montrer ce dont je voudrais être capable? Et si elle ne le peut pas, ce que je tiens à accomplir aura-t-il seulement encore de la valeur à mes yeux?' " Roy has faithfully captured the essence of an adult daughter's thoughts:

> Christine desperately wants to achieve what her mother, a more traditional woman, could not do. She wants to make her mother proud of her, in a sense, to repay her for all of the pain endured in childbirth, for all of the emotional stresses involved in raising a child. Christine has become a mature woman, but she reamins a young girl in her own eyes and, as she believes, in the eyes of her mother. As so many daughters, she continues to try to prove her worth to her mother.[80]

Roy's short stories published after *La Route d'Altamont* show an interesting development in their female characters, a development that was initiated with Mémère and Eveline in their close rapport and, in effect, identification with certain aspects of nature, in particular, with trees and the seasonal cycle. In addition, as these more recently created fictional women express their need for natural surroundings, they also carry on even more persistently the role of the traditional female. Roy's creation of independent and liberated female characters, even of women with divided priorities, is here more tempered. The fundamental solitude of the woman, however, now alone in nature, is still consistently stressed.[81]

The epitome of this solitary woman in the midst of nature can be found in Maria Martha Yaramko of "Un Jardin au bout du monde." This old and sickly Ukrainian woman, living on the Western Canadian plains, feels that she has nothing left in her life to keep her company, except the flowers of her garden, symbol of creation, and her own thoughts. She reflects upon her past life: the voyage to Canada, so ardently desired by her; her husband, Stépan, with whom she once sincerely communicated but who has become a silent stranger to her; and her three children, belonging to her only during their early childhood, and now, perhaps, even ashamed of her. She tries to understand why her children have departed, called to the modern English-

Canadian world:

> Elle se prit à pleurer doucement. Elle se voyait pour ainsi dire
> sans parents et sans enfants. Quelle était la cause d'une telle
> solitude. Trop de progrès trop vite? Ou pas assez? Tout ce
> qu'elle croyait entrevoir c'est que, un jour sans doute, des êtres
> issus d'elle [here, her grandchildren], mais assez loin de leur origine
> pour se sentir à l'aise dans le pays, n'auraient peut-être pas honte,
> eux, de la vieille grand-mère immigrée.

Martha never expected much from life and as a true self-effacing
female, never wanted to disturb anyone: "Surtout elle répugnait
à attirer l'attention sur elle, d'être l'objet de soins, d'importance
peut-être. Sa vie ne lui paraissait pas en mériter autant, la peur
la saisissait à la seule idée du moindre dérangement à cause
d'elle." But now despite her love of and confidence in life,
she begins to question its true meaning, to ask why she has even
lived.[82]. Such a new awareness, if it can even be categorized
as a feeble revolt, comes too late, for Martha dies alone.

The last group of women to be created by Gabrielle Roy
in her short stories appears in *Ces Enfants de ma vie* as the
mothers of the young school boys taught by the new teacher.
The only such character, however, who receives any significant
development is the mother of André Pasquier, the boy who is
forced into adult responsibilities at home. Mme Pasquier is a
proud, emotional woman who, pregnant with her third child,
must remain in bed, sacrificing herself with maternal resignation
for her unborn child. When, in addition, she speaks to the
teacher of the painful and interminable childbirths of one of
her neighbors, the two women, reflecting upon such difficulties,
are both deeply moved: "Tout à coup je [the teacher] n'en
pouvais plus moi-même et pleurai avec elle sur la misère féminine."[83]

The female characters of the typical Royan short story are
mothers, schoolteachers, and future writers, or young girls envisioning such roles for themselves. They are overtly content
with their lives and traditionally resigned to the maternal destiny
of women. They silence any desires for greater freedom and
independence and suffer intensely when they are left alone
without their children. Increasingly, they take solace and refuge
in nature. These women, however, would never relinquish their
maternal and familial roles, for they can at least displace upon

their children, and especially upon their daughters, all of their thwarted dreams.

From 1939 until 1983, Gabrielle Roy lost neither her deep preoccupation with female characters nor her sensitivity to their problems. While feminist literature in Quebec, as elsewhere, has relatively recently become concerned with the creation of independent, liberated, and self-assertive fictional women, as well as with its authors' involvement in female/feminist writing, Roy's feminist awareness and depiction of women dissatisfied with their lot or determined to be more independent first occurred in her early short stories of the late 1930s and early 1940s. Subsequently, she was viewed as more opposed to recent women's movements, that is, more as a "feminine," traditional writer than as a feminist. It is true that in both her novels and collections of short stories, she created traditional women, trapped in their predetermined destiny and apparently resigned to or voluntarily accepting their fate. The women of her novels struggle to survive, and those of the short stories essentially transfer their desires to their daughters. But although the anguish and dispair depicted in the novels are clearly more acute, one must also note that all of these women live in intense solitude, longing for a new beginning, but aware of its impossibility. This persistent atmosphere of isolation, along with an often useless martyrdom and self-effacement, causes one to question the author's personal attitude toward the traditional female condition. With "feminine humanism," Gabrielle Roy did love her female characters, just as she adored all of her literary creations. She did, in addition, underscore the joys of motherhood. But she clearly did not whole-heartedly support a woman who sacrificed her own life for others. Such a destiny, at certain times imposed and at other times chosen, only seemed to result in deep sorrow and pain, especially if the woman did not possess any other firm relationship in her adult life.

Contributing to the Royan female's difficult situation is the fact that she must usually face alone the problems arising in her life, without being able to depend upon any outside source of strength. In this sense, she must be seen as a strong, independent, and self-sufficient individual, often placed in contrast to a weaker male. It has often been mentioned that in Gabrielle Roy's works, male characters, when they are even present, are either poorly developed or are themselves purposely portrayed as weak, vulnerable, impractical, tormented, asexual persons, either lost children or, at best, not yet fully adults.[84]   In addition, in this predominantly female adult world, even when male characters do occupy the primary role in a given work, they are often surrounded by female symbols, as they search for a maternal figure in their lives.   One must not, however, underestimate the importance of certain Royan males, for just like Rose-Anna, Eveline, and Elsa, at least Alexandre Chenevert, Pierre Cordorai, and Sam Lee Wong are, too, unforgettable literary creations.

Before analyzing these three male figures, however, one cannot ignore the other men in Roy's fiction, beginning with those who people her early short stories.   Since this early fiction is dominated by strong, independent female characters, it is not surprising that the males are depicted either in a relatively negative light or, at least, as firmly tied to women.   Of course there are a few male characters in these stories who are portrayed with good, positive traits; interestingly enough, these five such men were all created in 1940 or early 1941. In addition, only one male is presented as cruel: Nick who, always drunk, beats his wife and daughter.[85]

Often the men in these early works appear simply as ridiculous, clearly treated with amusing irony.   In "La Justice en Danaca et ailleurs," for example, they think that they alone are competent, but impractical, they cannot even perform "women's tasks" and are always forced to turn to the female.   Jean-Baptiste of "Bonne à marier" is also seen as an egocentric male who believes that any woman will want to marry him because of his wealthy, eligible status.   He is treated as a man who, typically, cannot live alone and is, therefore, reduced to marrying the mother of the young women whom he unsuccessfully courts. Other men in these early stories are ridiculously obsessive, confused, and easily dominated.[86]

The most interesting of these early characters are the male chauvinists who voice their exaggerated opinions of women. Henderson of "Cendrillon '40," for example, is the eligible bachelor who sells vacuum cleaners to women: " 'Nous avons à coeur de lui épargner tout ouvrage fatiguant et malpropre. Nous voulons qu'elle ait de nombreux loisirs à consacrer à sa beauté et à sa tenue qui doit être toujours élégante si elle veut conserver le coeur de celui qu'elle aime.' "   Portrayed with a similar tone of sarcasm is Alain, the condescending, cynical male character of "Les Petits Pas de Caroline" who falls in love with the militant feminist, Judith, but intelligently wins her esteem and affection. Influenced by the traditional, ro-mantic trash written by Caroline, but desirous of "conquering" Judith, Alain is usually half-serious and half-mocking whenever he speaks of women in front of this feminist: " 'Ah, voilà com-ment j'aime les femmes; douces, confiantes, pas trop encom-brantes. . . .' " He will even quote from Caroline's novels es-sentially to irritate Judith: " 'Caroline dit justement à ce sujet . . . attendez que je trouve le paragraphe. . . . Ah voici: "La femme éprouve le besoin d'être dominée. Elle n'aura d'admira-tion que pour quiconque la réduira par force, et d'un mauvais traitement elle conservera souvent un souvenir attendri." ' " Alain is annoying, but he is also amusing.[87]

Three of Roy's early short stories published in 1946 and 1948, later than most of her others, must be placed in a separate category as direct precursors of her major fiction, essentially because of the depiction of a pathetic male character. The two 1948 tales, in fact, can be seen as preliminary studies for *Alexandre Chenevert.* Adrien of "La Justice en Danaca et ailleurs" is an insignificant man who works too much. At one point in his life, he works overtime, does not declare the extra income, is audited, and insults the auditor. After his ten-minute revolt, he calmly returns to his role as another *fourmis* of the country. Constantin Simoneau of "Feuilles mortes" is the most direct ancestor of Alexandre. He is a solitary, timid man who, without harboring any revolt within him, works too hard, fears losing his job, and accumulates debts. He lives with a constant sense of guilt and paranoia, the feeling that he is being judged. An insignificant man, Constantin is pathetically por-trayed.[88]

The most completely developed male character in Roy's early short stories and, in addition, one of the weakest and most pitiful is Dr. Vincent Raymond of the 1946 two-part novella, "La Source au désert." Married to Nathalie whom he hates and desires to kill and obsessively in love with Anne who refuses to flee with him, Raymond has become a stranger even to himself, a self-hating man addicted to morphine. He honestly believes that he is typical: in contrast to women who will always attempt a *recommencement,* a man "lorsqu'il est devant le désespoir, se tue d'un seul coup, ou bien, le fait à petit feu, se livrant à l'alcoolisme et encore comme lui à cette mort graduelle, inévitable par la drogue." Raymond lives solely for Anne, and when he realizes that he can no longer be with her, he literally departs toward his solitary death, toward a cabin in the extreme North, without provisions, and already in a feverish and hallucinatory state.[89]   If the power of true love is exalted but seldom achieved by the female characters in Gabrielle Roy's major fiction, it is equally essential but, at times, poignantly destructive in her early short stories.

Love also causes deep anguish in *Bonheur d'occasion:* Florentine is almost destroyed because of her love for Jean but manages to salvage her life by marrying Emmanuel; and Jean, although cruel toward Florentine, is obsessively attracted to her.   The character of Jean Lévesque, in fact, has been uniformly described by critics as dislikable, mean, sarcastic, and rebellious.   He is likened to violence, freedom, escape, ascension, virility, and, therefore, to the symbols of wind, boats, trains, and canals.   Even Roy herself, in reflecting upon her novel, stated that in Jean she had incarnated "le refus des responsabilités sociales, l'égoïsme qui conduit l'être social à accepter les avantages de la société sans lui sacrifier la moindre parcelle de sa liberté."   He is an excessively ambitious young man who exploits and dominates those whom he despises.[90]

In the beginning of her novel, however, Roy clearly describes Jean's dual nature, and, therefore, the reasons behind his cynical demeanor:

> C'est qu'il venait de se voir à travers les yeux de Florentine: blagueur, méchant garçon, dangereux même, attirant sans doute, comme tout danger réel. . . . le personnage qu'il s'était créé aux yeux de tous, celui d'un garçon astucieux, qui étonnait par ses vantardises, ses débauches supposées, un gars qu'on admirait. Le vrai Jean Lévesque était tout autre. C'était un silencieux, un têtu, un travailleur surtout. C'était celui-là qui lui plaisait davantage au fond, cet être pratique qui aimait le travail, non pas pour lui-même, mais pour l'ambition qu'il déculpe, pour les succès qu'il prépare. . . .

Jean is determined to prove himself to others, to show them that he is different, superior, successful.   In order to fulfill his ambition, he needs total independence and solitude, no attachment to a family or to a woman.[91]

His attraction to Florentine, therefore, causes great tension and confusion within his thoughts and creates an additional duality in his character:

> Et à la fin, cette obsession était devenue si vive qu'il n'avait plus
> vu qu'un seul moyen d'en être délivré: se montrer volontairement
> cynique et dur envers la jeune fille, l'obliger à le haïr, l'engager à
> le craindre, à s'éloigner de lui afin qu'il n'eût pas à faire lui-même
> cet effort.

His decision is useless, for despite his cruelty toward her and
her own realization of his destructive effect upon her, Florentine
continues to pursue this young man whom she sees as her savior.[92]
     When Jean finally submits, both to Florentine's demands
and to his own powerful desires, and goes to the young woman's
home, it is as though he has walked into a past that has returned
to haunt his memory. He recalls the poverty, misery, and solitude of his childhood, first in an orphanage and then with his
foster mother. Reminding himself of his vow to become a
solitary, self-made man, he becomes angry at himself for having
been moved enough by Florentine to visit her here:

> Il savait maintenant que la maison de Florentine lui rappelait ce
> qu'il avait par-dessus tout redouté: l'odeur de la pauvreté, cette
> odeur implacable des vêtements pauvres, cette pauvreté qu'on
> reconnaît les yeux clos. Il comprenait que Florentine elle-même
> personnifiait ce genre de vie misérable contre laquelle tout son
> être se soulevait. Et dans le même instant, il saisit la nature du
> sentiment qui le poussait vers la jeune fille. Elle était sa misère,
> sa solitude, son enfance triste, sa jeunesse solitaire; elle était tout
> ce qu'il avait haï, ce qu'il reniait et aussi ce qui restait le plus
> profondément lié à lui-même, le fond de sa nature et l'aiguillon
> puissant de sa destinée.[93]

His seduction-rape of the young woman will symbolize both
his need to merge with his past destiny and his brutal and violent reaction against it.
     Jean's confused thoughts after his sexual relations with
Florentine create in him feelings of anger, bitterness, pity, and,
in particular, guilt. The more he thinks about this woman,
the more determined he becomes to forget her, to flee from
this object of his obsession and this obstacle to his ambitious
future. He convinces himself both of the need of total and

solitary independence and of the necessity to leave Saint-Henri. With persistent excuses, defenses, and guilty feelings, he follows his logical decision, leaving Florentine to transfer her urgent need for salvation onto Emmanual.[94]

Throughout *Bonheur d'occasion,* Jean is constantly placed in contrast to his good friend, Emmanual Létourneau. Jean is cruel, and Emmanuel is sweet and tender. Jean is egocentric and ambitious for himself alone; Emmanual is an idealist, concerned about others and the world, and, in Roy's own eyes, a hero and a humanist. If Jean ultimately represents failure and destruction in Florentine's life, then Emmanuel symbolizes salvation and security for her. Jacques Blais, in fact, sees these two young men as enemy-brothers, portrayed in the novel in several parallel scenes. They are both awakeners of consciences, Jean for Florentine, and Emmanuel for his peers, although in the final analysis, Jean is identified with collapse and Emmanuel with *recommencement.* Ironically, however, Roy saw Jean as succeeding after the close of the novel, while Emmanuel would die in the war, sacrificing himself for his ideals.[95]

It is Emmanuel's idealistic humanism, in fact, especially when he decides to enlist in the army, that enlightens the reader about this young man's character. Raised in Saint-Henri but belonging to a middle class family, Emmanuel has retained certain conservative notions prevalent at that time in Quebec, in particular a fidelity to France and to her traditions and, therefore, a strong desire to aid her during times of crisis. In addition, Emmanuel loves humanity, is aware of universal misery, and wants to fight in this war in order to preserve justice, beauty, and fraternity. He fears, however, that such problems of the world surpass his ability even to comprehend. He remains alone, painfully cognizant of his ignorance and his naïveté.[96]

If Emmanuel's ideals for the world appear to be sincere but somewhat immature, his love for Florentine is equally honest but resounds with a certain shallowness. Emmanuel is attracted to Florentine just as he has always been drawn toward the world of poverty that he does not understand:

> Ce désir de pénétrer l'âme du peuple, il l'avait toujours éprouvé, mais jamais avec une telle intensité, comme si en allant vers le peuple, en restant avec lui, il continuait sa recherche de Florentine, une recherche qui le mènerait à une plus grande compréhension de la jeune fille et qui détruirait entre eux tous les obstacles.

> Oh, trouver une voix, entendre une voix ce soir, n'importe laquelle,
> mais qui lui parlât le langage de Florentine, le langage du peuple!

With this disturbing and condescending attitude of pity and superiority toward Florentine, Emmanuel desires to protect her and to spoil her. He is in love and does marry her, despite the objections of his family, but if Florentine considers him to be her savior, one has the distinct impression that he sees himself in a similar role.[97]

Certain parallels can be made between Emmanuel, Florentine's husband, and Azarius Lacasse, her father. Like the younger man, Azarius is a naive idealist who possesses a deep love for France and a blind, optimistic faith in some, as yet unknown individual who will save that country from the German peril. Azarius, in fact, seems to be more distressed about the distant European conflict than about the constant financial problems facing his own family. It is easier to worry about World War II; he does not have to witness it daily. It is not that Azarius is unaware of or insensitive to familial concerns, but a weak person, forever lost in daydreams, he simply does not want to accept reality. He continues to *jongler,* as Rose-Anna describes his favorite activity, and maintains his joyous and confident aura of youth.[98]

On three occasions, Roy has stressed the fact that Azarius is not lazy but, as the victim of wide-spread unemployment, is simply not able to practice his chosen trade of carpentry. He is, however, vain, and because of the joy that he once experienced in his work, he refuses any other type of employment. Despite his reputation in the neighborhood as a man who cannot support his family, Azarius prefers to pass his time at the local café, speaking eloquently on all subjects, and losing neither his confidence nor, however, his sense of vengeance: "Il leur montrerait à tous qu'il était capable de faire vivre sa famille ... une de ses grandes entreprises, le vengerait de tout le dédain, de toute la honte qu'il sentait peser sur lui." For Azarius Lacasse does feel discouraged and ashamed. He tries to disguise his true feelings even from himself, but at certain moments he catches a glimpse of reality: "Il regarda le misérable logis. . . . 'Rose-Anna n'a pas confiance, non plus,' se dit-il. 'Elle n'a jamais eu confiance. Personne a confiance.' Il eut peur de se réveiller [from his life-long daydream] et de se voir tel qu'elle l'avait jugé depuis vingt ans, tel qu'il était peut-être." He does sincerely love his wife, and he knows that he has made her suffer.   He becomes determined to ameliorate her situation.[99]

The method that Azarius chooses to better Rose-Anna's life is entirely in accordance with his nature.   For a man who is perpetually lost in daydreams, unable to support his family, and ashamed of his destiny in life, the perfect solution is escape, freedom from all responsibilities: "Il souhaita n'avoir plus de femme, plus d'enfants, plus de` toit. . . . Il souhaita l'aube qui le surprendrait l'homme libre, sans liens, sans soucis, sans a- mour."   And Azarius has discovered the ideal form of escape, while ironically finally being able to support his family: he enlists in the army in order to fight for his beloved France.   With a sense of self-pity, he announces to his wife: " 'Le plus beau de toute, c'est que tu vas être débarrassée de moi.' "   Either sym- bolically or melodramatically, on the same day that she has given birth to her eleventh child, and on the same day that Daniel has died, Rose-Anna will lose, in effect, her oldest child. Azarius, in turn, will gain what he has always desired:

> Libre, libre, incroyablement libre, il allait recommencer sa vie. . . .
> Il évoqua jusqu'aux champs de bataille fumants de sang humain,
> mais où un homme se révélait dans sa force.   Il eut un grand
> besoin d'aventure, de périls, de hasards, lui qui avait si misérable-
> ment échoué dans les petites choses.

At the desired dawn of his new life, Azarius will experience a *recommencement,* this time with the feeling of being a man.[100]

In her seond major work of fiction, *La Petite Poule d'eau,* Gabrielle Roy does not add much more strength to the male character of Hippolyte Tousignant, Luzina's husband.   Like Azarius, he is little more than an oldest son to his wife, is re- proached by her for having no practical sense, and as the con- stant impregnator of Luzina, obviously imposes himself only in bed.   Hippolyte, however, is neither a dreamer nor a pathetic individual as is Azarius.   During his wife's "vacations" to give birth, in fact, he does fulfill her authoritarian role.   He is, in addition, justly proud to have made three rational decisions about his children's education: it is his idea to write to the government to obtain permission for their school and teacher; he is the one who decides where to build the school; and finally he gives the school its official name.   Hippolyte is not a strong male character, but he complements well his powerful wife.[101]

Stépan Yaramko, the husband of Martha in "Un Jardin au bout du monde," cannot be classified as a weak and dominated male figure in the home, but, interestingly, his attempts at being strong have failed, and he essentially removes himself from familial concerns. He has become, as a result, a hostile, angry man, bitter toward his children who have departed from the home and who will unfairly benefit, as Stépan believes, from the work of the Canadian pioneers of his generation. He is also jealous of his wife's former close rapport with their children, as well as of her fundamental love for life. Under the influence of alcohol, he reproaches her, in particular, for dying first, for he is afraid that she will speak against him in heaven. As she approaches her death, therefore, he does begin to help her in a modified tender manner, although he still refuses both to serve her meals and to speak to her. Even fear is not sufficient to alter his brutish nature.[102]

All of the adult male characters discussed thus far are present in a home situation but are either weak and dominated or uselessly display their strength. There is one Royan spouse and father, however, who is frequently absent from his home, and when he does return, the atmosphere of the entire household changes:

> Papa était absent. Souvent il restait au loin tout un mois et même davantage. Papa était un homme estimé, honorable; cependant, il n'y a pas à dire, la maison était beaucoup plus gaie quand mon père n'y était pas . . . il n'aimait pas le bruit, et il voulait des repas servis à l'heure, de l'ordre dans la maison, les mêmes, toujours les mêmes choses aux mêmes heures et de jour en jour. . . .

In effect, Christine's father in *Rue Deschambault* is associated with *la misère:* he is much older than his wife, has a somber, morose, and sometimes violent nature, and remains essentially incommunicative, except to his daughter, Agnès. He personally prefers nighttime and, therefore, is somewhat jealous of the fact that his children, enamored of daylight, are more similar to Maman.[103]

There is, however, another aspect to Papa's nature. Although he can complain about having had children, he can also be unusually understanding of them, especially of Christine and of her, at times, melodramatic emotions. He is also the one who purchases a glass mobile for his youngest daughter when she is ill, and he is the remarkable man whom Maman praises during her trip to Quebec. And yet he is still never seen as joyous by his children, only as a tired and sad man.[104]

The joyous aspect of Papa's nature does exist, however, but it is only visible when he is away from home, happily working, and even at times singing, with his beloved Western Canadian immigrants to whom he has become an almost god-like figure. His gaiety at work then parallels that of Maman at home: "Car, si papa s'était comporté parmi nous comme parmi les étrangers, et maman avec lui comme en son absence, est-ce qu'ils n'auraient pas été parfaitement heureux ensemble? . . ." But they are not happy together, for Papa truly loves only this chosen work that, in addition, involves extensive travel. It is, however, precisely for this last reason that he also needs the stability of his home. He needs to know that his wife and family are there whenever he is to return home; therefore, he resents Maman's leaving at any time. She, in turn, sometimes resents this chauvinistic attitude on her husband's part, but as a traditional couple, they maintain their respective roles in this Royan fictional household.[105]

Despite the importance of the male characters discussed thus far, none of them constitutes the focus of a particular literary work, for they are essentially necessary for the total depiction of a female character. The predominantly female world of Gabrielle Roy contains, in fact, only three major male figures who exist for themselves. Ironically if Roy has always been considered as more successful in her creation of women, her first male character, Alexandre Chenevert of the 1954 novel of the same name, is undoubtedly one of her most powerfully developed literary creations.

Alexandre Chenevert is the story of an insignificant, mediocre, Montreal bank teller who is well aware of his imperfections, dislikes the weaknesses and the lack of self-confidence that he sees in himself, and yet remains a prisoner of his inferiority complex. This middle-aged man considers himself, in effect, to be a small and inoffensive nobody, ashamed of his unimportant job, obscurely and unheroically disappearing into the shadows, and when he suffers, doing so without even a sense of nobility. Chenevert is, in addition, paranoid: fearful of and curious about what other people think of him. In his work, however, he has a tendency to treat his customers, especially those whom he innately judges to be timid, in a nasty and abrupt manner, but true to his nature, he admits that what he is attacking are the negative traits of his own personality that he observes in others. Alexandre Chenevert is a masochist.[106]

If the aforementioned qualities of inferiority were fully to describe this character, however, he would not be the fictional success that he is. Related both to his concern about other people's opinion of him and to his often intolerant attitude toward many of those around him, is Chenevert's additional sense of superiority and egotism. For this insignificant individual suffers, both for himself and for the problems of the world and of humanity. He is proud of and feels a grandeur in this constant and obsessive suffering because he believes that he is the only person to be so tortured in his thoughts. He is, therefore, different, and not made for the period of time in which he is living. With what one can call a twentieth-century *mal du siècle,* as well as a Romantic René-complex, Chenevert "s'imaginait avoir du moins choisi d'être malheureux. Il en tirait une sorte de fierté. S'il ne dormait pas [because of his compulsive worrying], c'est qu'il avait l'âme trop sensible, la conscience déliée, qu'il n'avait pas, Dieu merci, l'insouciance de la plupart des hommes." Other people do not care about international events, but Chenevert worries about them all, pities, especially, the great leaders of the world, and, in effect, sees a resemblance between himself and both the Pope and Mahatma Gandhi. When the latter is assassinated, the bank teller feels as though a part of himself has died. In this distasteful but pitiful identification, Chenevert's egotism is unmistakably evident.[107]

Egocentric superiority is also a part of this man's relationship with his wife, Eugénie. Chenevert treats Eugénie with an attitude of scorn because he is obsessed with the international news that he hears on the radio and reads in the newspapers, while she happily listens to serials. What he hates about his wife is her contented well-being in such a confusing world. When the woman becomes ill, he is initially unaware of her problems and then worries solely about the financial costs involved. With a subsequent sense of guilt about his own attitude, however, he does begin to treat her in a more gentle manner, but this change is temporary, lasting only as long as Eugénie's sickness. Chenevert soon returns to his former insulated self, unable to communicate with anyone. It is only when he is about to die that Chenevert honestly begins to worry about his wife and, especially, her financial status after his death, as he tries to make amends to her. At the same time, he becomes understanding and cognizant of the pain and suffering that he has transmitted to his daughter, Irène, to whom he has also never related. But with both personal relationships, it is now too late to rectify past faults.[108]

If Alexandre Chenevert's unlikable but pitiful egotism and attitude of superiority are evident in his rapports with his family, they are even more greatly emphasized in his sole friendship with a peer, Godias. Chenevert is, in fact, surprised that Godias desires to be his friend, for one could never imagine two individuals more dissimilar. Just as Chenevert is thin, sickly, an insomniac, pessimist, and compulsive worrier and malcontent, Godias is happy, well-fed, healthy, and genuinely friendly toward others. For twenty years, Chenevert has complained about Godias, for he cannot understand how his friend can remain so oblivious to the unhappiness of the world. In a sometimes maternal and at other times tyrannical tone, the teller preaches to Godias, as he attempts to alter his friend's outlook on life. Chenevert is, in effect, pathetically and snobbishly desirous of influencing Godias, of molding at least one individual who could then begin to think as he does:

> Car, s'il était un homme au monde qui avait pu profiter de l'expérience d'Alexandre Chenevert, s'enrichir au contact des pensées, des lectures qu'il lui communiquait, s'il était un homme qui eût dû penser comme Alexandre, c'était Godias. Depuis vingt ans qu'il s'épuisait à lui ouvrir les yeux, à le faire réfléchir, à se projeter dans cette autre existence, et qu'en restait-il chez ce gros homme insignifiant qui lui faisait face? Son impuissance à influencer Godias, aujourd'hui plus que jamais lui rendit ce dernier insupportable.[109]

With characteristic sarcasm, Roy underscores the egotism of her insignificant hero.

Chenevert's attitude becomes even more pronounced when he enters the hospital, for he sincerely believes that Godias will miss him when he dies. The patient actually expands his circle of friendships, in fact, as he suddenly senses a new self-importance. Soon to die, Chenevert recieves visits from hitherto unknown friends; he proudly realizes his worth, since others have begun to talk about him.[110]. Perhaps he was not as alone during his life as he had always sadly but egotistically believed.

Once again, however, Alexandre Chenevert's lucid assessment of his past life occurs too late, for given the circumstances of his personal situation, as well as his own attitude formed by the frenetic, modern world, his mediocre life, typified by his profession as a bank teller, has been one of insignificance and solitude. Entrapped daily in his transparent teller's cage, Chenevert performs his job out of habit, with extreme orderliness and exactitude, but without any thought. Fearful of any change in his routine, especially of any promotion, he is resigned to the fact that, as most people, he will remain in this one job throughout his life. Seen both as a machine—and specifically as a calculator—with a long line of customers before his teller's cage, and himself as a part of the endless line of modern urban humanity, Chenevert is usually lost in his own lofty thoughts of eternity. With a general lack of regard for others whom he must see as disturbing his serious reflections, the teller usually treats his customers rudely and impolitely. He remains within his desired isolation.[111]

Alexandre Chenevert's almost predestined and yet voluntary emprisonment within the boredom of his job reaches its culmination when he makes a one-hundred-dollar error in his daily calculations. His initial reaction is one of relief: he will certainly lose his job and, therefore, will no longer have a problem with the unknown, that is, of deciding how to leave his job in the future. But when he admits his error to his boss, M. Fontaine, the pathetic teller is disillusioned. Instead of being allowed to resign—a fate that he views as being worthy of his financial mistake after so many years of hard work—Chenevert is advised to retain his job and to repay the money in small installments. Characteristically obsessed with this debt, he is forced to find a second job, thereby becoming doubly entrapped in his work and in his financial worries.[112]

After years of a dislike of and a resignation to his routine job, it is only when Chenevert is in the hospital and aware of the fact that he is dying that he desires to return to his former insignificant life: "Plus encore que d'être heureux, plus encore que la grandeur, il désira se trouver dans sa cage." Chenevert begins to see the bank as a haven of solidarity among the employees and between the workers and their customers. Now that he can no longer work there, he is anxious to hear both news about the bank and, egotistically, what people are saying

about him. With the new interest that all of these individuals
have shown in him, Chenevert regrets that he was so severe
toward them all and would like to repay them in some way.[113]
But preferring boredom to death, he becomes concerned about
the importance of personal relationships too late in his life.

For during that life, Alexandre Chenevert has always
worried more about people whom he does not know, more
about humanity in general, than about those close to him. A
product of modern, urban society, he is deeply influenced,
or rather bombarded, by the news on the radio and in the press
and has, as a result, become an insomniac, unable to sleep because of his obsessive anxieties about the state of the world.
He worries about Communism, Russia, and the Jews of Palestine. He maintains that he loves humanity and desires peace
for all people, but then he voices his particular dislike of English-
Canadians, French, Jews, Americans, and *Québécois.* Chenevert
does not sincerely love humanity; he merely, and egotistically,
feels responsible for it.[114]

In effect, Alexandre Chenevert is a compulsive worrier
because he is never content. He is always anxious to see the
arrival of another stage of life, and yet he deeply fears the
onset of old age. He feels, therefore, that life is both too short
and too long. In addition, life should be divided into two distinct existences: one for necessities and the other for meditation and lofty thoughts. In a brilliantly depicted scene, Chenevert yearns for such a separation but confuses these two desired lives even further, to the extent that one cannot tell which
is the significant existence and which is the insignificant:

> Dans la salle de bains, il se prit à réfléchir plus intensément. Il
> considérait ses doigts de pieds déformés par des cors. . . . Il fut
> frappé encore une fois par le déliement de l'esprit qui se manifeste
> à certains instants les moins opportuns, les moins dignes de la vie.
> De penser à l'immortalité de l'âme tout en contemplant ses orteils
> lui paraissait presque inconvénient. . . . Il y avait de l'ironie dans
> tout cela. Un homme ne devrait pas penser; ou bien ne pas avoir
> à éliminer de déchets.[115]

Chenevert underscores even more greatly the ironies of life
when he confuses daily reality with his obsessive, international
concerns and actually begins to see immigrant Jews, on their
way to Palestine, drowning in his bathtub. This insignificant

bank teller does, in fact, suffer from a combination of ills, both medical and worldly, that are often indistinguishable from one another. Both stomach pains and widespread propaganda, for example, affect him profoundly. He feels, however, that he does not have a right to be so unhappy, given the fact that others do not have either a country or enough food to eat. Chenevert's suffering, in the first third of the novel, is, indeed, a privileged suffering, but no less painful nor less symptomatic of deeper ills.[116]

After his momentous vacation at Lac Vert where he experiences a feeling of rebirth, Chenevert returns to Montreal and to his worries about the world. He decides, however, that mere worry is insufficient and that he must act in order to effect changes: he gives money to charity and fasts in order to protest war and violence. As his suffering becomes real, however, and he becomes increasingly ill with cancer, Chenevert begins to worry even more about the state of the world. His pitiful distinction from other people now stems from the fact that he treats so seriously a period of time that he is not fated to have to endure much longer. Egotistically once again, the more "il allait vers sa fin, et plus Alexandre s'inquiétait de l'état dans lequel il laisserait l'univers." It is only when he enters the hospital and accepts the fact that he is dying that his personal concerns become more urgent to him than those of humanity. His worrying never stops, but the weight of the world has finally been taken off his shoulders.[117]

Alexandre Chenevert's ultimate escape, therefore, will come only in his sickness and then in his death. Throughout most of his life, any hope for escape from tedious reality was in the form of a dream, the dream of a tranquil forest or a deserted island where alone with nature, he could attain peace and happiness. When he discovers terrestrial paradise at Lac Vert, his faith is restored: happiness may not last, but at least he now knows that it does exist. Like the Royan female character, this man is convinced that even if only temporary, a *recommencement* or a *renouvellement* of his life is possible.[118]

Chenevert's resemblance to the typical Royan female does not involve solely their common desire for and belief in a new life. In a novel devoted to a male character, the author has also chosen to surround her teller with female imagery, as she places him on a quest for a maternal figure, for a symbolic replacement for his late mother. Agnes Whitfield has recognized

Chenevert's maternal complex specifically in his dreams of forests and islands and in his vacation at Lac Vert. It is, in fact, obvious that in this country refuge, he rediscovers a sense of childhood and innocence, as he is surrounded by the maternal security and warmth of nature and the home. Gérard Bessette sees the influence of Chenevert's mother on him while the teller is still in Montreal. Chenevert knows that he resembles this woman and at times does not like what he sees of her in himself. Her suffering has been transmitted to him, and he, in turn, has passed this pain on to Irène and, through her, to his grandson, Paul. At other times, he wants to be like his mother and, indeed, does often treat Godias in a maternal manner. Chenevert also experiences joy in his thoughts of this woman, as in his memories of youth, so with a reaction of both happiness and pain, he is reminded of her whenever he sees certain individuals in his current life, in particular, his customers, Violette Leduc and Mme Huberdeau. Finally this middle-aged man prays to his late mother and cries out to her. With a sense of guilt, he feels that he never loved her enough and that, ultimately, he was responsible for her death.[119]. As a male hero, therefore, he must atone for the disappearance of the maternal female.

He must also atone for modern society, urban life, and the twentieth century in general, for if Alexandre Chenevert is an insignificant, ordinary individual, his true literary force lies in the fact that he represents humanity, or what one once called "modern man" or "Everyman." He is a universal, archetypal figure who, as a alienated Charlot, or Chaplinesque being, lives in a Zola-like, determined, and mecanized world. He is the modern, urban commuter who on the tram assumes "une curieuse pose de supplicié," for he is "loin, toujours de plus en plus de sa primitive insouciance" and symbolizes "le non-sens, la fatalité, la gratuité de la misère de son époque." With no mother and no communication with his wife, Chenevert also represents the disintegration of the family, as well as of the individual who searches for a purpose in a purposeless world. When he is about to die, he pities the others who must continue their difficult and false lives. Alexandre Chenevert is the nobody who is all of us.[120]

It is logical, therefore, that, as the post-World War II tragic individual, Chenevert is seen as living in a Kafkaesque cage, enduring Sartrian *nausée,* struggling against the Camus-like absurdity of life, and, especially, experiencing a constant "sensation d'étrangeté." Throughout the novel, there are numerous references to the fact that this modern urban prisoner feels "si étranger, si hostile à lui-même"; he is, as well, "un homme qui aurait pu être," a mysterious stranger to his wife. Chenevert, in addition, views the human condition as unbearable and wonders what his role could be in such a pitiless world, for suffering in absolute solitude, he remains a stranger even in his own city of Montreal, just as if he were in a foreign city. He assesses his life with bitter irony: "Ce qui lui arrivait était pire que la solitude: comme un atroce malentendu." Like Meursault, Camus's hero of *L'Etranger,* Alexandre Chenevert's existence is one of total absurdity, impossible to understand but, in the end, necessary to be accepted with all of its imperfections.[121]

Chenevert does ultimately become resigned to the absurdity of life, humanity, and the world when, once again, he lies dying in the hospital. At the same time, his role in this absurd society becomes clear. The insignificant, anonymous bank teller not only symbolizes humanity, but also becomes its needed scapegoat, its social and religious martyr. Indications of this role as a guilty and innocent victim have occurred throughout Chenevert's life. He has, first of all, always been paranoid, feeling that even silence is reproaching him and that he is forever on trial. Secondly, he is a man with the gift of misfortune, "trop délicat pour ce monde" and "fait pour souffrir." And thirdly, it is his doctor who diagnoses Chenevert's illness: " 'Vous êtes au bord d'un désastre. . . . Vous pensez trop. Vous raisonnez trop. Que diable,' fit-il, 'vous portez le monde sur vos épaules!' " It is only when he travels to Lac Vert and sleeps well that he is liberated from both God and humans: "Alexandre n'avait plus à répondre du péché originel, non plus que de ces armes d'aujourd'hui, si dangereuses qu'on va les essayer en des îles désertes."[122]

But this freedom from social and religious martyrdom does not last, for the interiorization of society's ills becomes more gravely pronounced in Chenevert's prostate cancer, and this new Christ must make amends to humanity, his priest, and God once he enters the hospital. At first stating that he would sacrifice himself for a better world, he then questions his true feelings and wonders if he does not prefer his own personal security to the common advancement of people. But he does sense a need to be with other suffering patients: "Sa propre misère ne lui avait jamais paru très méritoire. Mais celle d'un autre, inexplicable, il s'en couvrait en cet instant comme de son seul recours." True to his nature until the very end, Alexandre Chenevert assumes the misery of others and plays the role of society's martyr. At the same time he egotistically and proudly basks in humanity's suffering. He dies as the eternally pre-destined and voluntary scapegoat.[1 2 3]

It is interesting that the major characters, both female and male, of Gabrielle Roy's novels are portrayed more as symbols or archetypal figures than as individuals. In addition, they all represent some form of martyrdom: Rose-Anna Lacasse and Elsa Kumachuk are maternal martyrs, and Alexandre Chene-vert is the martyr of modern society. Similarly, the male hero of Roy's third novel, Pierre Cordorai of *La Montagne secrète,* is never fully individualized but remains the archetype of the artist, once again in a state of self-sacrifice, both for the perfect work of art and for humanity.

Maintaining a separate analysis of Royan male characters, one can distinguish numerous similarities between Cordorai and Chenevert. They are both proud and egotistical men who remain enigmas to themselves. Both are on an obsessive, life-long quest toward a goal that they do not understand: Alexandre toward a vague notion of peace and contentment for himself and for humanity; and Pierre toward a monumental concept of perfect aesthetic beauty and happiness. Once again like Rose-Anna and Elsa, these two men offer little verbal exchange with others, for Cordorai, in particular, prefers to communicate through his drawings. They both live in solitude—Alexandre in Montreal and then at Lac Vert, and, especially, Pierre in the extreme North of Canada and then in Paris. As loners maintaining their distance from others, however, they both feel a closeness to humanity, as well as a desire to communicate: Chenevert needs Godias, and Cordorai relates first to his friend, Steve, and then to the painter, Stanislas. The bank teller's wish to communicate with others, however, comes especially when he is in the midst of nature at Lac Vert, while for the artist, this desire pursues him throughout his life but becomes particularly intense when he discovers *la Resplendissante,* the perfect mountain of God's creation that the painter so desperately wants to recreate on paper. For both men, the paralyzing anguish of their lives has finally but temporarily been dissolved as they experience, at these respective moments, a sense of liberation. Such a tempo-rary release from obsessive anxiety can, in addition, be viewed for both male characters as the culmination of their common search for a maternal figure. During their lives, both Chenevert and Cordorai have renounced female tenderness: Chenevert in his lack of a rapport with Eugénie; and Cordorai in his refusal of Nina. If Chenevert's sensation of childhood and security at Lac Vert can be seen as a return to a maternal refuge, Cordorai's quest for and discovery of the ideal mountain has also been interpreted as that of a similar emphasis on the maternal female in a predominantly male novel.[124]

As both male heroes pursue their lives of compulsive sacrifice, their similarities continue. Chenevert's social anguish assumes the form of cancer, while Cordorai's obsession with the perfect work of art leads to his own serious heart ailment. The bank teller returns to Montreal, essentially in order to die, and the artist leaves northern Canada for Paris, likewise in order to die. Both are surprised that near death, they are surrounded by so many friends, for without having done anything against humanity, both are afflicted with what Cordorai's friend, Steve, calls "la pire souffrance de l'homme," that of self-hatred. At the point of death, Cordorai experiences a feeling formerly sensed by Chenevert, that of a possible new beginning. The artist becomes certain that, like the bank teller, he still has enough time "pour s'acquitter envers le monde," to clear himself of all charges made against him by and for humanity and to repay the world for his existence. In a second state of liberation, both Chenevert and Cordorai escape into a premature death, sacrificing themselves for an unknown, impossible, and essentially absurd goal.[125]

If Pierre Cordorai is the epitome of the obsessive and martyred artist, he is also the independent adventurer who flees modern civilization and seeks total solitude as he travels further North. As such, he is part of a group of Royan male characters, mostly secondary, who can be labelled as loners. One encounters these men throughout Roy's fiction: the old and somewhat strange Gédéon of *La Montagne secrète;* in *La Petite Poule d'eau* Nick Sluzick, Abe Zlutkin, Isaac, and Bessette; Gustave of "Un Vagabond frappe à notre porte"; and, especially, the crabby, old Ian of "La Rivière sans repos" who having fled from the modern, White world that is influencing the Eskimo way of life, prefers to live a solitary and primitive existence.[126]

In the Royan world, there is, in addition, a third major male character who must also be classified as a loner. He is

not, however, a strongly independent adventurer, but rather
a timid, pathetic, Chinese immigrant who, ultimately admired
for his honesty, perseverance, and understanding nature, appears
to be pushed along in his life by the incessant wind of fatality.
Sam Lee Wong of "Où iras-tu Sam Lee Wong?" can be likened
in several ways both to Alexandre Chenevert and to Pierre
Cordorai. Like the bank teller, he is poignantly depicted as an
insignificant man who rarely communicates with others and
who becomes increasingly serious and frenetic as modern prosperity invades his rapidly expanding town. Like Cordorai, Sam
Lee Wong prefers a simple life closer to nature, specifically and
nostalgically closer to the hills of his homeland of China. This
restaurateur's tormented search for such hills on the flat western
plains of Canada is, once again, seen as a quest for the past, for
a sense of childhood within a maternal refuge, as well as for a
return to the female earth. Sam Lee Wong is, in fact, alone,
without a wife because of Canadian immigration laws. The
only person with whom he can discuss his concerns is another
pitiful man, Smouillya, himself a lonely immigrant who, before
meeting Sam, a sincere listener, was avoided by everyone because
he talked too much about himself in an indecipherable accent.
In what Smouillya calls "une fatalité fraternelle," these two
solitary men honestly communicate. Ironically, however, it
is Smouillya who, because of a misunderstanding—like the
"atroce malentendu" of Chenevert's life— is responsible for his
friend's departure from the town. He organizes a farewell party
for Sam who, with no intention of leaving, is forced to do so in
embarrassment. He must travel into deeper solitude, still far
from his beloved hills.[127]   With Sam Lee Wong, as with all
of the other Royan male characters, life continues to be filled
with isolation and anguish. The male figures present in Roy's
works may indeed be weaker than the women, but they are
often equally poignant.

   In *Cet Eté qui chantait* Roy writes of all creatures of
nature: "Tout ce qui vit veut vivre à deux. A besoin de son
semblable. Ou, à défaut de son semblable, de quelqu'un d'autre." It is true that throughout Gabrielle Roy's fiction, characters do exalt true love, yearn to be part of a couple, or given
the innate solitude of individuals, desire to communicate with
at least one other person. Most couples depicted in these works,
however, appear to be unsuccessful. In defense of this tragic
characterization, Roy maintained that she simply wrote about

what she saw around her and had seen throughout her life. There were, in Roy's opinion, few couples deeply in love. Those who truly exhibited this emotion were, in addition, boring.[128]

Ironically, along with the creation of more independent women in her early short stories, Roy peoples these tales with a greater number of unsuccessful couples than in her later works. It is only in "Le Monde à l'envers," "Le Joli Miracle," and "A Okko," however, that the couples depicted present the totally joyous image of honest and happy love. The spouses of "Une Histoire d'amour" were also content in their youth and have remained together, but they are now portrayed as being pitiful in their old age. The power of love is equally strong between Bunny and Frederick in "La Sonate à l'aurore," but it is tragically destroyed by war. And finally, as has been seen, Dr. Raymond and Anne of "La Source au désert" are deeply in love, abandoning themselves to the permanent presence of the other within their individual natures, but allied forever, they realize that they form an impossible pair.[129]

Such impossible or mismatched couples increase in number in Roy's major fiction. The need to be part of a pair is still present, but either the desire itself is thwarted, or the two people living together lead parallel existences, without any communication. Florentine Lacasse, for example, desperately wants to find a boyfriend and be part of a couple. Masochistically, she choses Jean who rejects any possible pairing in his life. As a result of her tragic experience with Jean, the young woman bitterly views men and women as natural enemies but immediately decides to try to conquer Emmanuel and, thus, to form another mismatched couple, soon separated by war. Florentine has, of course, no model to follow in her life, for despite her parents' happiness and love at the beginning of their marriage, their relationship has evolved into one of two solitary existences. Marriages in *Bonheur d'occasion* are a failure.[130]

The Tousignant's marriage in *La Petite Poule d'eau* is more successful, although it appears to be based more upon convenience than upon the love and respect that Roy believed was essential to a good union. Only at one point, during a dance at a Metis celebration, do Luzina and Hippolyte rediscover their past youth, with its joyous and honest conjugal love. For the rest of their marital life, it is routine that dominates. Routine and convenience also form the basis of one of Roy's most pitiful couples, the Cheneverts. Alexandre and Eugénie are not only surrounded by mutual incompatibility and indifference, but they are also physically mismatched:

> Elle était plus grande que lui et, depuis nombre d'années, plus forte aussi de taille. Il avait été gêné toute sa vie de sortir en public avec Eugénie. . . . Il l'avait toujours lu dans le regard des autres: ils étaient de ces couples que les gens s'arrêtent pour voir passer, avec de l'étonnement, un peu de pitié, toutes sortes de spécula-tions.

They are, in addition, strangers to one another: "Il lui jetait alors un regard fermé, de ces regards sans communication comme peuvent surtout en avoir entre eux les gens qui ont vécu très longtemps ensemble." It is only with illness, old age, and the threat of death that these individuals begin to appreciate one another and discover "à cet instant, si tard, qu'ils s'aimaient."[131]

There is also no deep love between Christine's parents in *Rue Deschambault,* only honest respect and mutual admiration. Maman admits to her friend, Idole, that she married too young, chose a man much older than she, and experiences no passionate love for him. Only with time has she discovered his good quali-ties. As opposite as day and night, according to their daughter, Maman and Papa can never communicate, can never understand one another. They can be happy, but never happy together. This same pairing of entirely different individuals and the same subsequent lack of communication can be seen with Martha and Stépan Yaramko of "Un Jardin au bout du monde." Martha herself wonders: "Et qu'était-ce que cet amour qui, dans la jeunesse, alliait parfois les natures les plus opposées?" Now they do not speak to one another, do not even know how to begin to communicate. It has become impossible for them even to address one another by their first names, as if the use of the words, "husband" and "wife," would appear to offend their former love. The entire story of their lives is presented in this novella through their individual thoughts. The Royan couple has culminated in the existence of two entirely separate beings.[132]

It is Florentine Lacasse who, seeing men and women as innate enemies, also believes that they call a truce to their hostilities only during sexual relations. But in the Royan world, such a relationship inevitably leads to an even more profound separation between the two partners of a couple. Roy herself has stated that love or marriage based solely on physical needs must result in mutual scorn and hatred; sexual intimacy is not sufficient to sustain a true union.[133]   In fact, both the portrayal of sex in Roy's fiction and her characters' attitude toward physical relationships are not at all positive.   Sex is used for procreation which, as has been seen, produces too many pregnancies and too many children.   In all other situations, sexual relations are associated with rape and incest, resignation, joylessness, guilt, and shame.

Throughout *Bonheur d'occasion,* for example, Florentine exudes deep sensuality, is sexually audacious by inviting Jean to her home, calculatingly uses her sexuality to entrap Emmanuel, and yet expresses a great fear of physical contact.   The seduction-rape between Florentine and Jean is, in addition, surrounded by poverty and symbolizes a violent insult to and transgression of both social and religious norms.   A sense of guilt and shame, therefore, torments both young people afterwards.   One year later in "La Source au désert," in fact, Roy would specifically portray voluptuous, physical love as an evil perversion.[134]

In *Alexandre Chenevert,* sexual relations between Eugénie and her husband are as pathetic as everything else in their marriage.   Alexandre is, in effect, relieved that he no longer needs to make love.   In his opinion, men are not comfortable with sex and speak about it only with false carefreeness or with vulgarity. For Alexandre himself, sexual relations were always "une obsession alors, ce triste besoin physique, une espèce de contrainte beaucoup plus qu'une chose belle et saine. . . ."   Ironically and tragically, however, he feels guilty about Eugénie, for "elle avait été en quelque sorte irritée contre l'amour, par le manque de joie qu'il éprouvait, de spontanéité aussi.   Ah! que tout avait été triste entre eux, alors qu'ils se livraient à une sorte de ruse hypocrite l'un envers l'autre. . . ."   Eugénie was, therefore, in Alexandre's opinion, always too tired to resist, or else too fearful, for religious reasons, of not submitting.   She resigned herself to what she must have seen as the horrible act of love.[135] In her husband's eyes, she has always been a female martyr.

Physical sexual violence, always linked with characteristic female resignation, occurs on two significant occasions in "La Rivière sans repos."   The countryside of this Eskimo land is, in fact, described as not being suitable for making love, so to these people, sex is a natural, simple act, occurring solely by chance.   It is logical, therefore, that Elsa fully accepts the rape by the G.I. behind the bushes, a rape that leads to the inevitable divisiveness in her life. This resignation to the first transgression of the mores of White society is followed by the poignant acceptance of a second transgression, that of incest between Elsa and her uncle, Ian:

> Elle comprit qu'au grand froid il était venu chercher à épuiser, autant que l'angoisse, un besoin physique, resurgi encore brûlant. Ses propres sens furent mis en émoi par le violent désir de l'homme.
>
> Ils rentrèrent l'un derrière l'autre. A peine à moitié dévêtus, ils s'unirent dans une hâte qui projetait au plafond une immense ombre agitée.

The sight of this shadow of incestuous love traumatizes Jimmy who rejecting his mother with her new odor of physical shame, cries bitterly. Both Jimmy and Elsa, as well as Ian, will subsequently not be allowed to reach their desired paradise of Baffin Island in the extreme North of Canada, for this supreme agression against all morals is also the supreme sin against true human love.[136]

For Gabrielle Roy this human love is " 'le chemin mystérieux par lequel on est conduit à sa propre découverte. Tel qui commence dans une pauvre terre peut donner une fleur rare.' " Like a flower, human love can flourish or die, for everything "fructifiait peut-être donc en ce monde selon l'amour qui lui était accordé."[137] The distressing problem in the Royan literary universe is that despite an ideal of love for these adult creations and despite the author's apparent humanistic love for all of her characters, the love encountered by her poignant creatures seldom gives a rare flower or bears sweet fruit. Love does exist in Roy's fiction, but it is primarily between parents and children —and usually between mothers and daughters—among siblings, or between a teacher and her pupils. Adult women are too preoccupied with their maternal role to concern themselves with any overt love for their spouses, and adult men are either too weak to express their love to their wives, too indifferent to them, or too involved with purely physical desires. In the Royan adult world, women do dominate, and men are indeed present, but, sadly, there seem to be very few successful couples who experience any form of deep and honest love.

NOTES

[1] Gabrielle Roy, *Ces Enfants de ma vie* (Montréal: Editions Internationales Alain Stanké Ltée, 1977), p. 191.

[2] Jimmy of "La Rivière sans repos" will also decide to leave home and, like some of the young adults of *Bonheur d'occasion,* will choose to go to war, in his case to Vietnam.

[3] Gilles Dorion et Maurice Emond, "Dossier Gabrielle Roy: Questionnaire," *Québec Français,* No. 36 (décembre 1979), p. 35.

[4] It is Phyllis Grosskurth who speaks of Roy's maternal concern and her "mother's-eye view" of the world. See *Gabrielle Roy,* Canadian Writers and Their Works (Toronto: Forum House, 1972), p. 57. See also pp. 58-61; Phyllis Grosskurth, "Gabrielle Roy and The Silken Noose," *Canadian Literature,* 42 (1969), 7-13; Gérard Bessette, *Une Littérature en ébullition* (Montréal: Editions du Jour, 1968), pp. 224-227; Gérard Bessette, *Trois Romanciers québécois* (Montréal: Editions du Jour, 1973), pp. 182, 207, 208; François Ricard, *Gabrielle Roy,* Ecrivains canadiens d'aujourd'hui, No. 11 (Montréal: Editions Fides, 1975), pp. 31-32; Monique Genuist, *La Création romanesque chez Gabrielle Roy* (Montréal: Le Cercle du Livre de France, 1966), pp. 19, 31, 53, 57, 139-140; Michel-Lucien Gaulin, "Le Thème du bonheur dans l'oeuvre de Gabrielle Roy," Thesis Université de Montréal 1961, pp. 129-144; Joseph-Marie Le Vasseur, "Gabrielle Roy, peintre de la famille canadienne-française," Thesis Université de Montréal 1960, pp. 39-61; Paula Gilbert Lewis, "*Street of Riches* and *The Road Past Altamont:* The Feminine World of Gabrielle Roy," *Journal of Women's Studies in Literature,* 1, No. 2 (Spring 1979), 133-134; Jeanette Urbas, "Equations and Flutes," *Journal of Canadian Fiction,* 1, ii (1972), 69-73.

[5] Gabrielle Roy, "Cendrillon '40," *La Revue Moderne,* 21, No. 10 (février 1940), 8, 9, 41, 42; Gabrielle Roy, "Le Roi de coeur," *La Revue Moderne,* 21, No. 12 (avril 1940), 6, 7, 33-39; Gabrielle Roy, "La Grande Voyageuse," *La Revue Moderne,* 24, No. 1 (mai 1942), 12, 13, 27-30; Gabrielle Roy, "Six Pilules par jour," *La Revue Moderne,* 23, No. 3 (juillet 1941), 17, 18, 32-34; Gabrielle Roy, "Embobeliné," *La Revue Moderne,* 23, No. 6 (octobre 1941), 7, 8, 28, 30, 33, 34.

[6]Roy, "Cendrillon '40," pp. 41, 42; Gabrielle Roy, "Avantage pour," *La Revue Moderne,* 20, No. 6 (octobre 1940), 5, 6, 26.

[7]Roy, "Le Roi de coeur," pp. 7, 33, 35, 36, 38, 39; Gabrielle Roy, "Bonne à marier," *La Revue Moderne,* 20, No. 2 (juin 1940), 41, 42. The importance of marrying one's daughters, as well as the shame of not having a husband, is also treated in Gabrielle Roy, "La Grande Berthe," *Le Bulletin des Agriculteurs,* 39, No. 6 (juin 1943), 5, 9.

[8]Gabrielle Roy, "La Conversion des O'Connor," *La Revue Moderne,* 21, No. 5 (septembre 1939), 4; Roy, "La Grande Berthe," pp. 7, 8; Gabrielle Roy, "Les Mennonites," *Fragiles Lumières de la terre: Ecrits divers 1942-1970,* Collection Prose Entière (Montréal: Les Editions Quinze, 1978), pp. 45-47, 52-53. This last short story was originally published as "Femmes de dur labeur," *Le Bulletin des Agriculteurs,* 39, No. 1 (janvier 1943), 10, 25. Gabrielle Roy, "La Fuite de Sally," *Le Bulletin des Agriculteurs,* 27, No. 1 (janvier 1941), 9, 39.

[9]Roy, "La Grande Berthe," pp. 7, 39-40; Gabrielle Roy, "Sécurité," *La Revue Moderne,* 29, No. 11 (mars 1948), 13, 68; Alice Parizeau, "Gabrielle Roy, grande romancière canadienne," *Châtelaine,* 7, No. 4 (avril 1966), 120.

[10]Gabrielle Roy, "La Source au désert," *Le Bulletin des Agriculteurs,* 42, No. 10 (octobre 1946), 34, 10. See also pp. 11, 30, 32-36, 38-39, 41, 43-45, 47. Gabrielle Roy, "La Source au désert," *Le Bulletin des Agriculteurs,* 42, No. 11 (novembre 1946), 46; Personal interview with Gabrielle Roy, 29 June 1980; Marc Gagné, *Visages de Gabrielle Roy* (Montréal: Librairie Beauchemin Limitée, 1973), pp. 143-144.

[11]Gabrielle Roy, "Le Monde à l'envers," *La Revue Moderne,* 21, No.6 (octobre 1939), 6, 34; Gabrielle Roy, "A Okko," *La Revue Moderne,* 22, No. 12 (avril 1941), 8, 9, 41, 42; Gabrielle Roy, "Le Joli Miracle," *Le Bulletin des Agriculteurs,* 26, No. 12 (décembre 1940), 8, 29-30. Roy treats other working women, in particular, the difficult life of the rural schoolteacher, in one of her journalistic articles published during this same period. See Gabrielle Roy, "Pitié pour les institutrices," *Le Bulletin des Agriculteurs,* 38, No. 3 (mars 1942), 7, 45-46.

[12]Gabrielle Roy, "Les Petits Pas de Caroline," *Le Bulletin des Agriculteurs,* 26, No. 10 (octobre 1940), 45. See also pp. 11, 46, 48, 49.

[13]Roy, "Six Pilules par jour," pp. 17, 18, 32-34; Roy, "Embobeliné," p. 8; Roy, "La Grande Berthe," pp. 41, 49; Gabrielle Roy, "La Pension de vieillesse," *Le Bulletin des Agriculteurs,* 39, No. 11 (novembre 1943), 8, 32, 33, 36; Roy, "La Grande Voyageuse," pp. 29, 30.

[14]Parizeau, pp. 120, 123. See also pp. 44, 118. Roy continued to maintain that she was one of the first supporters and remained a strong advocate of liberation for women. Personal interview with Gabrielle Roy,

29 June 1980.

[15]Robert Morissette, "Interview avec Gabrielle Roy," in "La Vie ouvrière urbaine dans le roman canadien-français contemporain," Thesis Université de Montréal 1970, p. 166; Parizeau, p. 120.

[16]Parizeau, pp. 120, 122. See also pp. 123, 121; Personal interview with Gabrielle Roy, 29 June 1980. In this 1980 interview, Roy also expressed a traditional attitude toward current Québécois feminist literature, seen as being too obsessive and, therefore, extremist.

[17]Gabrielle Roy, Bonheur d'occasion (1945; rpt. Montréal: Librairie Beauchemin Limitée, 1973), pp. 241, 66. See also pp. 20, 79, 81, 104, 109, 137-139, 146, 149, 206-207, 230-231, 246, 251; Grosskurth, Gabrielle Roy, pp. 11-15. Rose-Anna continued to be one of Roy's favorite characters. Personal interview with Gabrielle Roy, 29 June 1980.

[18]Roy, Bonheur d'occasion, pp. 149, 314. See also pp. 76-78, 143, 145, 309; André Brochu, "Gabrielle Roy," Notes from course on author, Université de Montréal, Printemps 1978, taken by one of his students; Antonine Maillet (Soeur Marie-Grégoire), "La Femme et l'enfant dans l'oeuvre de Gabrielle Roy," Thesis Université Saint-Joseph de Memramcook 1959, pp. 88-89; Marie du Rédempteur, Soeur (Pierrette Seers), "Le Thème de la solitude dans l'oeuvre de Gabrielle Roy," Thesis Université de Montréal 1963, pp. 44-52.

[19]Roy, Bonheur d'occasion, pp. 322, 323. See also pp. 77-78, 321-329; Bessette, Une Littérature en ébullition, pp. 261-266; Gabrielle Pascal, "La Condition féminine dans l'oeuvre de Gabrielle Roy," Voix et Images, 5, No. 1 (automne 1979), 150-151.

[20]Roy, Bonheur d'occasion, p. 86. See also pp. 60, 83-90, 106-107, 211, 247-251.

[21]Roy, Bonheur d'occasion, pp. 143-144, 149-159, 168-170, 172-177, 312, 328. Paul Socken, "Use of Language in Bonheur d'occasion: A Case in Point," Essays on Canadian Writing, No. 11 (Summer 1978), pp. 67-68.

[22]Roy, Bonheur d'occasion, pp. 172, 173, 176. See also André Brochu, "Thèmes et structures de Bonheur d'occasion," in L'Instance critique (Montréal: Leméac, 1974), pp. 229-233; Pascal. pp. 149-150.

[23]Roy, Bonheur d'occasion, pp. 146, 245, 232. See also pp. 62-66, 106, 145, 199-202, 259, 305-307, 315, 317; Grosskurth, Gabrielle Roy, pp. 11-15; Brochu, "Thèmes et structures de Bonheur d'occasion," pp. 211-216; Jacques Blais, "L'Unité organique de Bonheur d'occasion," Etudes Française, 6, No. 1 (février 1970), 29-33, 39-46.

[24]Roy, Bonheur d'occasion, p. 205. See also pp. 204, 243; Gabrielle Roy, "Bonheur d'occasion aujourd'hui," Le Bulletin des Agriculteurs, 44, No. 1 (janvier 1948), 6; Bessette, Une Littérature en ébullition, pp. 291-293. Another traditional mother figure in this novel is Mme Philibert. See

Roy, *Bonheur d'occasion,* pp. 30-31.

[25]Roy, *Bonheur d'occasion,* pp. 172-173, 78. See also pp. 65, 247-251; Roy, *"Bonheur d'occasion* aujourd'hui," pp. 7, 23. It is in this article that Roy states that although Rose-Anna should not retain any illusions about the social reality that she does not really understand, she does, in effect, maintain some semblance of optimism. Sadly, the author has no answers for her character. See also Sainte-Marie-Eleuthère, Soeur, *La Mère dans le roman canadien-français* (Québec: Les Presses de l'Université Laval, 1964), pp. 174-180; Suzanne Paradis, *Femme fictive, femme réelle: Le Personnage féminin dans le roman canadien-français, 1884-1966* (Québec: Editions Garneau, 1966), pp. 45-52. This repetition or echo of advice from one generation of women to another is typical in Roy's fiction. The author believed, however, that, sadly, one could not teach experience to a child. Personal interview with Gabrielle Roy, 29 June 1980.

[26]Roy, *Bonheur d'occasion,* pp. 223, 239. See also pp. 20, 77-78, 103, 104, 106-109, 147, 228. Florentine's last comment refers specifically to her friend, Marguerite, who is portrayed as both nasty and compassionate toward Florentine. Marguerite is, in addition, content with her life and, therefore, totally different from the Lacasse woman. See Roy, *Bonheur d'occasion,* pp. 15-16, 236-237. See also Pascal, pp. 153-155; Annette Saint-Pierre, *Gabrielle Roy: Sous le signe du rêve* (Saint-Boniface, Manitoba: Editions du Blé, 1975), pp. 13-20; Bessette, *Une Littérature en ébullition,* pp. 261-266; Sainte-Marie-Eleuthère, pp. 174-180; Blais, pp. 39-46. Emmanuel's mother, Mme Létourneau, is also seen as a prisoner of her female condition. See Pascal, p. 150.

[27]Roy, *Bonheur d'occasion,* p. 222. See also pp. 226, 233, 236, 258, 291, 294, 300, 303; Brochu, "Thèmes et structures," pp. 218-220.

[28]Roy, *Bonheur d'occasion,* pp. 220, 26. See also pp. 11, 12, 16-17, 21, 75-76, 115, 118-121, 163-164, 183, 228, 269, 290-292; Saint-Pierre, pp. 13-20; Brochu, "Gabrielle Roy"; Albert Le Grand, "Gabrielle Roy ou l'être partagé," *Etudes Françaises,* 1ère année, No. 2 (juin 1965), pp. 51-56, 58-59. This duality in Florentine's name and nature can be seen as an additional example of Le Grand's interpretation of Royan characters as divided beings.

[29]Roy, *Bonheur d'occasion,* p. 69. See also pp. 70-73, 100, 112-113, 342; Roy, *"Bonheur d'occasion* aujourd'hui," pp. 22-23; Brochu, "Thèmes et structures," pp. 235-239; Socken, pp. 68-70.

[30]Roy, *Bonheur d'occasion,* p. 102. See also pp. 13, 101, 103, 224; Grosskurth, *Gabrielle Roy,* pp. 11-15; Brochu, "Thèmes et structures," p. 240.

[31]Roy, *Bonheur d'occasion,* pp. 92-94, 99, 125, 162-167, 177-187, 217-228, 232-235.

[32] Roy, *Bonheur d'occasion,* pp. 301, 302, 305. See also pp. 227, 239-240, 288-305; Saint-Pierre, pp. 13-20; Brochu, "Thèmes et structures," pp. 229-233.

[33] Roy, *Bonheur d'occasion,* pp. 306-307. See also pp. 308, 336, 340-345.

[34] Gabrielle Roy, *Alexandre Chenevert* (1954; rpt. Montréal: Beauchemin, 1973), pp. 14, 22, 113, 114, 116, 131. See also Paradis, pp. 56-59.

[35] Roy, *Alexandre Chenevert,* pp. 114, 120.

[36] Roy, *Alexandre Chenevert,* pp. 127, 146. See also pp. 129-130, 134-135, 139-142, 145; Pascal, pp. 152-153. In Roy's third novel, *La Montagne secrète,* one meets an unmarried woman, Nina, who described as a new Eve, has learned much about bitter life from men. She is in fact, flattered when she realizes that Pierre Cordorai, unlike other men, does not desire her sexually. For this independent vagabond, Nina symbolizes, instead, the warmth of the home. She does eventually marry his friend and does become pregnant, but Pierre's attitude toward her, as toward all women, remains consistent. While later staring at a painting of Eve by a Flemish master, for example, Pierre's reaction is emotional: he sees the female body as pure, delicate, and pathetic and the fragile woman as the trembling mother of all types of men. As an artist, he feels that he can understand the female destiny, and he offers a look of sympathy and consolation to the image before him. In this melodramatic scene, the hero does betray some of his chauvinism, although Roy does also seem to be attempting to endow her male character with a certain sensitivity for the female condition. Gabrielle Roy, *La Montagne secrète* (1961; rpt. Montréal: Librairie Beauchemin Limitée, 1974), pp. 33-35, 37-39, 69, 100, 137-138, 156.

[37] Gabrielle Roy, *La Rivière sans repos* (Montréal: Librairie Beauchemin Limitée, 1971), p. 137. See also pp. 124-136. Elsa was another of Roy's favorite characters. Personal interview with Gabrielle Roy, 29 June 1980. Although Roy's entire work is entitled *La Rivière sans repos,* the novel of the same name, and to which one is referring here, appears with three short stories, jointly called "Nouvelles esquimaudes," and each with its own title. These short stories do not appear in the English-language edition.

[38] Roy, "La Rivière sans repos," p. 137. See also pp. 138-147.

[39] Roy, "La Rivière sans repos," pp. 155, 162. See also pp. 148-151, 153-171. Ironically, Jimmy will later echo similar words in reference to Elsa. See p. 278.

[40] Roy, "La Rivière sans repos," p. 174. See also pp. 172-180, 204-216, 228-229, 231-234, 239-249. Ironically, when Elsa decides to leave new Fort-Chimo and return to the old Eskimo way of life in old Fort-

Chimo, she opposes her mother once again. Winnie hates the ways of the past and tries to keep Jimmy with her by tempting him with candy if he will say that he loves his grandmother more than his mother. Elsa's jealousy of her mother, therefore, may be well founded. Her jealousy of the white nurse who cares for Jimmy upon his return from the North, however, is simply that of an overly devoted mother. This latter situation also reminds one of Rose-Anna's jealousy of Daniel's anglophone nurse, Jenny. See Roy, "La Rivière sans repos," pp. 185-187, 197-198, 253-255; Roy, *Bonheur d'occasion*, pp. 199-202.

[41] Roy, "La Rivière sans repos," p. 272. See also pp. 255-266, 270-271; Brochu, "Gabrielle Roy."

[42] Roy, "La Rivière sans repos," p. 282. See also pp. 277-291. Jimmy is crying precisely because of his mother's story about the American soldier. One does not know if he believes this tale.

[43] Roy, "La Rivière sans repos," pp. 299, 301. See also pp. 292-301. Elsa, in fact, begins to look more and more like Winnie, also addicted to cigarettes.

[44] Roy, "La Rivière sans repos," pp. 310, 313. See also pp. 304-305; 311-315; Ricard, pp. 134-137; Marc Gagné, "*La Rivière sans repos* de Gabrielle Roy: Etude mythocritique incluant 'Voyage en Ungava' (extraits) par Gabrielle Roy (suite)," *Revue de l'Université d'Ottawa*, 46, No. 2 (avril-juin 1976), 181-189; Pascal, pp. 155-156.

[45] Roy, "La Rivière sans repos," p. 191. See also pp. 148-152, 156-158, 187-193, 221-223, 230-231; Pascal, p. 150.

[46] Gagné, *Visages de Gabrielle Roy*, p. 34; Roy, "Pitié pour les institutrices," pp. 7, 45-46. In this same article, Roy discusses the equally difficult and important role of the rural nurse and midwife. It must also be remembered that before becoming a journalist, Roy herself practiced this profession of a schoolteacher, as did her sisters, Anna, Marie-Anna, and Bédette. This career was that desired by her mother, Mélina Roy, for all of her children, and in particular, for her daughters. See Bessette, "Interview avec Gabrielle Roy," in *Une Littérature en ébullition*, p. 305; Marie-Anna A. Roy, *Le Miroir du passé*, Collection Littérature d'Amérique (Montréal: Editions Québec/Amérique, 1979), pp. 32, 55, 67, 118, 163. Gabrielle Pascal sees the Royan schoolteacher as a mythical figure in this fiction. See Pascal, pp. 143-144, 158-160.

[47] Gabrielle Roy, *La Petite Poule d'eau* (1950; rpt. Montréal: Librairie Beauchemin Limitée, 1970), pp. 42, 47, 49-54, 58, 63, 68. See also Jean-Joseph Bureau, "Le Complexe de la maternité chez Luzina dans *La Petite Poule d'eau* de Gabrielle Roy," Thesis Université de Montréal 1961, pp. 55-58.

[48] Roy, *La Petite Poule d'eau*, pp. 151, 78, 83, 89. See also pp. 70-75,

85-88; Brochu, "Gabrielle Roy"; Bureau, pp. 58-60; Maillet, pp. 50-54; Jacques Allard, "Le Chemin qui mène à *La Petite Poule d'eau*," *Cahiers de Sainte-Marie*, No. 1 (mai 1966), pp. 62-65. Luzina actually tries to paint a negative image of her children so that Mlle Côté will not become too attached to them. The teacher defends her pupils, however, and they are automaticlly drawn to her. She has become a symbolic mother, independent and only temporarily tied to children. See Pascal, p. 144.

[49] Roy, *La Petite Poule d'eau*, pp. 91, 154. See also pp. 92-101, 107-108; Bureau, p. 60; Maillet, pp. 55-60. Maillet's interpretation of Miss O'Rorke is partially valid but exaggerated. She sees this teacher as an egotist and a misanthrope, filled with self-pity. In addition, her life is a symbol of refusal, since she views the world and herself as enemies. She is a pitiful and solitary old woman, devoid of a sense of humor, and living without love, children, and ideals. Maillet does believe, however, that the psychological truth in this character saves her from becoming a caricature.

[50] Roy, *La Petite Poule d'eau*, pp. 140, 146. See also pp. 111-125, 133-137, 139, 141-142. This last statement concerning the mission to educate the "infortunés" and the "ignorants," however, does suggest the disturbing tone of a missionary zeal.

[51] Gabrielle Roy, "Gagner ma vie. . . ," *Rue Deschambault* (1955; rpt. Montréal: Librairie Beauchemin Limitée, 1974), pp. 283, 288. See also pp. 281-282, 284-285, 287, 289.

[52] Roy, *Ces Enfants de ma vie*, pp. 139, 45. See also pp. 7-8, 14-16, 28-29, 43, 44, 63-72, 79-81, 97-98, 131-132, 134; Gabrielle Roy, *Cet Eté qui chantait* (Québec-Montréal: Les Editions Françaises, 1972), pp. 179-189. Roy herself experienced periods of discouragement as a teacher. Personal interview with Gabrielle Roy, 29 June 1980.

[53] Roy, *Ces Enfants de ma vie*, pp. 140, 35. See also pp. 9-10, 12-16, 19-33, 37, 94, 95, 99, 101, 102, 105-106, 125, 144, 147-148, 151, 206-209.

[54] Roy, "De la truite dans l'eau glacée," *Ces Enfants de ma vie*, pp. 174-175. See also pp. 135-136, 150-151, 157-158, 163, 166-167, 169-173. M. Eymard's sarcasm and bitterness stem, in part, from the fact that his wife and Médéric's mother, half Indian, left them soon after her son's birth and returned to her people.

[55] Roy, "De la truite dans l'eau glacée," *Ces Enfants de ma vie*, p. 181. See also pp. 177-186; Paula Gilbert Lewis, "The Fragility of Childhood: Gabrielle Roy's *Ces Enfants de ma vie*," *The American Review of Canadian Studies*, 9, No. 2 (Autumn 1979), 151.

[56] Roy, "De la truite dans l'eau glacée," *Ces Enfants de ma vie*, pp. 210, 212. See also pp. 188-192, 197-198, 200-202, 209, 211; Lewis, "The Fragility of Childhood," pp. 151-152; Brochu, "Gabrielle Roy"; Gabrielle Poulin, "Une Merveilleuse Histoire d'amour: *Ces Enfants de ma vie* de

Gabrielle Roy," *Les Lettres Québécoises,* No. 8 (novembre 1977), p. 6.

[57] Roy, *La Petite Poule d'eau,* pp. 31, 115, 240. See also pp. 22, 26-27, 32-34, 70, 93-97, 108, 119-120, 132; Ricard, pp. 70-74; Genuist, pp. 40-43; Grosskurth, *Gabrielle Roy,* pp. 23-26; Sainte-Marie-Eleuthère, Soeur, pp. 181-186; Bureau, pp. 44-82, 93-109. Luzina was another preferred character of Roy. Personal interview with Gabrielle Roy, 29 June 1980.

[58] Roy, *La Petite Poule d'eau,* pp. 138-139, 151. See also pp. 162, 235, 247-250, 252, 260.

[59] Roy, *La Petite Poule d'eau,* pp. 240-241. See also pp. 36, 105, 111, 155, 248-249; Bureau, pp. 83-92. The Capucin de Toutes-Aides agrees with Luzina's complaints and, therefore, counsels her husband: "Selon la coutume des Canadiens français, le capucin désignait les femmes par ce terme qu'il trouvait poli. . . . Les créatures n'étaient point faites pour satisfaire les passions sans frein des hommes, ni reproduire la face humaine sans arrêt, sans repos. Le bon époux prenait en considération la santé de sa femme, les difficultés de la vie." The priest also recounts the story of a nineteen-year-old Finnish woman who gave birth in his presence. Deeply affected by this experience, he expresses his feeling that this woman was not created in order to endure such suffering. See Roy, *La Petite Poule d'eau,* pp. 243-244.

[60] Roy, *La Petite Poule d'eau,* pp. 14-15, 21, 23, 43; Bureau, pp. 1-43.

[61] Roy, *La Petite Poule d'eau,* pp. 146-147, 162. See also pp. 142-143, 149, 151-152, 154-155, 160-161, 163; Saint-Pierre, pp. 43-47; Genuist, pp. 40-43; Bureau, pp. 44-55. Pascal describes Luzina's life, in fact, as that of literary sublimation. See Pascal, pp. 157-158.

[62] Seen as an ideal, Luzina reminds one of Mme Le Gardeur of *Alexandre Chenevert,* also the symbol of the hospitable, happy, talkative, and yet isolated maternal figure. See Roy, *Alexandre Chenevert,* pp. 238-245. See also Donald Cameron, "Gabrielle Roy: A Bird in the Prison Window," in *Conversations with Canadian Novelists* (Toronto: Macmillan of Canada, 1973), pp. 131-132, for Roy's comment about *La Petite Poule d'eau* as life as it could have been. Interestingly, Roy, in her later years, stated that she was not so sure that *La Petite Poule d'eau* was a mere dream. Personal interview with Gabrielle Roy, 29 June 1980.

[63] Roy, *Rue Deschambault,* pp. 9. 15-17, 20-23, 29-33, 71, 172, 205. Many of Maman's characteristics are evident as of the initial story of the collection, "Les Deux Nègres," when the woman reacts both to her having a black man as a boarder in her home and to the affect of this man's presence on her family and on neighbors. Many of Maman's comments do suggest an unconscious tone of liberalism, streaked with racism.

[64] Roy, *Rue Deschambault,* pp. 72, 176. See also pp. 11, 13, 32, 40,

42, 44-45, 49, 57-60, 62-65, 96, 130-131, 134, 171, 174, 177. Only at one point does Christine refer to her mother's attitude of resignation toward a woman's role in life: "(Quelquefois j'avais entendu ma mère, parlant de quelque pauvre femme déjà chargée d'enfants, malade, et qui venait d'en mettre un autre au monde, observer en soupirant: 'C'est dur, mais c'est le devoir. Que voulez-vous! il faut bien qu'elle fasse son devoir!')" See Roy, *Rue Deschambault*, p. 39. It is, in addition, ironic and sad that Alicia, before becoming insane, also represented a mother figure to Christine: ". . . Alicia m'a prise dans ses bras; elle m'a bercée sous l'un des chênes qui bruissaient un peu au vent, et j'eus l'impression que le chêne, le ciel bleu, une inépuisable tendresse me berçaient." See Roy, *Rue Deschambault*, p. 169. It is interesting that Roy uses all of these maternal symbols in reference to an older sister-mother figure, rather than to Maman herself.

[65] Roy, "Le Jour et la nuit," *Rue Deschambault*, pp. 266-269.

[66] Roy, *Rue Deschambault*, pp. 121, 216. See also pp. 60-65, 127, 129, 213-217; Brochu, "Gabrielle Roy"; Maillet, pp. 67-76; Lewis, "The Feminine World of Gabrielle Roy," pp. 133-136. Maman is trying to convince Georgianna not to marry a particular young man, but the daughter follows her own instincts. Maman's words about true love are inspired by Mme Sariano, her Italian neighbor so deeply loved by her husband. Maman envies this woman, the symbol not only of that rare beloved female, but also of Italy, for Maman, the land of love. Such love, in Maman's opinion, is inaccessible in other countries. Ironically, however, being loved is not sufficient for Mme Sariano, for she remains unhappy, nostalgic for her homeland. See Roy, "L'Italienne," *Rue Deschambault*, pp. 215-221.

[67] Roy, *Rue Deschambault*, pp. 229, 239. See also pp. 227, 228, 237-238, 240; Lewis, "The Feminine World of Gabrielle Roy," pp. 136-137.

[68] Roy, *Rue Deschambault*, pp. 245-247, 135. See also Maillet, pp. 67-76.

[69] Roy, "Les Déserteuses," *Rue Deschambault*, pp. 99, 106. See also pp. 107-108, 113; Paradis, pp. 60-62. A similar resentment toward one's husband can be seen in Tante Thérésina, Maman's sister-in-law and wife of her brother, Marjorique. Constantly sick and complaining, but directing her household while sitting a chair, this woman is, in effect, the victim of her husband's desires to move continuously throughout their married life. Her travels finally cease in her desired moved to California, where she dies. See Roy, "Ma Tante Thérésina Veilleux," *Rue Deschambault*, pp. 181-202.

[70] Roy, "Les Déserteuses," *Rue Deschambault*, pp. 100-103, 109-111, 117-119, 122-125, 130-131, 134. Pascal sees the preparations for Maman's trip as an initiation before the adventure-quest. See Pascal, pp. 145-146.

[71] Roy, "Les Déserteuses," *Rue Deschambault*, p. 118. See also pp. 101-103, 122-124; Pascal, pp. 145-146. This traditional importance of having a husband can also be seen in the preoccupations of Mme Nault, Maman's cousin by marriage, to have her daughters marry well. See pp. 118-119.

[72] Roy, "Les Déserteuses," *Rue Deschambault*, pp. 136-138; Parizeau, p. 123. See also Pascal, pp. 147-148.

[73] Gabrielle Roy, *La Route d'Altamont*, Collection L'Arbre, No. 10 (Montréal: Editions HMH, 1966), pp. 28-29; See also pp. 14, 30-31, 54-55; Gagné *Visages de Gabrielle Roy*, p. 85; Bessette, *Trois Romanciers québécois*, pp. 185-187; Brochu, "Gabrielle Roy." The characterization of Mémère as an old woman will be treated in Chapter IV. The mountain is a typical maternal symbol in Roy's fiction.

[74] Roy, *La Route d'Altamont*, pp. 28-31, 216-221.

[75] Roy, *La Route d'Altamont*, p. 52. See also pp. 51, 53; Lewis, "The Feminine World of Gabrielle Roy," p. 137. The links among these generations, in reference to the role of memory, will be analyzed in Chapter VII.

[76] Roy, *La Route d'Altamont*, p. 229. See also pp. 89, 157, 159-160, 162-164, 185-186, 205-206, 211, 223, 228; Gagné, *Visages de Gabrielle Roy*, p. 166; Ricard, pp. 120-123. An analysis of Eveline as an elderly woman, especially in the last short story of this collection, will be found in Chapter IV.

[77] Roy, *La Route d'Altamont*, pp. 212, 148, 235-236.

[78] Roy, *La Route d'Altamont*, p. 236. See also pp. 94-95, 98-99, 212.

[79] Roy, *La Route d'Altamont*, pp. 337-343; Lewis, "The Feminine World of Gabrielle Roy," pp. 138-139.

[80] Roy, *La Route d'Altamont*, pp. 254-255, 248-249; Lewis, "The Feminine World of Gabrielle Roy," p. 139. See also Roy, *La Route d'Altamont*, pp. 199, 252-253; Paula Gilbert Lewis, "Trois Générations de femmes: Le Reflet mère/fille dans quelques nouvelles de Gabrielle Roy," L'Héritage français en Amérique Section, American Association of Teachers of French, Lille, France, 27 June 1983.

[81] One is referring here specifically to five female characters created after *La Route d'Altamont* and leading toward Martha of "Un Jardin au bout du monde." As a typical Eskimo woman, Deborah of "Les Satellites" needs to be close to the harsh nature of her northern homeland and feels suffocated within the enclosed home. She also manifests a traditional attitude of acceptance, a resignation to her destiny both as a woman and as an individual about to die. She cannot, in addition, understand White culture where, to her chagrin, it is often the female who gives orders. See Roy, "Nouvelles esquimaudes," *La Rivière sans repos*, pp. 23-25, 55-

57. The intimate relationship between women and nature can also be clearly seen in the characters of Berthe and the narrator of *Cet Eté qui chantait*. Both women are extremely sensitive to and understanding of all of nature, especially its animals. See Roy, *Cet Eté qui chantait*, pp. 16-20, 31-32, 49-51, 60-61, 106-107. Berthe's sensitivity toward animals is also treated in Gabrielle Roy, *Courte-Queue* (Montréal: Editions Internationales Alain Stanké Ltée, 1979). Martine, also of *Cet Eté qui chantait* and the heroine of "Le Jour où Martine descendit au fleuve," reminds one of both Mémère and Eveline, since she is described as a bending reed who has given birth to children, as big and as solidly planted as trees. Martine is also proud of her maternal accomplishments: " 'J'en ai eu quatorze,' nous dit Martine, 'quatorze enfants. Aujourd'hui, avec deux ou trois à é- lever, les femmes se plaignent: "C'est trop cher; c'est trop de besogne. . . ." Moi, j'en ai élevé quatorze,' reprit-elle avec fierté." See Roy, *Cet Eté qui chantait*, p. 153.

[82] Gabrielle Roy, "Un Jardin au bout du monde," *Un Jardin au bout du monde* (Montréal: Librairie Beauchemin Limitée, 1975), pp. 179, 168. See also pp. 157-159, 161-163, 165-173, 175-181, 186, 188, 192, 201-206, 214-217; Pascal, p. 149. It should be noted that the only negative remarks voiced about Martha are those of her husband. He describes her as a jealous and easily angered woman who silenced by him during her life, should be equally silenced in her death. See Roy, "Un Jardin au bout du monde," pp. 197-200; Personal interview with Gabrielle Roy, 29 June 1980. Martha's old age and relationship with her flowers will be treated in Chapters IV and V, respectively. Roy has indicated that the character of Martha is based both upon the image of a real woman, seen by the author during a trip to the town of Völkyn and upon Roy's neighbor and friend, Berthe, the character of *Cet Eté qui chantait* and *Courte-Queue*. Personal interview with Gabrielle Roy, 29 June 1980.

[83] Roy, *Ces Enfants de ma vie*, p. 119. See also pp. 118, 126-127; Pascal, pp. 151-152.

[84] Parizeau, p. 137; Genuist, p. 53; Bessette, *Une Littérature en ébullition*, pp. 225-227, 243, 263; Brochu, "Gabrielle Roy"; Maillet, p. 100.

[85] Gabrielle Roy, "Une Histoire d'amour," *La Revue Moderne*, 21, No. 11 (mars 1940), 8, 9, 36-38; Gabrielle Roy, "La Dernière Pêche," *La Revue Moderne*, 22, No. 7 (novembre 1940), 8, 9, 38; Roy, "Le Joli Miracle," pp. 8, 29-30; Gabrielle Roy, "La Sonate à l'aurore," *La Revue Moderne*, 22, No. 11 (mars 1941), 9, 10, 35-37; Roy, "A Okko," pp. 8, 9, 41, 42; Gabrielle Roy, "La Lune des moissons," *La Revue Moderne*, 29, No. 5 (septembre 1947), 12, 13, 76-80. Nick is the male character of this last short story. It should also be mentioned that Roy stresses male camaraderie, difficult physical work, and the importance

of having sons to whom a father can bequeath the family trade of fishing in "La Dernière Pêche," as well as in one journalistic piece. See Gabrielle Roy, "Une Voile dans la nuit," *Le Bulletin des Agriculteurs,* 40, No. 5 (mai 1944), 9, 49, 53. This essay also appears as "Les Pêcheurs de Gaspésie" in Roy, *Fragiles Lumières de la terre,* pp. 87-100.

[86] Gabrielle Roy, "La Justice en Danaca et ailleurs," in *Les Oeuvres libres* (Paris: Librairie Arthène Fayard, NS, No. 23, 1948), pp. 165, 171; Roy, "Bonne à marier," pp. 13, 40-42. See also Roy, "Cendrillon '40,'" p. 9; Roy, "Le Roi de coeur," pp. 6, 7, 33-39; Roy, "Six Pilules par jour," pp. 17, 18, 32-34; Roy, "Embobeliné," pp. 7, 8, 28; Gabrielle Roy, "Sécurité," *La Revue Moderne,* 29, No. 11 (mars 1948), pp. 12, 13, 66, 68. The four women of "Le Roi de coeur" are initially seen as being grateful to Ted for having dominated them and having put a sense of order into their extremely disordered lives. Eventually, as has been seen, however, it is Ted who succumbs to the confusion of these women and, in this sense, becomes dominated by their female life style.

[87] Roy, "Cendrillon '40,'" p. 40; Roy, "Les Petits Pas de Caroline," pp. 47, 48. In the second story see also pp. 45, 46, 49.

[88] Roy, "La Justice en Danaca et ailleurs," pp. 168-171, 174, 178-180; Gabrielle Roy, "Feuilles mortes," *La Revue de Paris,* 56e année, No. 1 (janvier 1948), pp. 46-55. In addition to these two early short stories, Roy also sees "Sécurité" as a precursor to *Alexandre Chenevert.* Personal interview with Gabrielle Roy, 29 June 1980.

[89] Roy, "La Source au désert" (octobre 1946), pp. 10, 33-36, 38, 39, 43, 44; Roy, "La Source au désert" (novembre 1946), pp. 13, 46-47. The few successes of true love in these early short stories will be treated later in this chapter as part of a discussion of Royan couples.

[90] Roy, *"Bonheur d'occasion* aujourd'hui," p. 23. See also Morissette, p. 168; Saint-Pierre, pp. 20-25; Bessette, *Une Littérature en ébullition,* pp. 239-254, 270-273, 282-287; Brochu, "Thèmes et structures," pp. 218-219, 222-233, 239-240; Le Grand, pp. 51-57; Blais, pp. 29, 33-44; Brochu, "Gabrielle Roy"; Gaulin, pp. 63-69.

[91] Roy, *Bonheur d'occasion,* pp. 23-24. See also pp. 10-12, 25-27, 30-31, 34-36, 40-42, 94-96.

[92] Roy, *Bonheur d'occasion,* p. 25. See also pp. 26-27, 72, 101-103, 148, 162-167, 224.

[93] Roy, *Bonheur d'occasion,* p. 183. See also pp. 179-182, 184. Saint-Pierre sees Jean as having an excess of masculinity in him but a lack of love. Brochu identifies him with violent virility and sex. Bessette relates him to a phallic symbol but without any body or any sensuality. Throughout this scene, in Bessette's interpretation, Jean is searching for a maternal figure because of his past, devoid of a real mother. His anti-domestic

nature, therefore, would be seen as a defense. See Saint-Pierre, p. 168; Brochu, "Thèmes et structures," pp. 222-224, 226-228; Bessette, *Une Littérature en ébullition*, pp. 239-254, 270-273. Bessette also identifies Jean first with Roy herself, also a stranger to Saint-Henri, and then with Petite Misère, that is Christine of *Rue Deschambault*. See Bessette, *Une Littérature en ébullition*, pp. 282-287.

[94] Roy, *Bonheur d'occasion*, pp. 184-192. Florentine's brother, Eugène, is similar to Jean in his egotism and attitude of superiority. He is, in addition, haunted by the image of his mother, Rose-Anna, whom he would like to aid but seems too often to forget. Eugène, however, does not have the cruel and cynical nature of Jean. See Roy, *Bonheur d'occasion*, pp. 207-217.

[95] Roy, *Bonheur d'occasion*, pp. 49, 54-55, 94-95, 118-121; Roy, "*Bonheur d'occasion* aujourd'hui," p. 23; Blais, pp. 29, 33-44; Brochu, "Thèmes et structures," pp. 239-241.

[96] Roy, *Bonheur d'occasion*, pp. 266, 281, 285-287. Emmanuel's concerns for the world in these passages remind one of Rose-Anna's concerns for all women of the world, especially in times of war. Emmanuel has also been seen as Roy herself, as the conscience of the novel.

[97] Roy, *Bonheur d'occasion*, p. 269. See also pp. 252-261, 280-305. Emmanuel's desire to hear a voice that speaks the language of the people occurs during his wandering around Montreal, while dreaming of Florentine. The only other young men who appear in Roy's major fiction are the aforementioned Alphonse, Boisvert, and Pitou of *Bonheur d'occasion*, Armand Dubreuil of *La Petite Poule d'eau*, and Wilhelm of *Rue Deschambault*. Dubreuil has already been seen as a gifted teacher who prefers not to teach. He is more interested in hunting. See Roy, *La Petite Poule d'eau*, pp. 111-115, 117, 118, 121-124, 137-138. Wilhelm is the object of Christine's first adolescent love. See Roy, *Rue Deschambault*, pp. 225-226.

[98] Roy, *Bonheur d'occasion*, pp. 38, 40, 61, 79, 80, 83-84, 149-153, 230, 262-266, 311-312, 324. See also Saint-Pierre, pp. 32-35. The father in "Un Vagabond frappe à notre porte" is also an impractical daydreamer who is pathetic when he is forced back into bitter reality. See Roy, *Un Jardin au bout du monde*, pp. 11-58.

[99] Roy, *Bonheur d'occasion*, p. 142. See also pp. 43, 136-143, 250, 313; Roy, "*Bonheur d'occasion* aujourd'hui," p. 20; Morissette, pp. 164-167; Dorion et Emond, p. 34; Le Vasseur, pp. 30-36; Marie du Rédempteur, Soeur, pp. 65-72. Azarius has caused Rose-Anna to suffer because of both her numerous pregnancies and his persistent daydreams and impossible projects. She is, therefore, a female victim because of her husband, just as Florentine is a victim of Jean's passion and cruelty.

[100] Roy, *Bonheur d'occasion*, pp. 143, 334-335. See also pp. 142, 242, 331-335. One can see in Azarius' delight about becoming a soldier a "macho-like" attitude toward this traditionally masculine role. As for Roy's beliefs, it is doubtful that she agreed with her male character, especially considering her negative opinion of war throughout the novel and, at the end of the book, her annoyance about women at home in war time, while their spouses and sons sent money to them.

[101] Roy, *La Petite Poule d'eau*, pp. 17, 19, 21, 42-43, 50, 56, 95-96, 115-117, 139, 145, 228, 244-245. See also Bureau, pp. 1-6; Le Vasseur, pp. 14-21. Alexandre Chenevert, of Roy's third major work of fiction, is also a father who is present in the home, but although not dominated by his wife as are Azarius and Hippolyte, he does not appear to be at all involved in domestic affairs.

[102] Roy, "Un Jardin au bout du monde," pp. 160-165, 180, 188-189, 191-200, 207-210, 214. See also Dorion et Emond, p. 34. Médéric's father in *Ces Enfants de ma vie* is also portrayed as being brutish, strong, angry, and bitter, especially toward his former wife. The sexual and cynical tone of his words addressed to his son's teacher, in addition, do make him look like a pitiful fool. He does, however, have a deep affect on his son who both loves him and hates him. See Roy, "De la truite dans l'eau glacée," *Ces Enfants de ma vie*, pp. 169-175. In this same collection of short stories, the young Demetrioff's father is seen as angry, violent, and menacing toward his son. He does begin to abandon this guise, however, and attempts a basic tenderness toward and rapport with his son, when the boy makes him proud by beautifully tracing letters on the board. The sole example of an open love and tenderness between a boy and his father is presented in the characters of Vincento and his father. It is quite feasible that such a display of overt affection stems from the fact that these two male characters are Italian, prone to true and natural love, in the opinion of Maman in *Rue Deschambault*. See Roy, *Ces Enfants de ma vie*, pp. 10-11, 68-72, 77, 86-89.

[103] Roy, *Rue Deschambault*, p. 102. See also pp. 37, 44-45, 57, 105-106, 136-138, 141-144, 269, 273, 275-276; Le Vasseur, pp. 22-29. Many of the negative traits of the fictional Papa have been suggested as being those of Roy's own father, Léon. See Marie-Anna A. Roy, pp. 10-11, 17, 29-31, 53, 55, 58.

[104] Roy, *Rue Deschambault*, pp. 38, 39, 43, 81, 122-124, 144. See also Adrien Thério, "Le Portrait du père dans *Rue Deschambault* de Gabrielle Roy," *Livres et Auteurs Québécois* (1969), pp. 237-243. Roy's sister defends their father in stating that he was, in fact, very tender and sensitive, with a love of storytelling and singing. See Marie-Anna A. Roy, pp. 20, 35-36, 76-77, 200-201.

[105] Roy, *Rue Deschambault,* p. 108. See also pp. 106-107, 113, 136-138, 142-145. "Le Puits de Dunrea" in this collection deals exclusively with Papa at work. See pp. 139-161. Within those traditional roles, of course, Papa becomes the impregnator of Maman when he is at home, although one does not see this woman as a true victim, like Rose-Anna and Florentine. There are, however, female victims in *Rue Deschambault,* especially Tante Thérésina Veilleux who, although sickly, is forced to follow her husband, Marjorique, on his continual moves throughout Canada and, ultimately, to California. Like Rose-Anna, she is the victim of her husband's dreams. She is also, specifically, the victim of his travels and, therefore, can be compared both to Mémère of *La Route d'Altamont,* who followed her husband to Manitoba, and to Mme Beaulieu of "La Rivière sans repos," who moves with her husband to Fort-Chimo in the extreme North of Canada. It is Elsa of the same novel, however, who must be seen as the ultimate female victim in Roy's literary world.

[106] Roy, *Alexandre Chenevert,* pp. 18, 27-28, 49-51, 59, 61, 78, 93, 95, 102-103, 116-117, 123, 145-147, 173-174, 294, 310, 316, 335, 341-345, 366-367, 374. See also Ricard, pp. 79-82; Genuist, pp. 48-49; Gaulin, pp. 44-47.

[107] Roy, *Alexandre Chenevert,* p. 31. See also pp. 10-11, 17-18, 27-28, 142-144, 284-287, 308-309; Genuist, pp. 48-49; Grosskurth, *Gabrielle Roy,* pp. 27-37; Brochu, "Gabrielle Roy." What one has labelled a René-complex refers, of course, to Chateaubriand's pre-Romantic hero, *René,* where it is stated that "une grande âme doit contenir plus de douleur qu'une petite." See Chateaubriand, *Atala/René* (Paris: Garnier-Flammarion, 1964), p. 155. Like René's *récit* of his life, Chenevert desires at one point in his life, to tell others of his experience, in particular, of his attainment of peace and hope at Lac Vert, after a life of worry and anxiety in Montreal. But this modern man cannot express himself sufficiently and merely falls asleep. See Roy, *Alexandre Chenevert,* pp. 249-255. This aspect of communication will be treated in Chapter VIII. Gabrielle Roy has agreed with this interpretation of her character as a proud, egotistical, Romantic, unlikable, distasteful, and yet pathetic individual. Personal interview with Gabrielle Roy, 29 June 1980.

[108] Roy, *Alexandre Chenevert,* pp. 14, 22, 113-117, 120, 125-126, 129-136, 145, 149-151, 311, 344, 377.

[109] Roy, *Alexandre Chenevert,* p. 70. See also pp. 63-78, 84-85.

[110] Roy, *Alexandre Chenevert,* pp. 339-340, 347-348, 358-361. An analysis of Chenevert's illness, hospital stay, and death, as well as his relationship with his doctor, Dr. Hudon, will be found in Chapter IV.

[111] Roy, *Alexandre Chenevert,* pp. 38, 40-42, 44, 48-52, 55-58. See also Agnes Whitfield, "*Alexandre Chenevert:* Cercle vicieux et évasions

manquées," *Voix et Images du Pays,* 8, (1974), 112-114.

[112]Roy, *Alexandre Chenevert,* pp. 83-84, 87-88, 93, 96-99, 101, 107-108, 119, 121. M. Fontaine, the stereotype of the successful business man, is ironically depicted. He is an obnoxious, disdainful individual who with an attitude of superiority, sets himself up as a model for others to follow. Fontaine is, in effect, the packaged product of advertisements for success and youth. He is always in control of himself and lives according to specific formulas and slogans. He can represent the depersonalized and institutionalized English-Canadian. Fontaine is, however, somewhat understanding of Chenevert's plight, especially in light of the teller's age, and with a mixture of sympathy and disdain, he allows the pitiful man to repay his debt. He does not realize that he is causing additional anguish to his employee. See Roy, *Alexandre Chenevert,* pp. 88-102. See also Eva Kushner, "Dossier Gabrielle Roy: De la représentation à la vision du monde," *Québec Français,* No. 36 (décembre 1979), p. 38.

[113]Roy, *Alexandre Chenevert,* p. 316. See also pp. 314-315, 318, 335, 341-345, 349-350, 358-361.

[114]Roy, *Alexandre Chenevert,* pp. 9, 11-14, 16, 18-21, 23, 41-42, 62-63; Personal interview with Gabrielle Roy, 29 June 1980. Chenevert does admire the industrious nature of the Japanese, but then he recalls their attack on Pearl Harbor. He also complains about his personal acquaintances. Interestingly, the only individual whom he ultimately decides to admire is Constantin Simoneau whom he barely knew and who is now dead. Simoneau is, of course, the pathetic hero of Roy's early short story, "Feuilles mortes," and already mentioned as a precursor of Chenevert.

[115]Roy, *Alexandre Chenevert,* p. 15. See also pp. 72, 81-82.

[116]Roy, *Alexandre Chenevert,* pp. 15-16, 154-157, 165. See also Grosskurth, *Gabrielle Roy,* pp. 34-37.

[117]Roy, *Alexandre Chenevert,* p. 282. See also pp. 269-270, 273-274, 283-289, 336-339, 364-365. Chenevert's trip to Lac Vert, to the country, will be treated in Chapter V, as will be the role of the city in his life.

[118]Roy, *Alexandre Chenevert,* pp. 10, 24, 26, 33-35, 86-87, 118, 151-152, 178, 181-183, 196, 236-237, 369-370. See also Gagné, *Visages de Gabrielle Roy,* pp. 73-78. Such daydreams will be more fully discussed in Chapter VII.

[119]Roy, *Alexandre Chenevert,* pp. 15, 43, 45-47, 51, 65, 86-87, 144-145, 209-213, 218, 220, 222, 374; Whitfield, pp. 144-125; Bessette, *Trois Romanciers québécois,* pp. 204-237; Pascal, pp. 149, 153.

[120]Roy, *Alexandre Chenevert,* pp. 167-168. See also pp. 25, 26, 47, 102-103, 223, 249-255, 261, 274, 275, 292-295, 314-315, 351-356, 367-368, 372, 384; Personal interview with Gabrielle Roy, 29 June 1980;

Gagné, *Visages de Gabrielle Roy,* p. 72; Ricard, pp. 79-82; Grosskurth, *Gabrielle Roy,* pp. 27-33; Brochu, "Gabrielle Roy"; Gaulin, pp. 10, 44-47; John Hind-Smith, *Three Voices: The Lives of Margaret Laurence, Gabrielle Roy, and Frederick Philip Grove* (Toronto: Clarke Irwin, 1975), pp. 100-101; Ben Shek, "L'Espace et la description symbolique dans les romans 'montréalais' de Gabrielle Roy," *Liberté,* 13i (1974), 90-96.

[121] Roy, *Alexandre Chenevert,* pp. 18, 78, 363, 268. See also pp. 30, 149, 151, 201, 216, 247, 294, 295, 361-362; Gagné, *Visages de Gabrielle Roy,* pp. 59, 64-69; Ricard, pp. 79-82; Grosskurth, *Gabrielle Roy,* pp. 27-33; Whitfield, pp. 107-114; Kushner, p. 38; Marie du Rédempteur, Soeur, pp. 75-80; D. G. Jones, *Butterfly on Rock: A Study of Themes and Images in Canadian Literature* (Toronto: University of Toronto Press, 1971), pp. 143-144; Jack Warwick, *L'Appel du nord dans la littérature canadienne-française,* trans. Jean Simard, Collection Constants (Montréal: Editions Hurtubise HMH, 1972), pp. 206-213. Roy herself rejected the use of the word, "absurd," to characterize life. Personal interview with Gabrielle Roy, 29 June 1980. See a discussion of this matter in Chapter X. At one point in the novel, the sensation of being a stranger to himself is seen as being positive. When he discovers peace at Lac Vert and realizes that this feeling is itself strange to his worries as a human being, Chenevert also finds within himself a new stranger whom he likes. This new self, however, will be suppressed upon Chenevert's return to Montreal.

[122] Roy, *Alexandre Chenevert,* pp. 177, 173, 209. See also pp. 31, 61, 96-97, 154-157, 172, 174, 201, 210-213, 318; Gagné *Visages de Gabrielle Roy,* pp. 53-64; Ricard, pp. 82-85; Grosskurth, *Gabrielle Roy,* pp. 27-33; Hind Smith, pp. 100-101. Roy herself stated that she was still haunted by Alexandre Chenevert who reminded her never to turn her back on suffering. See Dorion et Emond, p. 34.

[123] Roy, *Alexandre Chenevert,* p. 331. See also pp. 323, 326-330, 354, 384; Brochu, "Gabrielle Roy." Chenevert's relationship with God and with the Abbé Marchand, as well as his role as a religious martyr, will be more fully treated in Chapter IX. Given the complexity of Chenevert's nature, both ordinary and superior, it is not surprising that Roy appeared to prefer him to all of her characters. She was, in fact, almost haunted or obsessed with Chenevert. She stated that only her most sensitive readers and critics loved him and, most importantly, that of all of her literary beings, Chenevert was herself. Personal interview with Gabrielle Roy, 29 June 1980.

[124] Roy, *La Montagne secrète,* pp. 15, 24, 28-29, 54-57, 61, 62, 70-72, 106, 169-171. See also Saint-Pierre, p. 53; Grosskurth, *Gabrielle Roy,* pp. 44-50; Gaulin, p. 47; Bessette, *Trois Romanciers québécois,* pp. 187-199; Brochu, "Gabrielle Roy." Bessette also identifies Pierre's hunt for a

caribou as that for a maternal figure. It must be mentioned, however, that when asked about this association between the mountain and the woman or mother, Roy denied any such interpretation. See Bessette, *Une Littérature en ébullition*, p. 307. It should be noted that the character of Pierre Cordorai is here being briefly analyzed as that of a man. A more detailed discussion of his qualities, in particular those that are more allegorical, will be found in subsequent chapters: his rapport with nature in Chapter V; his symbolic travel in Chapter VI; the role of the artist and the work of art in Chapter VIII; and religious connotations of the novel in Chapter IX.

[125] Roy, *La Montagne secrète*, pp. 78, 220. See also pp. 188-189, 215-217, 219-222; Saint-Pierre, p. 87. Despite her mention of a comparison between *La Montagne secrète* and *Le Mythe de Sisyphe* of Camus, Roy still disavowed any acceptance of a definition of the world, life, or goals as absurd. Personal interview with Gabrielle Roy, 29 June 1980.

[126] Roy, *La Montagne secrète*, pp. 15-21; Roy, *La Petite Poule d'eau*, pp. 22, 30, 37, 54-55, 143-145, 178, 227-229, 257, Roy, "Un Vagabond frappe à notre porte," *Un Jardin au bout du monde*, pp. 11-58; Roy, "La Rivière sans repos," pp. 184-185, 199, 205-221, 233-241, 246-249.

[127] Roy, "Où iras-tus Sam Lee Wong?," *Un Jardin au bout du monde*, p. 99. See also pp. 61-72, 77-81, 85-87, 90-95, 100-102, 105-123, 125-130. When a preference for Sam Lee Wong as a character was mentioned to Gabrielle Roy, she became emotional and stated: "Nobody ever speaks to me of Sam Lee Wong!" She described him as a dear, old man. Personal interview with Gabrielle Roy, 29 June 1980. There is one final group of male characters in Gabrielle Roy's fiction: doctors and priests. The former, primarily in the personage of Dr. Hudon in *Alexandre Chenevert*, will be discussed in Chapter IV under sickness. Priests will be analyzed in Chapter IX under religion: le Capucin de Toutes Aides of *La Petite Poule d'eau*, l'Abbé Marchand of *Alexandre Chenevert*, le Père le Bonniec of *La Montagne secrète*, and Reverend Paterson of "La Rivière sans repos."

[128] Roy, *Cet Eté qui chantait*, p. 121; Personal interview with Gabrielle Roy, 29 June 1980.

[129] Roy, "La Source au désert" (octobre 1946), pp. 31, 45, 47.

[130] Roy, *Bonheur d'occasion*, pp. 19, 21, 57, 79, 114, 117-121, 125, 136-139, 149-150, 178, 223, 261, 269, 302, 304, 312, 313. See also Brochu, "Thèmes et structures," p. 233; Gaulin, pp. 111-121. Roy maintained that Rose-Anna and Azarius still loved one another. Personal interview with Gabrielle Roy, 29 June 1980.

[131] Roy, *Alexandre Chenevert*, pp. 128, 137, 363. See also pp. 14, 22, 23, 113-117, 120, 129-132, 135, 136, 145-146, 187, 260, 275-276, 305, 311, 325, 344, 361-362. Roy, *La Petite Poule d'eau*, pp. 17-18, 43, 270.

See also Pascal, pp. 152-153.

[132] Roy, "Un Jardin au bout du monde," p. 161. See also pp. 160-164, 208-210, 212-213. Roy, *Rue Deschambault*, pp. 106-108, 122-124, 129, 141, 161, 267, 273. Roy believed, however, that Christine's parents loved one another. Personal interview with Gabrielle Roy, 29 June 1980. In this second collection of short stories, Oncle Majorique and Tante Thérésina are also opposites. Although true love does exist between M. Sariano and his wife, the husband dies suddenly and leaves his wife saddened and alone. There are no successful couples in *La Route d'Altamont* or in *La Rivière sans repos*, either, especially since Elsa is devoid even of the chance of being part of a pair. Sadly, the only "couple" that approaches pure love and communication is that of the schoolteacher and Médéric in *Ces Enfants de ma vie*, but, of course, society will not permit such a love to flourish.

[133] Roy, *Bonheur d'occasion*, p. 223; Parizeau, p. 123. See also Brochu, "Thèmes et structures," p. 228. Roy maintained that her attitude toward sex as the cause of a separation stemmed from a Catholic training that emphasized a separation between the body and the soul. Personal interview with Gabrielle Roy, 29 June 1980.

[134] Roy, *Bonheur d'occasion*, pp. 74-76, 118-119, 129, 164-166, 178, 182-184, 186-192, 218, 239, 302, 309; Roy, "La Source au désert" (octobre 1946), pp. 32-33. See also Bessette, *Une Littérature en ébullition*, pp. 253-254; Gaulin, p. 69.

[135] Roy, *Alexandre Chenevert*, p. 324. See also pp. 158, 325.

[136] Roy, "La Rivière sans repos," p. 241. See also pp. 117-119, 124-137, 146, 226-227, 242, 243, 271-272; Ricard, p. 135; Brochu, "Gabrielle Roy." Elsa and Ian are, in fact, associated with a shameful Adam and Eve, in Jimmy's eyes. For this boy, the promised Baffin Island is a Garden of Eden toward which the three of them are travelling across the tundra.

[137] Roy, "La Rivière sans repos," p. 164; Roy, "Un Jardin au bout du monde," pp. 158-159.

CHAPTER IV

The Resignation of Old Age, Sickness, and Death

The atmosphere of solitude that surrounds Gabrielle Roy's adult characters does not dissipate as they enter old age, but, rather, intensifies. Throughout her works, the author consistently paints old age as pitifully sad and yet proud. Her most frequently used symbol for this period of time is that of a solitary tree, "un pauvre vieux chêne isolé des autres, seul sur une petite côte." Mémère, M. Saint-Hilaire, and Eveline are all described as such, while Inès, the oldest Eskimo in old Fort-Chimo, is seen as even more aged than the trees. Old age is also compared to the wind, plaintively crying to Mémère, Thaddeus, and Martha. Maintaining her symbols of nature, Roy identifies the elderly with evening, winter, and, most effectively, *l'été des sauvages,* Indian Summer, that short period of time after the initial cold of autumn and immediately preceding the great, final cold of winter, that is, of death. Finally, in the Royan literary universe, old age is likened to a prison, entrapping, for example, Isaac in his wheel chair, as "un vieux roi . . . mais maintenant dépossédé."[1]

The elderly characters of Roy's fiction are, in fact, dispossessed, robbed of their youth and, therefore, of their former sense of usefulness. Their lives are described as being filled with boredom, solitude, regrets, nostalgia, a lack of any more desires, and a fear of total abandonment by their children. Mémère, for example, regretfully reflects upon her past:

> "C'est de l'ouvrage jamais fini, la vie. Avec tout ça, quand on n'est plus bonne à aider, qu'on est reléguée dans un coin, au repos, sans savoir que faire de ses dix doigts, sais-tu ce qui arrive? . . . Eh bien, on s'ennuie à en mourir, on regrette peut-être le 'barda' [housework], peux-tu comprendre quelque chose à ça?"

Her daughter, Eveline, understands the problems of the aged Mémère only as she, herself, grows old and becomes increasingly sensitive and fearful of isolation. Elsa's mother, Winnie, however, is perhaps one of Roy's most pathetically depicted old women, a "pauvre vieille femme," hiding behind cigarette smoke, "un peu déçue, un peu égarée," seen either as "seule et chétive" or as "seule et accablée," and caught between her desires both for tradition and for change. She dies with the same expression of sadness and confusion on her face that she had in life.[2]

Roy's old male characters are equally poignant. Like Mémère and Winnie, M. Saint-Hilaire is divided among his nostalgia for past times, his realization of the inevitability of change, and his lack of understanding of the modern era. He is described as a solitary old man, abandoned by his grown children, and always dressed formally, as if awaiting a visit from someone who never arrives. When he is asleep, he appears even older than he actually is. Christine's father, however, seldom sleeps, for he remains alone at night, as a pitiful old man who reflects upon his past life as a failure, sees no future, and remains isolated within his nocturnal illusions.[3]

As a result of this state of inactivity and uselessness, these characters react differently toward their old age and increasing infirmities. Some of them develop certain idiosyncracies: they complain, are always angry, suspicious of everyone, and easily insulted. Like M. Saint-Hilaire, they fear any excesses; like Gédéon, they enter into the second childhood of senility. Other characters express shame or embarrassment about their age and ill health. Both Mémère and M. Saint-Hilaire react in this manner: the old man, in particular, hides his wrinkled hand behind his back, as he whispers his age to Christine "comme s'il avait un peu honte d'être si vieux." Finally, there is much bitterness evident in the elderly Royan characters precisely because they have reached old age. Alexandre Chenevert feels that it is unfair that the world should be so well organized for old people, with retirement, social security, and, therefore, fewer financial worries, for then death arrives. The old characters of *Ces Enfants de ma vie* bitterly cling to their hope and dream of rediscovering youth within themselves, within what is described as the atrocity of old age.[4]

Since Gabrielle Roy depicts all facets of life, however, her elderly creations would not be realistic if they were portrayed solely in a negative light. They are seen, therefore, as essential individuals in every family and in every society. With their nostalgia and respect for, as well as their knowledge of, the past, old people serve as guardians of that past and of tradition. Thaddeus retains the old Eskimo way of life, as he continues to sculpt traditional figures; this past culture will disappear with the death of such old men. As representatives of this older world, these Royan characters bring a sense of experience, wisdom, and, therefore, superiority to the younger world. They also reflect certain values from that past: the economical Mémère maintains an aura of order, cleanliness, and discipline in her household, while M. Saint-Hilaire remains formal, prudent, and patient.[5]

As individuals age, they also become increasingly desirous of stability, although such needs often betray an envy, as with Eveline, of the freedom of youth. At the same time, older people express a determination to remain independent. If Roy's old characters are seen as pitiful, the majority of them are also deeply proud persons. Mémère, for example, continues to work in her home as in her youth, refuses to be dominated by her grown children, and until her progressive infirmities finally hamper her lifestyle, will not move to Eveline's home. Mémère, like most elderly people, simply needs to prove to herself and to others that she is still a useful, capable human being. She fully realizes this goal, in fact, when she becomes the epitome of creative ability in her six-year-old granddaughter's eyes and makes a doll for Christine fashioned from old material stuffed with oats. Delighted with having found something worthwhile to do, the old woman speaks to Christine as if in defiance: " 'tu vas voir si je ne suis pas capable de faire ce que j'ai envie de faire.' " As she constructs the doll, Mémère acts as though she is inspired: "Elle continuait à travailler, ses lunettes aux yeux, heureuse je pense bien, la chère vieille femme, comme au temps où des tâches urgentes la réclamaient du matin au soir. . . ." When the doll is completed, Christine is duly impressed:

> Il m'apparaissait qu'il n'y avait pas de limites à ce que savait faire
> et accomplir cette vieille femme au visage couvert de mille rides.
> Une impression de grandeur, de solitude infinie m'envahit. Je
> lui criai dans l'oreille: "Tu es Dieu le Père. Tu es Dieu le Père.
> Toi aussi, tu sais faire tout de rien."

Despite Mémère's rejection of such a resemblance, Christine notices that "malgré tout elle n'était pas offensée de ce que je l'avais comparée à Dieu le Père."[6]

The rapport that develops between Mémère and Christine in this touching scene from *La Route d'Altamont* is typical of this entire work that, more than any other of Roy's fiction, delves into the complex relationships between old age and youth. These rapports are, at times, negative. Mémère often has little tolerance for young people, becomes impatient with them, and cannot accept their emotions and hypocrisy. She admits, however, that she simply does not understand youth. Like Eveline, she is jealous of these younger individuals; like Martha, she is ashamed before them of her old age and her old ways; and like Martine of *Cet Eté qui chantait*, she defensively treats youth with cynical scorn. Her sarcasm, therefore, stems from a reaction against the treatment of older people by the young. When Eveline finally convinces her mother to come and live with her, for example, she treats the older woman as a child and is unintentionally cruel toward her by pushing her to rest. Mémère's response is filled with bitterness and cynicism: " 'Pensez-vous . . . que j'ai envie de passer ma vie assise maintenant? . . . Ne t'imagine pas que je vais m'éterniser ici.' " Typically, Christine will echo her mother's words when the latter becomes old: "Cent fois par jour, je disais à maman: 'Reposez-vous. N'en avez-vous pas assez fait? C'est le temps de vous reposer.' Elle alors, comme si je l'eusse insultée, répondait: 'Me reposer! Il en sera bien assez vite le temps, va!' " Only in her own old age does Eveline fully understand how she must have offended Mémère with these same youthful words.[7]

Eveline and Christine do not intend to be cruel toward their elderly mothers. They certainly do not resemble some of the younger characters of Roy's early short stories in which, for example, children are extremely nasty to "La Grande Berthe" in her old age, and the young members of a family disrespectfully call their Aunt Bédette, "Tante Bête." In Roy's major fiction, youth simply has little time for old people, fears them, or merely does not understand them and their needs. When Mémère finally comes to live with her daughter's family, she even begins to lose her individuality: she is no longer herself but simply "la vieille, vieille femme" or "la vieille personne chez nous." Similarly M. Saint-Hilaire is a stereotype of old age; he is seen as the proverbial cantankerous old man, correct but stubborn in his ways, as "ce vieil enfant."   As these elderly children grow older, problems arise for the youth around them, as families begin to quarrel about whether their old parents should live alone or with their offspring. The old seem to have become a burden, embarrassed at being at the center of all of this discussion about them.[8]

In light of this pathetic situation, therefore, it becomes even more imperative for the elderly to try to prove to youth that they remain capable beings. When they succeed in this desire, as does Mémère before Christine, they are deeply flattered by the attention and respect given to them by the young, and a mutual admiration and communication can then begin between the two generations. This warm rapport and mutual need between young and old does occur in several of Roy's works, both prior and subsequent to *La Route d'Altamont.* Luzina Tousignant expresses a deep desire, for example, to keep her youngest child, Claire-Armelle, near her as "le bâton de sa vieillesse." In *Rue Deschambault,* Christine develops a tender friendship with an elderly couple. The children of "Le Fauteuil roulant" happily push Isaac in his wheel chair, while Jimmy of "La Rivière sans repos" is fascinated by Thaddeus' sculpture and thrives on the deep relationship with his great uncle, Ian. Finally, the old people of *Ces Enfants de ma vie* desperately cling to the presence of Nil, with his beautiful voice. In all of these relationships, there exists a reciprocal need for contact with the other generation.[9]

It is in *La Route d'Altamont,* however, that Roy particularly underscores this intimate rapport, seen by several critics as a sense of belonging, a dialogue of respect and tenderness between young and old, and a mutual understanding and communication.[10] The most powerful of these relationships exist first between Mémère and Christine and then between the same young girl and M. Saint-Hilaire, although some of this warmth is retained between a grown Eveline and her mother and between a mature Christine and Eveline.

It has been seen that the deep rapport between Mémère and her granddaughter begins with the creation of the *catin* and with Christine's long-standing belief "que ce ne pouvait être un homme sûrement qui eût fait le monde. Mais, peut-être, une vieille femme aux mains extrêmement habiles." When Mémère moves into Christine's house, in fact, the young girl refuses to view her grandmother as an inactive woman; she can remember

her only as a vibrant creator.   To Christine, however, Mémère
has always been old, for the youth cannot understand the confusion of ages that she witnesses before her: both Mémère
and Eveline appear elderly to her, and yet Christine's mother
remains a child before her own mother whom she treats as her
offspring.   It is only when Mémère and Christine silently communicate while looking at an album of old family photographs
that the young girl begins to comprehend the passage of time
and of successive generations:

> Et voici qu'en tournant les pages, je la [Mémère] trouvai, elle,
> jeune encore, assise auprès de son mari et parmi ses enfants. . . .
> Je levai les yeux de l'album et comparai avec l'original.   Il n'y
> avait pas beaucoup de ressemblance. . . .
>   "Vous étiez belle dans ce temps-là."
>   Est-ce que ses yeux n'ont pas brillé un peu?

True and mutual understanding between Mémère and Christine
has occurred.   It is, in addition, noteworthy that with the entire
scene tenderly observed by Eveline, this "jeu de la rencontre,"
this link among three generations of females has been effected,
as with the cloth doll, because of a child's game, "comme nous
jouons tous peut-être, les uns avec les autres, à travers la vie,
à tâcher de nous rencontrer."[11]
     When Mémère dies, Christine is extremely unhappy. As if
to console herself, to fill her deep need for a relationship with
an elderly person, she meets and becomes good friends with
the eighty-four-old M. Saint-Hilaire, her "bon vieillard."   Initiated, once again, by a common love for games, here imaginary
travel, this friendship is beneficial to both individuals, for is it
not "naturel aux petites mains à peine formées, aux vieilles mains
amenuisées, de se joindre?"   With Christine's desire to be everything in the world for the old man, and with his longing for the
presence of youth near him, the two best friends, who are, in
effect, more than a grandfather and a granddaughter to each
other, make a one-day trip to Lake Winnipeg.   It is during this
momentous voyage that Christine, at eight years of age, suddenly passes from childhood into the initial stages of maturity, as
she begins to understand the concept of old age and death.
Having questioned M. Saint-Hilaire throughout the day, Christine
finds still another question to ask: " 'Ça fait mal d'être vieux?' "
The old man quickly responds: " 'On n'est pas tellement plus

mal vieux que jeune, tu sais. . . . Et toi,' me dit-il, 'en vieillissant
tu en sauras encore plus.' Mais je ne voulais pas vieillir, je voulais
tout savoir sans vieillir, mais surtout, j'imagine, je ne voulais
pas voir vieillir autour de moi." Christine has suddenly understood that old age inevitably leads to death, and she begins
to hate life that causes one to grow old and to die, in spite of
oneself.   She is deeply upset by the realization that the old
man and she are separated by seventy-six years, and she becomes
discouraged "par le sentiment de l'inégalité et de l'injustice en
cette vie.   Pourquoi aussi n'arrivait-on pas tous ensemble au
même âge?"   When M. Saint-Hilaire explains to her that life
would thus be boring, Christine regretfully accepts his words
as those of a wise and experienced man. She has learned much
from him, while he, in turn, has sensed a temporary feeling of
recommencement in the young girl's presence.[1][2]
   It is interesting that despite the emphasis on elderly characters throughout *La Route d'Altamont,* none of them are described as being sick, the normal infirmities of old age notwith-
standing. Gabrielle Roy, however, has peopled her other works
of fiction with the realistic presence of both young and old
characters who are ill. With such literary creations, she remains
within the tradition of modern *Québécois* fiction that has been
identified as being rampant with pathological images. Like that
other fiction, the Royan world of sickness may be indicative of
the moral, spiritual, social, economic, and political condition of
Quebec society, but it is more likely to be a recounting of what
the author observed around her in the world.[1][3]
   Rereading this major fiction with a sensitivity to its pathological images, one counts at least twenty-one characters who
are ill, but only four who enter the hospital and one who enters
an insane asylum. In addition, Roy has created only two nurses
and only one doctor, along with the vague presence of a surgeon
and a gynecologist. It is, of course, her sickest characters who
do seek medical advice and eventually require hospitalization.
The attitude of Royan characters toward these hospitals is extremely realistic: they fear and mistrust them and yet, at times,
find solace among so many other patients. Alexandre Chenevert's attitude toward hospitals is the most complex, essentially
because he spends so much time there. He worries about his
medical bills and, therefore, for a long time resists seeing a doctor
and entering the hospital. When he does finally submit, he
discovers a confusing world with too many forms to be com-

pleted and too many people taking care of him, talking about him, and constantly murmuring and whispering around him. With anguish and humiliation, Chenevert realizes that nothing remains private when one becomes a hospital patient. But despite such negative feelings, the bank teller, like his wife, does discover a rapport with the other patients and experiences at least a temporary sense of rest, prior to his final escape in death.[14]

In these hospitals, two of Roy's young male characters, Daniel and Jimmy, make the acquaintance of nurses. Afflicted with leukemia that the doctor links to vitamin deficiencies and malnutrition, Daniel Lacasse enters an English-speaking hospital where, in his confusion and fears, he turns toward Jenny, a patient, understanding, anglophone nurse who, the opposite of Rose-Anna, instills jealousy in Daniel's mother. The boy begins to believe that he has always known Jenny, that it is she who has given him all of his new toys. When the nurse is transferred to a different hospital ward, Daniel cries out for her and feels totally abandoned, especially since he is in the last stages of his illness: "Sa petite figure diaphane et tirée sur les os prenait une curieuse expression de vieillesse. Il était d'une maigreur effrayante. . . . Malgré les transfusions de sang et les ingestions de viande crue . . . le mal avait fait de rapides progrès." Roy does not spare her readers any details when she describes the illness of pitiful children. If Daniel's illness is related to the poverty of Saint-Henri, then Jimmy Kumachuk's sickness occurs immediately after the incestuous act of love between his mother and great uncle and during the trio's attempt to reach paradise on Baffin Island. The boy develops a high fever and experiences hallucinations. He enters the hospital and, to Elsa's chagrin, befriends a white nurse. Unlike Daniel, however, Jimmy survives his illness and returns to his mother.[15]

Christine's sister, Alicia, is not as fortunate, for the sickness that emprisons her, insanity, will create suffering both for her and for her family and will ultimately take the young girl's life. Alicia lives, in effect, in another world and has become a stranger even to herself. After having caused great embarrassment and even shame to her family, Alicia has to be sent to an asylum. Once interned, she remembers nothing of her past life, except when, as if in a miracle, she momentarily recognizes Christine and even pronounces the young girl's name. But from this joy of "un moment de lucidité," Alicia quickly returns to the dispair of her separate world:

> Elle a commencé de s'éloigner; et, tout à coup, une sombre rivière invisible s'est creusée entre nous. Alicia, sur l'autre rive, prenait de la distance . . . mystérieusement . . . elle se retirait. J'ai eu le goût de l'appeler, tant elle était loin déjà. Et elle, comme quelqu'un qui va disparaître, elle a levé la main, elle l'a agitée vers nous.

Mental illness is, perhaps, the most tragic of all.[16]

Given all of the illness present in these works, it is surprising that Roy created only one doctor, Dr. Hudon of *Alexandre Chenevert*. When the sickly bank teller finally decides to go to the district of Montreal that is populated predominantly by doctors, his initial impression is that Dr. Hudon's office resembles a travel agency, prefiguring Hudon's prescribed cure of a vacation at Lac Vert. Continuing in this pathetic irony, Chenevert worries about the cost of his visit and of any necessary medical treatment, as he relates his medical history and symptoms to a man who, typical of all doctors, does not like to discuss financial matters with his patients. But Hudon is a compassionate man who, ambitious and always tired, is sincerely devoted to and concerned about the suffering of humanity. His attitude toward Chenevert is, however, representative of most doctors: presenting himself as a figure of authority, he questions his patient with the air of a social worker, psychiatrist, priest, or even God. Chenevert feels that he is being severely reproached, as if he were on trial. But despite their authoritarian pose, doctors are not infallible. Although Hudon cannot initially discover anything wrong with the teller, Chenevert ultimately enters the hospital with prostate cancer. The doctor continues his condescending tone and remains optimistic in his consultations with his patient, while fully realizing that Chenevert will soon die. Despite his role as a surrogate god-like figure, Hudon knows that he has lost: Chenevert will submit to the inevitability of death and, therefore, will grant victory to the priest and failure to the medical profession.[17]

It is all facets of the medical profession that have fascinated Chenevert throughout his life. Faithful to his nature of a masochistic worrier, the middle-aged man is obsessed with illnesses and medicines. No sickness fails to interest him, since he is convinced that he will eventually die in a hospital room from stomach cancer. A true hypochondriac, Chenevert even goes so far as to desire to be sick, for sick people are the objects of great sympathy and understanding from others:

> Et il en fut, ce soir, à se demander avec sérieux s'il ne valait pas mieux en ce monde être malade plutôt que malheureux. . . . En perspective, assez éloignée de lui, la maladie l'attira presque autant que les îles: en avoir fini avec les chiffres, n'être plus coupable surtout. Lui-même ne se pardonnerait-il pas bien plus volontiers d'être malade qui triste et insupportable? . . . Ah! s'il eût pu seulement être malade!

But then he remembers the expenses involved in being ill and decides that the respectful silence, care, and understanding that he would receive should last only for a short time: "Il rêvait du bonheur, dès qu'il serait sur le point de quitter la terre, d'être soigné, compris, regretté peut-être. . . ." Alexandre Chenevert will see the fulfillment of his dreams.[18]

But first it is Eugénie who becomes ill, and Chenevert feels guilty: he had desired to be sick, had, therefore, offended *le malheur,* and now his wife is suffering for his crimes. Eugénie, however, recovers, and her husband finally goes to the doctor. The recounting of his medical history reveals that Chenevert comes from a sickly family, but Dr. Hudon still insists upon his diagnosis that the teller's illness is simply that of nerves, thought, martyrdom, and guilt. He prescribes "la permission d'être heureux . . . comme un médicament." Chenevert follows the doctor's advice and vacations at Lac Vert. He believes that he is cured, but after his return, he looks and actually becomes even sicker. Suffering without any sense of nobility, Chenevert notices that people, like his cab driver, are nicer toward him than in the past, and he interprets this solicitude as a pessimistic sign.[19]

He does, in fact, enter the hospital, not with stomach cancer but prostate cancer. He soon experiences the traumas of pain and humiliation, intensified by the necessity of wearing a colostomy bag after his operation and symbolized by his constant horizontal position. He first decides that it is cheaper to die than to remain alive with medicine, but then he realizes that he can continue to earn money if he lives; Chenevert choses life. His body, however, wants to die, but at the mercy of drugs and machines and under the hallucinatory influence of morphine and then of heroin, it is not allowed to submit. From a pathetic bank teller, Chenevert has become a grotesque looking patient, at the point of death: "La bouche restait entr'ouverte, comme prête à jeter un cri, les yeux d'Alexandre fixes, attentifs, tout entier absorbés par la connaissance de la douleur." His privileged, mental suffering has now become intensely real.[20]

His only solace is to be found in his newly discovered friendship with others who are also suffering. He finally begins to understand and to appreciate other people who, both sick and well, have taken a new interest in him because he is dying: "Jusqu'au bout, les uns et les autres, ils défendirent cette pauvre vie comme si elle avait été précieuse, unique, et en quelque sorte irremplaçable." But this change both in Chenevert's nature and in the perception of him by others occurs too late. The insignificant bank teller, who is sacrificed by and for humanity, submits to his final escape from suffering and dies. Because of his painful illness, however, he rises above his human condition and achieves a modest form of immortality in the memory of those who live after him.[21]

It is logical that with the presence of old age and illness throughout Gabrielle Roy's fiction, there exists the constant threat of death. It is not, however, only middle-aged and elderly characters who must deal with the concept of death in the Royan universe, for when Yolande Chartrand of *Cet Eté qui chantait* dies, for example, her young schoolmates must face the reality of this tragic situation. They calmly accept the event, with a combination of sadness, shock, and resignation, but find a deep need to discuss Yolande as she was in life, as if a dialogue about life can console a lack of understanding about death. This same inability to comprehend the inevitability of death, added to a macabre fascination for and fear of this finality, can also be seen in Christine. The eight-year-old child initially views death as a mere disappearance or absence of someone. When she sees first her mother and then M. Saint-Hilaire asleep, however, she begins to fear what she does not understand:

> Alors une de ses mains [of M. Saint-Hilaire] qui reposaient sur la nappe glissa de la table, tomba le long de son corps et resta là, pendante et comme morte. J'eus peur. . . . Qu'est-ce qui s'empara alors de moi? L'idée que jamais plus le vieillard ne s'éveillerait si je ne me dépêchais de le ramener de ce côté? . . . Je me mis à crier son nom. . . .

During her visit to Lake Winnipeg with the old man, Christine, suddenly aware of the inevitability of death, as of old age, finally asks the most pertinent question of all: " 'Quand on est vieux, vieux, est-ce qu'il faut mourir?' " M. Saint-Hilaire's answer is simple: " 'Mais, vieux, c'est naturel.' " Christine has understood, for soon thereafter while thinking about their friendship, she reflects that "c'est peut-être en ce moment que j'entrevis le mieux qu'elle ne pouvait pas durer."[22]

This sensitive young girl may be aware of and concerned about death, but she herself is not about to die. Those characters who are on the threshold of death possess a somewhat different attitude, often associated with a vague or natural religious interpretation. Daniel Lacasse, for example, faced with death, cannot possibly understand what is about to occur, and despite his sister's attempt at a religious explanation, the child's frame of reference is life:

> Alors, il parut troublé.
>
> "Au ciel, Yvonne, est-ce qu'il y aura Jenny?"
>
> "Oui, ta belle Jenny, ta bonne Jenny y sera un jour," répondit gravement Yvonne. . . .
>
> "Et maman?"
>
> "Maman, tu peux être sûr. . . ."
>
> "Et toi? . . ."
>
> "Oui," dit Yvonne en se penchant pour l'embrasser. . . .
>
> "Il y aura tout ce que t'aimes au ciel. . . . C'est ça le ciel: tout ce qu'on aime. Il y aura la bonne Sainte Vierge. Elle te bercera dans ses bras. Et tu seras comme un Enfant Jésus dans ses bras."
>
> "Mais j'aurai mon manteau neuf," l'interrompit-il avec ressentiment.
>
> "Si tu veux . . . mais t'auras d'autres choses bien plus belles. T'auras plus faim, non plus au ciel, Nini. T'auras plus jamais froid. T'auras plus de bobo. Tu chanteras avec les anges."
>
> Il ferma les yeux, fatigué des visions qu'elle faisait naître. . . . Dès lors, il fut indifférent, ne parlant plus, ne demandant rien. Un matin . . . la garde-malade . . . le trouva sans vie. Il s'était éteint tout doucement, sans plaintes, sans souffrances.

Daniel may not have fully understood Yvonne's words, but they seem to have guided him into peaceful stoicism.[23]

M. Saint-Hilaire is similarly resigned to his approaching

death, although at his age, he remains reticent as well:

> "On a comme le goût d'aller voir maintenant de l'autre côté."
>   "Ah! Parce que vous avez assez appris et aimé de ce côté-ci? . . . "
>   "Assez appris? . . . Assez aimé? . . . je ne sais pas. Peut-être qu'on n'a jamais assez appris et aimé. Je voudrais encore un petit peu de temps. Je suppose qu'on voudrait toujours encore un petit peu de temps."

M. Saint-Hilaire is both fearful of and curious about this "pays mystérieux" that he describes to Christine as a place where all beloved deceased ones meet again. In a religious interpretation, he associates death with immortality: " 'L'éternité des temps, c'est quand on meurt?' 'Mais non, c'est la vie qui ne finit plus.' " One does not know if the old man truly believes in a life after death, if he is trying to convince himself of its existence in order to dispel his fears, or if he merely desires to assuage the anxieties of his young friend. With any of these possibilities, however, he is attempting to be stoically philosophical.[24]

As a result of her increasingly ill health, Martha also contemplates the idea of her death and realizes that, for the first time in her life, she is paying attention to her own thoughts, to the fact that she possesses a human existence. But despite some sadness that nothing of her may remain after her death, she tends to deny the possibility of personal eternity:

> Se pouvait-il qu'en des régions inconnues survécussent les âmes? Pour certaines, cela était peut-être possible; pour des âmes hautes, de nobles et profondes intelligences. . . . Mais Martha! . . . Non elle ne pouvait s'imaginer vivant toujours, se survivant. La destination était trop haute, la fin trop grande pour la vie qu'elle avait vécue.

But like Alexandre Chenevert who will remain in the thoughts of others, Martha will soon confide her soul to the wind and will achieve her own form of modest immortality.[25]

Given his obsessions and then his own experience with illness, Chenevert, too, thinks about death. He generally prefers those who have already died, for he believes that people never love the living enough and, therefore, later sense deep regrets. Resigned to his own fate, this man does find peace within himself

and a profound love for humanity, but only when—as for his
predecessor in the early short story, "Sécurité"—it is too late.
But the macabre irony in Chenevert's story resides predominantly in the fact that, with his pain and humiliation and in spite
of his new found human tenderness, he wants to die, but the
medical profession is determined to keep him alive for as long
as possible. In this aspect of his life, Chenevert appears to be
closer to a culture other than his own, closer to the Eskimo
attitude toward death. Doctors, medicine, and hospitals must
be seen as the White obsession with life.[26]

The conflict between these two cultures and their respective
attitudes toward death is examined in *La Rivière sans repos*.
In "Les Satellites," the sick Deborah tries in vain to understand
why Whites desperately cling to life, while Isaac of "Le Fauteuil
roulant" is forced to endure his old age because of a pension
and a wheel chair, given to him by the White government. Inès
of "La Rivière sans repos" agrees that with this generosity on
the part of the government, it is not easy to accept death, as the
Eskimos have traditionally done. The norms of White, Western
culture have been imposed upon them, to the extent that, as Roy
observes in her "Voyage en Ungava," the Eskimos have begun
to believe the foolish notion that the Whites will one day prevent
them from dying at all.[27]

What the White establishment is actually trying to prevent
in these "Nouvelles esquimaudes" is an embarrassing disappearance, as that of Deborah, of another sick or old Eskimo.
To avoid another official inquiry into a voluntary death, therefore, the government refuses to let Isaac die. It is well aware of
the fact that Eskimos face the threat of death with passivity,
powerlessness, and submissiveness, for death, to these people,
can be splendid in contrast to a useless life. These were, in fact,
the beliefs held by Deborah who viewed her inevitable death
as a form of deliverance and happiness. She simply disappeared
one night into nature. Deborah was, in fact, profoundly influenced by the myth of "la Vieille" who, in the past, also
voluntarily disappeared. Listening to this story recounted by
Isaac, Deborah agreed that there is "une sorte de beauté dans
cette mort de la Vieille dans l'ombre, le vent et le silence. . . ."
In the old days, people were allowed to die, for what is better
for them: preventing them from death or helping them along
a bit toward the ultimate end? To la Vieille, Deborah, and even
Isaac, the latter, the Eskimo way of life, is preferable. At least

their people can voluntarily return to their origins in the myths of nature:

> Et il [Isaac] se prit à décrire la Vieille, telle que maintenant il se la représentait, intacte, assise au milieu de son socle de glace . . . et qui continuait à tourner, tourner au bout du monde . . . tout comme ces satellites d'aujourd'hui. . . .
>
> "C'est ce qu'elle est devenue," rêva-t-il, "j'en mettrais ma main au feu: un satellite."[28]

The relationship between nature and death that is underscored in Isaac's words is particularly characteristic of these works, both in their emphasis on the natural and, especially, in their fundamental orientation toward a cyclical interpretation of life and of the world.   Roy, of course, utilizes numerous symbols to describe the concept of death, and not all of them are circular in nature.   Death is associated, for example, with rest, sleep, and, specifically, "le grand repos."   It is also seen as a somber and silent void, as well as, in one instance, a trap for both animals and people and, in two works, the outcome of war.[29]

The majority of Royan symbols for death, however, seem to fall into two categories of a circular or cyclical pattern: those referring to nature, to its cycles and to its eternal presence; and those related to the notion of travel, to voyages that return an individual to a past and, therefore, to the possible closing of the circle of life.   Throughout Roy's fiction, there is, especially, a close rapport between the death of characters and the eternal cycle of nature.   Even in its utmost irony, such an association occurs when at the point of death, Chenevert believes that he is finally breathing pure mountain air; the hospital staff has, in effect, given him an oxygen mask.   In a less ironic vein, Roy sometimes sees death as a glacial, winter night, thick with fog, or as the Northern Canadian tundra, with its harsh climate. As Pierre Cordorai is dying,   for example,   he hallucinates: "Formes, images chéries, rêves, sortilèges et courleurs tourbillonnèrent: une neige dans la tempête; une neige vue au kaléidoscope."   At other times death is identified more positively with warmth, summer, flowers, and singing birds.   The death of Christine's father at dawn is, in addition, a symbolic return to the beginning of his life and of time.   At the moment of their deaths, both Chenevert and Cordorai envision mountains, for these, too, can symbolize death in the Royan literary world. Similarly hills, for Mémère, Eveline, Smouillya, and Sam Lee Wong, represent a nostalgia for their respective homelands and youth.   In returning to these hills, the characters hope to re-possess that past, as they meet with death:

> Il paraissait que c'étaient de très anciennes collines liées au plus vieux passé de la Terre.   Sous les étoiles, avec leurs têtes rondes et blanches [with snow], elles éveillaient chez Sam Lee Wong une idée de vieillesse infinie, de passé profond, sans bornes, éternel, qui ancrait enfin l'errance de la vie.

And finally islands, both real and symbolic, can foster an image of death: the school children of "L'Enfant morte" form a circle around the young Yolande's coffin, thus creating the notion of an island of suffering and, with the presence of youth, of hope.[30]

Remaining within the realm of nature and death, Roy clearly describes a drought on the Western Canadian plains as "ce rond de malheur que l'on nomma le Desert Bowl." There exists a deathly silence in these abandoned towns that are prey to dust and wind. Even when these prairie villages are inhabited, the wind continuously makes its presence known, as it blows like a whirlwind across the plains. It is, therefore, the only form of eternity in death that Martha can understand:

> Presque toujours c'était par des temps d'automne qu'avaient lieu les enterrements et le vent fou emportait au loin la moitié des paroles de consolation. . . . Elle [Martha] écouta plutôt le vent. Qu'il se souvienne parfois d'elle qui l'avait tant aimé, qu'en par-courant le pays, en remuant les herbes, il dise quelque chose de sa vie . . . que le vent dans son ennui se console encore en elle et elle en cet esprit errant. . . . Martha croisa les mains. Elle eut un soupir. A cette humble immortalité de l'air, du vent et des herbes, elle confia son âme.[31]

Water imagery is undoubtedly the most prevalent Royan circular symbol for death in nature, as well as for birth and re-birth. When Chenevert discovers Lac Vert, for example, he is reborn and finally believes in a terrestrial paradise, for he has found the place where he would like to die. Rivers are plentiful in La Montagne secrète, as is the ocean that carries Cordorai to Paris and to his death. When Mémère recalls "la petite rivière Assomption" of her youth in Quebec, it is noteworthy that in this return to the past prior to death, the old woman clings to the image of a river, itself representing the eternally circular and rocking motion of nature. This natural movement also serves as the stimulus for a conversation in "Le Vieillard et l'enfant." As Christine sits on the banks of Lake Winnipeg, discussing old age and death with M. Saint-Hilaire, she wonders first whether she is looking at the same wave, moving toward her and then receding, and then whether the lake has a beginning or an end. The old man explains that, with neither a beginning nor an end, the lake is perpetual and, along with everything else, forms "un grand cercle, la fin et le recommencement se rejoignant." Finally, as Eskimo women, perhaps even closer to nature than are others, both Winnie and Elsa are, too, intimately linked with water, with the river Koksoak that flows through their town. When Winnie dies, she is found with her face turned toward her beloved body of water. As for Elsa, her life is actually equated with the flow of the river, for she is always walking along its banks:

> Toujours solitaire, toujours en marche le long de la Koksoak, elle avait parfois l'impression de descendre elle aussi le cours de sa vie vers son but ultime, vers sa fin. Elle aurait pu imaginer que sa propre existence, issue comme la rivière de loin derrière les vieilles montagnes rongées, coulait aussi depuis une sorte d'éternité.

Like the old Martine of *Cet Eté qui chantait* who, before dying, puts her feet in the water of a river and is reborn into the immensity of nature and of the past, Elsa is humanity, marching within the flowing eternity of nature and of time.[32]

In addition to being symbols both of nature and of death in Roy's fiction, wind and water are related to the equally important concept of travel, in particular of circular or return trips consistently made by these characters to their past. Death itself is referred to as a departure, as the last trip, as a long voyage to the unknown, as "la grande découverte" in the distant land of "le pays de l'amour." More complexly, it is identified with the wagon of a household mover whom Christine accompanies on one of his trips. With this initial contact with separation—that is, with the leaving behind of the stability and security of the home, both for her and for the family that is moving—Christine metaphorically experiences what will eventually be her entrance into the realm of death, with Mémère, M. Saint-Hilaire, and Eveline:

> The wagon upon which Christine sits with all of the old furniture represents, therefore, the chariot of death. It symbolizes death, in addition, in that it is a reminder of the dead past before the use of automobiles. Christine has the strange sensation of a mixture of time, past and present, as she moves along on the old wagon. She herself becomes the past. In a circular motion, she returns to death, just as she is heading toward the future of life's experiences and of the inevitable end.[33]

Most of Gabrielle Roy's symbols for death, therefore, correspond to a basic belief that time, humanity, and the universe function in a circular or cyclical manner as a spiral, pendulum, or whirlwind. The presence of what one can call the great circle of life, death, and rebirth has already been suggested in relation to a return to youth through children, heredity, the ability or at least the desire of Royan adults for *recommencement,* and the effective links among generations in their mutual rapports of communication and understanding. Associated with these images are two additional concerns that relate even more specifically to the concept of immortality: memory and the work of art. As for death, linked to nature and to travel, it can be seen as one of the great tragic events of life, but also as part of the infinite circle of time and life, continuously reborn and repeated.[34]

Throughout Gabrielle Roy's fiction, many of her characters—especially those who are old or about to die—present the image of a circle, with their own youth and old age holding hands, joining together prior to death. Alicia's insanity returns her to her childhood before she dies, while old age, in reference to Mémère and to M. Saint-Hilaire, is described as a second childhood. Martha, aware that she is going to die, turns around within herself, searching for her true being in her lost youth. Even Pierre Cordorai, on the road toward old age, has the bizarre impression of meeting himself as he was in the past, of exchanging ideas and news with his other self, significantly, on the banks of a river. One of the most striking images of this concept of circular life and death within an individual can be found in the portrait of the dying Chenevert: "Le visage était aussi mince que celui d'un enfant, mais d'un très vieil enfant à peau jaunie et séchée dont le regard paraissait s'être collé à la vie à force de désillusions."[35]

It is noteworthy that Christine, who so effectively represents youth in the Royan literary universe, is the one who best understands the nature of this circular phenomenon. Even as a child, when she mentally returns almost to the beginnings of life while she is being rocked in a hammock, she wonders if she has the right to survive this sensation of total happiness. As she matures, Christine reflects more profoundly upon the inevitable cruelties of old age, life, and death, here in relation to her own mother:

> Et comment se fait-il que l'être humain ne connaisse pas en sa vieillesse de plus grand bonheur que de retrouver en soi son jeune visage? . . . En quoi pouvait-il être bon, à soixante-dix ans, de donner la main à son enfance, sur une petite colline? Et si c'est cela la vie: retrouver son enfance, alors, à ce moment-là, lorsque la vieillesse l'a rejointe un beau jour, la petite ronde doit être presque finie, la fête terminée.[36]

But despite this aura of tragedy that accompanies the constant presence of death, these works remain optimistic, precisely because of the circular nature of humanity and of the world. One must not forget that, since the works remain open at their end, there is always hope, always a new dawn, always a possibility of *recommencement.* Similarly, the circle of life and death can never truly close, as long as there exist children to inherit traits from their parents, to repeat certain facets of these past lives, and to accomplish what the older generation was not able to do. Memories, as well, will prevent the closing of the circle, since, as shall be later analyzed, they create a form of eternity or immortality. Rather than being depicted as a circle, therefore, this universe is more accurately seen as cyclical, as a series of concentric or superimposed circles, all within one infinite circle encompassing humanity, nature, and time. This ultimate circle will never close.[37]

NOTES

[1] Gabrielle Roy, "Ma Grand-Mère toute-puissante," *La Route d'Altamont*, Collection L'Arbre, No. 10 (Montréal: Editions HMH, 1966), p. 54; Gabrielle Roy, "Le Fauteuil roulant," *La Rivière sans repos* (Montréal: Librairie Beauchemin Limitée, 1971), p. 104. See also Roy, *La Route d'Altamont*, pp. 13, 62, 133, 205-206; Roy, *La Rivière sans repos*, pp. 130, 225; Gabrielle Roy, "La Pension de vieillesse," *Le Bulletin des Agriculteurs*, 39, No. 11 (novembre 1943), 33; Gabrielle Roy, *Un Jardin au bout du monde* (Montréal: Librairie Beauchemin Limitée, 1975), p. 178; Gabrielle Roy, *Ces Enfants de ma vie* (Montréal: Editions Internationales Alain Stanké Ltée, 1977), pp. 48, 51; Marc Gagné, *Visages de Gabrielle Roy* (Montréal: Librairie Beauchemin Limitée, 1973), p. 162; Paula Gilbert Lewis, "*Street of Riches* and *The Road Past Altamont*: The Feminine World of Gabrielle Roy," *Journal of Women's Studies in Literature*, 1, No. 2 (Spring 1979), 137, 138.

[2] Roy, *La Route d'Altamont*, p. 29; Roy, "La Rivière sans repos," pp. 266-269. See also Roy, *La Route d'Altamont*, pp. 11, 14, 28-31, 33, 42-43, 47, 237-241; Roy, "Un Jardin au bout du monde," pp. 169, 178.

[3] Roy, "Le Vieillard et l'enfant," *La Route d'Altamont*, pp. 62, 71-76, 79, 90, 114, 126-128, 131, 149, 151; Gabrielle Roy, "Le Jour et la nuit," *Rue Deschambault* (1955; rpt. Montréal: Librairie Beauchemin Limitée, 1974), pp. 265-270, 274-277.   The father in "Un Vagabond frappe à notre porte" is similarly described as being pitifully lost in his memories and daydreams.   See Roy, *Un Jardin au bout du monde*, pp. 55-56.

[4] Roy, *La Route d'Altamont*, p. 138. See also pp. 13, 48, 51, 117, 132; Roy, "La Pension de vieillesse," pp. 35, 36; Gabrielle Roy, "La Grande Voyageuse," *La Revue Moderne*, 24, No. 1 (mai 1942), 13, 27, 28; Gabrielle Roy, *Bonheur d'occasion* (1945; rpt. Montréal: Librarie Beauchemin Limitée, 1973), pp. 172-176; Gabrielle Roy, *Alexandre Chenevert* (1954; rpt. Montréal: Beauchemin, 1973), pp. 81-82, 96-97, 99, 281, 375; Roy, "L'Alouette," *Ces Enfants de ma vie*, pp. 53-54.

[5] Gabrielle Roy, "Petite Ukraine," *Fragiles Lumières de la terre: Ecrits divers 1942-1970*, Collection Prose Entière (Montréal: Les Editions

Quinze, 1978), p. 80; Roy, "La Pension de vieillesse," p. 32; Roy, *La Route d'Altamont,* pp. 9-10, 24-25, 39, 47, 71-73, 75-76, 92-94, 114, 151; Roy, "La Rivière sans repos," pp. 180-182. The one exception to these characteristics of order, discipline, and formality in old age is Winnie of "La Rivière sans repos."

[6] Roy, *La Route d'Altamont,* pp. 18, 25, 27-28. See also pp. 17, 19, 21, 24, 26, 28-31, 34-35, 37-38, 44-45; Roy, "La Pension de vieillesse," p. 8; Lewis, p. 137. The light of life and communication is not only specifically evident during artistic creation, as for Mémère, but also normally reflected in the eyes of most of Roy's older characters. See especially Gabrielle Roy, "La Source au désert," *Le Bulletin des Agriculteurs,* 42, No. 11 (novembre 1946), 45, 48; Roy, *Rue Deschambault,* p. 53; Roy, *La Route d'Altamont,* pp. 62, 198-200.

[7] Roy, *La Route d'Altamont,* pp. 44-45, 200. See also pp. 9-13, 16, 18, 21, 22, 26-27, 33-39, 46, 199; Roy, "Un Jardin au bout du monde," pp. 178-179; Gabrielle Roy, "Le Jour où Martine descendit au fleuve," *Cet Eté qui chantait* (Québec-Montréal: Les Editions Françaises, 1972), pp. 148-149, 155.

[8] Roy, *La Route d'Altamont,* pp. 47, 96. See also pp. 9-11, 13, 20, 33-39, 42-43, 75, 92; Roy, "La Pension de vieillesse," pp. 8, 32, 33, 36; Roy, "La Grande Voyageuse," p. 27; Gabrielle Roy, "La Grande Berthe," *Le Bulletin des Agriculteurs,* 39, No. 6 (juin 1943), 4-9, 39-49.

[9] Gabrielle Roy, *La Petite Poule d'eau* (1950; rpt. Montréal: Librairie Beauchemin Limitée, 1970), p. 164. See also pp. 161, 163, 165; Roy, "Mon Chapeau rose," *Rue Deschambault,* p. 53; Roy, *La Rivière sans repos,* pp. 98-99, 101-106, 108, 181, 209-211, 247, 274-277; Roy, *Ces Enfants de ma vie,* pp. 35-37, 49-50, 53-54.

[10] Gagné, p. 153; Lewis, pp. 137-139; Paula Gilbert Lewis, "The Themes of Memory and Death in Gabrielle Roy's *La Route d'Altamont,*" *Modern Fiction Studies,* 22, No. 3 (Autumn 1976), 458; François Ricard, *Gabrielle Roy,* Ecrivains canadiens d'aujourd'hui, No. 11 (Montréal: Editions Fides, 1975), p. 123; André Brochu, "Gabrielle Roy," Notes from course on author, Université de Montréal, Printemps 1978, taken by one of his students; Bertrand Lombard, *"La Route d'Altamont,"* *La Revue de l'Université Laval,* 21, No. 2 (octobre 1966), 197-198; Gilles Marcotte, *Les Bonnes Rencontres: Chroniques littéraires,* Collection Reconnaissances (Montréal: Editions Hurtubise HMH, 1971), p. 151; Paul Socken, " 'Le Pays de l'amour' in the Works of Gabrielle Roy," *Revue de l'Université d'Ottawa,* 46, No. 3 (juillet-septembre 1976), 309-310.

[11] Roy, "Ma Grand-Mère toute-puissante," *La Route d'Altamont,* pp. 31, 56-57; Gagné, p. 85. See also Roy, *La Route d'Altamont,* pp. 10-11, 17, 19, 21-23, 25-30, 33-34, 36-37, 44, 46, 51-55; Paula Gilbert Lewis,

"Trois Générations de femmes: Le Reflet mère/fille dans quelques nouvelles de Gabrielle Roy," L'Héritage français en Amérique Section, American Association of Teachers of French, Lille, France, 27 June 1983.

[12]Roy, "Le Vieillard et l'enfant," *La Route d'Altamont,* pp. 118, 68, 132-133, 138-139. See also pp. 61-67, 74-76, 92-94, 96-97, 102-110, 120-131, 141-144, 151-152. Eveline, in her old age, also needs the presence of the youthful Christine and cries out to her: " 'Reste jeune et avec moi toujours, ma petite Christine, afin que je ne devienne pas trop vite tout à fait vieille et disputeuse.' " Christine, therefore, always remains a child in her mother's eyes and will continue to try to prove herself to the older woman. See Roy, "La Route d'Altamont," pp. 229, 199-200, 206-207, 237-241, 242-255. The attitude of people toward old age, as discussed thus far, concerns only White, Western culture. The attitude toward old age in Eskimo culture is related to that toward death and, therefore, will be treated later in this chapter. Finally, the relationship between old age and memory will be examined in Chapter VII.

[13]Jane Byers Moss, "Pathological Images in the Quebec Novel," *The American Review of Canadian Studies,* 10, No. 1 (Spring 1980), pp. 39-41, 45-46; Paula Gilbert Lewis, "Response: Pathological Images in the Quebec Novel," Literary Perspectives Section, Fifth Biennial Conference of the Association for Canadian Studies in the United States, Washington, D.C., September, 1979.

[14]Roy, *Alexandre Chenevert,* pp. 133, 151-152, 308-312, 323, 330-331, 339-345. The other hospitalized characters to whom one is referring are Daniel Lacasse, Deborah, of "Les Satellites" in *La Rivière sans repos,* and Jimmy Kumachuk. It is, however, Rose-Anna who fears and mistrusts hospitals in *Bonheur d'occasion.* Alicia is the character who enters an insane asylum. See Roy, *Bonheur d'occasion,* pp. 198-203, 325; Roy, *La Rivière sans repos,* pp. 36-37, 247; Roy, "Alicia," *Rue Deschambault,* pp. 174-180. In addition, Constantin Simoneau speaks of the cost of hospitilization in Gabrielle Roy, "Feuilles mortes," *La Revue de Paris,* 56e année, No. 1 (janvier 1948), p. 47. Deborah, in Roy's journalistic "Voyage en Ungava," also enters the hospital, as does a sick Eskimo child. See Marc Gagné, "*La Rivière sans repos* de Gabrielle Roy: Etude mytho-critique incluant 'Voyage en Ungava' (extraits) par Gabrielle Roy (suite)," *Revue de l'Université d'Ottawa,* 46, No. 3 (juillet-septembre 1976), 373, 377, 380. See also Socken, p. 319.

[15]Roy, *Bonheur d'occasion,* p. 318. See also pp. 82, 192-203, 231, 316, 319-321; Roy, "La Rivière sans repos," pp. 238-240, 245, 247, 253.

[16]Roy, *Rue Deschambault,* p. 179. See also pp. 165-168, 171, 175-177, 180; Lewis, "The Feminine World of Gabrielle Roy," pp. 135-136. The other important Royan characters who become gravely ill and die

are Deborah, of Roy, "Les Satellites," *La Rivière sans repos,* pp. 19-20, 25, 27-28; Martha, of Roy, "Un Jardin au bout du monde," pp. 157, 159, 167-168, 194, 196, 200; Tante Thérésina, of Roy, *Rue Deschambault,* pp. 187-189; and Pierre, of Gabrielle Roy, *La Montagne secrète* (1961; rpt. Montréal: Librarie Beauchemin Limitée, 1974), pp. 53-54, 188-189, 200, 204, 214, 215. Papa, of Roy, *Rue Deschambault,* p. 276, and Winnie, of Roy, "La Rivière sans repos," p. 218, are both sick but ultimately die of old age.   Gustave, of Roy, "Un Vagabond frappe à notre porte," *Un Jardin au bout du monde,* pp. 50-51, becomes delirious, while Christine, of Roy, *Rue Deschambault,* p. 81, has the whooping cough.   In her early short stories, Roy's "La Grande Berthe," pp. 44, 47; the heroine of Roy, "La Pension de vieillesse," pp. 33, 36; Nathalie, of Roy, "La Source au désert," p. 48; and finally Bunny, of Gabrielle Roy, "La Sonate à l'aurore," *La Revue Moderne,* 22, No. 11 (mars 1941), 9, 10, 35-37, are all ill.

[17]Roy, *Alexandre Chenevert,* pp. 108-109, 153, 159-165, 167, 169-170, 174-175, 177-180, 297-302, 333-334, 339-345. Eugénie's gynecologist is, likewise, condescending when he tells her that all of her problems are simply related to menopause. See Roy, *Alexandre Chenevert,* p. 114. Roy herself spoke ironically of doctors in general, stating that they treated only medical symptoms and illnesses, while forgetting about the individual, with specific problems and needs. She felt that doctors generally had a condescending air toward their patients. Personal interview with Gabrielle Roy, 29 June 1980.

[18]Roy, *Alexandre Chenevert,* pp. 110, 112. See also pp. 10, 17, 26-27, 29-30, 60, 63-65, 101, 111.

[19]Roy, *Alexandre Chenevert,* p. 179. See also pp. 113-115, 124-127, 151-152, 154-157, 172-173, 180, 217, 260-261, 276, 279-282, 290-291, 294, 303.

[20]Roy, *Alexandre Chenevert,* p. 375. See also pp. 311-312, 319, 333-334, 336-345, 355-356, 374.

[21]Roy, *Alexandre Chenevert,* p. 383. See also pp. 347-350, 375-377; Agnès Whitfield, *"Alexandre Chenevert:* Cercle vicieux et évasions manquées," *Voix et Images du Pays,* 8 (1974), 122; Personal interview with Gabrielle Roy, 29 June 1980.

[22]Roy, "Le Vieillard et l'enfant," *La Route d'Altamont,* pp. 128, 135, 142. See also pp. 56, 67-68, 109-110, 129, 134, 136-137; Roy, *Rue Deschambault,* pp. 41, 133-134; Roy, "L'Enfant morte," *Cet Eté qui chantait,* pp. 181-182, 186-189; Lewis, "The Themes of Memory and Death," pp. 463-465.

[23]Roy, *Bonheur d'occasion,* pp. 319-321.

[24]Roy, *La Route d'Altamont,* pp. 135-136, 110. See also p. 137; Lewis, "The Themes of Memory and Death," p. 465. Roy herself echoed

M. Saint-Hilaire's words about never having enough time in: Personal interview with Gabrielle Roy, 29 June 1980.

[25] Roy, "Un Jardin au bout du monde," pp. 214-215. See also pp. 59, 188, 206, 216-217.

[26] Roy, *Alexandre Chenevert*, pp. 21, 43, 55, 112, 151, 237, 281, 286, 289, 333, 336-345, 351-356, 359, 361, 369-370, 382-383; Gabrielle Roy, "Sécurité," *La Revue Moderne*, 29, No. 11 (mars 1948), 69. In associating eternity with nature, with the wind, Martha also reminds one of Eskimo culture.

[27] Roy, *La Rivière sans repos*, pp. 18, 20, 21, 38, 47-48, 92-94, 101-111, 225-228; Gagné, " 'Voyage en Ungava' (extraits) par Gabrielle Roy (suite)," p. 377.

[28] Roy, *La Rivière sans repos*, pp. 18, 49-50. See also pp. 16-23, 33-34, 42, 47, 51-54, 58, 92-94; Marc Gagné, "*La Rivière sans repos* de Gabrielle Roy: Etude mythocritique incluant 'Voyage en Ungava' (extraits) par Gabrielle Roy," *Revue de l'Université d'Ottawa*, 46, No. 1 (janvier-mars 1976), 91-99; John Hind-Smith, *Three Voices: The Lives of Margaret Laurence, Gabrielle Roy, and Frederick Philip Grove* (Toronto: Clarke Irwin, 1975), pp. 118-119. The Indian Mara, prior to *La Rivière sans repos*, is also anxious to die in order to learn the secrets of nature. See Roy, *La Montagne secrète*, p. 205.

[29] Roy, "La Pension de vieillesse," p. 36; Roy, *Rue Deschambault*, pp. 133-134, 159, 160; Roy, *La Montagne secrète*, pp. 43-45; Roy, *La Route d'Altamont*, p. 128; Roy, "La Rivière sans repos," pp. 224-228; Lewis, "The Themes of Memory and Death," pp. 463-464.

[30] Roy, *La Montagne secrète*, p. 222; Roy, *Un Jardin au bout du monde*, p. 102. See also Roy, *La Montagne secrète* pp. 219-221; Roy, *Un Jardin au bout du monde*, pp. 81-83, 92-95, 100-101, 126, 130; Roy, *Alexandre Chenevert*, p. 383; Roy, *Rue Deschambault*, pp. 159, 198, 202, 277; Roy, *Cet Eté qui chantait*, pp. 183-188, 193-198; Roy, *La Route d'Altamont*, pp. 193, 204-206, 224; Roy, "La Pension de vieillesse," pp. 33, 36; Gagné, *Visages de Gabrielle Roy*, pp. 154-155; Socken, pp. 321, 323; François Ricard, "De quelques avatars de Dieu," *Etudes Françaises*, 9, No. 4 (novembre 1973), 347.

[31] Roy, "Où iras-tu Sam Lee Wong?," *Un Jardin au bout du monde*, p. 97; Roy, "Un Jardin au bout du monde," pp. 216-217. In this same collection, see also pp. 98-102, 215. See also Roy, *La Rivière sans repos*, pp. 58-59, 201-203, Roy, *La Montagne secrète*, pp. 219-222.

[32] Roy, *La Route d'Altamont*, pp. 49, 50, 193, 121; Roy, "La Rivière sans repos," p. 301. In the first work, see also pp. 119, 122; in the second see also pp. 87, 266-269, 271, 281-282, 285-286, 304, 314-315; See also Roy, *Alexandre Chenevert* pp. 236-237; Roy, *Cet Eté qui chantait*, pp. 93,

95-96, 146, 155-160; Gabrielle Roy, "Mon Héritage du Manitoba," *Mosaic*, 3 iii (1970), 77, 79; Gagné, *Visages de Gabrielle Roy*, p. 160; Lewis, "The Themes of Memory and Death," pp. 465-466.

[33] Roy, *La Route d.Altamont*, pp. 142-143; Lewis, "The Themes of Memory and Death," p. 463. In the first work, see also pp. 93, 114, 136, 168-169, 242, 252, 255. See also Roy, *Rue Deschambault*, pp. 128, 133-134, 198; Roy, "La Rivière sans repos," pp. 240, 243; Roy, *Cet Eté qui chantait*, pp. 146, 156-157; Roy, *Un Jardin au bout du monde*, pp. 81-83, 92-95, 123; Ricard, *Gabrielle Roy*, pp. 26, 120-123. There is one additional symbol of death in Roy's fiction that, although circular, is related neither to nature nor to travel, but rather to the boredom of repetitive days and to the earth that turns: Rose-Anna's sewing machine, with its wheel and continual whirring sound. See Roy, *Bonheur d'occasion*, p. 149.

[34] Roy, *Bonheur d'occasion*, pp. 323, 330-331; Roy, *Ces Enfant de ma vie*, p. 185; Roy, "La Rivière sans repos," p. 299; Roy, *Un Jardin au bout du monde*, p. 99. Several critics have made reference to this circular or cyclical nature of Roy's works. See in particular: Gagné, "*La Rivière sans repos:* Etude mythocritique (suite)," (juillet-septembre 1976), p. 382; Lewis, "The Themes of Memory and Death," pp. 463-466; Lewis, "The Feminine World of Gabrielle Roy," pp. 137-139; Marcotte, pp. 151, 153; Socken, pp. 321, 323; Jacques Blais, "L'Unité organique de *Bonheur d'occasion*," *Etudes Françaises*, 6, No. 1 (février 1970), 41, 44-49; Donald Cameron, "Gabrielle Roy: A Bird in the Prison Window," in *Conversations with Canadian Novelists* (Toronto: Macmillan of Canada, 1973), p. 142; Phyllis Grosskurth, *Gabrielle Roy*, Canadian Writers and Their Works (Toronto: Forum House, 1972), pp. 20, 51-52, 55-56; Roland Charland et Jean-Noel Samson, *Gabrielle Roy*, Dossiers de documentation sur la littérature canadienne-française (Montréal: Fides, 1972), pp. 72-73. The role of nature, in general, in Roy's works will be examined in Chapter V, while the importance of travel will be discussed in Chapter VI. Memory, as related to heredity as well, will be treated in Chapter VII, and the role of the work of art in Chapter VIII. This section of Chapter IV, therefore, presents the fundamental concept of cycles and circles, to which one will subsequently refer, while it deals specifically with images of death.

[35] Roy, *Alexandre Chenevert*, p. 342. See also Roy, *Rue Deschambault*, pp. 178, 180; Roy, *La Route d'Altamont*, pp. 48, 96; Roy, "Un Jardin au bout du monde," pp. 211-212; Roy, *La Montagne secrète*, p. 198. It should be recalled that the young Daniel Lacasse, about to die, curiously resembles an old person.

[36] Roy, *La Route d'Altamont*, pp. 206-207. See also Roy, "Ma Coqueluche," *Rue Deschambault*, p. 86; Lewis, "The Themes of Memory and Death," pp. 461-462.

[37] Lewis, "The Themes of Memory and Death," p. 466; Personal interview with Gabrielle Roy, 29 June 1980.

CHAPTER V

The World of Nature

In 1967 Gabrielle Roy published an introduction to a photographic album dedicated to the Montreal World's Fair, *Terre des Hommes/Man and His World.* In this essay, she refers to the earth as "ce petit point dans l'ensemble de l'univers, notre pays, notre chez-nous." Five years later in her prose poem to nature, *Cet Eté qui chantait,* she refers to her readers as "les enfants de la Terre," as "enfants de toutes saisons à qui je souhaite de ne jamais se lasser d'entendre raconter leur planète Terre." Many of her characters were already listening to what she called, in 1961, "des ententes secrètes" between humanity and certain aspects of the universe, for Roy had always believed that one must remain open to an understanding of both human nature and the surrounding world.[1]

There exists a profound influence of environment—defined as one's physical and, at times, social milieu—upon all Royan characters, on both their actions and their thoughts. Whatever that surrounding location may be, there is a close rapport and even a communion between the individual and exterior space, to the extent that outside nature can be personified and become a character in its own right. In analyzing this important aspect of Roy's fiction, Paul Socken has indicated that since Royan characters, and in particular her urban characters, are fundamentally alone, alienated in an incomprehensible, modern world, and since they have become strangers to themselves and to nature, they have a deep need to adapt themselves to the natural world, to rediscover their surroundings so as to understand better both themselves and others. When one is sensitive to and aware of one's milieu, and when one perfects one's own explanation or description of the world, one possesses that world, makes it one's own, for the elements of nature, in Roy's fiction, reflect distinctive human emotions. Socken believes that, for Gabrielle Roy, there exists in the universe a basic harmony and unity to which humanity belongs. An ideal, therefore, is to be found in a mutual reconciliation between the world of people and, predominantly, the natural world.[2]

In order to convince her readers that such a reconciliation is possible, Roy must powerfully and realistically depict both her characters and their world. The individuals who people these works are both distinct beings and archetypal figures. As for her talent in describing exterior environment in her works, Roy has been seen as a social realist and as a quasi-photographic writer. She herself has spoken of the importance that her early journalistic writings had on her formation as an author, since these articles afforded her the opportunity to travel, research, and minutely observe everything around her both in Quebec and in Canada. She believed that influenced by the nineteenth-century French novelists of the movement of Realism, she was merely a realistic observer who wrote about what she saw and then added her own natural, creative sense of imagination.[3]

One can, however, pursue this influence even further. It is true that like Honoré de Balzac, Gabrielle Roy depicts her exterior and interior, that is, psychological, spaces as being mutually reflective. But, more specifically, that exterior space, the physical and social milieu into which her characters have been placed greatly determines the lives of her literary creations. Given the power of that outside influence, along with the inevitable presence of heredity within a particular family, one can state that there exists in the Royan literary universe a determinism or fatality that is not unlike that of Emile Zola and his quasi-scientific theory of Naturalism in literature. Her urban characters suffer because, living in an artificial milieu, they lack any contact with the natural world of the country, while her rural creatures also endure their own form of isolation but possess daily opportunities to relate to their natural surroundings.[4]

Throughout Roy's fiction there does exist an oscillation between the city and the country, with the sensation of loneliness and yet solidarity in the former locale and with freedom and yet solitude in the latter. The author has stated that most everything in her life and in her works could be traced back to the fact that she was born on the little rue Deschambault where, at one end, was a stop for the tram that could take her to Winnipeg and, within fifteen minutes, to humanity. At the opposite end of the street was a small group of trees and the beginning of wild nature to which she could go whenever she needed solitude and contact with the natural world. As a child, she spent much time walking back and forth along that street, drawn toward nature and then, when tired of it, able to frequent the world of people. Considering her deep need for both locations, therefore, she found it unjust that she had always been accused of hating the city, of depicting it in an entirely negative light in her creative works. She maintained, to the contrary, that cities, especially with their cross-section of ethnic groups, were fascinating and exciting. What Roy disliked about large metropolises was modern urban planning that preferred apartment buildings and cement to, for example, parks. To put a stop to the hell that modern people were creating for themselves, one must not abolish cities, but, in Roy's opinion, countrify them.[5]

These mixed feelings toward the city are evident in Roy's four 1941 journalistic articles describing the city of Montreal and serving as a source of information to the future novelist for her 1945 *Bonheur d'occasion*. As she stated in an article treating her early years in Montreal, Gabrielle Roy discovered this urban metropolis alone and on foot, during numerous walking tours of the entire city. Unaware of any aspect of Montreal, she was interested in everything that she saw: "En pèlerin, émue, éreintée, je l'ai traversée en entier, je l'ai connue dans son plus laid, dans son plus tragique, dans son plus altier du haut de la montagne, dans son meilleur, dans son pire et, quand je m'y attendais le moins, dans sa gaieté irrésistible." Her 1941 articles, are, in fact, thus described, as though her readers themselves were walking alongside the journalist. She writes of all quarters of the city and, most interestingly, of the rue Sainte-Catherine, depicted as though it were a person. She speaks of the poverty in Montreal, of "la plainte du peuple," as in retrospect, of hearing "soupirer le peuple." In "Du port aux banques," she portrays the constant hurrying of people who work as termites, enslaved by their new addiction to material comfort. Life in a large city is frenetic: "Il ne faut pas que le bruit cesse. Il ne faut pas que l'agitation tombe. Il ne faut pas s'arrêter. Il ne faut pas penser." "Après trois cents ans," Roy's fourth article on Montreal, presents a history of the city, underscoring its formation by two nations and suggesting, as explicitly stated in her more recent remembrances, that both cultures can benefit from a willing exchange:

> Il [Montréal] est français dans son exubérance et sa confusion
> politique, anglais dans les affaires, cosmopolite au port, amé-
> ricain dans la rue Sainte-Catherine, provincial dans l'est, puri-
> tain à Westmount, snob à Outremont, nationaliste au Parc La-
> fontaine, canadien-français le 24 juin, saxon à Noël . . . bilingue
> quand il le faut et profondément hybride dans l'âme. Nul doute
> que cette ville étonnante ne soit l'oeuvre de deux nations.[6]

Despite the obvious fact that, during her initial years in
Montreal, Roy learned to love the city, even with its distasteful
facets, it is essentially the negative that she stresses in her major
fiction, and specifically in three of her novels. *Bonheur d'occasion* is the tragic story of rural people, represented by the Lacasse
family, who have left the country with the naive hope of bet-
tering themselves in the large, increasingly industrialized city
of Montreal. Never becoming fully adapted to the rapid progress
and to the frenetic, costly lifestyle surrounding them, they
stagnate, remaining, like both Azarius and Rose-Anna Lacasse,
neither rural nor urban. With large families that are increasingly
difficult to raise and that are slowly disintegrating, these individuals find themselves caught in Saint-Henri, a section of the
city that teems with poverty and misery. They are trapped in
the odors of filth and poverty that pervade their homes and,
pathetically, their intimate sexual lives. Even the clouds of
Saint-Henri are formed by a continual "tourbillon de suie,"
emanating from the surrounding chimneys and symbolizing
the enclosed circle that engulfs these people in their wretched
misery. Ashamed and yet often resigned to their fate, the
inhabitants of Saint-Henri, and especially the young, bitterly
condemn society for allowing such conditions to exist. They
specifically attack the fact that, with the widespread unemployment in these early 1940s, there is something innately
wrong with a social order that allows such a waste of human
energy. With no work and, therefore, little money, these people
tend to lack any sense of dignity or self-esteem and, like Azarius
and his younger friends, Pitou, Boisvert, and Alphonse, spend
much of their time sitting in bars, complaining about their
predetermined social and economic status, or dreaming of
possible escapes.[7]
    Contributing to this urban situation is the fact that the

inhabitants of Saint-Henri are daily faced with sight of West-mount and are painfully tempted by the rue Saint-Catherine. Using the technique of placing in opposition specific geographic locations, Roy often contrasts Saint-Henri and Westmount, as she opposes the French and English-speaking Montrealers:

> Mais au-delà, dans une large échancrure du faubourg, apparaît la ville de Westmount échelonnée jusqu'au faîte de la montagne dans son rigide confort anglais. Il se trouve ainsi que c'est aux voyages infinis de l'âme qu'elle invite. Ici, le luxe et la pauvreté se regardent inlassablement, depuis qu'il y a Westmount, depuis qu'en bas, à ses pieds, il y a Saint-Henri.

Within Montreal these two sections remain in conflict, for the people who live in Saint-Henri are jealously drawn toward the mountain—image, for Jean Lévesque and Emmanuel Létourneau in particular, of success and escape. But even Emmanuel, who is far wealthier than his peers in Saint-Henri, but who shoulders the burdens of his neighbors' poverty, cannot penetrate the calm and order of this section of the city and senses a profound uneasiness as he walks through its streets. Similarly, the material luxuries in the windows of the stores on the rue Sainte-Catherine continuously tempt and even mock the poor inhabitants of the city, especially Florentine. Advertisements tell them to buy, to become a part of a society of consumers, but if the city of Montreal is forever in movement and if the temptations and expensive distractions of this city continuously try to seduce them, these people remain inert within their own section of town and within their poverty.[8]

The image of the city of Montreal, therefore, and in particular of Saint-Henri within that city, both as depicted in *Bonheur d'occasion*, is that of a prison or cage, even a concentration camp, in which individuals are forced by outside circumstances and by heredity to live. In this claustrophobic atmosphere, people can barely breathe, as they are pushed into a concentrated space, as well as—given the passage of little more than three months within the novel and the feeling of urgency to make a decision about one's future in the face of war or pregnancy—into a sense of restricted time. Described by André Brochu as a series of concentric circles or spheres of existence, both individual and collective, the city of *Bonheur d'occasion* and the urban lives intertwined within it represent a hell from which the characters yearn to escape.⁹

The form of escape from this urban world of poverty depends upon the individuals who are attempting to leave, whether they are families, men, or women.   The families of Saint-Henri, in their hope of departure, participate in a phenomenon effectively described by Roy.   Every spring they move from one apartment to another, for, as Jean observes, with the arrival of spring in Montreal comes the season of pitiful illusions, of foolish hopes for *recommencement.*   Roy herself, in retrospect, affirmed that "la grande masse semblait partir de son plein gré, comme pour se donner l'illusion de la liberté. Ils en étaient malades. . . ."   But this annual *déménagement* is truly an illusion of freedom, for these poor families, in their horizontal moves from one sector or cage to another within the same sphere, remain locked inside their misery.¹⁰

Many of the male characters in this novel, however, do escape from the city.   It is evident from the beginning, in fact, that Jean, in particular, will succeed, will effect a vertical form of liberation, since he is consistently identified with wind, boats, and trains that pass through Saint-Henri without stopping to worry about poverty.   But Jean is the only person in the novel to negate his destiny and to leave Montreal, and he does so by relinquishing his sense of humanism and by profiting from that which destroys many of his peers.   For the other men of Saint-Henri who are able to escape from their misery do so only to go to war.   Once again, in their only form of salvation, they are the partially willing pawns of a society that has kept them within the circle of urban misery and now sends them away toward their death.   Part victim, part volunteer, most of them will not return to Saint-Henri.¹¹

It is, however, the female characters of *Bonheur d'occasion* whose destinies ultimately become identified with the city itself.   If Montreal can be seen as an enclosed circle, specifically as "l'inquiet tourbillon de Saint-Henri," then the fictional lives of these Montreal women, and especially of Florentine, are similarly described either as being engulfed within that spiral or as whirlwinds themselves: "A force de regarder danser la neige sous ses yeux, il lui [Jean] semblait qu'elle avait pris une forme humaine, celle même de Florentine, et qu'épuisée mais ne pouvant s'empêcher de tourner, de se dépenser, elle dansait là, dans la nuit, et restait prisonnière de ses évolutions."   Although Florentine will eventually raise her economic and social status by her marriage to Emmanuel, she will remain tied to her mother, Rose-Anna, and to the other women of Saint-Henri. Caught in the round, female structures of motherhood, crowds, and hereditary misery, therefore, these female characters will be forced to remain, as well, within the equally female, urban sphere of Montreal.[12]

This same city of Montreal, as depicted in Gabrielle Roy's second novel, *Alexandre Chenevert,* is not that of the horrid poverty in her first novel. It is, rather, that of a modern urban metropolis in which middle class, white collar workers, in particular, are continuously bombarded with dire national and international news on the radio and in the press and equally inundated with impersonal and commercial slogans of advertisements. When Chenevert returns to Montreal from a brief vacation, for example, and is faced once again with the disasters of the world, he raises his eyes to the sky, as if to seek help in the horizon or in God. He reads instead: "BUVEZ PEPSI COLA." Everywhere, in fact, religion is being sold, even marketed in the impersonal Christmas greetings from businesses. Poor, modern, urban dwellers have become slaves to these banal formulas and, like the bank teller, soon discover that they themselves can write only "dans le ton des messages publicitaires."[13]

Life in Montreal is also noisy. Chenevert hates these sounds that appear to be allied against him so as to disturb his sleep. He also dislikes the idea of so many people living in such close proximity, to the extent that, knowing one's neighbors by their particular noises, one cannot even argue in peace. The urban world of *Alexandre Chenevert* is, in addition, that of crowds, fighting, pushing, hurrying, and, especially, standing in long lines. Himself standing in a line at the North Western Lunch cafeteria, Chenevert closes his eyes:

> Et alors l'imagination folle d'Alexandre lui présenta l'entassement de la vallée de Josaphat [at the Last Judgement]; toutes les files de la terre, les patientes files de tous les temps s'allongeaient les unes aux autres. . . . Aucun bruit, aucun discours, aucun son dans la Vallée; seulement cette marche silencieuse, au pas, ce docile mouvement de la foule que d'elle-même obéissait encore à l'alignement.

Whether jostling one another or quietly standing in interminably long lines, however, the inhabitant of the modern city is miserable: commuting in a tram, "dans une curieuse pose de supplicié," distant from primitive carefreeness, and seeing families disintegrate, as people become mechanical, impersonal beings. In this sense, Chenevert is accurate in his assessment of human misery, for he is a part of it.[14]

Urban space in *Alexandre Chenevert* is essentially similar to that described in *Bonheur d'occasion,* only in this instance the character who is caught within this enclosed, claustrophobic, and circular structure is male. Most of the bank teller's urban settings, in fact, have been identified as interior and engulfing: his bathroom, apartment, tram, teller's cage, and cafeteria. Instead of depicting one major island of poverty within the larger city of Montreal, however, Roy has chosen in this novel to portray her hero, like other ubanites, as passing from one geographical concentric circle or cage to another, somewhat like the annual moves of the families of Saint-Henri, but remaining within the large urban sphere. In order to be able to breathe, therefore, Chenevert, like Roy's earlier urban characters, dreams of escape from his life in Montreal and finally decides to leave the city for the open nature of the nearby countryside, immediately symbolized by a river: "A gauche de la route, il y avait le pénitencier. Mais Alexandre se trouvait regarder du côté de la rivière. Et lui, qui ne connaissait pour ainsi dire rien d'autre au monde que la ville, ses poteaux, ses numéros, il la quittait, étonné, troublé, comme s'il sortait de prison. Que d'espace, de lumière, de liberté!"[15]

Alexandre Chenevert is not, however, a rural individual but a true urban dweller. Unlike Azarius and Rose-Anna, unlike many of the older couples of Saint-Henri, he is not attached to the country and, in effect, feels *dépaysé* in this linear displacement at Lac Vert. After a few days of total isolation, he realizes that he needs the city, needs to communicate with others, and needs to return to what he now sees as anonymity, as the comforting solitude of urban life, that is, the knowledge that thousands of others are similarly alone in Montreal. He even goes as far as becoming nostalgic about humanity: "Il rêva aussi de journaux, de magazines en grosses piles sur le trottoir, apportant les nouvelles du monde. Là était la vie, l'échange perpétuel, émouvant, fraternel." Without ever truly relating, the inhabitants of the city represent human solidarity.[16]

The Montrealer returns, of course, to the grotesque artificiality of urban life, symbolized by an electric figure of Christ on the side of the highway.   As Chenevert's bus approaches Montreal, there is increasing traffic, confusion, and stagnant air.   When he finally arrives in the bus station, he realizes that he is experiencing something even worse than solitude.   He is feeling the absurd misunderstanding of being one among many unknown others in the city: "Il eut la curieuse sensation qu'il ne pourrait pas être plus à l'étranger à Moscou, à Paris. . . . 'Voyons,' pensa Alexandre: 'j'ai vécu toute ma vie à Montréal; je suis né ici, j'y mourrai probablement.   Il éprouva la terrible ingratitude de la ville à son endroit."   He decides, therefore, that one should never leave the city, never take a vacation in the country, for one's determined home and one's urban existence, appear too monstrous when one does return.   For Alexandre Chenevert, in particular, this return, or rather this need to return to the city will bring him to his final escape into the enclosed, structured, urban, and here male circle of death.[17]

If Chenevert voluntarily returns to Montreal in order to die, then Pierre Cordorai of *La Montagne secrète* is likewise sent to Paris, never to leave.   A fiercely independent, solitary, rural being, Cordorai will meet, for the first time in his life, other artists with whom he can communicate, but who are seen by him as prisoners of the city and, therefore, according to his friend, Stanislas, as not well equiped for life.   Encountering the modern annoyances of traffic, noise, and neon signs, this Canadian adventurer and painter will experience in this urban metropolis a new, more frightening sensation of isolation, "la si mystérieuse solitude des rues emplies de monde, de pas et de lumières!"   Like Chenevert, Cordorai will need to leave the city, will take one glorious vacation in the countryside, and will return to the city to dream of the open, wild nature of his beloved Canadian mountain but to remain in his small, enclosed apartment in order to die.   Once again, the structured, atypically male urban circle will close.[18]

It is noteworthy that Gabrielle Roy's two major male characters both return from traditionally maternal, protective, and yet open nature to the city and to their death, while her two heroines, Rose-Anna and Florentine, are also associated with the confines of urban structure, not necessarily as a place to die, but rather to continue the needless struggle to find happiness.   This unusual combination of male and female circular imagery for the city, both of which are enticing but destructive, is especially interesting in the works of an author who, increasingly, has preferred to place her characters in the open surroundings of nature. In *Cet Eté qui chantait*, an ode to that nature, the elderly Martine is, in fact, seen as having been exiled for fifty years in a city apartment "sans air ni horizon." She returns to the country, to her dear river, and then, like the male characters, goes back to the city before dying: "Martine à peine de retour dans l'étroit logis sans horizon et sans lumière, s'en alla vers les espaces ouverts que toute sa vie elle avait désirés."[19] It seems as though many Royan characters need to return to the country prior to death and then back to the city in order to die in an enclosed space, before eternally returning into open nature.

Despite the evident oscillation that exists between the city and the country, there is, as well, an intermediate geographic location that exhibits both urban and rural characteristics, while it creates its own form of society: the small town or village, especially on the Western Canadian plains. Having been born and raised in Saint-Boniface, Manitoba, Roy logically depicts life in that town near Winnipeg when she writes of her semi-fictionalized youth in *Rue Deschambault*. If Saint-Henri can be seen as a village in the middle of Montreal—but as as a grotesque caricature of the truly rural town—Saint-Boniface, described in one of Roy's memoirs as an island in the middle of the plains, is seen in this collection of short stories as a place of maternal order and protection. Its society, however, is provincial, especially in its curiosity, unconscious racism, and narrow-minded chauvinism toward outsiders and, in particular, toward those who are different from the inhabitants of the town. The black boarder in Christine's house, for example, is possessively and jealously referred to as "notre Nègre," that is, until Maman sees him taking a walk with her older daughter. Similarly, Christine's boyfriend, Wilhelm, is disliked by her family predominantly because he is Dutch and, therefore, a foreigner, not one of them. In smaller towns, these attitudes are even more prevalent toward any stranger, anyone who does not come from the same locale: Christine, the new teacher, is looked upon as an unmarried curiosity by the inhabitants of Cardinal; those who live in Ely regard the journalist with both curiosity and suspicion, and the social norms of the village in *Ces Enfants de ma vie* are so powerful that any actions by the new schoolteacher are malevolently and insinuatingly discussed by the local gossips.[20]

Life in a small town, such as Rorketon or Codessa, can also seem as frenetic as in a city, especially to someone who is used to the peace and silence of the isolated countryside. When, in addition, progress and prosperity suddenly arrive in a town, a new animation infects the inhabitants, as they become more materialistic, more serious, and more harried. Sam Lee Wong witnesses such a change when oil is discovered near his town of Horizon. Once a wealthy wheat village and then a dust-filled, deserted place, Horizon, to the restaurateur's chagrin, soon resembles a modern boom town.[21]

In Gabrielle Roy's fiction, there are two particular small towns that are as important as the city, since they represent several of the author's major concerns: tradition versus progress; the conflict or clash between two cultures, one primitive and the other modern; and inevitably and tragically, the disappearance of the former. In *La Rivière sans repos,* this antithesis, as manifested in the two opposing towns, can be seen as either binary or tertiary. The Eskimos of this area originally lived in Old Fort-Chimo, on the banks of the Koksoak River. During World War II, a White military post was established on the opposite bank, and slowly most of the native inhabitants moved to New Fort-Chimo, leaving only a few independent individuals in the original settlement. The new town itself became divided into two distinct ethnic quarters. Throughout Roy's texts, one sees the image of the Koksoak flowing between the two towns, as between primitivism and modernism, while the Eskimo characters, vacillating between these two poles, are also drawn toward the purely White section of town that they can never fully attain. In their eyes, the Whites represent power: the government, the law, the police, the Church, education, the military, the medical profession, and commerce, with the enticing presence of the Hudson Bay Company. White culture is identified, therefore, with progress, and many of the Eskimos cannot seem to decide if they desire or are fearful of this "maître difficile," of this "long chemin parcouru pour atteindre un peu plus de douceur et d'agrément de vivre," of this "force térrifiante qui était peut-être au delà de toute endurance humaine," that makes people sad, and is entrapping their own race.[22]

Considered by Roy as a prologue to her novel, "Les Nouvelles esquimaudes" prefigure many aspects of the conflict that is central to "La Rivière sans repos." Already seen as possessing the traditional Eskimo attitude toward the link between death and nature, Deborah is also portrayed as caught between two cultures: the North, with its beautifully harsh countryside; and the South, with its modern showers, soap, hair brushes, and cigarette tobacco that dirties the fingers and confuses the mind. A precurser to Winnie with this last habit, Deborah is content to return home from the sweet but boring life in the South but cannot seem to rid herself of the desire for White luxuries. Continuing to use material objects as symbols of this cultural clash, Roy next introduces her readers to Barnaby who is fascinated by, fearful of, and eventually obsessed with his new toy, a telephone. Reverting to a child-like nature—true to Roy's opinion of Eskimos as innocent, grown children— Barnaby plays with the phone, deriving great pleasure from bothering certain authoritarian Whites whom he both reveres and despises. Prefiguring Ian and, in part Elsa, Barnaby eventually decides that he can no longer be enslaved to this foolish object. He leaves New Fort-Chimo, crosses the Koksoak, and rediscovers a life of simplicity and freedom, as his telephone continues to ring, unanswered. More pathetically, Isaac also becomes entrapped within another symbol of White progress and civilization: his wheel chair. With his old age and the increasing power of the White government, however, Isaac will not be able to escape.[23]

With "La Rivière sans repos," Roy creates not only characters who are torn between tradition and progress, but also one individual who, himself, symbolizes this tragic conflict. When Jimmy Kumachuk, with his blue eyes and blond hair, is born to Elsa after her rape by an unknown American G.I. with, like all G.I.'s to Elsa, these same physical traits, he initially represents a golden age for the Eskimo people, a true fusion of two disparate cultures. As he matures, however, he begins to realize that he is neither Eskimo nor White and, therefore, never fully accepted by either race. But he is determined to be more white and leaves for the South, only to return briefly, with his newly acquired American accent, in an airplane. The story of his return visit justifiably and symbolically becomes exaggerated in the Eskimo town, as Jimmy is transformed into the myth that his birth has always destined him to be.[24]

The airplane in which Jimmy returns is the last in a long series of material objects, beginning with those of "Les Nouvelles esquimaudes," that symbolize the continual encroachment of the White World into the Eskimo culture. The first and perhaps most significant of these material objects in "La Rivière sans repos" is the film that Elsa and her friends watch immediately before the young girl is raped. Not only do the Eskimos believe that all Whites resemble those who are stereotypically, almost mythically, portrayed in the movies, but Elsa herself also views her own life, since the rape and the birth of Jimmy, as a comedy or dream, later to be clouded by more White inventions, cigarettes and beer. Elsa's mother, Winnie, is likewise dependent upon cigarettes, while her grandfather, Thaddeus, recalls the drunkenness felt by the Eskimos when they first drank hot tea. Clothes are also significantly utilized in the novel to demonstrate the influence of White culture: Elsa dresses Jimmy in expensive clothing, specifically in blue, while, most noteworthy, at Winnie's funeral, at the death of the older generation, Elsa uses the occasion to wear her most stylish dress, patterned after an illustration in a catalogue, her high-heeled shoes, and a hat given to her by her white friend, Mme Beaulieu. Symbolically, when she and Jimmy temporarily return to Old Fort-Chimo, the boy dresses in the traditional Eskimo fashion and remains dirty.[25]

The clash itself between the two cultures is reflected in the image of conflicting material objects. Thaddeus, for example, sculpts little animals and figures as the Eskimos have traditionally done. Similarly, Elsa will make Eskimo souvenirs, dolls and blankets, fabricated, ironically, on a modern sewing machine. While constructing these traditional objects, Elsa surrounds herself and her son, in their Quonset hut, with symbols of the White world: a refrigerator, ground beef, white bread, and a baseball outfit for Jimmy. Like the playpen that Elsa once bought for her son, like the medicine, the penicillin that Ian sees as entrapping free beings, the material world of White, Western, or rather Southern, modern civilization has imposed itself upon these natural people.[26]

In general, therefore, the image of Whites in this novel is that of artificiality. It is a world of film rather than of reality, a world of reflections in the windows of the Hudson Bay Company, a transparent world of glass windows in Mme Beaulieu's home that look out upon nature but prevent one from becoming too close to it. White culture is also identified with the color blue: Whites have blue eyes, and they travel in the blue sky in airplanes. They represent, as well, *la clarté*, the dawn of a new era: health for Jimmy, roads leading out of Fort-Chimo, and progress toward modern civilization. Contrasted to this world is that of the Eskimos, close to nature, to the harsh tundra, to the earth. These people cannot return, however, to their primitive ways on the tundra, as is evident in Elsa, Ian, and Jimmy's failure to reach Baffin Island. They must eventually cross the Koksoak—separating primitivism and modernism, but itself symbolizing the eternal flow of nature and humanity— and must remain in New Fort-Chimo. Even Ian realizes that his revolt, his determination to live as "un vieux réactionnaire acharné à combattre ce qui faisait avancer les hommes" is useless, for modern progress will eventually install its power, and no true synthesis, no mutual reconciliation will occur between the two cultures. The Eskimos will disappear as a distinct people. Their only true dialogue with White civilization will remain in the cemetery:

> Ici, Esquimaux et Blancs reposaient côte à côte, sous les mêmes croix, dans de pareils enclos ceints de minces lattes un peu espacées et finement travaillées au couteau en naïves dentelles et fleurs de bois. Les Blancs avient fourni l'humble pin devenu ici matière rare, et les Esquimaux, l'artiste. . . .[27]

The literary representation of this clash between two cultures in a rural setting is a unique case in Roy's fiction. The important role of the country itself as a geographic location, however, is consistently underscored throughout her works. After having written about the suffocating city in *Bonheur d'occasion,* in fact, Roy decided to place her characters in the desperately needed, almost utopian countryside of *La Petite Poule d'eau,* thereby contrasting the enclosed urban structure with an open, elevated, or ascending environment where, as for Chenevert at Lac Vert and Cordorai in Northern Canada, humanity and nature can finally become reconciled. All Royan characters dream about an escape to the country, whether it is to a peaceful forest, to a deserted, tropical island, to a high mountain, to the Western Canadian plains, to the protective hills of Quebec, or to a beloved river, for, as a fellow traveller explains to Chenevert, "la vie des hommes semblait être de sortir de leur campagne afin de faire assez d'argent dans la ville pour pouvoir venir refaire leur santé à la campagne."[28]

There is in Roy's writing as well, especially in her earlier works and in her journalistic writings, a deep love not only for nature in general, but for the land itself. She speaks of the collective richness of agriculture, of farmers working in harmony with the earth. She is, however, always aware of the difficulties in cultivating the land, as she is of the indifference and even hostility of nature toward humanity. Saskatchewan is seen as a province of earth and fire, of dangerous winds that can force the fire across the plains and destroy the agricultural marvels of rural pioneers. At the same time, there are those insensitive individuals who exploit the countryside, upset the balance of nature with their search for natural resources, torment or kill animals, and pollute the water and air. The countryside may be, at times, romanticized, but it is also realistic.[29]

Life in the country is likewise faithfully depicted. Most characters do thrive in the middle of a natural environment, for they adore the peace, tranquility, silence, and solitude that it brings. Chenevert, however, is somewhat surprised at this new experience of total isolation: "Et alors, sans plus de subterfuges possibles, il sut qu'il était devant celle qui l'avait appelé, séduit, trompé, que parfois il avait cru aimer, que dans le fond, il n'avait jamais rencontré: la solitude." He is confused: "La solitude parut absence; absence de tout: des hommes, du passé, de l'avenir, du malheur, du bonheur; complet dépouillement." He has encountered one of the most fundamental problems of living in the country: Roy's rural characters do love their solitary existences, but they also suffer deeply from the intense isolation and, at times, boredom of such a static life, whether it be on a farm or alone in the Canadian wilderness.[30]

Once characters are placed in the country, they are faced with an additional conflict, a choice among the type of landscape that they prefer: the plains, tundra, mountains, or rolling hills. Such a decision is sometimes difficult, given the attraction and repulsion of all of these geographic locations; at other times, there is no choice, for characters are often forced, by their destiny, to live in a countryside that they abhor. Many of Roy's literary creations prefer the immensity of the Western Canadian plains, a love most likely due to their creator's own passion both for the endless Manitoban sky that "invite à connaître et à aller voir, toujours, ce qui est au bout de l'horizon" and for the prairie that makes one feel so small and yet with "le coeur soulevé d'aise." Her characters, in fact, generally love immense spaces, whether they be reflected in the immensity of Canada itself, the openness of Ungava and the Northern tundra, or the vastness of the world.[31]

Images of the Canadian plains occur throughout Roy's fiction, but their extraordinary power over people and their association with departure, freedom, and adventure are particularly evident in three of her works. Christine, like her mother in her youth, is extremely attracted to these immense spaces in which one can recognize oneself and one's desires: "Moi, j'aimais passionnément nos plaines ouvertes. . . . Cette absence de secret, c'était sans doute ce qui me ravissait le plus dans la plaine, ce noble visage à découvert ou si l'on veut, tout l'infini en lui reflété . . . l'appel imprécis mais puissant que mon être en recevait vers mille possibilités du destin." In "Un Jardin au bout du monde," Martha believes that "la plaine était absorbée dans un grand rêve de choses à venir, et chantait la patience et la promesse que tout, en temps et lieu, serait accompli." And finally, the schoolteacher of *Ces Enfants de ma vie* adores the Manitoban plain as it is seen from the top of the hill:

> Comment en oublierais-je la vision? . . . je n'ai jamais si bien vu la plaine, son ampleur, sa noble tristesse, sa beauté transfigurée. . . . Pourtant, ce n'était par aucun de ses aspects même les plus rares que la plaine prenait le coeur, mais au contraire, parce que, à la fin, ils disparaissaient tous en elle . . . presque tout indice de vie humaine, presque tout détail, dans le plan infini de la plaine . . . . Et sans doute est-ce comment elle m'a si souvent rendu heureuse.

In all of these observations, the Canadian plains are clearly identified with an optimistic faith and hope in a future of unlimited choices and the possibility for *recommencement.*[32]

One of the most enticing and yet elusive landscapes in this countryside is the mountain, in particular the high, solitary mountain, with its snow-covered summit in the clouds, of *La Montagne secrète.* Interpreted as being the symbol of the attainment of age or maturity, of God, the creator, Olympus, or of the perfect work of art, this mountain was not, however, seen by Roy herself as a literary symbol, for she believed that the existence of such a splendid work of nature was powerful enough in itself. But although she did not intend to create a symbol when she wrote of this mountain, she has admitted that readers and critics may attribute to it what she herself may have unconsciously suggested. Whatever the truth may be, Cordorai's mountain is undoubtedly god-like, "une haute montagne isolée que le soleil rouge embrasait et faisait brûler comme un grand feu clair." Falling to his knees, as if before a divinity, Pierre sees the menacing pride of this perfect creation that he first names "la Solitaire" and then "la Resplendissante." Instead of scaling its lofty summit, Pierre, as an artist, needs to paint this mountain, to recapture on paper what has been created in nature, to make "la Resplendissante" his own. Despite the fact that the mountain appears to reproach him for attempting to recreate it in art, Pierre will continue to see it as an ideal goal, as on the plains, a light on the distant horizon that beckons to him and calls him toward the future.[33]

Critics have also interpreted "la Resplendissante" as being maternal, a symbol for Pierre of his mother and, therefore, of his past childhood. Despite Roy's denial of such an interpretation, there is evidence that mountains, or more precisely the memory of mountains, in two of her other works are similarly linked to one's past, to maternal protection, to one's childhood, to one's homeland, and, therefore, to a place to which one desires to return in order to close the circle of life and to die: the Pyrenees of "Où iras-tu Sam Lee Wong?" and the Montagnes Humides of "La Vallée Houdou." What is in question here, however, is actually the use of the word, "mountain," for in Royan nature, the word, "hill," that is, small, gentle, rolling hills, are more often associated with such nostalgic notions, especially since this particular landscape is usually placed in contrast to the vast, open plains.[34]

Once again, it is predominantly in *La Route d'Altamont, Un Jardin au bout du monde,* and, to a lesser extent, *Ces Enfants de ma vie* that this opposition between the plains and hills occurs. In the first two works especially, the sight of a countryside of hills reminds Roy's characters of Quebec, China, the Basque country, and Russia and transports them into the stable, secure, maternally enclosed world of their childhood. Rising like a spiral on the open plains, hills are able, for Sam Lee Wong, for example, to "bercer la vieille détresse des hommes." To Sam and his friend, Smouillya, without the existence of this protective landscape "qui ancrait enfin l'errance de la vie," humanity would be lost. It is only hills that can save people, hills "qui par leur noblesse et leur immuabilité obligeait [sic] l'espèce humaine à s'arrêter de tourner perpétuellement en rond." Humanity can finally cease its endless wandering, like a whirlwind of dust and wind on the plains, and can return to the infinite and eternal circle of nature and time.[35]

In this literary countryside, hills are also described as a landscape in movement, in revolt against the monotony of the prairie. In contrast to the absence of any secrets on the open plains, hills are exalting, "jouant avec nous un jeu d'attente, de surprise, nous tenant vraiment en suspens." The association between hills and the child-like game of hide-and-seek is noteworthy because this protective nature is likewise identified with clouds, with the mere mirage of hills sighted on the plains, as for the Doukhobors of "La Vallée Houdou," with an escape into fantasy, and, therefore, with the play of illusion and reality. When Eveline initially finds herself in the Pembina hills of Manitoba, she is confused: "Se crut-elle transportée dans le paysage de son enfance [Québec], revenue à son point de départ, et ainsi toute sa longue vie serait à refaire? Ou bien lui parut-il que le paysage se jouait de ses désirs en lui proposant une illusion seulement?"[36] Eveline is in a real chain of hills, but she also has the illusion of having returned to her past, an illusion that will become reality only when she dies.

Eveline, like her own mother, like Mme Beaulieu, the Doukhobors, Sam Lee Wong, and Smouillya, has spent much of her adult life in a natural environment that she does not particularly like. All of these characters, in fact, have been forced by circumstances, by family obligations or by their dreams as immigrants, to live surrounded by immensity when they prefer and desperately search for the comfort of hills. To these individuals, the plains, like the Northern landscape for Mme Beaulieu, are silent, motionless, boring, barren, harsh, insensitive, and cruel; they represent an immense void. Ironically, this natural enemy, about which one complains and in which one will never feel at home, exerts almost a macabre attraction for these characters. Elizabeth Beaulieu spends much of her time, "pensive et triste à sa baie vitrée, incapable de s'arracher à la fascination qu'exerçait sur elle le morne horizon glacial," while Mémère can never leave the Manitoban plains that repulse her but attach her to the memory of her productive years as a spouse and mother. Mme Beaulieu will finally leave the immensity of the North, but Mémère will die, engulfed in this vastness of space.[37]

Since, as has been seen, childhood is identified with springtime; adults continually attempt some form of *recommencement* in their lives; old age is linked with autumn; death is likened to winter; the entire cycle of life, death, and rebirth is associated with cyclical nature; and finally since the exterior environment has a direct influence upon the lives of individuals, it is logical that human actions and thoughts in Roy's fiction be developed against a backdrop of powerfully depicted seasonal changes. It has been stated that there are only two seasons in Canada, winter and summer. In Gabrielle Roy's world of nature, however, all four seasons receive their just literary treatment.

Of the four seasons, autumn appears the least in Roy's fiction. It is predominantly a transitory period of time during which people work together for the harvest, birds fly South, and the wind begins to ravage flowers as it announces the arrival of winter. Cold Canadian winters are extremely prevalent in the Royan world—in the city, on the Manitoban plains, and in the extreme North of the country. They are, in fact, deeply loved by Chenevert, Cordorai, the Eskimos, and most Royan children. Whether it be in Montreal or on the tundra, however, winter brings an abundance of snow, a cosmic negation in its universal whiteness, and a symbol of the cold that is contrasted with the warmth of the home. In Roy's fiction, snow also helps Elsa and Ian to hide in the immensity of the tundra, while it creates enormous difficulties for Courte-Queue who is trying to protect her kittens.[38]

Most importantly for these characters, with winter come the typical Royan *tourbillons,* the powerful winds, and the dangerous snowstorms or *tempêtes.* In every one of her fictional works, these agressive forces of nature surround her characters who struggling against them as if their very existences were being threatened, are also attracted to such a demonic display of power. Florentine, for example, is often caught in and even equated with the cold *tourbillon de neige* against which she fights but that will inevitably engulf her. Chenevert looks through his hospital window and watches a passer-by struggling against the raging elements but managing to continue toward his personal affairs; the bank teller envies this stranger. Dr. Raymond of "La Source au désert" actually abandons himself to a furious snowstorm so as to assuage his own suffering. Cordorai, in Paris, misses the violent storms of Northern Canada, while the teacher of *Ces Enfants de ma vie* sees these forces of nature as "les anges révoltés" but realizes that they call to her, to her deep sense of imagination. And finally the young Christine, lost in a raging snowstorm in Manitoba, is overpowered by its Luciferian and yet fascinating nature:

> L'exaltation que m'a toujours donnée la tempête était trop forte pour que le sentiment du danger pût avoir de prise sur moi. Debout près de la cabane, j'écoutais le vent, d'abord préoccupée de saisir ce qu'il disait, de définir ses grands coups de cymbale, ensuite sa pauvre plainte longuement étirée. Comment, sans autre instrument que lui-même, le vent produisait-il une telle variété de sons, un orchestre complet, parfois d'éclats de rire et de douleur![39]

Similarly, negative and positive aspects of spring and summer are depicted in the Royan literary world, although, once again, her characters are fundamentally drawn toward these seasons with their flourishing landscapes. Spring has, first of all, already been seen as the time for pathetic house moves, for the annual *déménagement* of people in whom is reborn the illusion of hope and freedom. More realistic, but no less negative, is the stifling image of the hot summer, seen as oppressive and suffocating, with no wind, for example, to cool M. Saint-Hilaire, nor to chase away the insects from the cows of *Cet Eté qui chantait.* When the wind does blow in the spring or summer, it can be powerful and angry as in a storm over Lake Winnipeg; it can destroy the flowers in Berthe's garden of *Cet Eté qui chantait* and in Martha Yaramko's garden:

> A deux pas de la maison, aux prises avec le vent, elle [Martha] ressemblait à quelque vague forme humaine engagée dans une tempête de sable au désert, et les fleurs autour d'elle, courbées dans le même sens, étaient comme des papillons déjetés. . . . Et parfois l'une d'elles, arrachée, se mettait à tournoyer comme dans une spirale invisible.

This "tempête de sable" reminds one that the winds of spring and summer are also associated with dust storms, especially across the plains. Throughout the stories of *Un Jardin au bout du monde,* Roy has created the *leit-motif* of this incessantly plaintive sound of the wind, this "tempête poudreuse," that "poussait en tourbillons la terre poudreuse," as well as the lives of the inhabitants of the plains, lives that are similarly described by Martha as "un immense exil poudreux. . . ."[40]

But spring and summer also bring the sun, the warmth of light and color, and the possibility for *recommencement,* as in the rebirth of nature and the dawn of each new day. Even in the city with the arrival of spring, there is a short period of human kindness and relaxation. In the country, nature and the world itself appear to be fresh and young; flowers, especially, seem child-like, "par leur naïveté, une sorte d'enfance éternelle de la création." Both the few days of spring in Montreal and the fragile nature of flowers, however, make one realize that this rebirth of the earth is temporary and that spring soon becomes summer, on its way toward autumn. Martha, particularly happy and relaxed at dusk rather than at dawn, sees her life as linked to these seasons, as "cette heure tardive de l'été et de sa vie." She thinks about summer, "à tout ce qu'elle avait fait dans sa vie en faveur de cette courte saison, pour la retenir, l'embellir, la voir resplendir. . . . L'été est un grand mystère, pensait-elle, autant que l'espoir, autant que la jeunesse." Like the *Enchanted Summer* that is beautiful but short-lived, the flowers of summer cannot last forever: "Il [a bouquet] disait le jeune été fragile, à peine est-il né qu'il commence à en mourir."[41]

Despite the temporary nature of the seasons and of the natural world, they are also cyclical and, therefore, eternal. It is, in fact, for both of these aspects of the environment that Royan characters express such a deep need to develop a rapport with their natural surroundings: they want to delight in nature before it disappears into a new season; and they desire to become a part of the permanence of creation. This second goal is that which is clearly suggested by Gabrielle Roy whenever she creates a resemblance between or a mutual existence of one of her fictional characters and a mountain or hill. Elsa is bent over, in the image of the distant mountains, while Sam Lee Wong assumes the form of the old hills, worn by time. As for Pierre and "la Resplendissante," they exist for one another. He has discovered the aesthetic ideal that will become the culmination of his life, while the mountain will be recreated by him for others:

> Je suis belle extraordinairement, c'est vrai, disait-elle. En fait de montagne, je suis peut-être la mieux réussie de la création. . . . Cependant, personne ne m'ayant vue jusqu'ici, est-ce que j'existais vraiment? Tant que l'on n'a pas été contenu en un regard, a-t-on la vie? . . .

Et par toi, disait-elle encore, par toi, enfin, Pierre, je vais
exister.[42]

Gaston Bachelard writes of this same power of a look, of
le regard, when he discusses the universal symbolism of water.
He equates a reflection on water with an aquatic eye on the
countryside, with the first vision of the world. Water will also
reflect the life cycles of humanity. It has been shown that
water imagery, in the Royan literary world, is typically linked
both to the birth and to the death of people: Chenevert is
reborn at Lac Vert before dying; Mémère recalls "la rivière
Assomption" of Quebec before she dies in Manitoba; Martine
bathes her feet in a river before her death; Elsa and Winnie
wander to their deaths alongside the Koksoak, symbol, with
Lake Winnipeg, of the circular and eternal nature of the universe
and of humanity. Roy herself has stated that the cycles of
life resemble the seas and the tides; both rivers and life are
in movement and, as such, are close to one another. Even
human emotions resemble the flow of water: "J'ai toujours
pensé du coeur humain qu'il est un peu comme la mer, sujet
aux marées, que la joie y monte en un flux progressif avec son
chant de vagues, de bonheur, de félicité; mais qu'ensuite, lorsque
se retire la haute mer, elle laisse apparaître à nos yeux une
désolation infinie."[43]

It is this "chant de vagues" that speaks to human beings
and initiates, therefore, a rapport of mutual communication.
With their eyes and desires turned toward the water in which
they see themselves reflected, M. Saint-Hilaire and Christine
listen to the "murmure infatigable" and to "la petite phrase
chuchotée" of Lake Winnipeg, as it poetically sings to them
what Roy later describes as "le plus ancien chant de la Terre."
The Koksoak also murmurs to Elsa, pathetically while she is
being raped, later while accompanied by her son, and finally
when she is alone on its banks, with her life then determined
and, like the river, without any possibility of changing their
mutual course toward the sea.[44]

Rivers, in their rapports with people, can represent not
only communication, but also separation, since the Koksoak
is seen as dangerous and tempestuous and divides the two Eskimo
towns. This same danger and power of water appear in the great
rivers of Ungava and in the rapids that carry Pierre and his boat
along and destroy his artistic tools. But it is precisely this force

that draws people toward the water, causes them to build communities on its banks, and, thus, creates a reflection, both positive and destructive, between a river and a people. Roy saw the Saint Lawrence River in this perspective:

> Mes randonnées [in Montréal] . . . aboutissaient presque toujours au fleuve, en un long tête-à-tête avec lui, vieux chant lui aussi de notre passé, mon Gange à moi. . . . Seules l'ont célébré quelques âmes très perceptives. Mais le plus souvent outragé, insulté, pollué, chargé de nos immondices et de notre dédain, on en a fait le reflet de notre plus triste condition.

Symbol of both collective origin and destiny, the Saint Lawrence will ultimately leave Quebec and make its way toward the purifying ocean, for, as Cordorai notes while looking at the Seine, "toutes les rivières sont-elles de même nature. . . . Toutes les rivières du monde ne sont-elles pas à tous, et pour tout confondre, tout réunir?" Water is the image of humanity and of nature, since it symbolizes the interdependence and unity of all of the elements of the world.[45]

Water also reflects the sky, with its clouds and, especially, its wind—like the water, furious and destructive, associated with birth, death, and eternity, but also gentle and warm in the joys of spring and summer. Also similar to water, the Royan wind speaks to people, has a true dialogue with Isaac, Thaddeus, and Elsa. With its plaintive cries and thirst for freedom, it speaks, in particular, to Martha who sees not only herself in the image of this nomad, but also all of humanity:

> Tous les mouvements de l'âme, la stérile révolte humaine l'ébranlant presque jusqu'à la folie, les grands coups d'ennui frappant de toutes parts, et aussi l'abandon, la douceur, le calme, il semblait que le vent connût tout cela et tour à tour cherchât à leur donner expression. "Il doit connaître les âmes, un peu de ce qui s'y passe," pensait parfois Martha, "car sans cela comment pourrait-il être si changeant, si impétueux, parfois soumis, mais toujous porté à chercher, à chercher. . . ."
>
> Et comme si le son de cette voix humaine eût attiré le vent, il franchit le seuil.[46]

Like the moving water, once again, wind is part of the eternal flow of nature and humanity, for it rocks people in their *balançoires,* just as it gently stirs the branches of trees, and thus provides a comforting motion, in *Cet Eté qui chantait,* for the crows who are perched upon this natural cradle. It is also the wind that, like a conductor, inspires and directs the music of summer:

> Jamais pour ainsi dire ne tarissait le vent du sud-ouest remplissant l'air du bruissement d'une rivière. . . . Ce vent béni, je l'imagine né dans un lointain pays heureux où les êtres ne se donnent plus la chasse, mais vivent tranquilles les uns à côté des autres. . . . Il y avait des accalmies. Alors, le vent se taisant, la musique des feuillages tombant d'un coup, on reprenait pied dans ce qu'on appelle le "réel. . . ." Mais bientôt renaissait à pleine atmosphère la musique stéréophonique de ces journées d'été à la campagne.
>
> En vérité, elle était complexe et exigeait une nombreuse participation. . . .
>
> A la fin, se joignent tous les instruments pour reprendre ensemble le thème de l'été triomphant. . . . Alors . . . chacun raconte une mystérieuse et secrète entente.[47]

As the wind rocks birds that are perched on the branches of trees, these animals are seen as navigating in a cradle-boat that offers them both stability and movement. Throughout the Royan rural landscape, trees, the symbol of both verticality and female roundness, of nature's shelter and nest, are associated with peace, maternal protection, hope, and unity. People can gather around a tree in order to converse, and even the two twin trees of *Cet Eté qui chantait* are themselves personified to the extent that they create their own musical dialogue. Elsewhere in Roy's works, human-like trees are grouped together as if they were exchanging news. Individual characters are, in addition, linked to trees—in particular, maternal and often elderly women to solid but solitary oak trees. Mémère, Eveline, and Martha are all seen as trees, while Alicia is identified, as well, with a protective oak, and Martine is a bending reed who has given birth to children, as strong as trees. But M. Saint-Hilaire, a parental figure to Christine, is also likened to a tree, while throughout the entire novel, Pierre Cordorai consistently resembles this solitary creature of nature.[48]

If there is any aspect of nature, however, that is the most prevalent in the Royan world, it is the flower, with its extension to bouquets and gardens. Seen as the world in miniature, flowers have even been made the titles of two of Roy's works: *Un Jardin au bout du monde,* translated as *Garden in the Wind,* and *La Rivière sans repos,* originally to be entitled *Fleur boréale* and, interestingly, translated as *Windflower.* The Royan garden does appear in only three instances—the Catholic priest's in Fort-Chimo, Martha's and Berthe's—but images of flowers, both wild and cultivated, occur in every work and possess numerous attributes. They offer friendship, communication, and happiness to humanity, since they symbolize youth, love, and the warmth of Southern places. A bouquet, or more poetically, "un mobile de fleurs," brings music and the color of life to people. Flowers also possess within them the mysteries of nature: from a seed is born the magnificence of natural beauty. And flowers are, sadly, fragile, delicate, and short-lived. Like the roses that are given to the dead child, Yolande, flowers will soon die in the autumn chill.[49]

In the humanistic world of nature depicted in Gabrielle Roy's fiction, it is logical that the author give to animals, at times, the status of a character. Images of animals are seen in Roy's earlier works, but it is predominantly in *Cet Eté qui chantait* and in her two stories for children that they become characters in their own right. Bossie, the cow, and Courte-Queue, the cat, are, of course, central to the children's tales, but in the enchanted summer of Royan nature, one also meets M. Toung, the frog, la Trotteuse, the Cow, Jeannot, the crow, Tontine, the dog, Grande-Minoune-Maigre and Mouffette, the cats, and a host of other unnamed animals. As characters in a natural environment of desired peace and reconciliation, these animals often have a close rapport with certain, sensitive human beings, especially with Christine or the narrator of several fictional works and with Berthe and Wilbrod of *Cet Eté qui chantait.* The blackbird is described as a friend; the animals of the surrounding countryside accompany their rural neighbors to mass; and the fireflies, with their fleeting but brilliant light aid their human companions: "S'éteignent, se rallument sans trêve sur l'herbe noire d'innombrables phares minuscules comme pour guider dans la nuit d'invisibles voyageurs. Ce pourrait être vous, ce pourrait être moi, qui avons souvent à chercher notre chemin."[50]

Not only do Royan animals relate to people, but they also possess human characteristics themselves. The dance of the prairie chickens resembles humans, while these birds, water hens, and ducks are all likened to the human soul. The crows perched together on trees do not communicate nor even know one another; they are like people. The fear, happiness, distress, and confidence of the plovers reflect the emotions of all of us. Reversing these similarities, people are seen as resembling individual types of birds, while the children of *Ces Enfants de ma vie* all sing as if they, too, were perched on trees.[51]

It is the specific identification or intimate rapport between a character and an animal, however, that is the most fascinating in Roy's fiction. In all of these relationships, one sees either the image of a free animal-person who is tamed, captured, or killed or the complex merger of the pursuer and the pursued. Médéric Eymard, for example, is closely associated with his horse, Gaspard, and especially, with the trout that allow themselves to be picked up and caressed by human hands. Birds are particularly prevalent in the Royan world, for these animals represent the freedom of the human body, mind, and soul: Maman is linked to sea gulls; Reverend Paterson is a bird of the tundra; Nil is a lark; and Pierre, as an artist, resembles a captured bird.[52]

The most intimate and complex association between a person and an animal, however, occurs in that between Pierre Cordorai and a caribou that he chases, wounds, and finally kills. At one point during this long pursuit, Pierre looks into the eyes of the animal and, in this reciprocal *regard,* sees both the laws of nature and a sense of fraternity with this creature who represents the sacrificial nature of all of life, of the animal and of the hunter-artist. Pierre understands and accepts this identification when he kills the animal:

> Les yeux du caribou écroulé se tournèrent vers lui, le fixèrent avec une détresse vivante encore, infiniment résignée, puis s'obscurcirent. Alors, transi de froid, Pierre se laissa glisser près du caribou mort qui doucement commença de le réchauffer. Dans l'étendue sans fin de la toundra, ils formaient une petite tache immobile et comme fraternelle. L'aube parut. L'intensité de sa faim ranima Pierre. Maintenant, après l'avoir réchauffé, le caribou allait lui devenir chair, sang et pensée.

Later in Paris Pierre recounts his adventure, speaking "d'un seul et même être, poursuivi et poursuivant." And finally, in the self-portrait painted before his premature death, Pierre actually draws himself as a human-animal: "Qu'avait donc voulu suggérer Pierre?   Quelle alliance étroite de l'âme avec les forces primitives?   Ou la haute plainte d'une créature en qui se fût fondue l'angoisse de tuer et d'être tuée?"   It is precisely this close alliance between the human and natural world that Cordorai-Roy is depicting.[53]

The outside environment, and in particular that found in the natural surroundings of a rural setting, is, in fact, so important in Gabrielle Roy's fiction that when nature becomes silent, the end of her story has arrived.   Her characters are never truly alone if they can communicate with their milieu, if they can create or rediscover links with their friends in nature, for one of Roy's literary goals was to "unir des paysages aux états d'âme."   There are, of course, certain Royan characters who are more at ease in their natural environment, who feel the immensity of the world reflected within their innermost selves, and who sense such an intimate harmony with their milieu that they tend to surpass the contradictions of the world: Alexandre at Lac Vert, Pierre in Northern Canada, Christine and M. Saint-Hilaire at Lake Winnipeg, Elsa, Barnaby, and Ian in Fort-Chimo, the narrator and Berthe during their enchanted summer, Martha in her garden, and children in general throughout Roy's works.[54]

As for the Tousignant family in *La Petite Poule d'eau*, they and the entire work have been viewed as a lost paradise in which perfect reconciliation between humanity and the natural world had been attained.   This peaceful universe has been seen, therefore, as a mere dream.   It is interesting to note, however, that Roy herself was no longer certain that the world described in this work was unreal; it may have been a humanistic goal, but it was not a dream.   This ideal was, in fact, attained at her summer residence, as depicted in *Cet Eté qui chantait*.   The world of nature and of human beings in this work is that of a pure garden, an enchanted circle, in which perfect understanding and communion, a child-like and almost primitive innocence and happiness are experienced.   But once again, although Gabrielle Roy may have had certain ideals, she was also realistic. The beauty attained in *Cet Eté qui chantait* only lasts for one summer, and during that season there exists for all creatures of nature not only joy and love, but also sadness and death.   If it were described in any other manner, this semi-fictional world would not be truthful: " 'Tous ne sont pas heureux au même moment. . . . Un jour c'est l'un, le lendemain l'autre. . . . Quelques-uns jamais, hélas! . . . Ici on est heureux. . . . Là-bas non. . . . Quand on sera heureux ensemble, ce sera le paradis . . . le paradis . . . le paradis. . . .' " Gabrielle Roy did not desire to return, nor did she want her characters to return, to a primitive paradise. It was enough to know, like Alexandre Chenevert, that, if even temporarily, paradise can exist.[55]

NOTES

[1] Gabrielle Roy, "*Terre des Hommes:* Le Thème raconté," *Fragiles Lumières de la terre: Ecrits divers 1942-1970,* Collection Prose Entière (Montréal: Les Editions Quinze, 1978), p. 203; Gabrielle Roy, *Cet Eté qui chantait* (Québec-Montréal: Les Editions Françaises, 1972), pp. VII, 76; Gabrielle Roy, *La Montagne secrète* (1961; rpt. Montréal: Librairie Beauchemin Limitée, 1974), p. 145. Roy's introduction was originally published as "Introduction: Le Thème raconté/The Theme Unfolded," in *Terre des Hommes/Man and His World* (Montreal and Toronto: La Campagnie canadienne de l'Exposition universelle de 1967/Canadian Corporation for the 1967 World Exhibition, 1967), pp. 21-60. See also Gabrielle Roy, "Le Long, Long Voyage," *Le Bulletin des Agriculteurs,* 41, No. 5 (mai 1945), 8-9, 51-52; Paul Socken, "Gabrielle Roy as Journalist," *Canadian Modern Language Review,* 30, No. 2 (January 1974), 98.

[2] Paul Socken, "L'Harmonie dans l'oeuvre de Gabrielle Roy," *Travaux de Linguistique et de Littérature* (l'Université de Strasbourg), 15, No. 2 (1977), 275-292; Paul Socken, "The Influence of Physical and Social Environment on Character in the Novels of Gabrielle Roy," *DAI,* 38 (December 1977), 3489A-3490A (University of Toronto); Paul Socken, " 'Le Pays de l'amour' in the Works of Gabrielle Roy," *Revue de l'Université d'Ottawa,* 46, No. 3 (juillet-septembre 1976), 317. See also Annette Saint-Pierre, *Gabrielle Roy: Sous le signe du rêve* (Saint-Boniface, Manitoba: Editions du Blé, 1975), p. 130; Monique Genuist, *La Création romanesque chez Garbielle Roy* (Montréal: Le Cercle du Livre de France, 1966), pp. 121-123.

[3] Personal interview with Gabrielle Roy, 29 June 1980. See also

Eva Kushner, "Dossier Gabrielle Roy: De la représentation à la vision du monde," *Québec Français,* No. 36 (décembre 1979), pp. 38-39; Guy Savoie, "Le Réalisme du cadre spatio-temporel de *Bonheur d'occasion,*" Thesis Université Laval 1972, pp. 104-106; Ben Shek, "L'Espace et la description symbolique dans les romans 'montréalais' de Gabrielle Roy," *Liberté,* 13i (1971), 78-86.

[4] André Brochu, "Thèmes et structures de *Bonheur d'occasion,*" in *L'Instance critique* (Montréal: Leméac, 1974), pp. 220-223; André Brochu, "Gabrielle Roy," Notes from course on author, Université de Montréal, Printemps 1978, taken by one of his students; Jacques Blais, "L'Unité organique de *Bonheur d'occasion,*" *Etudes Françaises,* 6, No. 1 (février 1970), 28-31; Réjean Robidoux et A. Renaud, *Le Roman canadien-français du vingtième siècle* (Ottawa: Editions de l'Université d'Ottawa, 1966), pp. 80-81; George-André Vachon, "L'Espace politique et social dans le roman québécois," *Recherches Sociographiques,* 7, No. 3 (septembre-décembre, 1966), 261-273; Socken, "L'Harmonie dans l'oeuvre de Gabrielle Roy," pp. 275-276. In the parallelism between individuals and masses, and in her creation of types, Roy has also been likened to Zola. See Shek, pp. 78-86. Roy herself said that there was no direct influence of Zola or Naturalism on her works, only a general similarity in that some form of determinism from environment and from heredity is present in the works of all novelists and short story writers. Roy's preferred text by Zola, by the way, was *Germinal.* Personal interview with Gabrielle Roy, 29 June 1980. See also Paula Gilbert Lewis, "Gabrielle Roy and Emile Zola: French Naturalism in Quebec," *Modern Language Studies,* 11, No. 3 (Fall 1981), 44-50.

[5] Personal interview with Gabrielle Roy, 29 June 1980. See also Shek, p. 96.

[6] Gabrielle Roy, "Le Pays de *Bonheur d'occasion,*" in *Morceaux,* ed. Robert Guy Scully (Montréal: Les Editions du Noroît, 1978), pp. 114, 117. See also pp. 115, 116. Gabrielle Roy, "Les Deux Saint-Laurent," *Le Bulletin des Agriculteurs,* 37, No. 6 (juin 1941), 40; Gabrielle Roy, "Du port aux banques," *Le Bulletin des Agriculteurs,* 37, No. 8 (août 1941), 11; Gabrielle Roy, "Après trois cents ans," *Le Bulletin des Agriculteurs,* 37, No. 9 (septembre 1941), 39. In this last work, see also pp. 9, 37, 38. See also Gabrielle Roy, "Est-Ouest," *Le Bulletin des Agriculteurs,* 37, No. 7 (juillet 1941), 9, 25-28; Savoie, pp. 18, 21-36; Marc Gagné, *Visages de Gabrielle Roy* (Montréal: Librairie Beauchemin Limitée, 1973), pp. 39-42. In her early short stories, Roy describes the city in a similar fashion, as possessing a power of attraction but creating anonymity and a need to escape. See Gabrielle Roy, "Le Monde à l'envers," *La Revue Moderne,* 21, No. 6 (octobre 1939), 6, 34; Gabrielle Roy, "Gérard le

pirate," *La Revue Moderne,* 22, No. 1 (mai 1940), 38; Gabrielle Roy, "La Derniere Pêche," *La Revue Moderne,* 22, No. 7 (novembre 1940), 9; Gabrielle Roy, "La Sonate à l'aurore," *La Revue Moderne,* 22, No. 11 (mars 1941), 36. In "Le Pays de *Bonheur d'occasion,*" in addition, Roy interestingly states that the Montreal, the Quebec that she discovered during those early years was that before any identity crises, before the Quiet Revolution of the 1960s, before "les prises de conscience." What she discovered was essentially an ugly city, with islands of beauty. What she clearly realized, as well, was the basic distinction between the *Québécois,* with their laughter and gaiety, and the English-Canadians who had not learned to laugh at themselves. See especially pp. 114-115. It was this article that Mireille Dansereau was interested in making into a short documentary film on Montreal. Personal interview with Gabrielle Roy, 29 June 1980.

[7] Gabrielle Roy, *Bonheur d'occasion* (1945; rpt. Montréal: Librairie Beauchemin Limitée, 1973), pp. 32, 221. See also pp. 15, 20, 44, 83-88, 101-103, 122-123, 132-136, 149, 183, 186, 194, 230-231, 243, 247, 250, 270-280; Gabrielle Roy, "*Bonheur d'occasion* aujourd'hui," *Le Bulletin des Agriculteurs,* 44, No. 1 (janvier 1948), 6, 20-22; Roy, "Le Pays de *Bonheur d'occasion,*" p. 117; Kushner, pp. 38-39; François Ricard, *Gabrielle Roy,* Ecrivains canadiens d'aujourd'hui, No. 11 (Montréal: Editions Fides, 1975), pp. 62-64; Donald Cameron, "Gabrielle Roy: A Bird in a Prison Window," in *Conversations with Canadian Novelists* (Toronto: Macmillan of Canada, 1973), p. 131; Jean Paul Desrochers, "La Famille dans l'oeuvre de Gabrielle Roy," Thesis Université Laval, 1965, pp. 26-29, 38, 40-45; Michel-Lucien Gaulin, "Le Thème du bonheur dans l'oeuvre de Gabrielle Roy," Thesis Université de Montréal 1961, pp. 30-41; Maurice Lemire, "*Bonheur d'occasion* ou le salut par la guerre," *Recherches Sociographiques,* 10 (1969), 26-35; A. Vanasse, "Vers une solitude désespérante," *L'Action Nationale,* 55, No. 7 (mars 1966), 844-845. The only rural character in the novel who appears to be happy with her urban life is Florentine's friend, Marguerite.

[8] Roy, *Bonheur d'occasion,* p. 33. See also pp. 18-19, 31-32, 51-52, 113, 118-121, 252-254, 269, 285-286; Roy, "Le Pays de *Bonheur d'occasion,*" p. 116; Blais, pp. 28-31; Savoie, pp. 68-74, 120-127; Albert Le Grand, "Gabrielle Roy ou l'être partagé," *Etudes Françaises,* 1ere année, No. 2 (juin 1965), pp. 47-49. The tin flute so desperately desired by Daniel and given to him before his death, can be seen as a symbol of all of these urban seductions. See Lemire, pp. 26-35.

[9] Roy, *Bonheur d'occasion,* pp. 26-27, 53, 101-103, 150-151, 208; André Brochu, "La Structure sémantique de *Bonheur d'occasion,*" *Revue des Sciences Humaines,* 45, No. 173 (janvier-mars 1979), 37-47; Brochu,

"Gabrielle Roy"; Gagné, pp. 70-79; Ricard, pp. 55-58, 62-64; Le Grand, pp. 44-47.

[10]Roy, "Le Pays de *Bonheur d'occasion*," p. 121. See also Roy, *Bonheur d'occasion*, pp. 83-90, 188-189, 312; Brochu, "La Structure sémantique," pp. 37-47; Brochu, "Gabrielle Roy"; Ricard, pp. 55-57; as travel in Chapter VI. Similarly, Rose-Anna and Azarius's trip to their childhood countryside of Richelieu will last only one day and will return them to the reality of Saint-Henri. See Roy, *Bonheur d'occasion*, pp. 168-177.

[11]Roy, *Bonheur d'occasion*, pp. 12, 26-29, 32-34, 44, 53, 75, 101-102, 186, 204-205, 208, 221-223, 227, 252, 286, 291, 334-340, 344-345; Brochu, "Thèmes et structures," pp. 229-233; Brochu, "La Structure sémantique," pp. 37-47; Brochu, "Gabrielle Roy"; Ricard, pp. 55-57; Le Grand, pp. 44-47; Gaulin, p. 36; Savoie, pp. 36-37, 42-47, 57-64.

[12]Roy, *Bonheur d'occasion*, pp. 12, 26-27. See also pp. 75-76, 93, 102, 110, 119, 222-223, 230, 232, 240, 291, 344; Brochu, "Thèmes et structures," pp. 220, 224, 225, 228-239. Analyses of both male and female characters in reference to their identification with *la droite* or *le cercle* and, therefore, with direct or circular roads, will be found in Chapter VI. It should be noted that the one contented rural character in this urban setting, Marguerite, also sees her life as a happy and "perpétuelle ronde de *sundaes*," served to her customers, one of whom will hopefully become her husband. The positive roundness or circularity of her life, however, is scornfully viewed by Florentine. See Roy, *Bonheur d'occasion*, p. 16.

[13]Gabrielle Roy, *Alexandre Chenevert* (1954; rpt. Montréal: Beauchemin, 1973), pp. 270, 252. See also pp. 11-12, 14, 23, 26, 94, 251-255, 269-272, 303-305.

[14]Roy, *Alexandre Chenevert*, pp. 58, 167. See also pp. 25, 31-33, 52-53, 57, 59, 62, 113, 168, 185, 271-272, 367-368; Genuist, pp. 76-77; Brochu, "Gabrielle Roy"; Desrochers, pp. 31-33; Vachon, pp. 261-273; Phyllis Grosskurth, *Gabrielle Roy*, Canadian Writers and Their Works (Toronto: Forum House, 1972), p. 29.

[15]Roy, *Alexandre Chenevert*, p. 191. See also pp. 38, 47-48, 121, 189, 265; Agnes Whitfield, "*Alexandre Chenevert:* Cercle vicieux et évasions manquées," *Voix et Images du Pays*, 8 (1974), 107-120, 125; Ricard, pp. 79-82, 84-85; Saint-Pierre, pp. 54-55; Gagné, pp. 70-79; Genuist, p. 95.

[16]Roy, *Alexandre Chenevert*, p. 259. See also pp. 105-106, 203, 261; Socken, "L'Harmonie dans l'oeuvre de Gabrielle Roy," pp. 281, 286; Vachon, pp. 261-273.

[17]Roy, *Alexandre Chenevert*, p. 268. See also pp. 263-276; Gagné, pp. 53-70. Like the Létourneau family in *Bonheur d'occasion*, there are

characters in *Alexandre Chenevert* who, in contrast to main characters, do succeed socially and economically in the city: Godias, Dr. Hudon, and M. Fontaine. It is, of course, the last who, along with the bank itself and its founder, represents the English-Canadian sector of Montreal. It is interesting that Roy, a woman writer, identifies more with this male character than with any other character. This may help to explain her atypical use of the cage or circle as masculine in this novel. Personal interview with Gabrielle Roy, 29 June 1980.

[18] Roy, *La Montagne secrète*, p. 140. See also pp. 150-151, 153-154, 157-159, 167, 171, 177-182.

[19] Roy, *Cet Eté qui chantait*, pp. 146, 160.

[20] Gabrielle Roy, "Les Deux Nègres," *Rue Deschambault* (1955; rpt. Montréal: Librairie Beauchemin Limitée, 1974), pp. 12, 15, 16, 25-26. See also pp. 21-23, 32-33; Roy, "Wilhelm," *Rue Deschambault*, p. 232; Roy, "Gagner ma vie. . . ," *Rue Deschambault*, pp. 284-285, 287-289; Gabrielle Roy, "Souvenirs du Manitoba," *La Revue de Paris*, 62e année, No. 2 (février 1955), pp. 77-79; Roy, "Le Manitoba," *Fragiles Lumières de la terre*, pp. 103-106, 110, 115-118; Gabrielle Roy, "Ely! Ely! Ely! ," *Liberté*, 21, No. 3, année 1979, No. 123 (mai-juin 1979), 15, 17-18, 20-21, 23; Gabrielle Roy, *Ces Enfants de ma vie* (Montréal: Editions Internationales Alain Stanké Ltée, 1977), pp. 93, 145, 162-163, 166-167, 172, 181, 185-189; Ricard, pp. 22, 62-64; Saint-Pierre, p. 93; Vachon, p. 266.

[21] Gabrielle Roy, *La Petite Poule d'eau* (1950; rpt. Montréal: Librairie Beauchemin Limitée, 1970), pp. 25, 181; Gabrielle Roy, *Un Jardin au bout du monde* (Montréal: Librairie Beauchemin Limitée, 1975), pp. 69-72, 74, 97-98, 103-110, 115-118, 125-130, 179, 195-196. In the second work, the village of Volhyn is described as isolated and uncivilized. In the first, the Métis village of Portage-des-Prés is seen as being ruled by the merchant, Bessette, who gives the inhabitants credit in his store and then allows them to repay with valuable furs, the true worth of which is unknown to them. Even in a small village, exploitation and corruption occur. See Roy, *La Petite Poule d'eau*, pp. 211-214, 221-226.

[22] Gabrielle Roy, *La Rivière sans repos* (Montréal: Librairie Beauchemin Limitée, 1971), pp. 161, 186, 192. See also pp. 15, 24, 76-80, 86-88, 159-160, 162-163, 179-180, 183-185, 190-191, 219-221, 225-234, 246-249, 287-288, 302-303; Ricard, pp. 133-137. Marc Gagné sees the actual structure of the work as binary and tertiary in rhythm, as antithesis, as well as synthesis. See Marc Gagné, "*La Rivière sans repos* de Gabrielle Roy: Etude mythocritique incluant 'Voyage en Ungava' (extraits) par Gabrielle Roy (suite)," *Revue de l'Université d'Ottawa*, 46, No. 3 (juillet-septembre 1976), 385, 388-389. Ironically, one of the reasons that this

work was not published in the United States was that it was seen not to represent faithfully Eskimo life. Personal interview with Gabrielle Roy, 29 June 1980. It is noteworthy that, as of 1980, the Quebec Government has officially changed the name of Fort-Chimo to Kuujiuaq, an Inuit name.

[23] Roy, *La Rivière sans repos*, pp. 38-46, 56-57, 63-80, 84-88, 91-94.

[24] Roy, "La Rivière sans repos," pp. 124-128, 135, 138-141, 143-147, 159-163, 174-178, 246-249, 263-266, 273-280, 285, 306-311. See also Marc Gagné, "*La Rivière sans Repos* de Gabrielle Roy: Etude mythocritique incluant 'Voyage en Ungava' (extraits) par Gabrielle Roy," *Revue de l'Université d'Ottawa*, 46, No. 1 (janvier-mars 1976), 92-99, 105-106. Not only do all American G.I.'s look alike to Elsa, but white people in general are seen as having a certain air about them, an air that Elsa begins to assume as she turns toward the White world. She becomes thinner, looks harrassed and preoccupied, and sets for herself increasingly difficult goals. See Roy, "La Rivière sans repos," p. 165.

[25] Roy, "La Rivière sans repos," pp. 122-123, 136, 138-141, 157, 166-171, 212-213, 267-268, 296-301.

[26] Roy, "La Rivière sans repos," pp. 123-124, 159-163, 180-183, 246-249, 253-262, 270.

[27] Roy, "La Rivière sans repos," pp. 248, 202-203. See also pp. 235-249; Brochu, "Gabrielle Roy."

[28] Roy, *Alexandre Chenevert*, p. 263. See also pp. 24, 181-183, 189, 191, 196, 215, 237, 265, 368-369, 383; Roy, *Bonheur d'occasion*, pp. 83, 150-151, 311; Roy, *La Montagne secrète*, pp. 97, 157-159, 180, 190; Gabrielle Roy, *La Route d'Altamont*, Collection L'Arbre, No. 10 (Montréal: Editions HMH, 1966), pp. 79-84, 117; Gabrielle Roy, *Ma Vache Bossie* (Montréal: Editions Leméac, Inc., 1976), p. 23; Ricard, pp. 65-74, 82-87; Saint-Pierre, pp. 54-55; Grosskurth, pp. 14, 21-24, 33; Whitfield, pp. 114, 116. This opposition between the city and the country is further developed in Roy's fiction with an opposition between East and West or North and South.

[29] Gabrielle Roy, "Plus que le pain," *Le Bulletin des Agriculteurs*, 38, No. 2 (février 1942), 33-35; Roy, "Les Hutterites," "Le Manitoba," "Terre des Hommes," *Fragiles Lumières de la terre*, pp. 26, 105, 107, 226; Roy, *La Petite Poule d'eau*, p. 174; Roy, *Alexandre Chenevert*, pp. 202, 205-207; Roy, *Rue Deschambault*, pp. 39, 113, 123, 151-153, 159, 218; Roy, *La Montagne secrète*, pp. 33, 115, 121; Roy, "La Rivière sans repos," pp. 220-221; Roy, *Cet Eté qui chantait*, pp. 27-28, 53-55, 72, 97-98, 107-111; Gagné, *Visages de Gabrielle Roy*, pp. 28-29, 34; Kushner, p. 39.

[30] Roy, *Alexandre Chenevert*, pp. 203, 204. See also pp. 201, 205-207, 228-230, 237-245, 257-259; Roy, *Fragiles Lumières de la terre*, pp. 30, 51,

55; Roy, *La Petite Poule d'eau,* pp. 12-14, 23, 32, 73-74, 104, 153, 156, 169, 211, 230, 232; Roy, *Rue Deschambault,* pp. 90, 117, 206; Roy, *La Montagne secrète,* pp. 11-18, 169.

[31] Roy, "Souvenirs du Manitoba," p. 83; Roy, "Le Manitoba," *Fragiles Lumières de la terre,* p. 109. In this last work see also pp. 107-108, 110, 112, 118-120. Roy also spoke of her own love for the plains in Alice Parizeau, "Gabrielle Roy, grande romancière canadienne," *Châtelaine,* 7, No. 4 (avril 1966), 44; Personal interview with Gabrielle Roy, 29 June 1980. For her characters' love of immensity see Roy, *Rue Deschambault,* pp. 113, 244; Roy, *La Montagne secrète,* pp. 89-90, 157-159, 167; Roy, *La Rivière sans repos,* pp. 32, 87, 184-185, 240, 268; Roy, *Un Jardin au bout du monde,* pp. 62, 64, 82-83; Gabrielle Roy, *Ces Enfants de ma vie* (Montréal: Editions Internationales Alain Stanké Ltée, 1977), p. 95; Gagné, *Visages de Gabrielle Roy,* pp. 110-115.

[32] Roy, *La Route d'Altamont,* pp. 191-192; Roy, "Un Jardin au bout du monde," p. 181; Roy, *Ces Enfants de ma vie,* pp. 156-157. See also Roy, *Rue Deschambault,* pp. 44, 58; Roy, *La Route d'Altamont,* pp. 83, 162-163, 170, 180, 189-191, 207, 215, 219, 251; Roy, "Un Jardin au bout du monde," pp. 201-204; Roy, *Ces Enfants de ma vie,* p. 102; Paula Gilbert Lewis, "The Incessant Call of the Open Road: Gabrielle Roy's Incorrigible Nomads," *The French Review,* 53, No. 6 (May 1980), 820-821. Gaston Bachelard associates the plains with a sentiment of "avec-moi" and "avec-nous." He feels that the sight of this immensity makes one grow, both in domination and in dispersion. Plains are pacifying, calm, and restful. See Gaston Bachelard, *La Poétique de l'espace,* Bibliothèque de philosophie contemporaine (Paris: Presses Universitaires de France, 1978), pp. 172, 184-188; Jean Chevalier et Alain Gheerbrant, *Dictionnaire des symboles* (Paris: Robert Laffont/Editions Jupiter, 1982), p. 762. A similar passion is evident in Roy's fiction for what is described as the tragic beauty of the cold, immense, and harsh tundra, although this particular geographic landscape is not as prevalent as the plain, familiar to Roy herself. See Roy, *La Montagne secrète,* pp. 117-121; Roy, "La Rivière sans repos," pp. 236, 240; Gagné, " 'Voyage en Ungava' par Gabrielle Roy," p. 370.

[33] Roy, *La Montagne secrète,* pp. 100, 103. See also pp. 101-102, 107, 108, 115, 122-124, 198; Personal interview with Gabrielle Roy, 29 June 1980; Gagné, *Visages de Gabrielle Roy,* pp. 218-221; Gérard Bessette, *Trois Romanciers québécois* (Montréal: Editions du Jour, 1973), pp. 306-307; Chevalier et Gheerbrant, pp. 645-649. The elderly Isaac also experiences happiness and freedom as he sits in his wheel chair at the top of a high hill. See Roy, *La Rivière sans repos,* pp. 99-106. Related to tall mountains and their summits are islands that attract one to them as if in

a dream, call people to them for discovery, are silent and primitive, and can, as Pierre's mountain, suggest a vague *malheur*. See Roy, *Cet Eté qui chantait*, pp. 193-198. An interpretation of this intimate rapport between Cordorai and the mountain as that between the artist and the work of art will be examined in Chapter VIII.

[34]Bessette, pp. 187-194; Gagné, *Visages de Gabrielle Roy*, p. 220; Roy, "La Vallée Houdou" and "Où iras-tu Sam Lee Wong?," *Un Jardin au bout du monde*, pp. 77-78, 81-83, 113, 137, 146-149.

[35]Roy, *Un Jardin au bout du monde*, pp. 126, 102, 82. See also pp. 61-63, 65, 81, 83, 92, 100-101, 109-111, 125, 130; Roy, *La Route d'Altamont*, pp. 49, 189-191, 193, 205-207, 229, 254; Roy, *Ces Enfants de ma vie*, pp. 155-156, 170; Chevalier et Gheerbrant, p. 269.

[36]Roy, *La Route d'Altamont*, pp. 203, 204. See also pp. 62, 200-202, 224; Roy, *Un Jardin au bout du monde*, pp. 67, 69, 145; Roy, *Ces Enfants de ma vie*, pp. 155-156, 176.

[37]Roy, "La Rivière sans repos," p. 186. See also pp. 117-119, 147, 149, 152, 156, 158, 189, 230; Roy, *La Route d'Altamont*, pp. 15-16, 39, 62, 116, 189-192, 215-221; Roy, *Un Jardin au bout du monde*, pp. 44, 58, 67, 69-71, 74, 77-78, 81-83, 94-98, 100-102, 109, 133-141; Lewis, p. 824.   Martha Yaramko prefers life on the Canadian plains, although she does speak of its straight and sad roads, as well as of the endless wind and dust. See Roy, "Un Jardin au bout du monde," pp. 153-154, 171-172.

[38]Roy, *Bonheur d'occasion*, pp. 26-27, 34, 75-76, 129; Roy, *La Petite Poule d'eau*, pp. 29, 133-134, 159-160; Roy, *Alexandre Chenevert*, pp. 121, 292, 313-315; Roy, *Rue Deschambault*, pp. 187, 188, 196; Roy, *La Montagne secrète*, pp. 38, 41-42, 49-53, 75-76, 97, 114-115, 158, 195; Roy, *La Route d'Altamont*, pp. 42-46, 71, 76, 192-193, 211, 212, 215; Roy, *La Rivière sans repos*, pp. 44, 49, 235-236; Roy, *Un Jardin au bout du monde*, pp. 101-102, 127, 178, 192, 211, 213, 214; Roy, *Courte-Queue* (Montréal: Editions Internationales Alain Stanké Ltée, 1979), pp. 24, 26, 27, 29-31, 33-36, 39; Bachelard, pp. 52-57.

[39]Roy, *Ces Enfants de ma vie*, p. 181; Roy, "La Tempête," *Rue Deschambault*, p. 255. In the first work see also pp. 33, 37, 109, 177-186. In the second see also pp. 89-90, 123, 134, 151-152, 183-184, 193, 251-253, 256-259, 285, 289, 291-293. See also Roy, *Bonheur d'occasion*, pp. 63, 93, 101-103, 110, 119, 148, 186, 291; Roy, *Alexandre Chenevert*, pp. 106, 292-203, 287, 313-315; Roy, "La Source au désert," *Le Bulletin des Agriculteurs*, 42, No. 10 (octobre 1946), 30, 34, 40; Roy, *La Montagne secrète*, pp. 61-62, 77, 121-122, 196; Roy, "La Rivière sans repos," pp. 130, 184, 242-244; Roy, *Courte-Queue*, p. 29; Gagné, *Visages de Gabrielle Roy*, pp. 120-123; Chevalier et Gheerbrant, p. 960.

[40]Roy, *Un Jardin au bout du monde*, pp. 183-184, 186, 68, 188.

See also pp. 69. 71, 74, 97-99, 100-102, 154-156, 160-163, 187, 189; Roy, *Bonheur d'occasion,* pp. 44, 83, 85, 188-189; Roy, *Rue Deschambault,* pp. 19, 193; Roy, *La Route d'Altamont,* pp. 13, 71, 76, 78-79, 89-90, 101, 107, 145-148, 150, 170; Roy, *Cet Eté que chantait,* pp. 115-118.

[41] Roy, "Un Jardin au bout du monde," pp. 170, 203, 211; Roy, *Ces Enfants de ma vie,* p. 212. In the first work see also pp. 168-169, 201-202, 204, 215. In the second see also pp. 47, 198-199, 209-211. In this work, spring is also linked to music. See also Roy, *Bonheur d'occasion,* pp. 19, 26, 145, 217-220, 228; Roy, *Alexandre Chenevert,* pp. 106-107, 180; Roy, *Rue Deschambault,* pp. 190-191, 196, 198, 201-202, 206-207, 220, 222, 266-267. In this last work, all positive aspects of spring and summer are identified with Maman. See also Roy, "Mémoire et création: Préface de *La Petite Poule d'eau,*" *Fragiles Lumières de la terre,* pp. 193-197; Roy, *La Montagne secrète,* pp. 55-59, 67-69, 100; Roy, *Cet Eté qui chantait,* pp. 75-76. *Enchanted Summer* is the English title of this last work. See also Gagné, *Visages de Gabrielle Roy,* pp. 85, 150-151; Gaston Bachelard, *La Poétique de la rêverie,* Bibliothèque de philosophie contemporaine (Paris: Presses Universitaires de France, 1974), pp. 100-101.

[42] Roy, *La Montagne secrète,* p. 102. See also pp. 89-90, 101-104, 219-222; Roy, *La Rivière sans repos,* pp. 27-29, 58-59, 99-106, 301, 314-315; Roy, *Un Jardin au bout du monde,* pp. 100-102; Brochu "Gabrielle Roy."

[43] Roy, *La Route d'Altamont,* p. 179. See also Cameron, p. 142; Roy, *Cet Eté qui chantait,* p. 93; Bachelard, *La Poétique de l'espace,* pp. 187-190; Bachelard, *La Poétique de la rêverie,* pp. 159-163, 169-173, 177. In her fiction see especially Roy, *Alexandre Chenevert,* pp. 195, 351-352, 371; Roy, *Rue Deschambault,* pp. 40, 143-144; Roy, *La Route d'Altamont,* pp. 49, 91, 101, 116-122, 145-147, 193; Roy, *La Rivière sans repos,* pp. 27-29, 58-59, 265-269, 271, 280-281, 285-286, 301, 304, 310, 314-315; Roy, *Cet Eté qui chantait,* pp. 145-148, 156-160. See also Saint-Pierre, pp. 41-45, 55-59, 63-64; Brochu, "Gabrielle Roy"; Gagné, *Visages de Gabrielle Roy,* pp. 158-161; Chevalier et Gheerbrant, pp. 374-382.

[44] Roy, *La Route d'Altamont,* pp. 115, 123; Roy, *Cet Eté qui chantait,* p. 95. In the first work see also pp. 86-87, 94, 106-107, 114, 116, 119, 130, 133, 145, 150. In the second see pp. 11, 49-51, 89, 96. See also Roy, "La Rivière sans repos," pp. 124, 125, 166-171, 271, 280-281, 294-296; Saint-Pierre, pp. 118-122; Brochu, "Gabrielle Roy."

[45] Roy, "Le Pays de *Bonheur d'occasion,*" p. 115; Roy, *La Montagne secrète,* p. 159. See also pp. 116-117 in the first work and pp. 36-39, 83-85, 179 in the second. See also Roy, *"Terre des Hommes," Fragiles Lumières de la terre,* pp. 223, 225; Gabrielle Roy, "Mon Héritage du Manitoba," *Mosaic,* 3iii (1970), 77; Roy, "La Rivière sans repos," pp. 180,

198-201, 205; Socken, "L'Harmonie dans l'oeuvre de Gabrielle Roy," pp. 280-281; Le Grand, p. 43. It should be noted, as well, that both in her apartment in Quebec City and in her summer home at Petite-Rivière-Saint-François, Roy herself had chosen to live with a view of the Saint Lawrence.

[46] Roy, "Un Jardin au bout du monde," pp. 177-178. See also pp. 171-181, 205-206; Roy, *La Rivière sans repos,* pp. 99-101, 105-106, 130, 137, 200-201, 229; Roy, *Rue Deschambault,* pp. 38, 82-84; Chevalier et Gheerbrant, pp. 997-998.

[47] Roy, *Cet Eté qui chantait,* pp. 49-51. See also pp. 39-47, 66-72; Roy, *Rue Deschambault,* pp. 168-169; Roy, "Un Jardin au bout du monde, pp. 162-163.

[48] Roy, *Bonheur d'occasion,* p. 189; Roy, "La Source au désert," p. 32; Roy, *La Petite Poule d'eau,* p. 19; Roy, *Rue Deschambault,* pp. 149, 168-169, 261, 285; Roy, *La Montagne secrète,* pp. 23-25, 30-31, 43-45, 64, 84, 148, 167, 183, 185, 200, 213, 217; Gagné " 'Voyage en Ungava' par Gabrielle Roy," p. 372; Roy, *La Route d'Altamont,* pp. 28, 43, 54-55, 62, 191. 205-206, 221-222; Roy, "Mon Héritage du Manitoba," p. 74; Roy, *La Rivière sans repos,* pp. 30, 31, 37, 117-119, 201-202; Roy, *Cet Eté qui chantait,* pp. 39-51, 105-111, 153; Roy, "Un Jardin au bout du monde," p. 205; Gagné, *Visages de Gabrielle Roy,* pp. 161-169; Ricard, pp. 138-140; Bachelard, *La Poétique de l'espace,* pp. 93-103, 182-184, 209-214; Chevalier et Gheerbrant, pp. 62-68.

[49] Roy, *Cet Eté qui chantait,* p. 79. See also pp. 12-13, 17-20, 29-31, 66-72, 118, 188-189; Roy, "Est-Ouest," p. 25; Roy, *Fragiles Lumières de la terre,* pp. 42, 58; Roy, *Bonheur d'occasion,* pp. 219, 311; Roy, "La Source au désert," pp. 35-36; Roy, *Rue Deschambault,* pp. 20, 145, 167, 197, 205; Roy, *La Rivière sans repos,* p. 82; Roy, *Un Jardin au bout du monde,* pp. 145, 157-160, 185-189, 192; Roy, *Ces Enfants de ma vie,* pp. 24, 31, 122, 209-212; Bachelard, *La Poétique de l'espace,* pp. 145-146, 148, 152, 159, 163-165; Brochu, "Gabrielle Roy"; Gagné, *Visages de Gabrielle Roy,* pp. 154-158; Gagné, "*La Rivière sans repos* de Gabrielle Roy: Etude mythocritique," (juillet-septembre 1976), p. 367; Chevalier and Gheerbrant, pp. 447-449. Roy herself was quite knowledgeable about flora and had attempted to be accurate when she composed *Cet Eté qui chantait.* A friend of hers who was an expert on trees, plants, and flowers, however, pointed out to her the inaccuracies in the book. After having been initially disturbed, Roy accepted the fact that, as long as her work was accurate in general, she had the freedom to add her own creative imagination. Personal interview with Gabrielle Roy, 29 June 1980.

[50] Roy, *Cet Eté qui chantait,* p. 174. See also pp. 13-20, 22-23, 35-36, 42-45, 49-51, 59-60, 65-72, 74, 83-92, 98-101, 107-111, 121-124, 127-132,

136-141, 145-146, 163-170, 175, 201-203; Roy, *Rue Deschambault,* pp. 41, 243; Roy, *La Route d'Altamont,* pp. 132, 159, 174-177, 183. Both Bossie and Courte-Queue are based upon real animals, the cow as a present to Roy when she was a child, and the cat as an independent, heroic animal who lived at Roy's summer residence and disappeared for long periods of time. Roy had been accused of being merely romantic in *Cet Eté qui chantait* and not at all realistic in her depiction of animals. She strongly believed, however, that what she had described of fauna in her book, based upon the surrounding nature of her own summer home, was totally real, even the sound of a guitar made by the frog. She also personally felt a close rapport, especially to "her" local robin. Personal interview with Gabrielle Roy, 29 June 1980.

[51] Roy, *La Petite Poule d'eau,* pp. 13, 254-256, 260; Roy, *Cet Eté qui chantait,* pp. 45, 74, 76, 163-168; Roy, *Ces Enfants de ma vie,* p. 42. See also Saint-Pierre, pp. 41-45.

[52] Roy, *Rue Deschambault,* pp. 99-100; Roy, *La Montagne secrète,* pp. 112-113; Roy, *La Rivière sans repos,* p. 178; Roy, *Ces Enfants de ma vie,* pp. 47, 107, 142, 144, 145, 148-154, 159-161, 177-186, 195. See also Gagné, *Visages de Gabrielle Roy,* pp. 123-125; Saint-Pierre, pp. 48-49, 79, 83.

[53] Roy, *La Montagne secrète,* pp. 120, 201, 213. See also pp. 43-45, 49-52, 115-122; Ricard, p. 106; Bachelard, *La Poétique de l'espace,* pp. 187-190; Bachelard, *La Poétique de la rêverie,* p. 141; D. G. Jones, *Butterfly on Rock: A Study of Themes and Images in Canadian Literature* (Toronto: University of Toronto Press, 1971), pp. 145-147; Jack Warwick, *L'Appel du nord dans la littérature canadienne-française,* trans. Jean Simard, Collection Constantes (Montréal: Editions Hurtubise HMH, 1972), pp. 147-148.

[54] Gabrielle Roy, "Témoignage," in *Le Roman canadien-français: Evolution-témoignage-bibliographie,* eds. Paul Wyczynski, Bernard Julien, Jean Ménard et Réjean Robidoux, Archives des lettres canadiennes, Tome III (Montréal: Fides, 1977), p. 304. See also Roy, *Alexandre Chenevert,* pp. 202-213, 235-237; Roy, *Rue Deschambault,* pp. 38-39, 243; Roy, *La Montagne secrète,* pp. 29, 81, 128, 180, 196, 205; Roy, *La Route d'Altamont,* pp. 90, 109, 111-113, 132, 144, 230; Roy, *La Rivière sans repos,* pp. 86-88, 137, 224; Roy, *Cet Eté qui chantait,* pp. 14-23, 163-168, 170, 201-203; Roy, "Un Jardin au bout du monde," pp. 153-155, 185, 210; Roy, *Ces Enfants de ma vie,* pp. 103-104, 157-158; Bachelard, *La Poétique* de l'espace, pp. 166-167, 170-173, 176, 179; Socken, "L'Harmonie dans l'oeuvre de Gabrielle Roy," pp. 276-292.

[55] Roy, *Cet Eté qui chantait,* pp. 203-204; Personal interview with Gabrielle Roy, 29 June 1980. See also Roy, "Mémoire et création: Préface de *La Petite Poule d'eau," Fragiles Lumières de la terre,* pp. 196-197; Ricard, pp. 66-69, 142-150; François Hébert, "De quelques avatars de Dieu," *Etudes Française,* 9, No. 4 (novembre 1973), 346-348.

CHAPTER VI

Divided Creatures: The Call of the Open Road
and the Protective Home

In describing her early years as a writer, as well as her later life, Gabrielle Roy underscored what is perhaps the most fundamental conflict plaguing many people and, in particular, her literary beings:

> Je cherchais déjà, je cherche encore à concilier le besoin de liberté dont nous ne pouvons nous passer avec l'affection qui attache, la tendresse qui retient, les liens de solidarité qui ne doivent se défaire. Et voilà notre vie! Nous voulons les opposés, les inconciliables. Et arrange-toi comme tu peux entre tes désirs qui s'entredéchirent!

Royan characters are, in effect, antithetical creatures, equally divided between their obsessive need for freedom, for travel on the open road, and for the security of the protective home, with its links of solidarity. Albert Le Grand places all of these creatures under the sign of "un être double" or "l'être partagé," individuals who are in a state of constant tension, torn between the dual attraction of, for example, childhood and adulthood, day and night, city and country, civilization and primitivism, North and South, plains and hills, solitude and solidarity, and, above all, structure and freedom. Roy's characters, both male and female, "long for the security of the home, the warmth of a small interior space. At the same time, they are dissatisfied with their present structured lives and dream of escapes, either in a distant past or in an ambitious future of total freedom." Essentially malcontents, therefore, they continuously search, move, or travel, but periodically return.[1]

After having read an essay devoted to this obsession with voyages in her fiction, Roy herself indicated that she had never realized the extent to which her characters were vagabonds.

She added that, if her literary creations were what could be seen as "incorrigible nomads," they had honestly inherited this trait from her. Stemming from her constant wandering back and forth on the rue Deschambault, Roy's later years were still filled with movement. She often left her home for long walks during which she jotted down on scraps of paper numerous ideas and fragments for future works. She described these ideas as running ahead of her and herself as attempting to catch up with them. In addition, as she composed a work of fiction, she saw and constantly ran after a common thread that appeared to race in front of her throughout a story. Gabrielle Roy viewed her professional life, as her works and her characters, as being in perpetual motion.[2]

When one fully analyzes this fiction, one becomes aware of the fact that almost all its characters possess a sensitivity toward the world and a compassion for others essentially because of their own inner conflicts that result in a continual search for a better life. Such a profound need is typically represented by an incessant call to depart, to travel along the open road. It is a call that comes to them from the outside world, as well as, most importantly, from their innermost selves. As early as 1940, Roy writes of the "nécessité du voyage. La route. Les hasards . . . cet appel, le vertige de l'inconnu." Six years later, her vagabond, Gustave, speaks of his obedience "au mystérieux appel des routes." And among numerous other references to such a powerful attraction, to one's "maître," one's "tyrannique possesseur," Christine identifies her own need: "Je l'avais entendu déjà, parfois, l'appel insistant, étranger—venant de nul autre que moi pourtant—qui, tout à coup, au milieu de mes jeux et de mex amitiés, me commandait de partir. . . ." The outcome of this, at times, involuntary desire is a life equated with a constant quest and a deep love for a nomadic existence. Most Royan characters are, therefore, "naturellement voyageurs," delighted "par le simple fait d'être en route," and, as notes Christine, obsessively nostalgic for the open road: "Etre à la dérive au fil de la vie! Ressembler aux nomades! Errer dans le monde!"[3]

This wandering occurs throughout Roy's writings, beginning even with the geographic orientation of most of her titles. Her characters utilize all modes of transportation: roads, rivers, cars, taxis, buses, bicycles, wheel chairs, dog sleds, carriages, wagons, trains, boats, kayaks, airplanes, and, especially, walking. Roy stresses the fundamental importance of these means of travel in one of her last short stories: "Le premier lien d'un pays ne serait-il pas un lien physique: fleuve, rivière, sentier, route, chemin de fer?"   Royan characters, therefore, make numerous trips and are, in addition, surrounded by symbolic images of the road, voyages, and freedom. When they do actually travel, their trips are usually significant ones: they move their lodgings; they migrate to the West; they are beckoned to the East, South, or, in particular, the North; or they simple walk endlessly.[4]

From 1940 to 1945, while employed as a journalist by *Le Bulletin des Agriculteurs*, Gabrielle Roy travelled extensively, researching articles concerning various regions of the Province of Quebec and of Canada.   Two major series of publications resulted from this work: "Peuples du Canada," accounts of the numerous immigrant groups that had migrated to that vast country; and Roy's four articles on the city of Montreal. Her own travels throughout Canada, her promenades in the urban metropolis, and the sensitively portrayed journeys of her immigrant characters all suggest early in her career what will become an obsession in her fiction.[5]

Roy's early short stories of this same period likewise emphasize an interest in travel. Lizzie O'Connor, in 1939, flees from her home and family, only to return soon thereafter; vagabondage is the fundamental theme of "Un Noël en route," while the heroine of "La Fuite de Sally" departs in order to rediscover the happiness of her past. Even elderly characters make voyages: the heroine of "La Pension de vieillesse" travels to western Canada; and Bedette, "La Grande Voyageuse," constantly forced to move in order to live periodically with different family members, learns to enjoy this nomadic life. More symbolic is Roy's later novella, "La Source au désert," in which life in general is described as a walk in the desert, Dr. Raymond's life specifically as "une marche forcée dans le désert," and Anne's life as "un interminable voyage gris." Roy's early characters prefigure her major literary creations.[6]

Images of *la route,* therefore, continue to predominate on numerous levels throughout Roy's major fiction, with no apparent distinction between novels and collections of short stories. *Bonheur d'occasion* presents visions of frustrated or useless travel, leading nowhere: annual house moves, walks around the city, one trip to and return from Richelieu. Azarius dreams of freedom but, like other male characters, flees only to war. *La Petite Poule d'eau* has been seen as a triptych of three different types of journeys: Luzina's trip to give birth and, therefore, a child's entrance into the world; the voyages of the schoolteachers to bring education to the Tousignant children who will themselves ultimately depart; and finally the incessant travels of the Capucin de Toutes-Aides. This vagabond, with his preference for Saint Joseph, himself a nomad, indulges his "appétit de voyage" and considers it important in his life: "Il est vrai qu'après la musique rien n'ouvrait le coeur comme de voyager d'un pays à l'autre; c'était la meilleure façon de comprendre les peuples. . . ." Even Alexandre Chenevert dreams of trips to exotic places, makes one momentous voyage to Lac Vert, travels, tragically, in a taxi to the hospital, and, interestingly, forms a friendship with a former adventurer, just as the bank teller is about to die.[7]

With *Rue Deschambault,* trips abound: Christine travels to her aunt's home and in a snowstorm; she journeys with her mother to visit her sister and then to Quebec to see relatives and friends; her father travels in his job; and Oncle Marjorique drags his family throughout Canada and finally to California. Most family members in these stories, in fact, express a deep longing to travel. Christine speaks of her desires to be "libre, si légère, toujours, en voyage!" She is, as has been previously noted, influenced by Maman who, with her incessant need for liberty and her penchant for a nomadic existence, is also voluntarily tied to her home, family, and daily responsibilities. Maman presents, therefore, one of the strongest figures of a divided being in the Royan literary world. Pierre Cordorai is also divided, as he continuously and compulsively travels throughout northern Canada, to Paris, and toward the perfect work of art, while he overcomes, or at least suppresses, his desires for security, symbolized by Nina. As a male character, of course, Pierre, like Père le Bonniec, possesses the freedom to choose his life of adventure, while most female characters must remain at home, with persistent and painfully unfulfilled desires.[8]

La Route d'Altamont, as its title indicates, deals entirely with the notion of journeys: to Mémère's home, to Lake Winnipeg, with a household mover, and to the hills of Altamont. Underlying the four stories in this collection is the fact that Christine's family, because of her "trotteur de grand-père," originally migrated from Quebec to Manitoba. As pioneers, described by Roy in her memoirs as searchers of the horizon and of illusions, as attracted by the "souffle du monde lointain," these individuals bequeathed an "instinct migrateur" to subsequent generations, especially to Maman and to Christine. The older woman, with her "vastes désirs tournés vers l'eau, les plaines, les lointains horizons," has attempted to suppress her "passion de partir," to live her longings through her daughter, but she remains torn in two. As for Christine, she thrives on games of imaginary travel, participates in the sordid reality of a household move prior to her own voyage into the world, and finally journeys first to Quebec and then to France: "Du reste, toujours en fut-il ainsi dans notre famille: une génération alla vers l'Ouest; la suivante fit le trajet inversement. Toujours nous sommes en migration."[9]

Deborah travels to the South and then returns home; Isaac moves in his wheel chair; Barnaby and Ian retreat to Old Fort-Chimo; Elsa, Ian, and Jimmy journey to the tundra; the young boy escapes to the South; and Winnie and Elsa walk endlessly along the banks of the Koksoak. The characters of *La Rivière sans repos* are "toujours en marche" or "toujours en route," amusingly justifying what one of Gabrielle Roy's acquaintances once mistakenly called her work: "La Rivière fatiguée." Despite what seems to be a short repose in *Cet Eté qui chantait*, characters, both humans and animals, are seen as continuously strolling in the countryside, as dreaming of travels to mysterious islands, and as searching like lost children for a common shore. This work even opens with the sound of a train.[10]

If *Un Jardin au bout du monde* begins with the tale of a true vagabond who desperately needs the freedom of the open road, while maintaining ties with a family, the other stories of this collection recount the difficult travels of immigrants—Chinese, Russian, and Ukrainian—on the Western Canadian plains. Martha, in particular, is identified with the wind, and, resembling Elsa, is "engagée sur cette route si longue . . . tirée en avant. . . ." The children of *Ces Enfants de ma vie* walk long distances between their homes and school; the teacher and Médéric travel in a *berline;* and these two close friends await an inevitable departure into adulthood that, at times, seems never to occur. They are like "deux voyageurs ayant pris place sur une même banquette dans un train qui n'en finissait pas de ne pas partir." Finally, Roy's 1979 short story, "Ely! Ely! Ely!," opens and concludes with a train ride, a form of transportation that, in this instance, is actually set in motion.[11]

Since nearly all of Gabrielle Roy's characters do travel or at least desire to do so, one can easily distinguish the nature of their trips, on circular or direct routes. Circularity clearly dominates in Roy's fiction, whether it be in the form of an actual circle, a series of concentric circles, a spiral or whirlwind, or a cyclical pattern. The same predilection for such images occurs in reference to travel.

It is frequent that the circular routes chosen by or forced upon Royan characters imply a lack of any forward movement. The human species itself is described as turning "perpétuellement en rond," while the soul, like the night, is on a long voyage "autour de soi tournant, tournant. . . ." The actions of individuals and the milieux in which they live are also circular, with no progression and, therefore, no escape: the house moves of *Bonheur d'occasion* and "Le Déménagement" return families to their original sphere of existence; the urban world and even the isolated rural world are often seen as static and engulfing.[12]

But it is predominantly individual characters who are identified with the whirlwind of circular roads that lead nowhere. Florentine, like Rose-Anna and the other women of Saint-Henri, is slowly consuming herself, entrapped within a "tourbillon de neige" of hereditary misery, poverty, biological destiny, and solitude: "Un vent d'hiver, un vent de tourbillon soufflait sur elle. Personne n'était venu vers elle ce soir-là, à travers la tempête. Ni jamais d'ailleurs, personne n'était venu vers elle." She does want to escape, but wandering around the city of Montreal, she continuously finds herself back on a circular road to the middle of the spiral. At the same time, she desires to remain at the center of that whirlwind, as during her danse with Emmanuel, for she can attain certain heights only within the *tourbillon*. She exists, therefore, both forceably and voluntarily, inside what Le Grand calls a "démarche antithétique et symboliquement circulaire."[13]

Male characters are also equated with circular images of travel, with *tourbillons*. Alexandre Chenevert has been seen as being caught in claustrophobic, enclosed spaces, as attempting escapes to the past, but as continuing to turn around upon himself. Even Pierre Cordorai, the free adventurer, is described as dreaming of whirlwinds of snow, as meeting his past self on the banks of a river, and, at the point of death, as having the sensation of turning "en une ronde douce, presque agréable,"

while forms, "images chéries, rêves, sortilèges et couleurs tourbillonnèrent. . . ." Eveline, of course, merely dreams of travel,
remains a prisoner within her stable life, and when she does
venture outside her home, embarks solely on trips to the past.
Winnie, Elsa, Martine, and Martha are all similarly identified
with circular routes, those specifically related to nature and
upon which these women incessantly walk without arriving at
any other destination but death.[14]

Throughout the fiction of Gabrielle Roy, characters undertake trips that return them to their past. It is Christine who
identifies this need on the part of most people: "Et, au fond,
tous les voyages de ma vie, depuis, n'ont été que des retours
en arrière pour tâcher de ressaisir ce que j'avais tenu dans le
hamac et sans le chercher." If all trips, therefore, are essentially
attempts to recapture the joy once experienced, for example,
while being rocked as a child by the wind in a hammock, these
voyages are sometimes real and other times imagined, but always
filled with a mixture of happiness and sorrow, they are either
only temporarily successful or totally disastrous. One is reminded of the Lacasse family's horrible trip to Richelieu and
then back to Montreal and to ensuing tragedies; Chenevert's
voyage to Lac Vert and then back to the city; Maman's journey
to Quebec and back to Manitoba; M. Saint-Hilaire's travels to
Lake Winnipeg; Eveline's discovery of the hills of Altamont;
the Eskimos' return to Old Fort-Chimo; Elsa, Ian, and Jimmy's
attempt to reach Baffin Island on the tundra; and Martine's
difficult journey to the river.[15]

What stimulates the majority of these return trips to the
past is an ardent attempt to recapture one's youth and the related feeling of maternal security. Rose-Anna, M. Saint-Hilaire,
and Martine, for example, actually return to places that they
frequented in the past. Rose-Anna, in fact, appears to radiate
"quelque chose comme son ancienne joie de jeune fille," as
she travels further back toward her childhood home. Martine,
likewise, is transformed: "A un moment elle tourna vers nous
un visage sur lequel la jeunesse perdue mettait soudain le reflet
d'un soleil lointain." Chenevert does not return to a known
place from his past, but his trip to the country, to the natural
habitat of humanity, offers him an "impression d'enfance."
More complex are the two return trips made by Maman-Eveline.
Travelling back directly to her husband's past in Quebec and
indirectly to her own, with the visit to her childhood friend,

Odile, Maman experiences a profound change: "Et je [Christine] m'aperçus combien maman rajeunissait en voyage; ses yeux devinrent tout pleins d'étincelles. . . ." When Eveline discovers and then returns to the hills of Altamont, however, the association of these hills with her past youth, with the hills of Quebec, is effected in her mind. In fact, all of these voyages to youth, although actually undertaken, truly occur in one's memory and, therefore, cannot permanently succeed.[16]

Related to the desire to discover a circular route to one's childhood are the return trips made or planned to one's homeland. All of Roy's immigrant characters long to return to their land of origin, to the extent that, in a repetitive or circular motion, they migrate to Canada only to reestablish their old ways on the Western prairies. They maintain a sense of nostalgia for their roots but realize that they are in Canada to stay: "Parfois, se prenant la tête entre les mains, il [Smouillya] la secouait comme pour y ramener une idée consolante, car dans la cabane sombre . . . il ne voyait vraiment plus comment lui viendrait de l'argent pour payer ses dettes et acheter le billet de retour au pays." The most powerful attraction of one's homeland in the Royan world, however, comes from Quebec and, further back, from France, both calling to the Manitoban pioneers to return. Roy herself stated that the most beautiful voyage for her family was in the direction of Quebec. Significantly, it is Christine who recognizing that her family had abandoned a country when they moved to the West, eventually travels back first to Quebec and then to France, her "vieille mère patrie."[17]

Circular roads will also bring individuals back to a former way of life, for example, to the Eskimo ways of Old Fort-Chimo for Barnaby, Ian, and, temporarily, Elsa and Jimmy. Linked to this return trip is a voyage back to a former state of primitivism. Chenevert believes that he has recaptured this primitive state, this origin of himself, while he vacations at Lac Vert. Similarly, islands conjure up the image of a past, primitive life. The most effective example of an attempted return both to the ways of the past and to primitivism, however, occurs during Elsa, Ian, and Jimmy's voyage across the tundra toward Baffin Island. Travelling to this past, to a desired *paradis terrestre*, as well as to a desired future of simplicity and happiness, these three characters fail in their attempt. Ian becomes more savage, as he returns further back in time, while Jimmy almost dies. They have come close to becoming one with circular nature. Once that identification occurs and once one is successful in this particular return trip, one has reached the desired "pays de l'amour," the happiness of the past, and, as for Chenevert, Cordorai, Eveline, Elsa, Winnie, Martine, and Martha, the inevitable future closing of the circle in death.[18]

There remains one final type of a return trip that, in particular, stresses the importance of the repetitive nature of life and the eventual opening of the individual or familial circle into a larger, worldly circle or into direct routes. Luzina Tousignant's annual voyage back to her home does create happiness and a sense of sociability for her family, but since she carries back with her the gift of a newborn child, her circular road has returned her to the inevitable: not here to the past and, hence, to the closing of the circle of life and death, but to the cyclical future of progress, in education and civilization: "Just as Elsa's return from her unsuccessful trip to the tundra . . . will be followed by the loss of her son, Jimmy, to the modern culture of the South, Luzina's return will mean the inevitable and painful departure of her children, and of her youth, on route toward a new destiny." Life repeats itself, while direct roads have been introduced into the circular nature of travel.[19]

In *La Petite Poule d'eau* it is Luzina and the Capucin de Toutes-Aides who represent this attempted reconciliation between circular and direct routes. Both characters need the roads leading toward the family and sociability, while the priest thrives on his nomadic existence on direct roads in the North, and Luzina travels on a straight path to give birth and then lucidly accepts the road toward education and progress. The concept of progress is, in fact, one of the most powerful examples of a direct route in Roy's fiction. It can be destructive if it confuses and alienates people such as Alexandre Chenevert, Sam Lee Wong, and various immigrant groups, and when it calls one's children from home, but Roy also envisions an enlightened interpretation of the future: " 'Le vrai progrès, c'est celui qui tend vers une fraternité plus grande.' "[20]

All of Roy's direct roads will lead toward this fervently desired tenderness and understanding of and among others. Emmanuel wanders around Montreal but remains on a direct path toward a deep passion and love for humanity. The trip to Mémère's house and the road past Altamont merge to form one route of understanding among generations. And finally Martha, the one who so ardently desired to migrate to Canada but who is now herself confused by progress, still equates her life with human solidarity:

> Cependant, de se voir engagée sur cette route si longue qui, passé Codessa, continuait vers d'autres villages plus grands encore, atteignait des villes, elle se sentait tirée en avant, portée vers une fraternité humaine, une rumeur de voix; des idées de foule, d'animation, s'éveillaient en son esprit, elle en rêvait comme d'une chose fantastique, elle éprouvait au coeur un petit choc d'excitation, d'aventure. Il lui semblait s'en aller en direction du Canada.[21]

Martha's tempered excitement about being engaged upon a direct route toward the future reminds one that both freedom and a sense of adventure are two of the strongest attractions of travel.   If the female characters of *Bonheur d'occasion* have been identified with circular routes and with whirlwinds, the male characters of this novel can be seen as possessing the freedom to travel along a direct road outside of Montreal and to war. Both Emmanuel and Azarius effect such an escape, as the latter also dreams of wind and cargo ships, symbolic of a future of independence.   Jean, in particular, is associated with these same images, as well as with boats, trains, mountains, steeples, violence, ascension, mobility, and total freedom.   He is seen as moving along a straight, rectilinear road toward his sexual desires and ambition, as an adventurer escaping into exterior time and coldly destructive on the way: "Jean, il était le vent dur et cinglant, l'hiver. . . . Lui . . . il était entré dans sa vie [Florentine's] comme un éclat de bourrasque qui saccage, détruit. . . . Et Jean s'en allait comme si son oeuvre était accomplie, et qu'il ne lui restait plus rien à faire ici. . . ."[22]
There is also a sense of adventure and freedom when immigrants journey courageously toward a new home, as yet unknown.   When Eveline recounts to Christine the story of their family's migration from Quebec to Manitoba, the same excitement about being on the road, now nostagically recalled, is reborn in the older woman's words:

> "Donc, tu étais heureuse!"
> "Heureuse?   Oui, je le pense. . . .   Heureuse comme on l'est, quand on est jeune—et aussi moins jeune—par le simple fait d'être en route, que la vie change, va changer, que tout se renouvelle. . . ."
> Et elle me promettait que je connaîtrais moi aussi plus tard

ce que c'est de partir, de chercher à la vie sans trêve un recommencement possible. . . .

It is only direct routes that truly offer this deeply desired possibility for a new beginning.[23]

It is especially in *La Route d'Altamont* that there appears
this close rapport between the image of a direct route and the
future, in particular, one's chosen road in life leading toward
self-discovery, self-awareness, and an understanding and conquest
of one's own identity. Christine speaks of the "routes de section" across the Canadian plains that seem to call to her and to
her "confiance illimitée en un avenir lui-même comme illimité."
She writes of the numerous roads throughout Europe that remind her of her long journey toward self-knowledge. Even prior
to her voyage in Europe, Christine understood the importance
both of travel and of departure itself: "Je commençais à craindre
cet instant exaltant du départ qui est aussi celui où l'on prend
sa taille exacte dans le monde, si petite que le coeur peut nous
manquer. Pourtant cette vulnérabilité extrême me paraissait
et me paraît encore l'une des étapes les plus nécessaires à la
connaissance de soi."[24]

Like Christine, all of Gabrielle Roy's characters will depart,
and many of them will travel along the direct roads that culminate in a future of self-acceptance. If circular routes can lead
them to the closing of the circle of life and death, however,
direct routes will likewise bring Roy's literary beings to the
completion of their work: of a work of art and of their lives.
Pierre travels endlessly in Canada and to Paris in order to discover
and create the perfect aesthetic masterpiece. He finally envisions it but dies. Alexandre eventually understands and is understood by others; he then dies.[25]

Given this obsession with *la route* and with the call to depart, it is logical that the author create in her works numerous
images for the road and for a nomadic existence. It has already
been noted that many of her characters, fascinated by the open
road, express a deep sense of love toward the immensity of
open spaces, typified by the Western Canadian plains, with their
vast horizons and seemingly endless skies. Perhaps leading
nowhere or perhaps to the unknown, the prairie calls, with a
"signe intelligible," to the Royan character who is immediately
"prêt à partir." The individual wanders across these plains, as
though mysteriously drawn toward some distant notion of a

new beginning, associated, in addition, with dawn or morning. For Roy's characters, immensity is equated with an optimistic faith in the future.[26]

Travelling across the open plains as a companion of the Royan vagabond is the wind. This symbol of freedom and adventure is also a reflection of the changes of individuals: their revolts, searches, and wandering throughout life. It is the wind that has pushed the immigrant groups to and across the vast country of Canada, sometimes as a furious force, other times as a "simple voyageur," but always singing "un vent de voyage." The wind also sings to Christine, as it gently rocks her in her hammock, inviting her to dream of imaginary travels. It is, in addition, responsible for the movement and music of Christine's glass mobile, her "chanson de verre," itself a symbol both of stability and freedom. Music itself, in fact, is linked to travel. Le Capucin de Toutes-Aides views it, along with voyages, as the best means to understand others. When Nil sings the beautiful Ukrainian songs taught to him by his mother, he appears to designate "une route? une plaine? ou quelque pays ouvert qui donnait envie de le connaître." He points to "une route heureuse au bout de ce monde."[27]

The immensity of the tundra, too, can be seen as a symbol of *la route,* of freedom, and, specifically with Baffin Island, of an unknown but ideal destination. Life, and in particular Elsa's, is also viewed as a trek across this tundra: " 'Celui qui part à pied pour un long voyage à travers la toundra, bien suffisamment chargé dès le premier jour, se préoccupe-t-il . . . de ce qu'il aura . . . à porter au cinquième, au dixième jour. . . . Elsa, tu pars bien plus chargée dès le premier jour que tes braves ancêtres si sobres.' " The attraction to the tundra is related to the call of the North, especially for Pierre, the Eskimos, and le Capucin de Toutes-Aides: "Plus il [the priest] était monté haut dans le Nord, et plus il avait été libre d'aimer." For Thérésina, Mme Beaulieu, Jimmy, and Deborah, it is the South that urges them to move: "De tout cela elle [Deborah] avait surtout retenu un mot magique pour elle: le Sud. Elle en avait rêvé, tout comme des gens du Sud . . . rêvent, eux, du Nord, parfois. Seulement pour le plaisir du voyage, pour voir enfin comment était ce fameux Sud, elle se serait peut-être décidée." For the Canadian pioneers, it is the West that calls to them, while Christine desires to discover herself and to perfect her chosen career by travelling East. In short, all directions can become obsessions to individuals. And just as city dwellers long to escape into the country-side but encounter either disastrous results or only temporary success, all Royan characters will bring to their preferred locale their own successes and failures, along with their continuing, relentless need to depart.[28]

If the open plains beckon to some of Gabrielle Roy's characters, mountains and hills—in particular the roads to and through them, as well as their lofty summits—likewise call to other individuals. Sam Lee Wong is forever looking at or walking toward his beloved hills, symbol of the routes to his past. For the young people of Saint-Henri, Westmount appears as the path toward ambition and success in life. To Cordorai, "la Re-splendissante" represents perfection, the true liberation from his incessant quest for ideal, aesthetic beauty. Finally, hills sym-bolize the road to Quebec for Eveline, the freedom of childhood and adolescence for Médéric, and independence for Deborah and Ian.[29]

Three additional locations represent a love for *la route* in Roy's fiction: forests, islands, and water, the latter in the form of rivers, lakes, and oceans. It is not only the wind that Martha considers as her nomadic companion, but also a solitary tree on the plains that always appears to her as if it were "en marche, tel un moine [like le Capucin de Toutes-Aides or le Père le Bonniec], un pèlerin peut-être, quelqu'un en tout cas qui semblait venir de très loin à pied." This symbol of an isolated tree re-minds one of Chenevert's freedom in the tranquil forest at Lac Vert. The bank teller, of course, also dreams of an escape to a deserted, exotic island where he can attain total serenity and liberty, as if in paradise. Islands, in addition, conjure up life as it should be in *La Petite Poule d'eau,* while they serve as an inspiration to dreams of primitive life and adventurous voyages of discovery in *Cet Eté qui chantait.* For Roy, islands represent the hope for human communication and, once again, *recom-mencement.* This same possibility for a road toward rebirth can be seen in the image of water, transporting Royan charac-ters to their desired destinations, reflecting the nomadic exis-tence of both nature and humanity, and by extension, sym-bolically placing them together in time: "L'oiseau noir à son bord, moi dans ma chaise au jardin, nous avons passé bien des heures à voyager ensemble sur la même vague du temps."[30]

If Roy uses locations as symbolic images of travel, she also utilizes specific objects and sounds. In addition to obvious modes of transportation, wedding suitcases (related to the wedding *berline*), train tracks, and train whistles (the latter related to church bells and steeples)—all represent the obsessive urge to leave. The train whistle, announcing what one is about to see, reminds the traveller, in addition, that the trip is temporary. As during a house move, the illusion of a nomadic existence is often short-lived: " 'Pendant un temps . . . on est comme apparenté aux nomades . . . nulle part ne plongeant leurs racines. On n'a plus de toit. Oui, vraiment, pendant quelques heures du moins, c'est comme si on était à la dérive, au fil de la vie.' "[31]

Since Roy's characters are frequently identified with animals, it is understandable that the author choose certain creatures to symbolize humanity's longing for vagabondage. The bison of Manitoba, the firefly of enchanted summer, and Médéric's horse, Gaspard, all serve this function. It is, however, birds that are predominantly associated with the freedom to leave and, in addition, with the mind in its dreams and thoughts of departure and travel. The tale of Maman's trip to Quebec, "Les Déserteuses," for example, opens and ends with the image of seagulls:

> Vers le milieu du *pont* Provencher, maman et moi nous fûmes environnées de *mouettes;* elles *volaient* bas au-dessus de *la rivière* Rouge; maman prit ma main et la serra comme pour faire *passer* en moi un *mouvement* de son âme; cent fois par jour, maman recevait de la joie de l'univers; parfois ce n'était que *le vent* ou *l'allure des oiseaux* qui la *soulevaient*. Penchées sur le parapet, nous avons longtemps regardé *les mouettes*. Et, tout à coup, sur *le pont* maman me dit qu'elle aimerait pouvoir *aller où* elle voudrait, *quand* elle voudrait.

Maman will depart in this story, only to return to her family. Other characters, however, will leave permanently: "Vers ce temps de l'année où émigraient les oiseaux du Nord partit le premier des enfants Tousignant."[32]

Edmond Tousignant is, in fact, departing on a road in order to further his education. The powerful image of education itself, with the geography class, maps, postcards, books, and reading in general, are all associated with the notion of travel, as well as with several of the other nomadic symbols already examined. Like these symbols, education leads to freedom and to self-awareness. It also leads to an understanding of others, just as though two people had met in the same book:

> Par ailleurs elle [Elsa] était émue à la moindre trace du passage
> d'un autre lecteur: un trait pour souligner une phrase, des nota-
> tions, dans la marge. . . . Alors elle avait le sentiment, comme
> dans la toundra, à la vue de quelques pierres déplacées ou de la
> mousse de caribou foulée, qu'un être humain venait tout juste de
> traverser l'infini pays désert, qu'avec un peu de chance on pourrait
> peut-être encore apercevoir au loin sa silhouette en marche.[33]

This scene in which Elsa is so moved by her reading and by the
notations of another in a book is a typical example of Roy's
expansion of the antithetical nature of her characters to the
opposition between immensity and intimacy and between exterior and interior spaces.   With the light from a lamp inside
Ian's small hut, Elsa is reading, ironically, the story of *Ivanhoe,*
while a storm rages outside.   Throughout the Royan fictional
world, in fact, nomadic creatures inevitably encounter such
conflicts inherent in their obsession with *la route.* If many of
them—and in particular Luzina, le Capucin de Toutes-Aides,
Papa, Eveline, Christine, Pierre, and Gustave—are fascinated by
departure, direct routes, freedom, and vagabondage, all leading
toward exterior immensity, equally important is their attraction
to and need of belonging, reconciliation, circularity, stability,
permanence, and family ties—all symbolized by the image of
interior intimacy, as in the protective home.[34]

It is true that, at times, the Royan home does possess negative connotations, especially when, like a cage, it hampers the
freedom of Azarius, Eveline, Deborah, Ian, and Martine, or
when it is steeped in poverty.   The Lacasse's home in *Bonheur
d'occasion,* for example, is a place from which it is difficult
to escape, but which is located near the train tracks. Like the
pitiful "chez nous" of the poor family of "Le Déménagement,"
it is also, as fears Rose-Anna, a home predestined for unhappiness: "Il lui paraissait que certaines maisons prédisposent au
bonheur et que d'autres, par un enchaînement fatidique, sont
destinées à n'abriter que des êtres éprouvés." To add to this
concern is the depressing fact that both homes here discussed
do not fully represent stability, since their inhabitants are continually moving.   The concept of a home is important to the
Lacasse family, but it is a word filled with contradictions:

> Chez nous!
> Il était vieux ce mot-là, un des premiers qu'ils eussent appris,
> eux, les enfants. . . . Chez nous, c'était un mot élastique et, à
> certaines heures, incompréhensible, parce qu'il évoquait non pas
> un seul lieu, mais une vingtaine d'abris. . . . Il contenait des regrets,
> des nostalgies et, toujours, une parcelle d'incertitude. Il s'appa-
> rentait à la migration annuelle. . . . Il sonnait au coeur comme une
> fuite, comme un départ imprévu; et quand on l'entendait, on
> croyait entendre aussi, au fond de la mémoire, le cri aigu des
> oiseaux voyageurs.[35]

Generally, however, the Royan home is seen as a positive image, as what Gaston Bachelard describes as the warmth of a primitive, maternal, terrestrial paradise, an absolute refuge or nest of happiness and well-being. It is, in fact, Bachelard's analysis of the home as an intimate space that most closely corresponds to Roy's own depiction. For Bachelard, images of the home are reflected in other models of intimacy, in places and in objects: attics, corners, nests, certain rooms, shells, dressers, and chests. For both writers, the home is often symbolized by the light and warmth of the fire, stove, hearth, candle, lantern, and lamp. A light at the window, as well as the window itself, is likened to an eye, waiting and watching over the inhabitants. In addition, windows and doors can be closed or opened, representing the dialectic of interior and exterior space. The image of the home, for both Bachelard and Roy, is usually armed against the universe, against the cold, harsh exterior, while it looks out onto the immensity of that world.[36]

In three of Gabrielle Roy's works, the home is seen specifically as a warm but isolated house in the country. In a beautiful scene in *La Petite Poule d'eau*, for example, Armand Dubreuil reads aloud in Luzina's warm kitchen, while outside it is raining. Le Capucin de Toutes-Aides, himself such a vagabond, also adores the Tousignant's *foyer* where he can finally rest. The Le Gardeur home in *Alexandre Chenevert* is similarly seen as noisy, happy, hospitable, and most importantly, self-sufficient in winter. When Chenevert first enters his cabin at Lac Vert, however, it appears to be too small, but it soon seems to grow, as it creates a warm atmosphere of possession and friendship:

> Or, soudain, Alexandre découvrait une lueur . . . et que celle-ci
> provenait de sa lampe allumée dans la cabane . . . de ses fenêtres

éclairées qui semblaient lui signifier la douceur, l'attrait de la sécurité terrestre. . . .

"Mon feu," se dit-il, aimant le mot. . . .

Il marchait d'un pas allègre vers sa véritable demeure. . . .

Jusqu'ici, il avait pensé: la cabane.

Ce soir, il commença de dire: ma cabane. . . .[37]

Given the focal point in *Rue Deschambault* of both childhood and the maternal presence, it is logical that Roy place in this work varied images of the home. It is seen primarily as a warm kitchen, with its *poêle* around which the family congregates. It is also a small space that protects rather than encloses: "La liberté, est-ce que ce ne serait pas de rester en un tout petit espace d'où l'on peut sortir si l'on veut?" As a child, Christine cannot yet venture out from this protective place; she can only dream, preferring the immensity of the road and the sky that she sees when high up on her swing to the sensation of entrapment when the swing descends her into her small garden. But the prototype of this intimate space for Christine is her *grenier* to which she often flees in order to find herself and, especially, from which she can observe the sky, the clouds, and the trees, while listening to the wind.[38]

Christine also experiences the positive sensation of being in a small, warm schoolhouse, while a winter storm rages outside. Similarly, she is caught in a carriage, resembling a ship and referred to as "la cabane," during another violent snowstorm. With the light and warmth from both the lamp and from a sense of friendship inside this moving home, the interior appears to exist as though there were no exterior. These two images in *Rue Deschambault* remind one of *Ces Enfants de ma vie*, with its warm, protective schoolhouse and, especially, the trip in the *berline* made by the teacher and Médéric during a storm. Seen as both a cradle and a ship, with a lantern inside, this sled-carriage transports its two passengers through the snow, while offering them a feeling of shelter on the road. The most striking depiction of the protective home in this collection of short stories, however, is the isolated Pasquier house, with its "chaleureuse animation" and its miracle of "le seul feu timide de la lampe." Noting the tenderness, warmth, and light of familial love, as well as the presence of maternal and filial protection, the schoolteacher happily concludes that "la maison est bien gardée." As such, it typifies the power of Royan intimacy.[39]

If Roy's fictional homes thus far discussed often present the image of an interior space in contrast to the exterior, it is particularly in *La Montagne secrète* and *La Rivière sans repos* where this opposition is the most intense. Pierre's cabin, shared with his friend, Steve, is seen as a refuge of warmth, fire, and even thought from the harsh, northern Canadian winter climate. The men are viewed in hibernation in these small quarters, as Pierre will later be in his Paris studio, with its warm stove. He transfers, in fact, what he calls this law of the North to his urban lodgings, as he searches for and finally discovers an apartment without too much light. For this trapper-painter, light belongs solely outdoors:"l'immensité au dehors, au-dedans l'exiguïté."[40]

In *La Rivière sans repos* the Eskimo hut is described as being hermetically sealed against the winter, as its smoke struggles against the immense cold outdoors. Intimacy, however, can be suffocating, and Deborah, for example, longs to escape from the heat of this interior space. As for Winnie, she moves into a real house and expresses deep joy at being at home in it, rather than in a tent or an igloo. Both women are placed in contrast to Mme Beaulieu whose home opens onto the void of the North and receives, through its bay windows, the immensity of the landscape and horizon. Mme Beaulieu desperately desires a small, enclosed living space. It is precisely this intimacy that Elsa experiences when she spends one night in an igloo, contrasted with exterior immensity but fashioned from the cold, snow-covered tundra and "faisant corps avec le pays":

> Il se glissèrent à l'intérieur. La lampe à l'huile . . . l'éclairait de sa flamme douce. Elsa disposait les fourrures pour en faire de bons lits chauds. Sur le réchaud allumé commença à chanter l'eau du thé. . . . les yeux de l'enfant [Jimmy] eurent un rayonnement si lumineux que Ian, plein de rire, s'écria:
> "On pourrait éteindre la lampe, ménager l'huile. Le petit nous éclaire déjà bien avec ses yeux brillants. . . ."
> Le vent prit au dehors. Il criait en faisant le tour de l'igloo isolé dans la nuit sans fin. . . . Sa plainte intensifiait chez le petit garçon le sentiment d'être au chaud, en toute sécurité avec ceux en qui il avait pleine confiance.[41]

Like the igloo on the tundra, both Mémère's and Maman's homes on the Canadian plains are seen as secure, well-stocked shelters against the months of winter. Similarly, *Un Jardin au bout du monde* notes in its preface the importance of the *poêle* in the Manitoban home and opens with the tale of the vagabond who deeply needs the warmth of the narrator's home, with its stove and agreeable odors. It is near this fire that he invents and tells his stories to the family, while a snowstorm rages across the plains: "On voyait la neige accumulée déjà à la hauteur des fenêtres. Soudain une rafale s'y jetait comme pour chercher à éteindre par-delà la vitre le feu de la lampe, ce dernier signe encore visible de la vie luttant contre la passion déchaînée du blizzard." Royan characters, sheltered in their intimate spaces, will struggle against the outside world. They will fight to maintain this needed sense of security and warmth, at least until they themselves decide to depart from this maternal circle into exterior immensity. But it is precisely this atmosphere of the protective home that they, even while on the road, will attempt to recapture throughout their lives.[42]

Once these characters do depart from the home, they will encounter an additional immensity-intimacy conflict, as has already been examined, in the form of a love for roads through the open plains, accompanied by an equally deep love for the routes that lead to a countryside of protective hills. Although many of Roy's characters do delight in the "petite route droite" or in the "routes de section" across the prairie, increasingly in this fiction, these roads are placed in opposition to preferred paths into hills, symbolic of the sheltered, maternal home, a peaceful homeland, and a happy childhood that one desires to repossess. Roy's older characters—in particular, Mémère, Eveline, Sam Lee Wong, Smouillya, and Martha—yearn to rediscover these intimate, restful hills and mountains and express hatred for this "longue route de terre, droite et triste" or this "infinie route de terre, au delà d'une plaine sauvage. . . ." For these individuals, immense, direct roads lead first to solitude and then to death.[43]

There often exists, therefore, a sense of anxiety and haste while Royan characters travel along their roads. They must hurry on direct routes toward their goals before the circle of life closes, and yet this impatient pace will bring them more quickly toward the end of their lives. In addition, while travelling, they encounter still another conflict and remain divided: should they hasten in solitude toward self-discovery or with others toward mutual understanding? The Royan character has enjoyed the peace of a small, interior space but has experienced deep solitude there.   Departing to find oneself and others, however, can result, once again, in the same intense feeling of being alone.   At the same time, a sense of solidarity with others can be achieved in the protective home, as well as along the road.   Gabrielle Roy's characters need, hate, and experience both of these conflicting conditions.[44]

The author herself recognized this inevitable conflict within each individual: "Solitaire et solidaire, les deux mots qui disent l'essentiel de notre condition humaine. . . ."   She saw these two conditions, however, as related: "Solitude et solidarité. Paradoxe: on s'enfonce dans la solitude, on fuit les autres. . . . Mais pourquoi, sinon pour être digne de quelqu'un, de quelque chose . . . d'un jugement de qualité."   Not only does one need others, but one's own sensation of solitude aids in an understanding of other people.   One recognizes "la présence et la solidarité humaines dans l'infinie solitude environnante. . . . Le sentiment que l'on a de sa propre solitude, c'est ce qui nous fait pressentir la solitude des autres. . . . Sans la solitude, y aurait-il fusion, union, tendresse des coeurs?"[45]

Despite the anguish that it may bring, therefore, solitude is necessary to everyone. The void that one feels at the end of a day when a friend has departed causes one to appreciate companionship even more.   The departure that one undertakes alone, from Manitoba back to Quebec, for example, or from Montreal to the Manitoban town of Ely, carries an individual, in the first instance, back to one's origins and, in the second, toward renewed family ties.   In Roy's own experiences, as well as in the lives of most of her characters, solitude and solidarity conflicted and united with one another.[46]

Throughout Roy's writings, there is underscored this inherent conflict of humanity.   In *Bonheur d'occasion,* Jean desires to be alone, to be free of any human involvement, so that he may further his ambitious goals. He is, however, drawn toward Florentine.   This young woman, in turn, rejects the friendship of women and yet deeply fears solitude; she needs others, and particularly men, in order to exist.   Her father is similarly divided: he wants the freedom of being alone, without family obligations, but he desperately needs to converse with others.   This same opposition intensifies in *La Petite Poule d'eau* where Luzina chooses to live in a totally isolated region and yet, the epitome of the sociable person, has to leave periodically, not only to give birth, to populate her area more, but to seek contact with others. Le Capucin de Toutes-Aides, especially, thrives on his solitary, nomadic existence, but only to love and understand even more other human beings with whom he adores socializing.[47]

Alexandre Chenevert, surrounded by `people in Montreal, remains isolated in his urban anonymity. He travels to the countryside to be alone, to renew himself, and discovers true, absolute solitude. He realizes that he needs to relate to others with whom he suddenly feels a deep solidarity, achieved, in his eyes, solely in the city. He returns, only to die alone, but surrounded by new friends. The deep solitude that Chenevert first experiences at Lac Vert is depicted as a natural part of life for the Eskimos, isolated in Fort-Chimo. Some of them, like Elsa's uncle, Ian, prefer that loneliness to life with others in what Ian sees as a cage: a family, home, or town. As for Winnie, she spends her life surrounded by her own family and own people but, like Elsa, continuously walks alone along a solitary path.[48]

It is noteworthy that the three Royan works that deal the most extensively with the solitude-solidarity conflict were written in 1955, 1961, and 1966 and have been categorized as forming the second chronological group of Roy's fiction. The works examine, in addition, the quests of both youth and the artist toward self-discovery, human understanding, and perfection. The story of Pierre Cordorai, "l'Homme-Seul" who searches for and finds his splendid mountain, "la Solitaire," is that of an adventurer-artist whose human and professional condition is described as being "à la fois si proche . . . et si éloignée des hommes. . . ." As a man, Pierre needs to feel a certain solidarity with others and realizes that "la seule privation tout à fait intolérable, c'est celle d'un compagnon." Yet as an independent soul, Pierre desperately needs to be alone: "Comment faire comprendre à l'amitié que pour se connaître mieux, mieux mériter d'elle peut-être, se mieux accomplir, il lui fallait partir seul." Once again, what Cordorai sees as the marvels of solitude will hopefully result in a sense of solidarity with oneself and with others.[49]

It is these same joys of solitude that an adult Christine intially discovered early in her life: "Comment ne sait-on pas plus tôt qu'on est soi-même son meilleur, son plus cher compagnon? Pourquoi tant craindre la solitude qui n'est qu'un tête-à-tête avec ce seul compagnon véritable?" As an adult, on the road toward a literary career and toward self-knowledge, this sensitive individual knows that not only is it "dans la solitude seulement que l'âme goûte sa délivrance" but also that it is necessary to be "bien seul . . . pour se retrouver soi-même." Christine, however, is still too young and unrealistic to accept the fact that desired solitude and solidarity are often difficult to attain at the same time.   She remains naively optimistic:

> Mais j'espérais encore que je pourrais tout avoir: et la vie chaude et vraie comme un abri . . . le temps de marcher et le temps de m'arrêter pour comprendre; le temps de m'isoler un peu sur la route et puis de rattraper les autres, de les rejoindre et de crier joyeusement: "Me voici, et voici ce que j'ai trouvé en route pour vous! . . . M'avez-vous attendue? . . . Ne m'attendez-vous pas? . . . Oh! attendez-moi donc! . . ."[50]

With maturity, this optimism toward the future, toward a departure upon any path, does not necessarily disappear but does become tempered. It is, perhaps, the inevitability of finding oneself on a circular road or the possibility of not being able to reconcile solitude and solidarity that instills an attitude of ambivalence about departures in Roy's fiction. Even at the end of Christine's positive statement, there is clearly suggested a nagging fear that perhaps others may not wait for her, may not be able to offer her the solidarity that she needs while discovering herself in solitude. In all of Roy's works, there is an excitement about voyages, "but these feelings are increasingly accompanied by a sense of sadness, loss, and fear of *dépaysement.*" With age, this anxiety increases, and, therefore, the obsession that forces one to leave can cause profound anguish.[51]

The narrator expresses this duality in the conclusion of "Ely! Ely! Ely!," as she notes the chronological distinction in her attitude toward departure: "Les longs coups de sifflet des trains qui maintenant [1979] me déchirent le coeur, en ce temps-là [1940s] m'exaltaient. Dieu que j'étais heureuse, en mouvement, disponible, tout à l'inconnu de notre pays comme à tout l'avenir encore possible du monde." The youthful Roy, in her journalistic meanderings, believed in an enlightened future for humanity and for the world, to be discovered *en route.* By the time that she began writing her fiction, and increasingly throughout that fiction, her characters' attitude toward departures evolved into one of ambivalence. All of her fictional departures, even those depicted in her earlier works, are, in fact, charged with complex emotions: Yvonne's departure for a life of religion; that of the soldiers to war; Luzina's annual "vacations"; the pitiful departure of Miss O'Rorke; the departure of the Tousignant children; Alexandre's pleasure at leaving the city and then his advice never to depart; Odette's and Alicia's journeys from the home. Enthusiasm, anxiety, and despair surround all of this movement.[52]

In the 1966 *La Route d'Altamont,* Roy still endows her young character, Christine, with a sense of hope and adventure, an impatience to depart toward happiness and *recommencement.* For Christine, one always leaves in the freshness of morning, toward the transformation of the world, of things, and of oneself, but the sentiment of an imminent departure can still be "triste parfois, parfois joyeux." Reality has begun to touch Christine who melodramatically imagines a memorable departure by a poor family from their lodgings and witnesses, instead, a scene devoid of regret or of any emotion whatsoever. The young girl then soon learns from her mother that this need to depart is, indeed, an obsession that can cause misery: " 'Toi aussi tu aurais cette maladie de famille, ce mal du départ. Quelle fatalité! . . . Pauvre de toi. . . . Qu'adviendra-t-il de toi, pauvre, pauvre de toi!' " Christine's own attitude will alter as she matures, until she envisions paradise as "une région où il n'y a sans doute plus ni carrefour ni difficiles points de départs."[53]

Departures described in Roy's fiction subsequent to 1966 are progressively sad. If humanity is seen in 1972 as "des enfants perdus qui aspirent à un commun rivage," then people are increasingly searching for stability rather than for a nomadic existence, and even the thought of additional departures becomes painful. In 1975 when Sam Lee Wong, suddenly beloved by the inhabitants of Horizon, is forced to leave the town, he is anguished, embarrassed, and horrified even at hearing the words, "départ" and "retraite." This feeling of sorrow deepens in 1977, when the young schoolteacher must leave her pupils, thereby causing the inevitable separation among loved ones. And by 1979, Roy's narrator fears *la route* and its call to depart.[54]

NOTES

[1] Gabrielle Roy, "Le Pays de *Bonheur d'occasion*," in *Morceaux*, ed. Robert Guy Scully (Montréal: Les Editions du Noroît, 1978), p. 120; Albert Le Grand, "Gabrielle Roy ou l'être partagé," *Etudes Françaises*, 1ère année, No. 2 (juin 1965), pp. 39-41, 62-64; Paula Gilbert Lewis, "The Incessant Call of the Open Road: Gabrielle Roy's Incorrigible Nomads," *The French Review*, 53, No. 6 (May 1980), 818. See also Marc Gagné, *Visages de Gabrielle Roy* (Montréal: Librairie Beauchemin Limitée, 1973), pp. 97-98; François Ricard, *Gabrielle Roy*, Ecrivains canadiens d'aujourd'hui, No. 11 (Montréal: Editions Fides, 1975), pp. 8, 31; André Brochu, "Gabrielle Roy," Notes from course on author, Université de Montréal, Printemps 1978, taken by one of his students; André Brochu, "La Structure sémantique de *Bonheur d'occasion*," *Revue des Sciences Humaines*, 45, No. 173 (janvier-mars 1979), 43.

[2] Personal interview with Gabrielle Roy, 29 June 1980. The study to which one is referring is the article by Lewis cited in the previous note. The term, "incorrigible nomads," comes from Gabrielle Roy, *La Rivière sans repos* (Montréal: Librairie Beauchemin Limitée, 1971), p. 314.

[3] Gabrielle Roy, "Un Noël en route," *La Revue Moderne*, 22, No. 8 (décembre 1940), 32; Gabrielle Roy, "Un Vagabond frappe à notre porte," *Un Jardin au bout du monde* (Montréal: Librairie Beauchemin Limitée, 1975), p. 49; Gabrielle Roy, *La Route d'Altamont*, Collection L'Arbre, No. 10 (Montréal: Editions HMH, 1966), pp. 231, 164, 157. The second work was originally published in *Amérique Française* (janvier 1946), pp. 29-51. In the first work, see also pp. 33, 34; in the second, see pp. 43-45; and in the third, see pp. 163, 232, 237-241. See also Gabrielle Roy, *Rue Deschambault* (1955; rpt. Montréal: Librairie Beauchemin Limitée, 1974), pp. 196, 244; Gabrielle Roy, *La Montagne secrète* (1961; rpt. Montréal: Librairie Beauchemin Limitée, 1974), pp. 96, 190, 203; Roy, *La Rivière sans repos*, pp. 34-35, 235, 314-315; Gabrielle Roy, "Ely! Ely! Ely!," *Liberté*, 21, No. 3, année 1979, numéro 123 (mai-juin 1979), 26; Gagné, p. 130; Lewis, p. 818; Jack Warwick, *L'Appel du nord dans la littérature canadienne-française*, trans. Jean Simard. Collection Constantes (Montréal: Editions Hurtubise HMH, 1972), pp. 133-136. Ricard

states that Roy's works themselves, ending with a death or a departure, seem to call to the subsequent book to commence. See Ricard, p. 153.

[4] Roy, "Ely! Ely! Ely!," p. 15. See also Lewis, p. 820.

[5] The series, "Peuples du Canada," has been published as part of: Gabrielle Roy, *Fragiles Lumières de la terre: Ecrits divers 1942-1970*, Collection Prose Entière (Montréal: Les Editions Quinze, 1978). See also Lewis, p. 816; Roy, "Le Pays de *Bonheur d'occasion,*" p. 114.

[6] Gabrielle Roy, "La Source au désert," *Le Bulletin des Agriculteurs*, 42, No. 10 (octobre 1946), 30, 34, 38. See also Gabrielle Roy, "La Conversion des O'Connor," *La Revue Moderne*, 21, No. 5 (septembre 1939), 4-5, 32-33; Roy, "Un Noël en route," pp. 8, 32-34; Gabrielle Roy, "La Fuite de Sally," *Le Bulletin des Agriculteurs*, 27, No. 1 (janvier 1941), 9, 39-40; Gabrielle Roy, "La Pension de vieillesse," *Le Bulletin des Agriculteurs*, 39, No. 11 (novembre 1943), 32; Gabrielle Roy, "La Grande Voyageuse," *La Revue Moderne*, 24, No. 1 (mai 1942), 12, 13, 27-30; Lewis, p. 816.

[7] Gabrielle Roy, *La Petite Poule d'eau* (1950; rpt. Montréal: Librairie Beauchemin Limitée, 1970), p. 207. See also pp. 12-18, 29-30, 60-62, 66, 81-83, 91, 133-134, 141, 149, 155, 157, 161, 170-171, 177, 185, 216-217, 248; Gabrielle Roy, *Bonheur d'occasion* (1945; rpt. Montréal: Librairie Beauchemin Limitée, 1973), pp. 27, 44, 83-90, 153, 168-177, 192-195, 234, 244-261, 267-270, 280-287, 312, 334-339; Roy, "Le Pays de *Bonheur d'occasion,*" pp. 120-121; Gabrielle Roy, *Alexandre Chenevert* (1954; rpt. Montréal: Beauchemin, 1973), pp. 48, 63, 83, 117-121, 129, 148, 183-276, 302-305, 310, 314, 375-376; Lewis, pp. 816-817; John Hind-Smith, *Three Voices: The Lives of Margaret Laurence, Gabrielle Roy and Frederick Philip Grove* (Toronto: Clarke Irwin, 1975), pp. 94, 100.

[8] Roy, *Rue Deschambault*, p. 86. See also pp. 49-54, 57-59, 61-65, 99-138, 168, 173, 176, 191-198, 220, 247, 251-261, 276, 288, 292-293; Roy, *La Montagne secrète*, pp. 16-18, 21, 38-39, 61-63, 81-85, 99-100, 131, 139, 144-150, 157-159, 161-162, 167, 180, 185-189, 200; Lewis, pp. 817-818; Warwick, pp. 142-143.

[9] Roy, *La Route d'Altamont*, pp. 28, 212, 94, 148, 242; Gabrielle Roy, "Le Manitoba," *Le Magazine Maclean*, 2, No. 7 (juillet 1962), 114. In the first work see also pp. 30, 64-69, 73, 91, 95, 98-110, 113, 140-141, 155-159, 162-164, 167-173, 180-185, 189-192, 196-198, 214-216, 227, 243, 252-255. In the second see also pp. 103, 105, 109. See also Gabrielle Roy, "Mon Héritage du Manitoba," *Mosaic*, 3iii (1970), 70; Gabrielle Roy, "*Terre des Hommes:* Le Thème raconté," *Fragiles Lumières de la terre*, p. 233; Lewis, p. 817; Brochu, "Gabrielle Roy."

[10] Roy, *La Rivière sans repos*, pp. 204, 268; Personal interview with Gabrielle Roy, 29 June 1980. In the first work see also pp. 25-35, 44-46,

81, 97-99, 120, 166-171, 197-203, 233-249, 269, 281, 284-291, 295. See also Gabrielle Roy, *Cet Eté qui chantait* (Québec-Montréal: Les Editions Françaises, 1972), pp. 11, 44-45, 51, 83-102, 145-160, 174, 195, 198; Lewis, p. 817.

[11] Roy, *Un Jardin au bout du monde*, p. 172; Gabrielle Roy, *Ces Enfants de ma vie* (Montréal: Editions Internationales Alain Stanké Ltée, 1977), p. 199. In the first work see also pp. 82, 88, 102, 125-130, 154, 166, 171-173, 176-181, 217; in the second see also pp. 94-95, 101-105, 167-168, 177-186. See also Roy, "Ely! Ely! Ely!," pp. 13-26; Lewis, pp. 817-818.

[12] Roy, *Un Jardin au bout du monde*, pp. 82, 166-167. See also Roy, *Bonheur d'occasion*, pp. 83-90, 221-223; Roy, *La Route d'Altamont*, pp. 168-169, 180; Ricard, p. 123; Le Grand, pp. 44-45; Brochu, "Gabrielle Roy"; Brochu, "La Structure sémantique de *Bonheur d'occasion*," pp. 38-47; Phyllis Grosskurth, *Gabrielle Roy*, Canadian Writers and Their Works (Toronto: Forum House, 1972), pp. 55-56; Jacques Blais, "L'Unité organique de *Bonheur d'occasion*," *Etudes Françaises*, 6, No. 1 (février 1970), 41, 44-49. These annual house moves also ironically occur in springtime, a time of rebirth.

[13] Roy, *Bonheur d'occasion*, pp. 110, 291; Le Grand, pp. 51-56. In the first work, see also pp. 12, 15, 26-27, 34, 75-76, 93, 102, 119, 230, 232, 236, 240, 344. See also Lewis, p. 819; André Brochu, "Thèmes et structures de *Bonheur d'occasion*," in *L'Instance critique* (Montréal: Leméac, 1974), pp. 220, 224-225, 228-239; Guy Savoie, "Le Réalisme du cadre spatio-temporel de *Bonheur d'occasion*," Thesis Université Laval 1972, pp. 120-127. One year after the publication of her first novel, Roy described the life of Dr. Raymond as leading nowhere, as turning upon itself, and that of Anne as a refusal to flee, to travel. See Roy, "La Source au desért," pp. 10, 30, 39.

[14] Roy, *La Montagne secrète*, pp. 219, 222. See also pp. 122, 157-159, 198; Roy, *La Route d'Altamont*, pp. 94-95, 98-99, 148, 235-236; Roy, *La Rivière sans repos*, pp. 266-269, 281-282; Roy, *Un Jardin au bout du monde*, pp. 183-184; Lewis, p. 819; Gagné, pp. 120-123, 146; Agnès Whitfield, "*Alexandre Chenevert:* Cercle vicieux et évasions manquées," *Voix et Images du Pays*, 8 (1974), 108-119, 121-125; Brochu, "Gabrielle Roy"; Warwick, pp. 135-136.

[15] Roy, "Ma Coqueluche," *Rue Deschambault*, p. 84. See also pp. 99-138; Roy, *Bonheur d'occasion*, pp. 168-177; Roy, *Alexandre Chenevert*, pp. 195-276; Roy, *La Route d'Altamont*, pp. 101-152, 189-209, 245-252; Roy, *La Rivière sans repos*, pp. 197-204, 235-249; Roy, *Cet Eté qui chantait*, pp. 145-160; Lewis, pp. 819-820, 823; Ricard, pp. 55-56; Whitfield, pp. 119-120; Gagné, pp. 58, 102, 239-240; Paula Gilbert Lewis,

"*Street of Riches* and *The Road Past Altamont*: The Feminine World of Gabrielle Roy," *Journal of Women's Studies in Literature*, 1, No. 2 (Spring 1979), 138.

[16] Roy, *Bonheur d'occasion*, p. 168; Roy, *Cet Eté qui chantait*, p. 157; Roy, *Alexandre Chenevert*, p. 212; Roy, *Rue Deschambault*, p. 113. In the first work, see also pp. 149-159, 169-170, 193-194, 325-326, 334; in the second see pp. 156, 158-160; in the third see pp. 209-211, 213, 218-222; in the fourth see pp. 101, 126-128, 131, 133-138, 293. See also Roy, *La Route d'Altamont*, pp. 93, 164, 198, 204-207, 255; Roy, "Mon Héritage du Manitoba," pp. 72-73; Roy, "La Source au désert," pp. 11, 31, 34; Roy, *Ces Enfants de ma vie*, pp. 177-186; Lewis, "Gabrielle Roy's Incorrigible Nomads," pp. 819-820, 823; Gagné, pp. 101-103; Whitfield, pp. 114-120. Especially when these roads to the past are blocked, when characters can not actually voyage to places of their youth, they do have recourse to memories, dreams, and daydreaming. This power of imagined travel will be examined in Chapter VII.

[17] Roy, *Un Jardin au bout du monde*, p. 83; Roy, *La Route d'Altamont*, p. 238. In the first work, see also pp. 61-63, 81-82, 123-130, 153, 176-181; in the second see also pp. 28, 30, 217, 237, 239, 242, 245-255. See also Roy, "Le Manitoba," p. 116; Roy, "Mon Héritage du Manitoba," pp. 72-73; Gabrielle Roy, "Souvenirs du Manitoba," *La Revue de Paris*, 62e année, No. 2 (février 1955), p. 78; Roy, *Rue Deschambault*, pp. 107, 136-138; Roy, *La Rivière sans repos*, pp. 40-46, 230; Roy, "Ely! Ely! Ely!," pp. 24-25; Lewis, "Gabrielle Roy's Incorrigible Nomads," pp. 819-820, 823.

[18] Roy, *La Route d'Altamont*," p. 143. See also pp. 133, 142, 204, 255; Roy, La Rivière sans repos, pp. 87-88, 166-171, 179-180, 197-204, 211, 235-249, 266-269, 301; Roy, *Alexandre Chenevert*, pp. 181-183, 221, 226-227, 383; Roy, *Rue Deschambault*, pp. 134, 200; Roy, *La Montagne secrète*, pp. 198, 219-222; Roy, *Cet Eté qui chantait*, pp. 157-160, 194-197; Roy, *Un Jardin au bout du monde*, pp. 100-102, 123, 183-184, 215-217; Lewis "Gabrielle Roy's Incorrigible Nomads," pp. 819-820, 823; Gagné, pp. 103-105; Paula Gilbert Lewis, "The Themes of Memory and Death in Gabrielle Roy's *La Route d'Altamont*," *Modern Fiction Studies*, 22, No. 3 (Autumn 1976), 466; Marc Gagné, "*La Rivière sans repos* de Gabrielle Roy: Etude mythocritique incluant 'Voyage en Ungava (extraits) par Gabrielle Roy (suite)," *Revue de l'Université d'Ottawa*, 46, No. 2 (avril-juin 1976), 189-199. Roy has stated that she agreed with this attempted return to primitivism only if it were cyclically linked with a route toward the future. Personal interview with Gabrielle Roy, 29 June 1980.

[19] Lewis, "Gabrielle Roy's Incorrigible Nomads," p. 820. See also Roy, *La Petite Poule d'eau*, pp. 26-27, 29-30, 36, 146-147; Ricard, pp. 74-

75; Jacques Allard, "Le Chemin qui mène à *La Petite Poule d'eau,*" *Cahiers de Saint-Marie,* No. 1 (mai 1966), pp. 58-61, 63-69.

[20] Gabrielle Roy, 1970, as quoted in Gagné, *Visages de Gabrielle Roy,* p. 83.   See also Roy, *La Petite Poule d'eau,* pp. 17-18, 140, 146; Roy, *La Rivière sans repos,* pp. 186, 211; Roy, *Un Jardin au bout du monde,* pp. 176-181; Roy, *Ces Enfants de ma vie,* pp. 177-186, 205; Allard, pp. 58-69; Lewis, "Gabrielle Roy's Incorrigible Nomads," pp. 819, 822.

[21] Roy, "Un Jardin au bout du monde," p. 172.   See also p. 171; Roy, *La Montagne secrète,* pp. 21, 28; Roy, *Rue Deschambault,* pp. 43-44; Gagné, *Visages de Gabrielle Roy,* pp. 101-103; Lewis, "Gabrielle Roy's Incorrigible Nomads," p. 822; Savoie, pp. 121-127.

[22] Roy, *Bonheur d'occasion,* pp. 101-102.   See also pp. 12, 26-27, 29, 32-34, 44, 75, 148, 186, 208, 221-223, 227, 252, 291, 334-339; Lewis, "Gabrielle Roy's Incorrigible Nomads," pp. 818-819; Brochu, "Thèmes et structures," pp. 222-233, 235-240; Brochu, "Gabrielle Roy"; Brochu, "La Structure sémantique," pp. 40-43; Le Grand, pp. 46, 51-57. Luzina also views her direct road toward childbirth as a vacation and an adventure, but, of course, she is in no way destructive. Jimmy, however, escapes on a direct path to the South and, as a result, destroys his mother. See Roy, *La Petite Poule d'eau,* pp. 14-15; Lewis, "Gabrielle Roy's Incorrigible Nomads," p. 819.

[23] Roy, *La Route d'Altamont,* p. 164.   See also pp. 28, 30, 162-163; Roy, *Un Jardin au bout du monde,* pp. 61-63, 100-102; Roy, "Le Manitoba," p. 109; Lewis, "Gabrielle Roy's Incorrigible Nomads," p. 819.

[24] Roy, *La Route d'Altamont,* pp. 197-198, 242.   See also pp. 138-139, 144, 163-167, 196, 237-241, 253; Roy, *Rue Deschambault,* pp. 59, 134, 243-247; Roy, *La Montagne secrète,* pp. 21, 28, 186-189; Roy, *La Rivière sans repos,* pp. 261, 295-296; Lewis, "Gabrielle Roy's Incorrigible Nomads," p. 822.

[25] Lewis, "Gabrielle Roy's Incorrigible Nomads," pp. 822-823; Roy, *Alexandre Chenevert,* p. 188; Roy, *Rue Deschambault,* pp. 198, 200; Roy, *La Montagne secrète,* pp. 198, 219; Roy, *La Rivière sans repos,* pp. 266-269, 301, 304, 314-315; Roy, *Cet Eté qui chantait,* pp. 157-160, 175; Roy, *Un Jardin au bout du monde,* pp. 100-102, 125-130, 154, 215-217.

[26] Roy, *La Route d'Altamont,* pp. 196, 190.   See also pp. 158, 166, 189, 191-192, 197-198; Roy, *Alexandre Chenevert,* pp. 189-191; 218; Roy, *Rue Deschambault,* pp. 44, 51; Roy, *La Montagne secrète,* pp. 81-82; Roy, "Le Manitoba," p. 109; Roy, "Mon Héritage du Manitoba," pp. 71, 78-79; Lewis, "Gabrielle Roy's Incorrigible Nomads," pp. 820-821; Gagné, *Visages de Gabrielle Roy,* pp. 110-115. Related to this immensity of open spaces are the battlefields envisioned by Azarius Lacasse. See

Roy, *Bonheur d'occasion,* pp. 334-335.

[27] Roy, *Rue Deschambault,* p. 38; Roy, *Un Jardin au bout du monde,* p. 32; Roy, *Rue Deschambault,* p. 82; Roy, *Ces Enfants de ma vie,* pp. 49, 56. In *Rue Deschambault,* see also pp. 39, 83-86, 103, 193, 244, 251-261; in *Un Jardin au bout du monde,* see also pp. 68, 100-102, 153-154, 161, 167, 171-173, 177-181, 215-217. See also Roy, *Bonheur d'occasion,* pp. 44, 291; Roy, *La Petite Poule d'eau,* p. 207; Roy, *La Montagne secrète,* pp. 196, 219-222; Roy, *La Route d'Altamont,* pp. 87-90, 105, 170, 215, 232; Roy, *La Rivière sans repos,* pp. 58-59, 99-100, 229, 238, 314-315; Lewis, "Gabrielle Roy's Incorrigible Nomads," p. 819; Ricard, p. 31; Annette Saint-Pierre, *Gabrielle Roy: Sous le signe du rêve* (Saint-Boniface, Manitoba: Editions du Blé, 1975), pp. 43-50, 91.

[28] Roy, *La Rivière sans repos,* p. 176; Roy, *La Petite Poule d'eau,* p. 272; Roy, *La Rivière sans repos,* p. 20. In this last work, see also pp. 35, 54, 149, 230, 233-234, 236, 238, 243, 290-291. In *La Petite Poule d'eau,* see also pp. 37, 72, 119-120, 145. See also Roy, *Rue Deschambault,* pp. 196, 198; Roy, *La Montagne secrète,* pp. 23, 26-27, 29, 70, 76, 185; Roy, *La Route d'Altamont, pp.* 217, 242; Lewis, "Gabrielle Roy's Incorrigible Nomads," pp. 821-822; Saint-Pierre, pp. 41-50, 91; Gagné, *Visages de Gabrielle Roy,* pp. 206-209; Savoie, pp. 125-127.

[29] Roy, *Bonheur d'occasion,* p. 33; Roy, *La Montagne secrète,* pp. 89-90, 100-104, 123, 198, 219-222; Roy, *La Route d'Altamont,* pp. 29, 191-192, 206-209, 229; Roy, *La Rivière sans repos,* pp. 58-59, 99-100, 102-106; Roy, *Un Jardin au bout du monde,* pp. 61-63, 81-83, 125-130; Roy, *Ces Enfants de ma vie,* pp. 148, 170, 200; Gagné, *Visages de Gabrielle Roy,* pp. 117-120, 218-221.

[30] Roy, *Un Jardin au bout du monde,* p. 205; Roy, *Cet Eté qui chantait,* p. 51. In the second work, see also pp. 193-198. See also Roy, *Bonheur d'occasion,* pp. 297, 325-326; Roy, *Alexandre Chenevert,* pp. 105, 148, 182, 189-191, 195, 209-211, 219; Roy, *Rue Deschambault,* pp. 40, 99, 126, 179; Roy, *La Montagne secrète,* pp. 36, 83-85, 159, 186; Roy, "Le Manitoba," pp. 111-112; Roy, *La Route d'Altamont,* pp. 85, 99; Roy, "Mon Héritage du Manitoba," p. 77; Roy, *La Rivière sans repos,* pp. 87, 166-171, 180, 192, 266, 271, 281, 295, 301, 304; Roy, "Mémoire et création: Préface de *La Petite Poule d'eau,*" *Fragiles Lumières de la terre,* pp. 296-297; Gagné, *Visages de Gabrielle Roy,* p. 241; Whitfield, pp. 114, 116.

[31] Roy, *La Route d'Altamont,* p. 157. See also pp. 110, 168-169, 175; Roy, *La Petite Poule d'eau,* pp. 194-195; Roy, *Alexandre Chenevert,* pp. 185-186, 302; Roy, *Rue Deschambault,* pp. 12, 14, 18, 20, 22, 23; Roy, *Cet Eté qui chantait,* pp. 197-198; Roy, *Ces Enfants de ma vie,* pp. 167-168, 177-186; Roy, "Ely! Ely! Ely!," p. 14.

³²Roy, *Rue Deschambault,* p. 99; Roy, *La Petite Poule d'eau,* p. 134. In the first work, see also pp. 100, 108, 126, 138, 202. In the second, see also pp. 13, 44, 133, 254-256, 260. See also Roy, "Souvenirs du Manitoba," p. 79; Roy, *La Montagne secrète,* pp. 112-113, 155; Roy, *La Route d'Altamont,* pp. 38, 108, 159, 250; Roy, *Cet Eté qui chantait,* pp. 174-175; Roy, *Ces Enfants de ma vie,* p. 142; Lewis, "Gabrielle Roy's Incorrigible Nomads," p. 822; Ricard, pp. 24-25; Saint-Pierre, pp. 41-50. The italics in the first quotation have been added to emphasize all of the nomadic images in this passage.

³³Roy, "La Rivière sans repos," p. 216. See also Roy, *La Petite Poule d'eau,* pp. 20, 63, 65, 73, 79-81, 100-101, 109, 124-125, 129-132, 149, 151-152, 271; Roy, *Rue Deschambault,* pp. 245, 287-288; Roy, "Memoire et création: Préface de *La Petite Poule d'eau," Fragiles Lumières de la terre,* pp. 296-297; Lewis, "Gabrielle Roy's Incorrigible Nomads," p. 822; Brochu, "Gabrielle Roy."

³⁴See especially Lewis, "Gabrielle Roy's Incorrigible Nomads," pp. 823-824; Ricard, pp. 22-25, 31-36, 75, 120-124; Hind-Smith, pp. 74, 105. Roy uses the reading of the tale of adventure, *Ivanhoe,* just as she uses that of *Treasure Island* and *Robinson Crusoe* in other works.

³⁵Roy, *Bonheur d'occasion,* pp. 249-250, 244-245. See also pp. 61-62, 147, 229, 251, 310, 332. See also Roy, *La Route d'Altamont,* pp. 94-95, 103, 156, 170-173, 181, 182; Roy, *La Rivière sans repos,* pp. 55-56, 104, 108, 151-152, 184-185; Roy, *Cet Eté qui chantait,* pp. 160, 183-184; Roy, *Ces Enfants de ma vie,* pp. 12, 14, 75, 99.

³⁶Gaston Bachelard, *La Poétique de l'espace,* Bibliothèque de philosophie contemporaine (Paris: Presses Universitaires de France, 1978), pp. 17-20, 24-27, 30-44, 46-49, 52-59, 61-63, 72-75, 83-91, 93-103, 127, 130-135, 138, 145, 158, 178-181, 200-207; Gaston Bachelard, *La Poétique de la rêverie,* Bibliothèque de philosophie contemporaine (Paris: Presses Universitaires de France, 1974), pp. 117, 166-169; François Dagognet, *Gaston Bachelard,* SUP "Philosophes" (Paris: Presses Universitaires de France, 1972), pp. 45, 48-49; Lewis, "Gabrielle Roy's Incorrigible Nomads," pp. 823-824; Gagné, *Visages de Gabrielle Roy,* pp. 106-110, 130-133. The relationship between the intimacy of the home and daydreams will be examined in Chapter VII.

³⁷Roy, *Alexandre Chenevert,* pp. 221-222. See also pp. 24, 197, 216, 223, 237-245, 247; Roy, *La Petite Poule d'eau,* pp. 43, 67, 119-220, 159, 212, 236, 242-247, 252. The third work describing a country home is *Cet Eté qui chantait,* in which there appears the image of a home at night, with only candlelight dancing on the walls and inhabitants joyously communicating. In addition, one sees a little chapel that, with its open door, seems to allow the exterior to penetrate its small space. See pp.

130-132, 136-139.

[38] Roy, *Rue Deschambault*, p. 176. See also pp. 15, 38-39, 51, 63, 89, 92, 134, 135, 137, 160, 166-167, 169, 178, 243-244, 246, 258-261, 269-273, 281. In this same work appears, as well, the portrait of Tante Thérésina in her self-imposed interior prison, opposed to life outside. See pp. 188, 195, 197.

[39] Roy, *Ces Enfants de ma vie*, pp. 123, 125, 128. See also pp. 24, 57-78, 116-117, 124, 127, 167-168, 177-186; Roy, *Rue Deschambault*, pp. 252-255, 260, 291-293. The image of a warm school in the middle of a winter blizzard also appears in Roy, *La Montagne secrète*, pp. 62-63.

[40] Roy, *La Montagne secrète*, p. 193. See also pp. 42, 45-47, 54, 57, 68, 76, 194-195.

[41] Roy, *La Rivière sans repos*, pp. 237-238. See also pp. 15, 31, 55-58, 63, 124, 129, 141-143, 149, 156, 158-159, 188, 207-208, 215, 245, 254, 260-261. The warm home and the singing water for tea, seen in contrast to the cold, snowy winter outside, later appear, as well, in *Courte-Queue*. Here the cat and her kittens walk all night in the snow to get to Berthe's home, where they immediately retreat behind the stove that seems to meow like the animals. The teakettle purrs, and with winter outside, happiness and warmth remain indoors. Gabrielle Roy, *Courte-Queue* (Montréal: Editions Internationales Alain Stanké Ltée, 1979), pp. 2, 5, 39, 40, 43.

[42] Roy, *Un Jardin au bout du monde*, p. 51. See also pp. vii, 11-13, 15, 17, 30, 57, 71-75, 83, 88, 110; Roy, *La Route d'Altamont*, pp. 15, 41-42, 156, 157; Lewis, "Gabrielle Roy's Incorrigible Nomads," p. 824.

[43] Roy, "Souvenirs du Manitoba," p. 83; Roy, *La Route d'Altamont*, p. 197; Roy, *Un Jardin au bout du monde*, pp. 171, 153. See also Lewis, "Gabrielle Roy's Incorrigible Nomads," p. 824.

[44] Lewis, "Gabrielle Roy's Incorrigible Nomads," p. 824; Ricard, pp. 8, 21, 35-36, 86; Le Grand, pp. 42-44; Gagné, *Visages de Gabrielle Roy*, pp. 191-202; Saint-Pierre, pp. 54, 75, 123-125.

[45] Roy, *"Terre des Hommes:* Le Thème raconté," *Fragiles Lumières de la terre*, pp. 230, 204. The second quotation is taken from the unpublished Gabrielle Roy, "Carnets intimes" (été 1973), as quoted in Ricard, p. 21. See also Albert Camus, "Jonas," *L'Exil et le royaume* (Paris: Editions Gallimard, 1957), p. 183.

[46] Roy, *Cet Eté qui chantait*, pp. 12-13, 169-170; Roy, "Le Manitoba," pp. 118, 120; Roy, "Ely! Ely! Ely!," pp. 24-25. Once again, Roy described her own continued need for solitude and solidarity as stemming from her hours alone with nature at one end of the rue Deschambault and then her sense of being with humanity, closer to Winnipeg, at the opposite end of the street. Personal interview with Gabrielle Roy, 29 June 1980.

[47] Roy, *Bonheur d'occasion,* pp. 96, 127, 143, 181, 184, 187-190, 226, 236, 335; Roy, *La Petite Poule d'eau,* pp. 18, 21-23, 104, 132, 146, 171, 172, 178, 185. See also Lewis, "Gabrielle Roy's Incorrigible Nomads," p. 824.

[48] Roy, *Alexandre Chenevert,* pp. 117-119, 182-183, 195, 197, 201, 203-207, 268, 347-348; Roy, *La Rivière sans repos,* pp. 184-185, 268-269, 282, 314-315; Lewis, "Gabrielle Roy's Incorrigible Nomads," p. 824; Le Grand, pp. 42-44.

[49] Roy, *La Montagne secrète,* pp. 93, 103, 54, 63, 79. See also pp. 16-18, 25, 37, 39, 70-73, 76, 81, 92, 108, 140, 148, 163-164, 187, 191-192, 218-219. See also Lewis, "Gabrielle Roy's Incorrigible Nomads," pp. 824-825. The solitude-solidarity condition of Pierre as an artist will be treated in Chapter VIII.

[50] Roy, *Rue Deschambault,* p. 84; Roy, *La Route d'Altamont,* pp. 229-230, 206; Roy, *Rue Deschambault,* p. 247. In the first work, see also pp. 83, 134-138, 176, 178, 244, 246, 281; in the second see pp. 205, 235, 239, 253. See also Lewis, "Gabrielle Roy's Incorrigible Nomads," p. 825. One final conflict that occurs because of incessant travel or that, in fact, causes that wandering has previously been examined: the opposition between the city and the country. With the Lacasse family, Mlle Côté, Alexandre, Pierre, Mme Beaulieu, and Martine, this inherent conflict is seldom resolved.

[51] Lewis, "Gabrielle Roy's Incorrigible Nomads," p. 825.

[52] Roy, "Ely! Ely! Ely!," p. 26. See also Roy, *Bonheur d'occasion,* pp. 317, 336-339; Roy, *La Petite Poule d'eau,* pp. 14-15, 19, 106-108, 133-134, 140-149, 161, 165; Roy, *Alexandre Chenevert,* pp. 10, 189-191, 218, 274; Roy, *Rue Deschambault,* pp. 76-78, 179, 215-216, 221, 247.

[53] Roy, *La Route d'Altamont,* pp. 165, 185-186, 255. See also pp. 101-103, 141, 157, 164, 166, 174, 242; Lewis, "Gabrielle Roy's Incorrigible Nomads," p. 825.

[54] Roy, *Cet Eté qui chantait,* p. 198; Roy, *Un Jardin au bout du monde,* p. 122. In this last work see also pp. 113-118, 120-121, 123. See also Roy, *Ces Enfants de ma vie,* pp. 208-209; Lewis, "Gabrielle Roy's Incorrigible Nomads," p. 825.

CHAPTER VII

The Power of Imagined Travel: Memory, Dreams, and Daydreams

If the majority of Gabrielle Roy's characters are people who move, travel, and obey the call of the open road, they also spend much of their time, while at home, in imagined travel, with the call of the mind to memories, dreams, and daydreams. The author herself recognized this important facet of her literary beings: " 'Quand mes personnages ne peuvent voyager, ils rêvent; le voyage par excellence, c'est le voyage de l'âme.' " With the latter part of this admission, Roy was, in addition, underscoring the essential geographic nature of the imagination, for, as states Gaston Bachelard, "on rêve sur carte, on rêve en géographe." There are, in fact, numerous similarities between the preoccupations of Royan characters when they travel and when they remember, dream, or daydream, especially in reference to the fundamental immensity-intimacy relationship and conflict. In the intimacy of a small, protective, structured space, the mind either remembers the past and, therefore, returns to the immensity of primitive nature, equally protective, or it dreams of the future and opens up onto the wide horizons of the world and the infinite cosmos. The travels of the creative mind can be more grandiose than those of reality.[1]

Throughout the Royan literary universe, the important and powerful role of the imagination cannot be underestimated. Roy has noted the constant activity of her own memories of the past, and critics have seen her characters as expressing a Proustian need to search for and recapture past time. As for dreams and daydreams, the author believed that one could often learn more from them than from reality and that the dream, in particular, "plus que tout autre est commun aux hommes." If her characters are Proustian, they also exhibit a penchant for reverie, particularly in the form of self-illusions; they have been seen, therefore, as suffering from a variation of Flaubert's *bovarysme.* All Royan characters love to give their minds the freedom to wander.[2]

In a 1980 interview, Gabrielle Roy stated that the work done by Gaston Bachelard on dreams was, in her opinion, the most monumental and important of any on this subject. For the purposes of this study, therefore, it is logical to use his definitions of the states of mind associated with dreaming: with memory, dreams, and daydreaming or reverie. Memories are, of course, remembrances of the past and, in the Royan world, usually of a past, happy childhood or young adulthood. As for dreams and daydreams, Bachelard bases his observations upon the distinction originally made by Karl Jung between *animus* and *anima,* with the first related to *rêve* and the second to *rêverie.* In Roy's works, both of these states occur predominantly during the day, since, with a few major exceptions, the role of sleep and of the dreams occurring during that time of day is not as prevalent.[3]

For Bachelard, the dream, or *animus,* is typically associated with masculinity, tension, worry, and the determination and ambition for specific projects. Present in all people, one's *animus* is translated into a desire or goal for the future, to be constructed actively by the individual. Daydreams or reverie, linked with one's *anima,* are, in contrast, typically more female. They are manifested, and precisely in Roy's fiction, in one's thoughts of or wishes for a vague future or another life, perhaps possible, perhaps not. Bachelard defines this state as a penchant for happiness, peace, tranquility, and primitive purity. Lost in the solitude of reverie, one experiences a sensation of intimate warmth, along with expansion into or unity with the cosmos. The state of *anima* produces, therefore, a rapport rather than a conflict between immensity and intimacy. Conflict occurs solely when objective reality abruptly enters into this tender, personal world. As for Royan characters, one often finds them either deep in daydreams or preoccupied with the world of their memories, since they frequently seem to prefer those states to present reality. If each individual possesses both an *animus* and an *anima,* therefore, it is the latter that dominates in the personalities of many of Roy's literary beings.[4]

Throughout Roy's fiction, the role of memory is as pervasive as in the author's own life, documented in her numerous memoirs concerning her family's migration to and her own childhood in Manitoba. In a typically Proustian scene, for example, the semi-autobiographical narrator of *Cet Eté qui chantait* emphasizes this power of memory, involuntarily activated by chance and by exterior circumstances:

> La clochette a tinté fortement, tout près. Et pourquoi cela a-t-il brusquement éveillé en moi le souvenir—que je croyais mort—du temps où, enfant, lorsque j'arrivais pour les vacances d'été chez mes oncles sur leurs fermes au Manitoba, j'étais accueillie dès en descendant du train par le drelin d'une cloche à main qu'agitait sur le seuil l'hôtelier . . . et que j'en étais rendue heureuse mystérieusement. . . . voici que m'est redonnée cette curieuse joie de ma vie dont je ne sais toujours pas au juste de quoi elle est faite et pourquoi elle m'enchante encore.[5]

Given the importance and complexity of the role of memory, therefore, it is evident that one can distinguish numerous levels of remembrances in Roy's works. In a first level, elderly characters, like Mémère, M. Saint-Hilaire, and Martha, recall their youth and their years as spouses and as young parents. Secondly, older characters, such as Eveline, try to remember what they had been told about the past of their parents, while they think back upon their own youth and upon the image of those parents as they had appeared to them in the past. Young characters, like Christine, also recall the earlier days of their lives and attempt to understand those of older generations, of parents and of grandparents. And finally, an adult narrator, again like Christine, recounts her own matured memories of childhood, adolescence, and young adulthood, as she tries to recall anterior remembrances from her own mind as a child. All of these levels of memory, however, are closely interwoven into the typical Royan circle of time where particular moments or experiences appear to be frozen into one instant equaling all time, or where history is seen in a repetitive fashion. Memory, like reverie, produces timelessness: "J'ai dû passer tout l'été, presque tout l'été, au fond de mon hamac . . . et pourtant il ne m'apparaît que comme un seul instant chaud et tranquille, un instant fixé dans une petite musique claire comme le soleil."[6]

Timelessness, however, is only one of the varied attributes of memories in Roy's fictional world. As powerful as a "chant impérissable," one's memory is generally a deep and intimate secret, locked in one's mind, often seemingly lost in "les mystérieux abïmes du souvenir," but then suddenly, instinctively, and involuntarily activated. When an adult Christine accidently discovers a road that passes through the sole mountain chain of Manitoba, for example, the sight of this countryside causes Eveline to recall the beloved hills of her childhood in Quebec. What this road past Altamont actually represents, therefore, is a route to the past, accidently or involuntarily discovered by youth on behalf of the old. When Christine then consciously attempts to find this road again, she encounters difficulty. Rediscovery is not within her will: "Et certes, je savais déjà que les souvenirs heureux ne nous viennent pas de notre gré, qu'ils appartiennent à un autre monde qu'à celui de notre volonté. . . ."[7]

Precisely because of their involuntary nature, memories must be stimulated by some exterior key, themselves involuntarily encountered. In *La Route d'Altamont,* it is the town itself or, more specifically, the name of the town engraved on a post office sign that becomes similarly engraved in the older woman's memory, as it fixes itself "comme une flèche dans son esprit." In other works, odors, in particular those of poverty, fish, and flowers, inspire these imagined return trips to the past. The sound of music or a cow bell, the sight of hills or plains, and, as in "Un Vagabond frappe à notre porte," listening to tales recounted by an effective storyteller can all activate one's memory. Even more complexly, an older memory can be resuscitated by another, more recent remembrance. When Eveline later recalls the day when she and Christine discovered the Manitoban hills, for example, her mind travels further back into time, as she also begins to think about her earlier memory of Quebec.[8]

One of the most intriguing aspects of memory can be found in what the mind chooses to recall from the past. At times, it is only a seemingly unimportant detail that is remembered. Throughout Roy's semi-autobiographical works, in fact, the narrator's childhood is recreated as a montage of sketches: of specific people, incidents, and even moments. At other times, an individual retains only a vague impression of a past event. This obscurity of memory is often described as a light from the past: the flame from a candle, a light at the end of a long corridor, or "un grand morceau de temps" that from "l'oubli où il est tombé, obscur et impénétrable . . . remonte parfois comme une lueur."[9]

Related to the way in which the mind remembers the past are the embellishments or distortions that memories receive either from one's imagination or from the passage of time. Christine feels, for example, that her mother is probably exaggerating the beauty of the hills of Quebec, just as her entire family has continuously altered the story of her grandparents' migration to Manitoba. She describes this particular tale as a canvas or tapestry on which each family member has worked: "En sorte que l'histoire varia, grandit et se compliqua à mesure que la conteuse prenait de l'âge et du recul."[10]

Visions of the past can also be modified because of a confusion in memory, especially during old age. This infirmity, therefore, is often associated with senility or what one calls "second-childhood." "La Grande Voyageuse," the father in "Un Vagabond frappe à notre porte," Mémère, and M. Saint-Hilaire all suffer from this weakness of remembering, and the last two, in particular, are greatly embarrassed about it, especially in front of the young Christine. Mémère, for example, does have difficulty in recalling the names of her grandchildren but is determined to prove that she remains a capable and useful, although elderly, person. When she decides to make a doll for Christine, she becomes so inspired in her artistic endeavor that her excellent memory returns, and she is easily able to recall exactly where every needed item is located. Similarly, M. Saint-Hilaire becomes confused when he tries to recall the past, but he clearly understands his problem:

> He explains to Christine how numbers are easily lost in retrospect and how particular details will flash into one's mind without that person's being able to recall an entire incident. It is as though one were placed before numerous little unmarked roads where certain landmarks appear familiar. But one is not sure which specific route will lead . . . to the Manitoban mountain range and to the rediscovery of the true past.

One continues to wander in search of the accurate memory, but one remains fearful that all roads are blocked.[11]

Whenever one is not cut off from this past, however, memories can produce a sensation of joy and happiness, as one recalls, like Florentine and Alexandre, one's youth or, like Mémère, one's past achievements as a young adult: "Car, tout comme pour un être humain, le bonheur de sa vieillesse [of

Tontine, the dog] lui vient du souvenir d'avoir été jeune et pleine de vitalité." In the Royan world, the power of memory is evident even in animals. It is frequent, however, that feelings of nostalgia, sadness, regret, bitterness, or even pain will be the result of this mental return to the past. One recognizes the inevitability of the passing of time, the actual loss of past happiness and youth, and the changes that have occurred to render the present world one that the elderly, in particular, may have difficulty in understanding or accepting. Memories, like the years, are piled up in one's mind "comme un amas de feuilles épaisses et bruissantes, tombées au pied de l'arbre, à l'automne." One's past life, as states a dying Mémère, appears as nothing more than a dream, a vague and confusing dream, at times permeated with an overwhelming sense of melancholy.[12]

It is often difficult for younger persons to understand this attitude toward and this importance of accounts of the past, on the part of older individuals:

> Non, ce qui me [Christine] confondait le plus, c'était maman elle-même, son visage changeant, triste et doux quand elle parlait de grand-mère jeune, puis ensuite seulement triste et affaissé. Je ne comprenais presque plus rien à ce va-et-vient d'un être humain à travers le souvenir d'un autre être.

Youth, therefore, can sometimes reject remembrances related by the elderly but usually with maturity, will increasingly desire to comprehend and appreciate the true meanings and importance of the past. With old family photographs and continual questions, young Royan characters like Christine will attempt to communicate with aging people in the latter's mental wanderings into the past so that this younger generation can learn to respect both these memories and the links to traditions and roots that they represent.[13]

It is the maintenance of these traditions, the culture of one's homeland, and the knowledge and pride of a family's past that is one of the essential roles and purposes of memories. Recounted by the old, as guardians of the past, these remembrances, like stories, folklore, and music, will hopefully instill in the young a respect for their origins. Such tales will assure renewed ties with the past of Canadian immigrant groups and Quebecers who have migrated to the West.[14]

For an individual, the most fundamental purpose of retaining one's memory is the need to recapture the lost routes of the past and to experience, at least temporarily, a sensation of fixed time. For the majority of Roy's characters, and in particular for those of *La Route d'Altamont*, therefore, remembrances lead to a form of self-rediscovery, a new retention of one's former, youthful self and a temporary loss of one's present, older self. Memories permit one to travel back mentally toward a state of innocence, primitivism, and paradise where one was secure in a maternal world. As such, however, the Royan character is, at the same time, travelling forward along the circle of life and death that now incorporates both memory and heredity.[15]

Given Gabrielle Roy's vision of humanity and the universe as a series of concentric circles or cycles, it is not surprising that she describes the rapports among memory, life, birth, rebirth, and death in a similar fashion. Since one's memory is associated with a return to one's youth, an elderly person who is not able to rediscover this past, who experiences a failure of memory, fears the loss of this former childhood and, consequently, a self-abandonment into old age and death. When Christine has difficulty in finding the Altamont hills a second time, Eveline appears to age greatly, as though she finally and suddenly realizes and accepts reality. She has become too old, tired, and forgetful to continue to cling to the past, lost forever because she has arrived at the end.[16]

If one is successful in recapturing the past, however, in encountering one's own youth in the mind, there is the risk of abandoning oneself too deeply within these memories and of returning to a mental childhood in total senility. After having expressed satisfaction at seeing her mother's joy while in the mountains, Christine begins to worry that she is about to lose Eveline on this imagined return trip. The younger woman becomes anxious to leave the circular landscape of these hills and to return to the flat plains. Similarly, Martha, at the point of dying, remembers the past, significantly associated with cyclical summer, nature, music, tradition, and homeland:

> Dans ce peu de bien-être, ses pensées, comme déjà libérées, s'élevaient, s'en allaient dans le passé rejoindre un air de musique lointaine. Un air qui avait trait à l'été—toujours donc l'été, saison de la vie, saison du coeur—qui exaltait la chaleur, les cérisiers en fleurs et parlait aussi de jeunes hommes et de jeunes filles réunis

pour danser sur l'herbe d'un pré autour d'un arbre isolé. Ainsi, par quelques bribes de mélodie que retrouvait son souvenir . . . elle se sentait rejointe mystérieusement par une âme inconnue d'elle, dont la nostalgique tendresse était toute vivante dans ce vieux chant d'Ukraine. L'immortalité, était-ce donc vrai?

Martha's young self has joined hands with her old self, as her circle of life closes in death, and yet this cycle will continue within another cycle, since rebirth in the Royan world is infinitely possible.[17]

This concept of continual *recommencement* and, therefore, of a type of immortality for Gabrielle Roy's characters can be attained through the close and complex rapports that exist in her fiction among memories (of another), old age (of parents and grandparents), youth (of children and grandchildren), and heredity (among generations in a family). The most simple form of immortality that one can achieve is to be found in another's memory of that individual: Alexandre Chenevert, despite his insignificance, remains alive because others have not forgotten him and still mention his name from time to time. These cycles of life become more complex when an older person, like Mémère, relates stories of her youth to her child, Eveline, so that the younger person may gain some understanding of the past of the parent. The daughter then retells these memories, now her own, to her child, to Christine, who can then better understand the lives both of her mother and her grandmother. The love for the Rivière Assomption in Quebec and the momentous journey to Manitoba, like the visual memories contained in the old family photographs, are remembrances that have been passed on to the young so that links in time and communication among generations can be successfully effected.[18]

Associated with this recounting of memories to subsequent generations that adopt them as their own is the complex process by which one's memory of a parent tends to mature with the child, until a deeper understanding of the older person is reached. At the same time, there appears in the younger individual an increasing realization and acceptance of one's similarities with the parent. After Winnie's death, Elsa thinks about her mother, finally understands the older woman's distress, and, with age, begins to resemble her. Martha, likewise, remembers her aged mother as she had been in the Ukraine, when her children had departed for Canada. She imagines the elderly woman to be just like herself in the present: old and alone, abandoned, misunderstood, and perhaps even mocked by her modern offspring. And finally, only with her own increasing age does Eveline begin to understand Mémère and to discover their similarities:

> "C'est avec l'âge mûr que je l'ai rejointe, ou qu'elle-même m'a rejointe, comment expliquer cette étrange rencontre hors du temps. . . . Maintenant, peux-tu [Christine] honnêtement me dire que je ne ressemble pas étonnamment à ce portrait que nous avons de grand-mère à l'âge que j'ai atteint? . . ."
>
> "Par le caractère aussi . . . puisque devenue elle, je la comprends. Ah, c'est bien là l'une des expériences les plus surprenantes de la vie! A celle qui nous a donné le jour, on donne naissance à notre tour quand, tôt ou tard, nous l'accueillons enfin dans notre moi. Dès lors, elle habite en nous autant que nous avons habité en elle avant de venir au monde. . . . On se rencontre . . . on finit toujours par se rencontrer, mais si tard!"

What Eveline is stating is that, sadly, this "jeu de la rencontre" ultimately occurs solely in the mind.[19]

Eveline is, in addition, speaking of the role of heredity in this great circle or cycle of generations. As one ages, one can experience a renewed sense of youth in another, in one's child who, having inherited certain traits from the parent, continues along the path of life and death:

> "N'as-tu [Christine] donc pas encore compris que les parents revivent vraiment on leurs enfants?"
>
> "Je pensais que tu [Eveline] revivais surtout la vie de tes parents à toi."
>
> "Je revis la leur, je revis aussi avec toi. . . . c'est peut-être la partie de la vie la plus éclairée, située entre ceux qui nous ont précédés et ceux qui nous suivent, en plein milieu. . . ."

While remaining an individual in the present, one is also linked to the past and future that are kept alive both in the mind and in the continuing cycles of life. For Roy, in fact, one could never teach experience to a child. The young must learn for themselves, first as they recall the precepts of their parents from whom they have inherited their natures, and then as they echo the former generation's words and repeat their actions.

From Mme Laplante to Rose-Anna to Florentine, from Mme Chenevert to Alexandre to Irène to Paul, from Mémère to Eveline to Christine, from Winnie to Elsa, and from Martha's mother to Martha, all of life is ironically and yet optimistically repeated within the actual and mental circle of time.[20]

Related to the power of memory, or more precisely associated both with remembrances and with dreams or *animus*, as well as with reverie or *anima*, are dreams occurring while one is asleep and nocturnal thoughts, usually during insomnia. Bachelard describes the nocturnal dream as that which creates a state of self-dispersion, a return to the nothingness of our being until our self, our *je*, is lost and dissolved. Royan dreams appear to illustrate that interpretation. Nightmares, although rare in this fictional world, are described as a vague fog, a *brume*, surrounding the dreamer and in which an obscure sixth sense averts one to danger. Dreams themselves are seen as a state of submission to one's primitive past in infancy. When Chenevert finally falls asleep at Lac Vert, for example, he dreams of a return to a childhood of paradise, innocence, and peace, of a return to God. He experiences the sensation of being on a trip, of flowing on a river in the mind.[21]

Chenevert, however, is more frequently depicted as an insomniac, as a man who lives in an atmosphere where "il faisait nuit." He loves that night, in fact, and spends his days waiting for it to arrive so that he can freely worry about the problems of the world while remaining awake and alone. The bank teller is only one of several nocturnal characters in Roy's fiction, however, including Florentine, Nathalie, and Christine's father. All of these people prefer nighttime, whether it be a soothing time of day, a time that offers hope, as for Papa, a time, for this same individual, conducive to memories and daydreams, or, for the Royan lover of nature, an atmosphere of mysterious magnificence when one is on the threshold of infinity.[22]

Daydreams that occur during a sleepless state and the memories that are recreated at the same time or in sleep are, of course, pastimes of the imagination, as are often one's dreams formulated in nighttime. In order to be faithful to one's *animus*, therefore, one must move from a mental preoccupation with dreams of the future to an awakened determination to pursue such goals actively. This necessary transition is beautifully illustrated, both in Roy's journalistic writings and in her fiction, by the numerous immigrant groups of Canada. In her short story, "Ely! Ely! Ely!," an account of some of her early days as a journalist, the narrator announces, in retrospect, her antici- pated work on these ethnic groups. She knows that she will learn much about her country and its people, as she delves further into this reporting, and she states that such an interest is sufficient to occupy her for the remainder of her life. Whether it be in these articles or in her creative works, Roy's concern for Canadian immigrants did not wane.[23]

On the Canadian plains, especially in Manitoba, in Rorke- ton, in Winnipeg, in Horizon, in Volhyn, and in Ely, various immigrant groups, predominantly from parts of Russia and the Ukraine, have made this vast North American country a melting pot. Despite inevitable assimilation, however, Roy writes in particular of these people's determination to keep their distinct traditions and cultures alive in the new land. Such a goal is, at times, difficult and, as Martha states, often results in an indi- vidual's sensation of being neither fully Canadian nor, for exam- ple, fully Ukrainian. In addition, conflicts among generations are frequent in such situations: the youth of Rorketon are the ones who desire the survival of tradition in folklore, literature, and music, while the older people follow progress. In contrast, it is the older Ukrainians of Volhyn who remain faithful to their former way of life, although Martha admits that she would feel entirely *dépaysée* if she were to return to her homeland. She understands, therefore, but is saddened by the fact that her children feel equally out of place in Volhyn and now belong to the modern world of progress in Canada. She fears the future, however: "Sans ses enfants, Volhyn n'avait plus que quelques années, peut-être seulement des mois à se survivre. Peut-être même Volhyn mourrait-il définitivement le jour ou [sic] elle- même disparaîtrait."[24]

To add to this concern, immigrant groups can also en- counter problems with the Canadian government, in the name of laws and schools, viewed as an obstacle to their dreams of success. Roy writes that this government should aid these new- comers, especially since their communities are often a show- place for other immigrant groups, as is the case of Dunrea in *Rue Deschambault,* and since their productive work is an in- spiring example to everyone. In her journalistic writings in particular, Roy praises these agricultural cooperatives that are models of pacifism, collectivism, and communism.[25]

What Roy is essentially discussing, therefore, in both

her journalistic and fictional works concerning immigrants is the dream, the collective *animus,* of these people. They have migrated to Canada as if to the promised land and have maintained their confidence and faith in their ability to "recommencer la vie" or to "recommencer à neuf." These individuals are, fundamentally, dreamers, searchers of their "rêves chimériques" that, at times, become reality, at other times, bring discouragement and deception, and finally, sometimes provide a mere semblance of a truth that is sufficient for life. The Doukhobors of "La Vallée Houdou," for example, know that they have not actually discovered hills on the Manitoban plains, but only the play of light and clouds, but this illusion satisfies their deep need for a settlement in a protective and nostalgic countryside. For them, their dream has been fulfilled.[26]

For certain Royan characters, however, the mere illusion of having accomplished their dreams and their future, ambitious goals, will not suffice. Traditionally, Bachelard identifies this active, determined *animus* as masculine, and it is, in the Royan fictional world, essentially male characters who exhibit such tendencies, especially since they live in a society that historically encourages these desires on the part of boys and men. In the male sector of the world described in *Bonheur d'occasion,* for example, it is Jean Lévesque who is depicted as the most ambitious character, a young man anxious to begin anew, to become self-made, while Florentine views her dreams as dead. Similarly, Marjorique, Pierre, and, to a certain extent, Sam Lee Wong all actively pursue their respective goals, although success is never guaranteed in such quests, and failure can cause dreams to revert into daydreams. Interestingly, it is Christine who, as a young woman, transfers her daydreams, her *anima,* into a real goal, an *animus,* as she travels on the road toward a career as a writer.[27]

Christine will first, however, become a schoolteacher, thereby satisfying, like a dutiful daughter, her mother's wishes: "Quand on se connaît mal encore soi-même, pourquoi ne tâcherait-on pas de réaliser le rêve que ceux qui nous aiment font à notre usage!" Later, Christine will travel, will accomplish what her mother had always desired but was not able to do. Mothers, like Maman-Eveline, Berthe, Rose-Anna, Luzina, and Elsa, possess their dreams, too, but will typically place upon the shoulders of their children, and often upon their daughters, the task of fulfilling these imagined goals.[28]

It is noteworthy that four male Royan characters also express dreams for others, not for their offspring, as in the case
of female characters, but for humanity in general. Azarius speaks
of the humanitarian causes of war and of his confidence and
optimism in the glorious future of France. Emmanuel, likewise,
clings to naive and idealistic dreams of equality and justice
for everyone. Papa envisions a splendid paradise for his immigrants, while even Alexandre ultimately lives on his hopes of
possible happiness for all people. These dreams may have been
created by one's *animus,* but unrealistic, they are, in fact, chi-
meras, closer to vague daydreams.[29]

Similarly, some Royan characters imagine a future of
recommencement for themselves, but despite attempts to realize
these dreams, they fail, deceive themselves, thereby sadly remaining within the domain of illusions, or reach their goals only
at the end of their lives. The travel dreams of a young and
middle-aged Eveline have become the pitiful daydreams of an
elderly woman, while her husband thinks of buying a store
only when he has been forced to retire. Sam Lee Wong, at
least realizing that the grandiose projects for his restaurant are
mere daydreams, sees himself as an older spectator of his own
youthful plans. Azarius vacillates, in his thoughts, between
discouragement and hope for the future but ultimately escapes
from one reality into another only by going to war. And finally,
Alexandre's great dream of peace and restfulness is fulfilled
when he enters the hospital and dies. Since each individual is
said to possess both an *animus* and an *anima,* the distinction
between one's dreams and one's daydreams, or reverie is, at
times, difficult to perceive.[30]

This difficulty in detecting a clearly defined difference
between one's *rêve* and *rêverie* occurs primarily after the mental
process has been activated. Prior to the commencement of
these thoughts, it is the source of inspiration that distinguishes
a dream from a daydream, with one's inner, voluntary self as
that which stimulates one's *animus,* and with an exterior, often
accidental stimulus as the impetus for one's *anima.* In this
aspect, therefore, reverie is closer in nature to memory than to
dream.

In Gabrielle Roy's fiction, one can identify six major
groups of sources of insipration for reverie. The first group
contains images that are associated with nature: the countryside
in general and, more specifically, hills, islands, dusk, fog, the

sounds, sights, and odors of springtime, flowers, and gardens. The most powerful of these stimuli appears to be the snow-storm, or more precisely, the situation of being kept warm and secure during such a storm, as for Christine and for the teacher of *Ces Enfants de ma vie* whose imaginations wander through-out time and space, while they are prey to the furious elements of the outside world. Related to this initial group of natural stimuli, as well as to the second category of sources of inspira-tion associated with movement are birds in flight, water, trees, clouds, and wind. Listening to the song of the waves or tide and seeing one's reflection in a lake, the Royan character is lulled into a state of reverie. And whether it be for birds on the branches of trees or for Christine, gently rocked as she stares up at the clouds, the wind produces a movement that, in turn, easily activates one's dream-like thoughts.[31]

Christine is, of course, lying in her hammock, as she is rocked by the wind. Also found in this second group of sources of inspiration for reverie in movement, therefore, are the ve-hicles that provide this motion: hammocks, swings, rockers, wagons, and *berlines.* Royan characters, and especially females, love this sensation of being rocked, inviting them to daydream about a vague past, linked to their overwhelming *nostalgie du berceau.* Related to this reverie, bathed in an atmosphere of warmth and security, is the third group of exterior stimuli, all associated with the home or an intimate space. In Roy's fiction, candlelight, a lighted lantern, as in the *berline,* a fire, or Christine's attic hideaway all inspire a pleasant state.[32]

A fourth classification contains inspirations linked to religion. The image of the Virgin Mary and Jesus for Floren-tine and Jean, the Capuchin's sermon for Luzina, and the sight and sound of church bells in *La Petite Poule d'eau* all serve as external simuli for daydreaming. Similarly, intellectual or artistic pursuits can inspire one's *anima* and form, therefore, a fifth group. Reading and listening to a history lesson for Luzina, the sight of a work of art, or, especially, the sound of music, as of Nil's poignant Ukrainian songs, can create an atmosphere conducive to reverie. Finally, as a sixth classification, are artifi-cial stimuli: drugs, such as morphine and heroin, for Vincent Raymond and Alexandre Chenevert, beer, and tobacco, for Eskimo women. The effect of these exterior inspirations, soon internalized, however, is a pathetic state of vague and confused thoughts, linked more to hallucinations.[33]

A more typical effect of these inspirations for reverie, however, is the sensation of having discovered, in one's mind, an escape from the reality of a daily routine and an initiation into a state of release, that of happiness and peace. Bachelard writes of the sense of archaic well-being as one dreams in front of a fire, of purity, forgetfulness, and idealism when one dreams before a body of water, and of an opening onto the world as one watches images of flight. The result of this reverie, there-fore, is a mental return to one's childhood, to an anterior state, if the daydreamer is an adult, or a mental trip toward the world and into the cosmos, if the daydreamer is a child. In both instances, there occurs a detemporalization in which the past becomes the future in us, while the reverse process is simul-taneously achieved. Bachelard's interpretation, therefore, closely resembles Roy's own definition of reverie as a cyclical motion in which a return to primitivism is equated with one's future.[34]

The joy and repose that are attained are also associated, in Bachelard's analysis, with a flight or a liberation into another world, into an *ailleurs* or an *au-delà*. One experiences, in addi-tion, a duality of one's self, a reciprocity between one's now super-male *animus* and one's super-female *anima*. One returns to a primitive state of androgyny, as there occurs a mental diffusion of one's being, a sense of plasticity to one's *je*. This self-diffusion, however, is a positive experience, since it also unites the dreamer with the imagined world and cosmos, in mutual respiration, and, once again, provides an atmosphere conducive to a rapport between intimacy and immensity.[35]

As one reflects upon Roy's works, one realizes that the characters in them offer supportive evidence to Bachelard's discussions, both in the attributes of reverie and in its preva-lence. On three separate occasions, in fact, Roy stressed the importance and predominance of daydreams both to her charac-ters and to her readers. She viewed each reader of her fiction as a "cher enfant amoureux de songes," while all of her charac-ters were purposefully created as dreamers, since reverie was, in her opinion, most prevalent in such sensitive individuals.[36]

In her first novel, for example, Azarius has been seen as continually lost in childish mental meanderings, while Emmanuel conjures up visions of a beloved Florentine. Influenced by his deep love for Anne and then by morphine, Dr. Raymond increasingly exists solely in a world rich with illusion. Alexandre daydreams of peace and nature and remains, in fact, prey to thoughts of eternity, as he mechanically performs his job at the bank. Birds and cows seemingly abandon themselves to the reverie of an enchanted summer, while Sam Lee Wong, Smouillya, and the father in "Un Vagabond frappe à notre porte" are seen as needing their dreams of a past-future in order to endure the present. Finally, both the old and, especially, the young of *Ces Enfants de ma vie* encounter the fragile frontier between reality and daydream. The school-aged children and adolescents, in fact, cling to the liberty attained in these voyages of the imagination. As dreamers, like Christine, they give credence to Bachelard's statement that reverie is particularly prevalent in children and in poets.[37]

Bachelard should have added, however, that a penchant for daydreams is equally powerful in women. If the activation of the *animus* is seen by Bachelard as a male quality and, as such, is especially visible in Roy's male characters, the tendency to give free rein to one's *anima* is defined as a female characteristic and, indeed, is to be found as most prevalent among Royan female characters. Rose-Anna, for example, tries not to allow daydreams to enter her harsh world of reality but still describes herself as "trop rêveuse." She dreams of finding money, of locating a beautiful new home, of the happiness of her youth. The narrator explains that the Lacasse matriarch should not possess such illusions but does. In fact, in one scene she is lost in a reverie that is parallel but separate from that of her oldest daughter with whom, therefore, she does not communicate. As for Florentine, she adores these "rêveries paresseuses," broken by the abrupt entrance of reality, first in the person of her mother in the Quinze-Cents store and later in the older woman's admission of pregnancy immediately after Florentine's dream-inspiring kiss by Jean. Despite the young woman's consistent dreams of a new life, of *recommencement,* her imagination is never powerful enough to destroy the reality in which she is caught.[38]

Luzina Tousignant also possesses a "humeur rêveuse," as she imagines the future lives of her children and is easily inspired in thoughts of travel and heaven while listening to the words of others. Elsa, influenced by American films, views much of her life as an obscure daydream, enjoys the "nuages . . . tranquilles" of her reverie in nature, and increasingly learns to exist on both her illusions of the past with Jimmy and her imagined life for her son in the South. Martha, about to die, reflects upon her past life, as does Mémère, as if upon a long daydream. She also describes her thoughts themselves as "rêves plutôt que de réflexions, de vagues ombres amies." Like Maman-Eveline and most other Royan women, she lives in a zone between reality and dream.[39]

It is significant that the only two female characters exhibiting both a strong *animus* and *anima* are schoolteachers, a profession open to women even in past times, with one of these characters, even more significantly, determined to become a writer. The semi-autobiographical creation of Roy-Christine-teacher—the latter of *Ces Enfants de ma vie*—has a propensity for what can be called relaxing but creative reverie because of the profession, literary ability, and youth of its composite character. Christine, of both *Rue Deschambault* and *La Route d'Altamont*, revels in her imaginary wanderings, inspired, in particular, by a moving carriage in a storm or by her hammock:

> Je sommeillais d'un rêve à l'autre; parfois, j'emportais dans mon rêve inconscient le tissu fin et léger des rêves éveillés, et de même le rêve du fond marin me suivait au réveil et se mêlait aux nouveaux voyages que j'allais faire. Le bercement de mon hamac aidait la trame de mes contes. N'est-ce pas curieux: un mouvement lent et doux, et l'imagination est comme en branle! Docile, docile au moindre départ, un petit bercement lui suffit. . . .

The future writer and traveller are here described in their embryonic state.[40]

Similarly, the young teacher, rocked in an old wedding carriage during a snowstorm, is at the center of an effective literary scene in which her mind takes control:

> Je fermai les yeux, mais ce n'était pas par besoin de sommeil. C'était pour mieux rêver à mon aise. Ecartée maintenant l'idée de mourir ou même de vieillir, je me plus à m'imaginer parcourant la vie sans prendre d'âge. Je voyagerais, je voyagerais beaucoup, me disais-je, incitée sans doute à ce rêve particulier par le bercement de la berline. . . . Je visiterais des pays, des villes, des sites incomparables. Je me voyais atteindre un avenir élevé d'où je me retournais avec une certaine commisération vers la gauche petite institutrice de campagne que j'avais été.

From these circular visions of imagined travel, the young woman moves to a sensual, surrealistic experience in which she sees the reflection of Médéric in a lighted lantern, as he starts to brush away a lock of her hair: "Médéric semblait aussi flotter sur des îles de neige, et j'avais cette curieuse impression que tout ce que je voyais ne se passait que dans la lanterne, que c'était elle qui inventait ces jeux auxquels nous ne prenions vraiment part ni Médéric ni moi." Only in this instance, the daydream is real, as the teacher is forced to abandon her state of timeless reverie for present reality.[41]

No matter how powerful, therefore, daydreams are always temporary. It is for this reason that they are so necessary in the lives of Royan women who, entrapped more firmly than men within themselves and within their defined worlds of existence, desperately need this outlet in the mind. But although more intense and prevalent in the lives of Roy's fictional females, reverie, like memories and dreams, is important to all of her literary beings. In 1970, Roy herself admitted that one had to escape, at least for short periods of time, from even the best of lives. One needs, therefore, to remember, dream, or daydream. More recently, however, in 1980, the author refused to believe that the dreams of her characters were forms of escape. To the aging Roy, they were, instead, always positive creations of the imagination.[42]

There was, perhaps, an evolution in Roy's definition of and attitude toward the role of this imagined travel in her fiction, just as there had been a progression in her thoughts about departures and real travel. More logical an explanation, however, is to be found in a reconciliation between terms or interpretations, that is, between memories, dreams, and reverie as negative, an escape from or denial of a situation, or as a positive, temporary, and creative withdrawal from reality. It is Christine who, in speaking of her own family, offers this possible explanation:

> En fin de compte, au Manitoba, n'avons-nous pas toujours rêvé de quelque chose d'autre que ce que nous avions. . . . Ainsi avons-nous vécu là-bas, comme au reste un peu tout le monde, j'imagine, sur la face de la terre, peu satisfaits du présent, mais en attente toujours de l'avenir, et au regret souvent du passé.[43]

There is no doubt that the Royan character is a dissatisfied creature, a divided person who, no matter how successful, searches for something else, somewhere, at sometime. The source for the creation of this better self, better life, and better world is located within the mind, in remembrances of the past, dreams of the future, or relaxed, vague daydreams in which one gathers strength before tackling reality. In this sense, Royan characters are not escapists, but rather idealists, who, like the artist, will continuously, but realistically, quest for perfection, both for themselves and for humanity.

NOTES

[1] Gabrielle Roy, 28 janvier 1970, as quoted in Marc Gagné, *Visages de Gabrielle Roy* (Montréal: Librairie Beauchemin Limitée, 1973), p. 140; Gaston Bachelard, *La Poétique de l'espace*, Bibliothèque de philosophie contemporaine (Paris: Presses Universitaires de France, 1978), p. 185. See also Gaston Bachelard, *La Poétique de la rêverie*, Bibliothèque de philosophie contemporaine (Paris: Presses Universitaires de France, 1974), pp. 17-21, 50-65, 86-88; François Dagognet, *Gaston Bachelard*, SUP "Philosophes" (Paris: Presses Universitaires de France, 1972), pp. 45-50, 97-100; Annette Saint-Pierre, *Gabrielle Roy: Sous le signe du rêve* (Saint-Boniface, Manitoba: Editions du Blé, 1975), p. 76; Albert Le Grand, "Gabrielle Roy ou l'être partagé," *Etudes Françaises*, 1ère année, No. 2 (juin 1965), pp. 40-41.

[2] Gabrielle Roy, "Témoignage," in *Le Roman canadian-français: Evolution-témoignage-bibliographie*, eds. Paul Wyczynski, Bernard Julien, Jean Ménard et Réjean Robidoux, Archives des lettres canadiennes, Tome III (Montréal: Fides, 1977), p. 303. See also Gabrielle Roy, "Le Pays de *Bonheur d'occasion*," in *Morceaux*, ed. Robert Guy Scully (Montréal: Les Editions du Noroît, 1978), pp. 113-114; François Ricard, *Gabrielle Roy*, Ecrivains canadiens d'aujourd'hui, No. 11 (Montréal: Editions Fides, 1975), pp. 90-91; Roland Charland et Jean-Noël Samson, *Gabrielle Roy*, Dossier de documentation sur la littérature canadienne-française (Montréal: Fides, 1972), pp. 71, 75-77; Anne Srabian de Fabry, "A la recherche de l'ironie perdue chez Gabrielle Roy et Flaubert," *Présence Francophone*, 11 (1975), 95-96; Robert Morissette, "Interview avec Gabrielle Roy,"

in "La Vie ouvrière urbaine dans le roman canadien-français contemporain," Thesis Université de Montréal 1970, p. 167; Personal interview with Gabrielle Roy, 29 june 1980.

[3] Personal interview with Gabrielle Roy, 29 June 1980. See also Bachelard, *La Poétique de la rêverie*, pp. 17-21, 50-65; Saint-Pierre, p. 20.

[4] Bachelard, *La Poétique de la rêverie*, pp. 9, 10, 17-21, 26, 50-65, 183; Dagognet, pp. 33-35, 50, 52-53, 64, 69, 91, 103-105, 113; Bachelard, *La Poétique de l'espace*, p. 100; Saint-Pierre, p. 9. André Brochu analyzes four distinct states for Roy's characters: dream, reality, non-dream, and non-reality. The first state relates to the individual, the second to the family, the third to the world, and the fourth to society. See André Brochu, "Gabrielle Roy," Notes from course on author, Université de Montréal, Printemps 1978, taken by one of his students; André Brochu, "La Structure sémantique de *Bonheur d'occasion*," *Revue des Sciences Humaines,* 45, No. 173 (janvier-mars 1979), 43-47.

[5] Gabrielle Roy, *Cet Eté qui chantait* (Québec-Montréal: Les Editions Françaises, 1972), pp. 60-61.

[6] Gabrielle Roy, *Rue Deschambault* (1955; rpt. Montréal: Librairie Beauchemin Limitée, 1974), p. 83. See also Gabrielle Roy, *La Route d'Altamont,* Collection l'Arbre, No. 10 (Montréal: Editions HMH, 1966), pp. 14, 28-30, 36-37, 41-42, 49-50, 67, 82-84, 127, 140-141, 162-164, 189-193, 214-221, 245-248. In this work, Roy speaks of "le temps fixé dans la mémoire." See p. 192. See also Paula Gilbert Lewis, "The Themes of Memory and Death in Gabrielle Roy's *La Route d'Altamont,*" *Modern Fiction Studies,* 22, No. 3 (Autumn 1976), 458; Bachelard, *La Poétique de l'espace,* pp. 28-29; Saint-Pierre, p. 107.

[7] Roy, *La Route d'Altamont,* p. 152; Gabrielle Roy, *Bonheur d'occasion* (1945; rpt. Montréal: Librairie Beauchemin Limitée, 1973), p. 297; Roy, *La Route d'Altamont,* p. 246. In this last work, see also pp. 90, 116-117, 219-220, 245. See also Roy, *Rue Deschambault,* pp. 38, 43; Roy, *Cet Eté qui chantait,* pp. 60-61; Gabrielle Roy, *Un Jardin au bout du monde* (Montréal: Librairie Beauchemin Limitée, 1975), pp. 22-23; Lewis, pp. 458-459; Ricard, p. 96; Saint-Pierre, p. 103.

[8] Roy, *La Route d'Altamont,* p. 209. See also pp. 39, 208, 218; Roy, *Bonheur d'occasion,* pp. 163-164, 252, 291; Roy, *Cet Eté qui chantait,* pp. 60-61, 189; Roy, *Un Jardin au bout du monde,* pp. 14, 16, 17, 88, 156; Lewis, p. 459.

[9] Roy, *La Route d'Altamont,* p. 149. See also pp. 85, 120, 150; Roy, *Rue Deschambault,* pp. 58, 60, 62, 135, 178; Roy, *Un Jardin au bout du monde,* p. 215; Gabrielle Roy, *Ces Enfants de ma vie,* (Montréal: Editions Internationales Alain Stanké Ltée, 1977), p. 16; Phyllis Grosskurth, *Gabrielle Roy,* Canadian Writers and Their Works (Toronto: Forum

House, 1972), p. 37.

[10] Roy, *La Route d'Altamont*, p. 214.   See also pp. 163, 189-191; Lewis, p. 459.

[11] Lewis, p. 460.   See also p. 459; Roy, *La Route d'Altamont*, pp. 11-13, 22-24, 36, 49-50, 88, 90, 93-94, 112, 114; Roy, *Un Jardin au bout du monde*, p. 18; Gabrielle Roy, "La Grande Voyageuse," *La Revue Moderne*, 24, No. 1 (mai 1942), 28-30; Gabrielle Roy, "La Source au désert," *Le Bulletin des Agriculteurs*, 42, No. 10 (octobre 1946), 11, 34.

[12] Roy, *Cet Eté qui chantait*, p. 146; Roy, *Un Jardin au bout du monde*, p. 23.   In this first work, see also pp. 156-157; in the second see also pp. 22, 211-212.   See also Roy, *Bonheur d'occasion*, pp. 179-181, 289-292; Roy, "La Source au désert," pp. 31, 34, 38, 44; Gabrielle Roy, *La Petite Poule d'eau* (1950; rpt. Montréal: Librairie Beauchemin Limitée, 1970), pp. 108, 171; Gabrielle Roy, *Alexandre Chenevert* (1954; rpt. Montréal: Beauchemin, 1973), pp. 86, 144-145; Roy, *Rue Deschambault*, pp. 136-138, 165; Roy, *La Route d'Altamont*, pp. 14-15, 28-30, 49-50, 112, 127, 221; Gabrielle Roy, *La Rivière sans repos* (Montréal: Librairie Beauchemin Limitée, 1971), pp. 173, 286; Roy, *Ces Enfants de ma vie*, pp. 53-54, 171; Lewis, p. 460.   In some of the above examples, memories themselves are painful because they recreate in the mind a painful experience, such as Florentine's relationship with Jean.

[13] Roy, *La Route d'Altamont*, p. 37.   See also Lewis, pp. 460-461.

[14] Gabrielle Roy, "Petite Ukraine," *Fragiles Lumières de la terre: Ecrits divers 1942-1970*, Collection Prose Entière (Montréal: Les Editions Quinze, 1978), pp. 80-85; Gabrielle Roy, "La Pension de vieillesse," *Le Bulletin des Agriculteurs*, 39, No. 11 (novembre 1943), 32; Roy, *La Petite Poule d'eau*, pp. 81-83; Roy, *La Route d'Altamont*, pp. 48-50; Roy, *Un Jardin au bout du monde*, pp. 14, 16, 17, 21-23, 28, 30, 61-65; Lewis, p. 461.   The storyteller's role in this maintenance of ties to the past is particularly evident in "Un Vagabond frappe à notre porte."

[15] Roy, *Bonheur d'occasion*, pp. 84, 93, 151-152, 325-326, 329-330; Roy, *Alexandre Chenevert*, pp. 33, 86-87, 357-358; Roy, *Rue Deschambault*, p. 126; Roy, *La Route d'Altamont*, pp. 39, 192-193, 198, 205-207, 215; Gabrielle Roy, "Mon Héritage du Manitoba," *Mosaic*, 3iii (1970), 72-73; Roy, *Cet Eté qui chantait*, pp. 146, 156-157; Roy, *Un Jardin au bout du monde*, p. 109; pp. 461-462.

[16] Roy, *La Route d'Altamont*, pp. 245-250; Lewis, pp. 462-463.

[17] Roy, *Un Jardin au bout du monde*, pp. 215-216.   See also pp. 211-212, 217; Gabrielle Roy, "La Fuite de Sally," *Le Bulletin des Agriculteurs*, 27, No. 1 (janvier 1941), 39-40; Roy, *Rue Deschambault*, pp. 86, 126, 200, 273; Roy, *La Route d'Altamont*, pp. 48, 114, 192-193, 204-207, 255; Roy, *La Rivière sans repos*, pp. 86-88, 237-238, 285-286;

Roy, *Cet Eté qui chantait*, pp. 146, 156-160; Roy, *Ces Enfants de ma vie*, pp. 53-54, 183-185; Lewis, pp. 462-463.

[18] Roy, *Alexandre Chenevert*, pp. 144-145, 374, 384; Roy, *La Route d'Altamont*, pp. 49-50, 56-57, 189-190; Lewis, p. 462.

[19] Roy, *La Route d'Altamont*, pp. 226-227; Gagné, p. 85. In the first work, see also pp. 216-221, 224-225, 228. See also Roy, *La Rivière sans repos*, pp. 268-269, 298-301, 305; Roy, *Un Jardin au bout du monde*, pp. 22, 178-179; Roy, *Bonheur d'occasion*, pp. 84, 90, 130, 325-326; Lewis, p. 462; Paula Gilbert Lewis, "*Street of Riches* and *The Road Past Altamont:* The Feminine World of Gabrielle Roy," *Journal of Women's Studies in Literature*, 1, No. 2 (Spring 1979), 137-139; Grosskurth, pp. 51-52, 55-56; Donald Cameron, "Gabrielle Roy: A Bird in the Prison Window," in *Conversations with Canadian Novelists* (Toronto: Macmillan of Canada, 1973), p. 142; Paula Gilbert Lewis, "Trois Générations de femmes: Le Reflet mère/fille dans quelques nouvelles de Gabrielle Roy," L'Héritage français en Amérique Section, American Association of Teachers of French, Lille, France, 27 June 1983.

[20] Roy, *La Route d'Altamont*, p. 236. See also Personal interview with Gabrielle Roy, 29 June 1980; Lewis, "The Themes of Memory and Death," p. 466; Brochu, "Gabrielle Roy"; Paul Socken, " 'Le Pays de l'amour' in the Works of Gabrielle Roy," *Revue de l'Université d'Ottawa*, 46, No. 3 (juillet-septembre 1976), 321, 323. It should be noted that, with the exception of Alexandre Chenevert and his family, this round of generations is entirely female. The force of heredity in the Royan world can also be interpreted as a form of Naturalist determinism.

[21] Bachelard, *La Poétique de la rêverie*, pp. 9, 124-128, 145; Roy, *Rue Deschambault*, pp. 64, 91, 96, 135, 147; Roy, *Alexandre Chenevert*, pp. 33-35, 207-213, 371.

[22] Roy, *Alexandre Chenevert*, p. 9. See also pp. 10-35, 79-81, 206-207, 220; Roy, *Bonheur d'occasion*, pp. 154, 294, 300; Roy, "La Source au désert," p. 41; Roy, *Rue Deschambault*, pp. 265-268, 272-277; Roy, *Cet Eté qui chantait*, pp. 174-175.

[23] Gabrielle Roy, "Ely! Ely! Ely!," *Liberté*, 21, No. 3, année 1979, numéro 123 (mai-juin 1979), 22. Given Roy's continual portrayal of these immigrant groups, it is surprising that they have reacted little to her works. See Gilles Dorion et Maurice Emond, "Dossier Gabrielle Roy: Questionnaire," *Québec Français*, No. 36 (décembre 1979), p. 36.

[24] Roy, *Un Jardin au bout du monde*, p. 181. See also pp. 88, 117, 172-173, 176-180; Roy, "Petite Ukraine," *Fragiles Lumières de la terre*, pp. 77, 85, 86; Roy, *La Petite Poule d'eau*, pp. 82-83, 169, 182-183, 201-205; Gabrielle Roy, "Souvenirs du Manitoba," *La Revue de Paris*, 62e année, No. 2 (février 1955), pp. 79-81; Gabrielle Roy, "Le Manitoba,"

Le Magazine Maclean, 2, No. 7 (juillet 1962), 113-118; Roy, "*Terre des Hommes:* Le Thème raconté," *Fragiles Lumières de la terre*, pp. 214-215; Roy, *Ces Enfants de ma vie*, pp. 48, 73-78.

[25] Gabrielle Roy, "Plus que le pain," *Le Bulletin des Agriculteurs*, 38, No. 2 (février 1942), 9, 33-35; Roy, "Les Hutterites," "De turbulents chercheurs de paix," "L'Avenue Palestine," "Les Pêcheurs de Gaspésie: Une Voile dans la nuit," *Fragiles Lumières de la terre*, pp. 17, 18, 25, 29, 38-41, 58-60, 100; Roy, *Rue Deschambault*, pp. 145, 148-149; Roy, *Un Jardin au bout du monde*, pp. 64, 86-87; Roy, *Ces Enfants de ma vie*, pp. 73-78; Eva Kushner, "Dossier Gabrielle Roy: De la représentation à la vision du monde," *Québec Français*, No. 36 (décembre 1979), p. 39. It should be noted that Roy's knowledge of the problems and successes of these groups began early in her life, since her father, like Christine's, was a colonizing agent.

[26] Roy, "Plus que le pain," "De turbulents chercheurs de paix," *Fragiles Lumières de la terre*, pp. 33, 43; Roy, *Un Jardin au bout du monde*, p. VIII. In the first work, see also p. 34; in the second see pp. 34-35, 37, 41; in the third, for "La Vallée Houdou," see pp. 135, 137, 140, 145-149. See also Roy, "L'Avenue Palestine," "Petite Ukraine," *Fragiles Lumières de la terre*, pp. 56, 79; Roy, "Le Manitoba," p. 114; Paul Socken, "Gabrielle Roy as a Journalist," *Canadian Modern Language Review*, 30, No. 2 (January 1974), 97-98. Despite Roy's deep sensitivity to these ethnic groups, some of her individual immigrant characters can be seen as mere stereotypes: Sam Lee Wong and secondarily, but most emphatically, Abe Zlutkin and Isaac as Jewish immigrants. See Roy, *La Petite Poule d'eau*, pp. 30, 175, 178.

[27] Bachelard, *La Poétique de la rêverie*, p. 27; Roy, *Bonheur d'occasion*, pp. 10, 13, 23-27, 33, 70-73, 161, 167, 181, 187-191, 240, 306; Roy, *Rue Deschambault*, pp. 191-194, 243-247; Gabrielle Roy, *La Montagne secrète* (1961; rpt. Montréal: Librarie Beauchemin Limitée, 1974), pp. 21, 99-100, 104. See also Saint-Pierre, pp. 13, 22, 82-87, 106-109.

[28] Roy, *Rue Deschambault*, p. 284. See also p. 283; Roy, *La Route d'Altamont*, pp. 95, 98-99, 236, 252-255; Roy, *Bonheur d'occasion*, p. 90; Roy, *La Petite Poule d'eau*, pp. 139-140, 152, 162; Roy, *La Rivière sans repos*, pp. 174-175, 265. The fulfillment of the goal of becoming a teacher is also seen in *Ces Enfants de ma vie*.

[29] Roy, *Bonheur d'occasion*, pp. 39. 40, 49, 54-55, 83-84, 188-189; Roy, *Alexandre Chenevert*, p. 354.

[30] Roy, *Rue Deschambault*, pp. 99, 220, 274, 276; Roy, *La Route d'Altamont*, pp. 235-236; Roy, *Un Jardin au bout du monde*, p. 112; Roy, *Bonheur d'occasion*, pp. 61, 80, 136-143, 149-159, 175, 332, 334; Roy, *Alexandre Chenevert*, pp. 151, 361, 368-369.

[31] Roy, *Bonheur d'occasion*, p. 61; Roy, *Alexandre Chenevert*, p. 105; Roy, *Rue Deschambault*, pp. 82-86; Roy, *La Montagne secrète*, p. 159; Roy, *La Rivière sans repos*, pp. 166-171; Roy, *Cet Eté qui chantait*, pp. 42-44, 51, 96, 193-194, 196; Roy, *Un Jardin au bout du monde*, pp. 100, 166; Roy, *Ces Enfants de ma vie*, p. 106, 158, 181-185. See also Saint-Pierre, pp. 43-49, 56-59, 76-77, 98-99, 115-122; Gagné, p. 160; Dogognet, pp. 45-50, 97-100; Bachelard, *La Poétique de l'espace*, pp. 159-160; Bachelard, *La Poétique de la rêverie*, pp. 169-170.

[32] Roy, *Rue Deschambault*, pp. 82-86; Roy, *La Route d'Altamont*, pp. 168-169; Roy, *Cet Eté qui chantait*, p. 131; Roy, *Ces Enfants de ma vie*, pp. 105, 181-185. See also Saint-Pierre, pp. 105-108; Gagné, pp. 98-99; Dagognet, pp. 45-50, 97-100; Bachelard, *La Poétique de l'espace*, pp. 26, 135; Bachelard, *La Poétique de la rêverie*, pp. 117-120, 164-169. Related to movement is the reverie that is inspired, in *Ces Enfants de ma vie*, by fatigue from the exercise of walking. Roy herself adored the motion of swings and rockers, possessed several of them, and when questioned about this preference, exclaimed, "Ah! le berceau!" Personal interview with Gabrielle Roy, 29 June 1980.

[33] Roy, *Bonheur d'occasion*, pp. 179-181; Roy, "La Source au désert," pp. 10, 31; Roy, *La Petite Poule d'eau*, pp. 81-83, 207-210; Roy, *Alexandre Chenevert*, p. 375; Roy, *La Rivière sans repos*, pp. 40, 300-301; Roy, *Ces Enfants de ma vie*, pp. 42, 53-54, 59. See also Saint-Pierre, pp. 43-49, 93-94; Bachelard, *La Poétique de l'espace*, pp. 159-160.

[34] Bachelard, *La Poétique de la rêverie*, pp. 92-96, 166-173, 180; Personal interview with Gabrielle Roy, 29 June 1980.

[35] Bachelard, *La Poétique de l'espace*, pp. 33, 168-169; Bachelard, *La Poétique de la rêverie*, pp. 4, 8, 10-14, 49-51, 69-80, 89, 129-131, 140-146, 148-154.

[36] Gabrielle Roy, "Jeux du romancier et des lecteurs," L'Alliance française, Montréal, 1 décembre 1955, as quoted in Gagné, p. 264; Morissette, p. 167; Personal interview with Gabrielle Roy, 29 June, 1980. See also Le Grand, p. 57.

[37] Roy, *Bonheur d'occasion*, pp. 100, 136-143, 255, 256, 266-270; Roy, "La Source au désert," pp. 10, 30, 31, 34; Roy, *Alexandre Chenevert*, pp. 24, 45-48, 58, 112, 202, 317, 369; Roy, *Cet Eté qui chantait*, pp. 42-44, 51, 60; Roy, *Un Jardin au bout du monde*, pp. 12, 18-19, 22-23, 92-95, 100; Roy, *Ces Enfants de ma vie*, pp. 53-54, 106, 140, 143, 156, 180, 183-185; Bachelard, *La Poétique de la rêverie*, pp. 84-85. See also Saint-Pierre, pp. 26-27, 32-37, 56-62. The power of reverie in children, linked to the child-like character of Azarius, is also portrayed in Gabrielle Roy, "Gérard le pirate," *La Revue Moderne*, 22, No. 1 (mai 1940), 37.

[38] Roy, *Bonheur d'occasion*, pp. 146, 102. See also pp. 19, 21, 61,

77, 86, 90, 103, 148, 149, 174, 176, 245, 311, 324; Gabrielle Roy, "*Bonheur d'occasion* aujourd'hui," *Le Bulletin des Agriculteurs*, 44, No. 1 (janvier 1948), 6; Saint-Pierre, pp. 14-15, 17-19, 23-32.

[39] Roy, *La Petite Poule d'eau*, p. 77; Roy, *La Rivière sans repos*, p. 171; Roy, *Un Jardin au bout du monde*, p. 203. In the first work, see also pp. 26, 44, 52, 66, 120, 153; in the second see pp. 119-123, 157, 169-170, 272, 285-286, 295, 298-300, 312-314; in the third see pp. 166, 172. See also Saint-Pierre, pp. 43-49.

[40] Roy, *Rue Deschambault*, p. 85. See also pp. 82-85, 168; Roy, *La Route d'Altamont*, pp. 30-31, 63-69, 88, 159, 168-170, 174, 201-204; Saint-Pierre, pp. 98-100, 105-106, 108, 115-122.

[41] Roy, *Ces Enfants de ma vie*, pp. 183, 184. See also pp. 50, 56-58, 105, 158, 181-182, 185.

[42] Morissette, p. 167; Personal interview with Gabrielle Roy, 29 June 1980.

[43] Roy, *La Route d'Altamont*, p. 77.

CHAPTER VIII

Royan Aesthetics: The Roles of Language, The Writer-Artist, and the Work of Art

If Royan characters exhibit a propensity for both real and imagined travel, the discoveries made during these voyages do not remain within the private domain of the individual; that is, they do not remain unexpressed. They serve, rather, as the sources for art and as the basis for a deeply needed communication with others. It has been noted, in fact, that Roy herself became increasingly concerned about the literary-artistic process, as her vocation as a writer became one of the focal points of her works themselves. In 1980 she spoke at length of this chosen vocation and stated that all that she desired to do was to tell stories to others. She viewed herself and wanted to be seen by her public as "the last of the great storytellers, the last of the Mohicans." Communication, for Gabreille Roy was of utmost importance in her life.[1]

Roy desired to write for as wide a reading public as possible, both inside and outside Quebec and Canada. Her goal, in addition, was to reach all types of people: "Oui j'aime atteindre par mes écrits des gens de tous âges et si c'était possible à tous les niveaux de la société. Je suis d'une grande témérité, n'est-ce pas, d'espérer tant, car c'est une chose que peu ont réussi. N'importe, j'aime rêver que c'est possible." She addressed her works, therefore, to a composite, unknown reader whom she had envisioned as looking over her shoulder as she wrote and, earlier, as reading her fiction in another locale:

> Je m'imaginais avoir au moins un lecteur que je me représentais parfois me lisant dans la solitude de sa petite chambre comme je lui écrivais de la mienne, et cela suffisait pour me soutenir. E-trange! Je n'ai jamais cessé, je pense, de m'adresser à ce lecteur inconnu, peut-être un jeune homme fier que je ne connais ni de nom ni de visage, pourtant que je triche ou que je mente et il me

> le ferait savoir de quelque mystérieuse façon, comme il me fait parfois savoir dans le plus profond silence qu'il m'approuve. Qui est-il à la fin? Peu importe sans doute. L'essentiel est qu'il existe. Qu'il reste dans ma vie.[2]

Given this importance and need of communication, for Roy and within her fictional world, it is not at all surprising that she was deeply interested in the roles of language: the problems of and obstacles to language and communication between the text and its readers, as well as within the text itself; and the power of words to radiate an atmosphere of sociability, the past, and one's entire life. If Roy's primary goal was to reach a diverse public through language, therefore, it is logical that she had such a negative opinion of *Québécois* literature that was written entirely in *joual.* For Roy, such works did not affect enough people, could not appeal to a public outside the Province of Quebec, and, finally, could not be easily translated into other languages. If a writer desired to become part of a network of world literature, then a work of art, in Roy's opinion, had to be written in a language accessible to all.[3]

This statement does not mean, however, that a literary work should be devoid of specific geographic particularities of language. Roy herself was accused of having created a barrier between the text and its readers by the use of "le parler canadien-français," or what was once labelled "Canadianisms," throughout *Bonheur d'occasion,* and especially in dialogues, in order to depict faithfully the language of her characters living in Saint-Henri. In a study of this use of language, in fact, it has been shown that, despite some inconsistencies, Roy succeeded in giving an accurate representation of speech in that particular urban sector: its peculiarities of pronunciation, indicated in the novel through the use of altered orthography; the use of Anglicisms; the morphology and syntax of popular, modern French; and the archaic and dialectal elements stemming from the seventeenth-century *patois* spoken by the original French settlers of Nouvelle France. As a text certainly comprehensible to those who read modern French and successfully translated into eight languages, *Bonheur d'occasion* is also, linguistically, a manifestation of reality.[4]

There are many more problems with and obstacles to language and communication within the Royan text—that is, among her characters—especially if humanity is seen, as in the eyes of Smouillya, as "un immense manège où personne ne comprenait jamais personne." One of the fundamental causes for such difficulties is to be found in the presence of numerous immigrant groups in Canada. The journalist-writer speaks of the language problems encountered by these people and, in *La Petite Poule d'eau,* describes the immigrant settlement of Rorketon as a Babel of languages. Some of Roy's immigrant characters, like Martha, feel more secure using their own tongue and revert to it, especially for abstract concepts. Others, like the Ruthènes, consider people like Papa to be strangers until they can communicate with him in their native language. But ultimately, obstacles are overcome in this multilingual Royan world, and individuals, like Luzina and the family of Icelanders, do relate to one another, even without the presence of a common tongue.[5]

A second composite cause of obstacles in communication stems first from social and economic class distinctions—evident in the character of Florentine with her "accent peuple" and her ignorance of certain words—and secondly, and predominantly, from the bilingual nature of Montreal, Quebec, and Canada. Whether it be for the Lacasse family and Alexandre Chenevert in Montreal, the French-Canadians of northern Manitoba or Saint-Boniface, of whom the latter cannot decide upon the language of their preference, or the Eskimos, caught among the trilingualism of French, English, and Inuit, French-speaking Royan characters are surrounded by an English-speaking population that, in addition, is in control of their government, laws, and schools. All of Luzina's correspondence from the educational authorities in Winnipeg is written in English, and Miss O'Rorke, the Tousignant's second teacher represents all that is foreign to this gentle matriarch. This caricature of an anglophone Canadian insists upon communicating in her native language to a family that, in her opinion, should not continue to speak French in a country whose majority is English-speaking. It is, typically, only Luzina who learns to understand Miss O'Rorke's determination:

> Très opportuniste au fond, Luzina avait fini par découvrir au moins une qualité à son Anglaise: c'était l'anglais. Quoique incapable de l'apprécier, Luzina ne le tenait pas moins pour une qualité. Trouvait-on à redire de Miss O'Rorke, Luzina l'excusait:

> "Elle parle bien l'anglais, en tout cas."

Luzina, however, remains alone with her positive opinion of this foreign tongue.[6]

Living in Montreal, in particular, the francophone Royan character encounters linguistic problems not only with bilingualism but also with modern, commercial, and journalistic slogans, jargon, and banalities. It has already been seen that the urban metropolis to which Alexandre Chenevert has become enslaved is a mecca for such impersonal language, represented by the banal mottos of M. Fontaine: "*Play hard . . . work hard* était l'un de ses slogans. Il en avait plusieurs: Ne perdez pas une minute de temps, et le temps vous appartiendra; maintenez-vous en bonne santé, et la vie vous paraîtra digne d'être vécue."[7]

The sad result of having spent one's entire life in this linguistic environment is the inability to express oneself in any other manner. When Chenevert finally decides to communicate to others his personal experiences and discoveries at Lac Vert, he cannot do so:

> Rien ne lui venait. C'est-à-dire rien que des bouts de phrases qui avaient l'air de lui arriver en droite ligne de son journal à cinq cents, des slogans répandus dans les tramways. . . . et il était le premier à sentir que cela ne touche personne. Il semblait que le ton faux de la propagande eût mis sa griffe sur lui.

Chenevert is distraught: "Ainsi donc, le seul genre de prose qui lui était assez familier, était celui-là dont il n'avait pas le goût." Like Barnaby who is fascinated but frightened by the formulas of politeness that one uses on the telephone, and like both Barnaby and Elsa who do not know how to end their phone conversations or letters, respectively, Chenevert is a product and a victim of the language of modern times.[8]

If Alexandre Chenevert dies with certain regrets about his life, one of the major causes of his sorrow, therefore, is his past lack of communication with others. Having once expressed his feelings in a letter published in the newspaper, *Sol,* the quiet bank teller has retained this desire for self-expression but, feeling that he possesses no talent in this domain, has remained silent and frustrated: "Car la beauté [of his experiences at Lac Vert] était en lui. . . . Il ne lui manquait que les mots. Et comment se faisait-il qu'une émotion aussi profonde, aussi sincère, n'appelât point les moyens qui l'eussent rendue communicable?" When he tries to write, he encounters a void: "Sur la page blanche, il n'y avait rien." When he tries to speak to his daughter, Irène, he cannot, likewise, quite find the words to express his deepest feelings: "Le meilleur du coeur semble destiné à s'user en regrets [instead of in language], à se perdre comme les ruisseaux, les sources, les rivières, toute l'eau vive et fraîche de la terre dans l'amertume de l'océan."[9]

It is possible that, as Roy herself states, "il y a des choses que seuls savent dire les yeux," and it is true that many Royan characters do sincerely communicate with their eyes, without speaking, and without "la maladresse des mots" that are often inadequate and imprecise. But what is distressing is that, in a literary universe so filled with humanism and sensitivity, many individuals do not relate to others in any manner and do not succeed, in particular, in verbal communication. A few characters, like Nick of *La Petite Poule d'eau* and Pierre Cordorai, do not even desire to speak to others, but even many Royan couples lack any form of meaningful verbal exchange. Martha and Stépan Yaramko do not even know where or how to begin to speak to one another again. In other families, such as the Lacasses, the Kumachuks, and the Yaramkos, there is little communication between parents and children. Finally, Sam Lee Wong, to whom no one in Horizon bothers to speak, is the sole person to listen to Smouillya, avoided by everyone because of his practically unintelligible speech patterns. If communication among people can be seen as a "common rivage," it is, in Gabrielle Roy's realistic fiction, often a difficult shore to reach.[10]

In order to attain the ideal world that Roy so ardently desired, however, communication and, in particular, language are of major importance. Despite the problems encountered in verbal exchange, therefore, almost all of her characters exhibit some sense of sociability, as they search for an opportunity for conversation with others. Azarius and his male friends spend much of their time conversing at the Deux Records, while Florentine, usually distant from female acquaintances, turns to Marguerite as to someone with whom she can share her troubles. Luzina, like the Capucin, is the epitome of the talkative, gregarious individual who, also like Mme Le Gardeur, needs conversations with people in order to counteract her isolated existence in a rural area. Solitude also describes the life of Alexandre who, almost in spite of himself, still clings to the possibility of communication with Godias. Loners, such as Gédéon and Cordorai, enjoy occasions when they can relate to another human presence. The pitiful couple of Sam and Smouillya base their companionship upon conversation. Even the solitary train conductor needs to talk and thrives on human dialogue. Royan characters may remember, dream, and day-dream alone, but whenever possible and although often unsuc-cessfully, they do attempt to communicate with other people.[11]

With this intense need for sociability and conversation in the Royan fictional world come both a love for and the impor-tance and power of the word, spoken or written. The author herself expressed her own love for certain words, especially for those in the English language, such as "longing," "dusk," "nightingale," and "swallow," that either do not have an e-quivalent in French or, in her opinion, do not sound as beauti-ful. In her fiction, it is Christine who, as a sensitive young woman and a future writer, recognizes the fact that she has inherited her love for language from her mother: "Elle m'avait enseigné le pouvoir des images, la merveille d'une chose révélée par un mot juste et tout l'amour que peut contenir une simple et belle phrase." She has learned to use words "comme de ponts fragiles pour l'exploration [of oneself, of others, and of the world] . . . et il est vrai, parfois aussi, pour la communica-tion." Other Royan characters, as well, fully understand this power of language and regard or use words accordingly: Luzina, as the ability to involve a reader or listener; Alexandre, as the power to negate the sadness or tragedy of one's life; Pierre, as the capacity to create an air of adventure and space; and, similar-ly, Gustave, as the potential to suggest new, unknown routes and worlds.[12]

Given this sensitivity to the power of language, it is not at all surprising that Gabrielle Roy carefully chose the names of her characters and, at times, the locations that they inhabit. Several critics have, in fact, noted the symbolism of some of these names, especially of people. Jacques Blais has even gone so far as to propose the theory that there exists a distinction between the meaning of the first and last names of many characters, with one's given name as the symbol of hope for one's destiny and one's family name as an indication of heredity, of a pre-determined life of failure. Such a theory, however, if at all sound, is applicable only to certain Royan names. "Florentine," as in springtime, has already been contrasted with "Lacasse," not only, as in Jean's eyes, as a name associated with poverty, but also as suggestive of a state of being boxed in, thwarted, encaged. "Lacasse," therefore, can also be seen in opposition to the "Rose" of "Rose-Anna." Irony is evident in the choice of other names in *Bonheur d'occasion*. Jean Lévesque desires to achieve the stature and authority of a bishop but, despite his role as Florentine's saviour, certainly rejects any religious ties. Emmanual Létourneau, in his role as the agent of a possible rebirth for Florentine, is faithful to the symbolism of his last name as a starling, once again as springtime, but his naive nature is equally, and ironically, suggested by his name.[13]

One of the most obviously ironic uses of a symbolic name is that of Alexandre Chenevert. He has been identified as having a first name that is suggestive of a powerful and war-like conqueror. His last name is indicative of nature, with both its refreshing, seasonal colors and growth and its majestic and strong oak trees. It is, therefore, pathetically ironic that the insignificant bank teller cannot fashion his life upon the strength of his name, except, perhaps, in his unspoken and unwritten thoughts. Like the circumflex that is missing in his family name, Chenevert is lacking precisely in the traits that he attributes to the great leaders of the world, while he only temporarily achieves the rebirth suggested by this same composite word.[14]

Elsewhere in this novel, names are significantly utilized. The gentleness of the "vert" in Alexandre's last name is echoed in that of Godias Doucet. It is also clearly reflected in the bank teller's discovered paradise at Lac Vert, with its simple name and natural beauty. It is, in fact, at this locale that Chenevert makes the acquaintance of Etienne Le Gardeur, "un nom qui inspirait confiance et amitié, tout en exprimant la protection." Equally significant is the fact that Le Gardeur advertises his vacation retreat first as being at Lac des Iles, thus linking it to Chenevert's dreams of an exotic, tropical island, and secondly as being four miles from Saint-Donat, prefiguring the gift of a natural, religious experience for the teller in the countryside. This instinctive, personal discovery will later be contrasted to organized religion, in the person of the ironically named priest, l'Abbé Marchand.[15]

There are two symbolic names to be found in *Rue Deschambault*, both of which are nicknames for Christine. The sensitive child rejects the implications of the name, "Petite Misère," given to her by her unhappy father, while she loves the nickname, "Petite Fraise," once again, linking a character to spring. Two final examples of significant names are related to the obsession with roads, travel, and, therefore, life-long pursuits. Sam Lee Wong settles in the prairie town of Horizon, whose name is reflective of its environment and of the varied goals of its inhabitants. More powerful, however, is the choice of the name, Pierre Cordorai, for the trapper-painter who obsessively continues his search for an aesthetic ideal. Critics have seen his family name—perhaps exaggeratedly—as signifying "Qu'adorai," suggesting a Sisyphus-type figure who continuously pursues his voyage toward some unknown and impossible idol to be adored, and as "Qu'adorer," a man isolated and without a home. Roy herself compared her novel to *Le Mythe de Sisyphe* but did not comment on such an interpretation of her main character's name.[16]

If Roy's choice of the above proper names is significant, their articulation, as well as the articulation of other words, produces equally significant results. The importance and multiple symbolism of the words, "Chez nous," in *Bonheur d'occasion* have already been examined. In *La Petite Poule d'eau*, it is especially the naming of children, like Pierre-Emmanuel-Roger and Philippe-Auguste-Emile, that is effective:

> Les deux aînés n'étaient pas les seuls des enfants Tousignant à porter des prénoms composés. Comme pour mieux peupler la solitude où elle vivait, Luzina avait donné à chacun de ses enfants toute une kyrielle de noms d'après les grands de l'histoire ou tirés des rares romans sur lesquels elle avait réussi à mettre la main. Parmi les enfants . . . il y avait Roberta-Louise-Célestine, Josephine-Yolande, André-Aimable-Sébastien; le plus petit, un bébé de quinze mois, répondait au prénom de Juliette-Héloïse.[17]

The articulation of language is even more powerful in *Alexandre Chenevert*, since it creates a new form of immortality for the main character:

> Cependant, ailleurs que dans les églises, il arrive encore aujourd'hui, après ces quelques années, que le nom soit prononcé—et n'est-ce point chose mystérieuse et tendre, qu'à ce nom corresponde un lien. . . . Il arrive qu'ici et là, dans la ville, quelqu'un dise: "— . . .

Alexandre Chenevert. . . ."

If the power of the spoken word is here related to the eternity achieved in memory, it actually becomes a life-giving force in *Rue Deschambault,* as Papa, pronouncing the word, "maison," is suddenly brought back to life and renews his desire to defeat the threat of death during a devastating fire. Similarly, when Christine calls Alicia by her name, the insane young woman abruptly discovers a path out of the darkness enveloping her mind and manages, in return, to recognize her sister, as she pronounces her nickname, "la Petite." In this instance, however, the power of the word is only temporary, and Alicia soon drifts back into her former state.[18]

Finally, both Martha and Stépan Yaramko fully understand the effects of articulated language. Martha, like Luzina, needs to think and to speak of her children in order to negate her solitude: "Elle en venait à penser à ses enfants. Pour s'assurer de leur existence malgré le lien immensément relâché d'elle à eux, elle se répétait leur nom et aussi les noms des endroits où ils vivaient." As for the relationship with her husband, both spouses are unable to pronounce the words, "homme" and "femme," for such articulation would constitute an insult to their former love. When Stépan finally needs to speak to his bedridden wife, simply to inform her that her lunch has been prepared, he does not know what to do:

> Il espérait que tout se passerait sans qu'il eût à ouvrir la bouche. Car que dire? Et surtout comment la nommer, elle? Dire simplement: Martha, impossible. L'habitude en était depuis trop longtemps perdue. . . . Elle-même . . . parut sur le point d'ouvrir la bouche. Mais pour elle aussi sans doute il était trop difficile de parler.

Aware of the probable results of speech, that is, the renewal of their marital bond, the couple prefers to remain silent.[19]

This intense fear and, therefore, total lack of any articulated language are rare in Gabrielle Roy's fiction, for along with the power of the word usually comes the importance of the storyteller. Roy herself regarded the role of such an individual with the greatest respect, for not only did she see herself as practicing this vocation, but she also considered the presence of the storyteller to be the stimulus of human communication:

"Il me semble que le premier petit groupe amical a dû, sur terre, se former autour d'un conteur." If one can describe the act of living and experiencing as a straight road, then the act of recounting a tale is here seen as circular, as creating a warm and secure circle of people around the one who is speaking. Storytellers are, therefore, usually "conteurs-nés qui semblent n'exister que pour briller le soir, quand ils prennent la parole. . . ." Their desire is to "tâcher de se communiquer quelque chose d'unique en chacun d'eux et qui les rapprochait." Their effect on others, such as Christine, can be permanent: "C'est de ces soirées se déroulant comme des concours de chants et d'histoires que date sans doute le désir, qui ne m'a jamais quittée depuis, d'appendre à bien raconter, tant je pense avoir saisi dès alors le poignant et miraculeux pouvoir de ce don." The Royan nomads of real voyages and of travels in the imagination have become the spinners of tales from the past, often filled with journeys that come alive again with the power of spoken language.[20]

The importance of maintaining this past of one's family, traditions, and culture, as well as of one's individual life, unique and yet so similar to others, is the cause of such a prevalence of storytellers throughout Roy's texts. Associated with these gifts from the past is the warmth of the stove or fire around which so many tales are told. It is, in fact, the fire itself that seems to speak to Chenevert. In most of Roy's fiction, however, it is a member of an older generation who recounts stories of former days: Thaddeus and then Elsa to Jimmy; Mémère and then Maman to Christine. Given the semi-autobiographical nature or, at least, inspiration of many of Roy's works, it is tales of Manitoba, of migrations to Manitoba, or of a past in Quebec that predominate. Gustave, the vagabond, in particular, tells stories about the father's family in Quebec and thus not only instills a respect for this province in the hearts of the Manitobans listening to him, but also creates familial links and "notre parenté avec les hommes." His "voix ensorcelante" speaks, almost sings, as it captivates the audience. It does not matter that Gustave has created a fictitious world of goodness and happiness in Quebec, a fictitious world, even, of the family itself. The nostalgia and joy that he has brought with him far outweigh any wickedness in his having embellished reality.[21]

With both the author's and her characters' love for the role of the storyteller, it is logical that Roy uses the narrators of her fiction as a type of storyteller as well. In all of Roy's works, but especially in her first-person narratives, the presence of the narrator brings a certain lucidity and logic to the text. In *Rue Deschambault, La Route d'Altamont,* and, more recently, *Ces Enfants de ma vie,* the narrator is, in fact, a persona, a character participating within the story, as well as recounting the tale. As the unique and central conscience of the text and, therefore, with a heightened sense of perception, the narrator-Christine posses a dual self, a dual *je:* her present, adult self and her past, youthful self. Utilizing one of the major benefits of relating a story, the adult narrator of these works looks at her younger self and judges, comments, and criticizes her former actions and thoughts. Maintaining her distance, while conjuring up the past, the narrator-storyteller, like the writer, easily takes an ironic stance toward herself and toward others, as she achieves her fundamental desire of relating the story of her life.[22]

This personal need and goal are foremost in the minds of many of Roy's characters and narrators. In spite of or, perhaps, because of his solitary life, Pierre Cordorai recognizes this deep desire of everyone, when he first reads a passage from Shakespeare's *Hamlet:*

> Il releva la tête, se répéta à lui-même: *"To tell my story. . . ."*
> Oui, c'était le désir profond de chaque vie, l'appel de toute âme: que quelqu'un se souciât d'elle assez pour s'en ressouvenir quelquefois, et, aux autres, dire un peu ce qu'elle avait été, combien elle avait lutté. Tant d'agitation, de secrets et de tergiversations, pour en finir sur cette douce plainte: *to tell my story!*

Roy herself understood this need on the part of her characters, on the part of, for example, Nina of *La Montagne secrète,* Jim Farrell and Smouillya of "Où iras-tu Sam Lee Wong?," and Martha, of whom the latter asks the writer "ce que tous nous demandons peut-être du fond de notre silence: Raconte ma vie." Either in their own words, in those of fictional storytellers, through the intervention of a narrator, or, ultimately, because of the sensitivity of the writer, the lives or stories of many people are here beautifully told.[23]

The role of the writer in Gabrielle Roy's fiction, however, or of the painter in *La Montagne secrète,* is not simply that of a storyteller. It is a far more complex and important role, beginning with a Romantic-like call to this vocation-mission in life. Roy incarnates the epitome of the predestined artist in the character of Christine who hears a vague and natural "voix des étangs":

> Ainsi j'ai eu l'idée d'écrire. Quoi et pourquoi, je n'en savais rien. J'écrirais. C'était comme un amour soudain qui tout d'un coup, enchaîne un coeur. . . . je voulais écrire comme on sent le besoin d'aimer, d'être aimé. . . .
>
> Alors j'ai gravement annoncé à maman ce qu'il en était: que je devais écrire. . . .

Similarly, Pierre Cordorai is called both by nature to paint images of its beauty and happiness and by some unknown and interior voice to travel continously further toward an aesthetic ideal. The Royan writer-artist has a determined role to play in this world.[24]

In order to fulfill this partially chosen and partially involuntary role in life the writer-artist embarks upon a long, distant, and difficult road. Seen as typically Royan nomads, therefore, or as mythical *Québécois coureurs-de-bois,* these individuals undertake what Pierre calls an arduous exercise so that they may move closer toward self-discovery, maturity in artistic expression, and an awareness of the intimate rapports, as yet unknown, within the universe:

> Au vrai, ai-je jamais vraiment consenti à être écrivain? Je ne pense pas. J'avais déjà trop bien pressenti qu'embarqué dans ce chemin, on ne peut en voir le bout. On marche du colline en colline; chacune est un peu plus haute que la précédante, mais assez pour voir au-delà de celle qui vient.

With lives often filled with torment and suffering, these artists submit to "des plus mystérieuses épreuves" while *en route.* They can be likened to medieval heroes or to nineteenth-century French Romantic and Symbolist poets who must pass through stages of initiation before attaining their predestined, ideal goal of purity.[25]

One of the fundamental causes of the difficulty and torment of these aesthetic journeys can be found in the divided nature of the personality, life, and role of the writer-artist. An ordinary mortal among others and desirous of remaining as such, the Royan writer-artist is also proudly obsessed with an absurd goal of an unknown, aesthetic image of perfection. Pierre sees himself as "cet enfant rare entre les hommes," a superior being who, with the child-like innocence but genius of vision, is a Promethean figure, the giver of this perfection, fire, or knowledge to others. With the tranquility and objectivity of the artistic regard and the anguish of the subjective, artistic emotion, this chosen individual attempts to reconcile the opposing natures of the self and of humanity.[26]

The writer-artist in Roy's fiction is, therefore, even more than other characters, an "être partagé": both a spectator and an actor, one who looks, observes, and objectively reports and one who is living on stage. Painfully recognizing the inevitable dangers and unhappiness of this talent and duty of being both a *regardant* and a *regardé,* Christine's mother can only forewarn her daughter:

> "Ecrire," me dit-elle tristement, "c'est dur. . . . N'est-ce pas se partager en deux, pour ainsi dire: un qui tâche de vivre, l'autre qui regarde, qui juge. . . ."
>
> Elle me dit encore:
>
> "D'abord, il faut le don. . . . Car on dit le don, mais peut-être faudrait-il dire: le commandement. Et c'est un don bien étrange . . . pas tout à fait humain. Je pense que les autres ne le pardonnent jamais. Ce don, c'est un peu comme une malchance. . . ."

Since most people neither understand nor accept this artistic gift, the writer-artist suffers while remaining an actor in life, suffers pitifully like a *poète maudit,* and ultimately must sacrifice a part of life in order to succeed. As a sacrificial hero, the Pierre-caribou figure must abandon himself to the realm of art: "Comment! l'art exigerait le sacrifice de la vie chaude, souffrante et suppliante. A présent il convenait que c'était vrai, qu'une part du moins de la vie mourait en se fixant dans la beauté—et de là dans son âme une sorte de blessure grave."[27]

The most painful aspect of this suffering and sacrifice while on the road toward aesthetic discoveries is the fact the writer-artist must endure these hardships, and often desires to endure them, alone. He/she can be seen as a shy and somewhat neurotic individual who practices a chosen profession in total loneliness. For Maman, the gift of artistic talent resembles a misfortune " 'qui éloigne les autres, qui nous sépare de presque tous. . . . Ecrire . . . est-ce que ce n'est pas en définitive être loin des autres . . . être toute seule, pauvre enfant!' " Defined as a rupture or series of ruptures, as a separation, or as a wandering without roots, the act of writing in Roy's fiction has been aptly described by François Ricard as an experience of solitude, in that it is a renunciation or destruction of the writer's self in order to reconstruct and repossess an aesthetic universe. If one accepts this interpretation, then this act of writing can be viewed as Mallarméan.[28]

The successful recomposition of this aesthetic world discovered in solitude is useless, even non-existent, however, unless the writer-artist can communicate it to others. Pierre Cordorai realizes and accepts this necessity for a public of his art, just as he recognizes the similarly inevitable conflict within his divided self, as within all Royan beings, between solitude and solidarity, between his conditions of being "à la fois si proche . . . et si éloigné des hommes":

> Il s'aperçut qu'il pensait à des hommes, des inconnus, une multitude. Il rêvait d'eux, d'une entente entre eux et lui,—d'une entente avec des inconnus,—lui, qui, toute sa vie, jusqu'ici, s'était sans cesse éloigné des hommes.
>
> Eloigné? Ou rapproché?
>
> Tout à coup, l'inonda le sentiment d'avoir pour eux seuls osé ce qu'il avait fait. Et pour qui d'autre l'eût-il tenté?

Pierre, like all writers and artists, needs and desires to relate to others, to share emotions, experiences, and thoughts with the outside world precisely because of his solitary state and in order to vanquish that state. After having searched for and then endured solitude, therefore, the writer-artist can make an effort toward solidarity with others and can return to them with an offering of reconciliation, for as Ricard points out, this individual "part pour écrire, mais il revient en écrivant."[29]

Solidarity with humanity, therefore, is not necessarily a conflicting state with but often a natural progression from solitude. Once the writer-artist has attempted to communicate any discoveries, a public will, in Roy's opinion, realize first that this art expresses an ideal of self-liberation, beauty, and love and then that the writer-artist has, in fact, envisioned this new world for them. They, in turn, will now view this universe through the enlightened vision of "celui qui ouvre leurs yeux, celui qui ouvre aussi entre eux de grandes portes soudaines de communication." Once again like a Romantic or Symbolist prophet or guide, the Royan writer-artist, by telling the stories of humanity, will convey to others their uniqueness and their similarities, will create links and a sense of solidarity, and will, ultimately, make the world a more pleasant place to live.[30]

In order to effect this solidarity and in order to be this agent of communication, the writer must play the role of a prestidigitator, and the artist, like Pierre, must play that of "l'homme au crayon magique." The power of both roles will convince people that such a world is possible, at least in the aesthetic realm. In addition, the Royan creator, sensitive to the condition of humanity, is a revolutionary, a "protestaire; et d'abord contre le sort humain qui est de finir." Creating, therefore, a form of immortality in art, this individual accomplishes that which is sublime in this world, "un acte de protestation": "Créer . . . n'est-ce pas de toute son âme protester? A moins . . . à moins . . . que ce ne soit une secrète collaboration. . . ."[31]

As a magician, a creator of aesthetic immortality, and a protestor, the writer-artist encounters the second most fundamental cause of a life of difficulty and torment: the attempt at divine collaboration, at being the recreator of nature. Throughout *La Montagne secrète*, Pierre Cordorai's unique desire is to paint what he sees as simple life and nature, in particular, water and, of course, the splendid, solitary mountain. At the end of his life, he finally realizes that he has come close to successful recreation, not necessarily of the real world, but rather of his own inner, secret vision: "Sa montagne, en vérité. Repensée, refaite en dimension, plans et volumes; à lui entièrement; sa création propre. . . . Et sans doute ne s'agissait-il plus de savoir qui avait le mieux réussi sa montagne, Dieu ou Pierre, mais que lui aussi avait fait oeuvre de création." This artist is proud, as he has been during his entire life, not of being God but either of collaborating, of being a rival, or of being himself a type of divinity.[32]

Despite this sense of pride and precisely because of its powerful presence, Cordorai, this Mallarméan artist-writer, is fearful that he may be attempting to surpass his human limits in his goal of recreating aspects of nature. After having tried to capture the image of water on paper, for example, Pierre is carried along in his boat by the river rapids and loses all of his paints in the natural water. The artist's pride has temporarily been destroyed. Similarly, he desires to recreate "la Resplendis-sante" in art, but he is afraid: "La saisir donc! Il en avait peur maintenant. A sa joie profonde se mêlait de la timidité. L'ap-préhension de faire affront à la montagne, ou à soi-même. Il redoudait ce premier geste, ce premier trait, toujours si dé-concertant. . . ." When Pierre does finally paint images of the mountain, his work is destroyed by a bear, once again either by nature or by some superior force, as he hears "le reproche de la montagne":

> Depuis des siècles . . . je suis ici à attendre. Je n'existe vraiment que quelques semaines par année, au plus fort de l'été, lorsque mon front sort enfin des brouillards et de l'infinie solitude. Je n'existe qu'un moment, lorsque je suis belle et calme. Et toi qui m'as vue ainsi, tu n'as pas su fixer l'instant, la splendeur, l'exceptionnelle splendeur qui est ma vérité.

Even when certain elements of nature want to be recaptured in art, the artist is unable to succeed.[33]

Given both this fear of surpassing one's limits and this constant inability to reach one's aesthetic goal, the Royan writer-artist, in the person of Pierre, longs to destroy this in-cessant, absurd desire to recreate natural perfection. But once again, unmistakably resembling Mallarmé in his poetic torment, Cordorai remains obsessed, haunted by what he feels that he must do:

> "Mais les tableaux que tu n'as pas fait," se disait-il, "de loin à lui-même, qui les fera? Et cette oeuvre qui est en toi, est-ce que tu vas l'abandonner?" Sa pensée devenait chagrin, regret infini, solitude navrée pour ce qui n'était pas né—cependant en lui comme une graine dans la terre. La mort du présent n'est rien; c'est la perte de l'avenir en soi qui est déchirante.
>
> Il parvint à sortir de sa torpeur, à se mettre debout. . . . demain, il se mettrait en route. . . . Et la pensée de la montagne seule le soutenait.[34]

Like the true creator, faithful to an obsessive goal of artistic perfection, Cordorai will continue on this life-long journey that predestines him to a constant sense of failure. He feels the pain of inertia, absence, and nothingness, as if he cannot achieve nor ever has achieved perfection in art. He feels, therefore, that he has accomplished nothing of value. He fears, in addition, that he will die before his work can be done, and he senses that his task will, thus, never be completed. It cannot, of course, be completed because it is an impossible task. The artist is not God, for God will not tolerate any rivals. There exists, therefore, an air of sadness around Pierre, just as around Gabrielle Roy herself when she, too, lamented that she would never have enough time to complete all that she desired to write. The writer-artist, like all creators, is a perpetually dissatisfied person.[35]

This dissatisfaction, however, obsessively drives the Royan creator toward a final, often unknown goal, toward the story to be told as the work of art. In Gabrielle Roy's aesthetic vision, it is the act of creation and the existence of that artistic work that ultimately reflect a profound humanism. This work represents an idea, action, matter, desire, emotion, vision, and heart. It is initially "une émotion revécue en toute tranquillité": a form of self-expression, recreated with the temporal and spatial objectivity of self-distance, leading to self-liberation for the creator. As an observance of and a speaking for others, the work of art also becomes an expression of humanity, "le portrait sans cesse renouvelé de son semblable." This portrait that succeeds in creating "à travers un être imaginé tant d'êtres vivants et variés" reveals "ce que chacun possède à la fois d'unique et de plus semblable à tous. . . ." These characteristics of diversity and sameness that define the human condition are reflected in both their beauty and tragic sorrow. The liberation of the writer-artist, therefore, is transferred to others who, in their new knowledge and acceptance of the human state as manifested in art, overcome their sense of solitude and begin to relate among themselves. A work of art is, ultimately, a communicable message: "Voici que l'oeuvre de Pierre était un peu comme avait été la montagne, avant qu'il ne la contemplait, belle peut-être, mais qui le savait qui la connaissait?" To be effective, that message needs a public: "Il fallait lui donner la vie, ne pas la [the work of art] laisser, elle, mourir. Ce qui meurt d'inexprimé, avec une vie, lui [Pierre] parut la seule mort regrettable."[36]

What this desired public will discover in the work of art will be an aesthetic recreation of the colors of life and the soul, a rebirth of the light of the sky and of the primitive world, a breath of life and truth revealed in their unity. It is

Cordorai who envisions his artistic vocation in this sublime manner, as he paints a series of small pictures, each representing or, rather, trying to capture, a single facet of reality. In essence, however, these works portray what Cordorai's Parisian art teacher defines as "une sorte de résonance intérieure avec l'univers—elle-même au reste indéfinissable." The work of art is actually the recreation of a personal, inner vision, extended to include the universe and humanity. It is a "poème de la pensée" that "se plaisait donc à ces rencontres imprévues d'objets naturellement si loin les uns des autres." As a vision of reality and an adventure into the imaginary, it can transcend exterior reality and be more beautiful. For Pierre Cordorai, art is magic, a talisman for the memory, and that which will remain when all else has disappeared.[37]

It is for these characteristics of duration, permanence, and even immortality that the work of art is of utmost importance to its creator. It represents a doubling or a summation of the writer-artist's life, in the form of both a spiritual ascent and a psychological inquiry into the inner self. Like the self-portrait of Pierre at the end of *La Montagne secrète,* it is the creator's last testament, a mortal's attempt at perfection. The dream of the Royan writer-artist, therefore, like that of every creator, is to express everything, to speak of everything in one work: "Un dernier mot définitif, un tableau final: ce rêve le [Pierre] tenait." The ideal work of art in Roy's universe is *Le "Livre"* of Stéphane Mallarmé, the unique, sublime work that is all: "Qui n'a rêvé, en un seul tableau, en un seul livre, de mettre enfin tout l'objet, tout le sujet: tout de soi: toute son expérience, tout son amour, et combler ainsi l'espérance infinie, l'infinie attente des hommes!"[38]

This individual ideal work of art must represent the ultimate, the final masterpiece simply because it equals both life and death. As the story of the creator's life-long vision, the existing work is always only a partial fulfillment of one's dream. The dream itself of aesthetic perfection is an impossible goal, and the writer-artist must die with a sense of failure, without having achieved total success. At the conclusion of *La Montagne secrète,* Pierre Cordorai, about to die, finally envisions his ideal goal, a goal that, sadly, will remain unexpressed by him:

> Une douleur aiguë lui déchira la poitrine. Ses yeux grandirent d'un étonnement sans bornes. Il tendit la main vers le tableau.

> La douleur lui raidit le bras. Son âme resta un instant encore
> liée à l'oeuvre parfaite, enfin entrevue. . . . Il commença de s'af-
> faisser. . . . La haute montagne s'éloignait. Qui, dans les brumes,
> la retrouvera![39]

Pierre is fully aware that aesthetic goals of purity and perfection are mere dreams, giving a sense of purpose to an individual's life, but never as attainable ends. But he remains optimistic and idealistic. Like any individual creator, he may die without having expressed his ideal, but, as suggested at the conclusion of the novel, there is always the possibility that someone else will rediscover Pierre's mountain, hidden in the mist. Roy has described the novel as an iceberg "dont on dit qu'un huitième seulement de la hauteur totale émerge de l'eau": "C'est sa partie immergée, sur laquelle tout repose, et qui cependant n'a pas été dite, c'est ce vieux fond de rêve mi-obscur qui lui assure, s'il doit y parvenir, de flotter quelque temps. . . ." If all of the artistic world can be similarly seen as this partially expressed, partially unseen iceberg, then there will always be future creators to desire and to attempt to discover the as yet silent, submerged vision of humanity and the universe. It is this inevitable continuation of the artistic dream, in a typically cyclical fashion, that assures that art will endure forever.[40]

NOTES

[1]Personal interview with Gabrielle Roy, 29 June 1980. See also Réjean Robidoux, "Le Roman et la recherche du sens de la vie: Vocation: Ecrivain," in *Mélanges de civilisation canadienne-française offerts au professeur Paul Wyczynski,* ed. Pierre Savard, Cahiers du Centre de Recherche en civilisation canadienne-française, No. 10 (Ottawa: Editions de l'Université d'Ottawa, 1977), p. 225; Jack Warwick, *L'Appel du nord dans la littérature canadienne-française,* trans. Jean Simard, Collection Constantes (Montréal: Editions Hurtubise HMH, 1972), p. 149.

[2]Letter received from Gabrielle Roy, 27 March 1980; Gabrielle Roy, "Le Pays de *Bonheur d'occasion,*" in *Morceaux,* ed. Robert Guy Scully (Montréal: Les Editions du Noroït, 1978), p. 113. Personal interview with Gabrielle Roy, 29 June 1980.

[3]Personal interview with Gabrielle Roy, 29 June 1980. It is for this last reason that Roy was negative toward much modern, current literature, toward, in particular, *le nouveau roman.* She found such works to be cryptic and out of the realm of understanding of most people. Personal interview with Gabrielle Roy, 29 June 1980.

[4]Gabrielle Roy, *Bonheur d'occasion* (1945; rpt. Montréal: Librairie Beauchemin Limitée, 1973), pp. 48, 49. See also pp. 38, 263, 269; James E. La Follette, Jr. "Le Parler franco-canadien dans *Bonheur d'occasion,*" Thesis Université Laval 1949, pp. 1, 3, 14-17, 20-22, 33, 96-99, 112-113, 118, 139, 146-147, 168-175, 201, 205-232, 251-253, 293-294, 300-306, 316-318.

[5]Gabrielle Roy, *Un Jardin au bout du monde* (Montréal: Librairie Beauchemin Limitée, 1975), p. 82. See also p. 167; Gabrielle Roy, *La Petite Poule d'eau* (1950; rpt. Montréal: Librairie Beauchemin Limitée, 1970), pp. 33, 183, 256, 261; Gabrielle Roy, *Rue Deschambault* (1955; rpt. Montréal: Librairie Beauchemin Limitée, 1974), pp. 146, 155; Gabrielle Roy, "Les Sudètes de Good Soil," *Fragiles Lumières de la terre: Ecrits divers 1942-1970,* Collection Prose Entière (Montréal: Les Editions Quinze, 1978), pp. 72, 76; Gabrielle Roy, "Plus que le pain," *Le Bulletins des Agriculteurs,* 38, No. 2 (février 1942), 9.

[6]Roy, *Bonheur d'occasion,* p. 19; Roy, *La Petite Poule d'eau,* p. 100. In the first work, see also pp. 71, 95, 198, 202; in the second see also pp. 46, 57, 63, 65, 91-93, 97, 99, 101, 104-106, 131. See also Gabrielle Roy, *Alexandre Chenevert* (1954; rpt. Montréal: Beauchemin, 1973), pp. 19-20, 38-39, 49, 97, 307; Gabrielle Roy, "Souvenirs du Manitoba," *La Revue de Paris,* 62e année, No. 2 (février 1955), pp. 82-83; Roy, *Rue Deschambault,* pp. 122, 124, 194; Gabrielle Roy, "Voyage en Ungava," as quoted in Marc Gagné, "*La Rivière sans repos* de Gabrielle Roy: Etude mythocritique incluant 'Voyage en Ungava' (extraits) par Gabrielle Roy (suite)," *Revue de l'Université d'Ottawa,* 46, No. 3 (juillet-septembre 1976), 375; Gabrielle Roy, "Le Manitoba," *Le Magazine Maclean,* 2, No. 7 (juillet 1962), pp. 113-118, 120; Gabrielle Roy, *La Rivière sans repos* (Montréal: Librairie Beauchemin Limitée, 1971), p. 259; Gabrielle Roy, "Ely! Ely! Ely!," *Liberté,* 21, No. 3, année 1979, numéro 123 (mai-juin 1979), pp. 16, 20, 24. In this last work, the narrator describes herself as speaking a French from France and an English from England. She is, therefore, not fully Canadian, linguistically, for she does not communicate in the "doux parler du Québec."

[7] Roy, *Alexandre Chenevert*, p. 90. See also pp. 303-305.

[8] Roy, *Alexandre Chenevert*, pp. 251-252, 255. See also pp. 23,
249-250; Roy, *La Rivière sans repos*, pp. 65-75, 221-223, 296-299.

[9] Roy, *Alexandre Chenevert*, pp. 252, 251, 151. See also pp. 28-29,
66, 88, 96, 112, 117, 150, 155-156, 229, 368.

[10] Gabrielle Roy, *Courte-Queue* (Montréal: Editions Internationales
Alain Stanké Ltée, 1979), p. 40; Gabrielle Roy, *La Route d'Altamont*,
Collection L'Arbre, No. 10 (Montréal: Editions HMH, 1966), p. 204;
Gabrielle Roy, *Cet Eté qui chantait* (Québec-Montréal: Les Editions Fran-
çaises, 1972), p. 198. See also Roy, *Bonheur d'occasion*, pp. 61-62, 145,
148, 149, 230, 232, 236, 245, 258, 307; Roy, *La Petite Poule d'eau*, pp. 22,
24; Roy, *Rue Deschambault*, pp. 169, 176, 178, 179; Gabrielle Roy, *La
Montagne secrète* (1961; rpt. Montréal: Librairie Beauchemin Limitée,
1974), pp. 15-17; Roy, *La Rivière sans repos*, pp. 281, 284; Roy, *Un
Jardin au bout du monde*, pp. 74-75, 78-82, 113-115, 208-209, 212-213.

[11] Roy, *Bonheur d'occasion*, pp. 36-38, 131, 233-240, 245; Roy,
La Petite Poule d'eau, pp. 18, 20, 22, 25, 27, 31, 33, 132, 170, 178, 185,
232; Roy, *Alexandre Chenevert*, pp. 63-66, 134-135, 199-200, 229, 238-
245; Roy, *La Montagne secrète*, pp. 11-15, 70-72, 163-166; Roy, *Un
Jardin au bout du monde*, pp. 77-82, 85-87; Roy, "Ely! Ely! Ely!," p. 26.

[12] Roy, *Rue Deschambault*, p. 246; Roy, *La Route d'Altamont*, p. 233.
In this last work, see also pp. 55, 139. See also Personal interview with
Gabrielle Roy, 29 June 1980; Roy, *La Petite Poule d'eau*, pp. 119-120;
Roy, *Alexandre Chenevert*, pp. 11, 23, 150, 182-183, 249-255; Roy, *La
Montagne secrète*, p. 167; Roy, *Un Jardin au bout du monde*, pp. 38, 197;
Gabrielle Roy, "Pitié pour les institutrices," *Le Bulletin des Agriculteurs*,
38, No. 3 (mars 1942), 46.

[13] Roy, *Bonheur d'occasion*, p. 26. The name, "Pitou," was used by
Roy because of its popularity at that particular period of time. Emmanuel's
choice of the record entitled *Bitter Sweet* is clearly symbolic of his relationship with Florentine and, in a sense, is the reverse of the young woman's
name. See p. 291; Roy, "Le Pays de *Bonheur d'occasion*," p. 117. See
also Jacques Blais, "L'Unité organique de *Bonheur d'occasion*," *Etudes
Françaises*, 6, No. 1 (février 1970), 46-47; Roland M. Charland et Jean-
Noël Samson, *Gabrielle Roy*, Dossiers de documentation sur la littérature
canadienne-française (Montréal: Fides, 1972), p. 15; Anne Srabian de
Fabry, "A la recherche de l'ironie perdue chez Gabrielle Roy et Flaubert,"
Présence francophone, 11 (1975), 94. Even prior to the composition of
her first novel, Roy exhibited a preference for symbolic names, as in the
creation of Loubka, a name that signifies the word "love" and suggests
the promise of happiness but is constantly mispronounced by the young
woman's French-speaking landlady: "Madame Savard n'avait aucune sym-

pathie pour les noms qui n'avaient pas à ses oreilles canadiennes une résonance du pays. Et elle savait prononcer celui-là avec une espèce d'affecta-
tion comique, une teinte d'effroi et de gêne qui disait exactement sa pensée:
une étrangère." See Gabrielle Roy, "Le Joli Miracle," *Le Bulletin des
Agriculteurs*, 26, No. 12 (décembre 1940), 8.

[14]Roy, *Alexandre Chenevert*, pp. 39, 75. Interestingly, Chenevert
hates the use of the familiar, diminutive form of his name, "Alex." See
also Blais, pp. 46-47; Charland et Samson, p. 18; Marc Gagné, *Visages de
Gabrielle Roy* (Montréal: Librairie Beauchemin Limitée, 1973), p. 54.

[15]Roy, *Alexandre Chenevert*, p. 183. See also pp. 72, 182, 234, 320.

[16]Roy, *Rue Deschambault*, pp. 38, 212; Roy, *Un Jardin au bout du
monde*, p. 65; Blais, pp. 46-47; Richard M. Chadburne, "The Journey in
Gabrielle Roy's Novels," in *Travel, Quest, and Pilgrimage as a Literary
Theme: Studies in Honor of Reino Virtanen*, eds. Frans. C. Amelinckx
and Joyce N. Megay (Lincoln, Nebraska: Society of Spanish and Spanish-
American Studies, 1978), p. 257; Personal interview with Gabrielle Roy,
29 June 1980. Pierre Cordorai is also called "l'homme au crayon magique"
and "L'Homme-Seul." See Roy, *La Montagne secrète*, p. 93. The name,
"Pierre," also reminds one, first, of the Saint, and, therefore, of the artist
as a religious figure, and, secondly, of precious stones and, therefore by
extension, of the artist as an alchemist, magically turning metals-words-
paintings into gold. Jean Chevalier et Alain Gheerbrant, *Dictionnaire des
symboles* (Paris: Robert Laffont/Editions Jupiter, 1982), pp. 751-758.

[17]Roy, *Bonheur d'occasion*, pp. 244-245; Roy, *La Petite Poule d'eau*,
p. 23. In this last work, see also pp. 13, 24, 54-57.

[18]Roy, *Alexandre Chenevert*, p. 384; Roy, *Rue Deschambault*, pp.
160, 177-179. In the first work, the effect of the word, "merci," is also
described. See p. 54. In the second work, the connotations of the word,
"Canada," with its grandeur and immensity, are equally powerful. See
p. 114.

[19]Roy, *Un Jardin au bout du monde*, pp. 212, 208. See also pp. 85,
163. There are additional examples of the power of articulated language
in Roy's texts: prononciation of the word, "artiste," and of the names of
colors and rivers in Roy, *La Montagne secrète*, pp. 73, 186; that of the
names, Anastasie, Sans-Génie, and Altamont, in Roy, *La Route d'Altamont*,
pp. 25, 174-175, 209, 251-252; the teacher's sorrowful and sensual comment, " 'Ah! Médéric! Médéric!,' " as if to invoke the adolescent's presence
in Gabrielle Roy, *Ces Enfants de ma vie* (Montréal: Editions Internationales
Alain Stanké Ltée, 1977), p. 212; and the names from the past, Ely and
Dave, in Roy, "Ely! Ely! Ely!," pp. 13, 23.

[20]Gabrielle Roy, "Jeux du romancier et des lecteurs," l'Alliance
Française, Montréal, 1er décembre 1955, as quoted in Gagné, *Visages*

de Gabrielle Roy, p. 267; Roy, *La Route d'Altamont,* p. 213. Personal interview with Gabrielle Roy, 29 June 1980; Robidoux, p. 232. The circle of people gathered around the storyteller reminds one of that around the protective tree.

[21] Roy, *Un Jardin au bout du monde,* pp. 31, 32. See also pp. VII, 14-17, 21-25, 30, 35, 37-38, 46-48; Roy, *Alexandre Chenevert,* p. 223; Roy, *Rue Deschambault,* pp. 269-272; Roy, *La Route d'Altamont,* pp. 48-50, 162-164, 185, 214, 216-221; Roy, *La Rivière sans repos,* pp. 141, 170, 179-182, 262. Luzina, Armand Dubreuil, and le Capucin de Toutes-Aides also enjoy telling stories. See Roy, *La Petite Poule d'eau,* pp. 25, 77, 113, 119-120, 205, 231-235. See also Roy, *Cet Eté qui chantait,* pp. 130-131, 195; Roy, "De turbulents chercheurs de paix," "Petite Ukraine," "Une Voile dans la nuit," *Fragiles Lumières de la terre,* pp. 33, 85, 89; Gabrielle Roy, "Mon Héritage du Manitoba," *Mosaic,* 3iii (1970), 70, 71, 74, 75, 77.

[22] François Ricard, *Gabrielle Roy,* Ecrivains canadiens d'aujourd'hui, No. 11 (Montréal: Editions Fides, 1975), pp. 92-97; Charland et Samson, p. 72, Srabian de Fabry, pp. 90-95, 97-104; Warwick, pp. 23, 137; Ellen Babby, "The Narrator as Persona in Selected First Person Narratives of Gabrielle Roy," *Littérature québécoise* Section, Northeast Modern Language Association Convention, North Dartmouth, Massachusetts, March 1980; Paul Socken, "Art and the Artist in Gabrielle Roy's Works," *Revue de l'Université d'Ottawa,* 45 (1975), 344.

[23] Roy, *La Montagne secrète,* p. 147; Roy, *Un Jardin au bout du monde,* p. VIII. In the first work, see also pp. 36-38, 163-166; in the second see pp. 77-82, 85. See also Gagné, *Visages de Gabrielle Roy,* pp. 193-194.

[24] Roy, *Rue Deschambault,* pp. 244-245. See also Gabrielle Roy, "*Bonheur d'occasion* aujourd'hui," *Le Bulletin des Agriculteurs,* 44, No. 1 (janvier 1948), 6; Roy, *La Montagne secrète,* pp. 28-29, 38-39; Roy, "Le Joli Miracle," p. 30. René Richard, upon whom the character of Cordorai is based, also receives the call of destiny to become an artist. Luzina's destiny is described as that of writing letters, while Chenevert wants to be a writer but cannot. It is not in his particular destiny. See Gabrielle Roy, "Préface de *René Richard,*" in Ricard, p. 172; Roy, *La Petite Poule d'eau,* p. 63; Roy, *Alexandre Chenevert,* pp. 28, 249-255. See also Gagné, *Visages de Gabrielle Roy,* pp. 175-177.

[25] Roy, "Le Pays de *Bonheur d'occasion,*" p. 120; Roy, *La Montagne secrète,* p. 97. In the last work, see also pp. 21, 24-25, 177-179, 206, 218-219. See also Roy, *La Route d'Altamont,* p. 253; Gabrielle Roy, "La Source au désert," *Le Bulletin des Agriculteurs,* 42, No. 10 (octobre 1946), 42; Warwick, pp. 144-149; Marie Grenier-Francoeur, "Etude de

la structure anaphorique dans *La Montagne secrète* de Gabrielle Roy,"
Voix et Images, 1, No. 3 (avril 1976), 394-405; André Brochu, "Gabrielle Roy," Notes from course on author, Université de Montréal, Printemps 1978, taken by one of his students.

²⁶Roy, *La Montagne secrète*, p. 133. See also pp. 26, 99-100, 172-174; Gagné, *Visages de Gabrielle Roy*, pp. 183-189, 203-221, for a complete discussion of the Pierre-Prometheus figure; Grenier-Francoeur, pp. 394-405.

²⁷Albert Le Grand, "Gabrielle Roy ou l'être partagé," *Etudes françaises*, 1ère année, No. 2 (juin 1965), p. 39; Roy, *Rue Deschambault*, p. 246; Roy, *La Montagne secrète*, p. 206. Roy has stated elsewhere that the creator always relinquishes a part of life to one's creations. Similarly, the writer is often invaded by fictional characters. See Gabrielle Roy, "Les Terres nouvelles de Jean-Paul Lemieux," *Vie des Arts*, No. 29 (hiver 1962-1963), p. 42; Roy, "Le Pays de *Bonheur d'occasion*," p. 120. See also Warwick, pp. 144-148; Annette Saint-Pierre, *Gabrielle Roy: Sous le signe du rêve* (Saint-Boniface, Manitoba: Editions du Blé, 1975), p. 81.

²⁸Roy, *Rue Deschambault*, p. 246; Personal interview with Gabrielle Roy, 29 June 1980; Ricard, pp. 22, 26-30, 35-36, 83, 107-110. See also Roy, *La Montagne secrète*, pp. 24-25, 55, 140, 191-192, 216-219; Roy, *La Route d'Altamont*, p. 23; Saint-Pierre, pp. 71, 108-109, 123-125; Chadburne, p. 258. Cordorai is also described, as has been noted, as "L'Homme-Seul." See Roy, *La Montagne secrète*, p. 93.

²⁹Roy, *La Montagne secrète*, pp. 54, 112; Ricard, p. 29. In the first work, see also pp. 108-109, 135; in the second see pp. 21, 26-28, 30, 83, 86, 107-110, 121-124, 130. See also Roy, *Rue Deschambault*, p. 281; Roy, "Jeux du romancier et des lecteurs," pp. 270, 272; Personal interview with Gabrielle Roy, 29 June 1980; Gagné, *Visages de Gabrielle Roy*, pp. 176, 194-202; Saint-Pierre, pp. 53, 60-61, 72-75, 78-81; Robidoux, p. 232; Kathleen O'Donnell, "Gabrielle Roy's Portrait of the Artist," *La Revue de l'Université d'Ottawa*, 49, No. 1 (janvier-mars 1974), 70-77.

³⁰Roy, *La Montagne secrète*, p. 133. See also pp. 58-59, 113, 127-128, 216-217; Roy, "Jeux du romancier et des lecteurs," pp. 268-269, 271; Roy, *La Route d'Altamont*, p. 233; Roy, "*Terre des Hommes:* Le Thème raconté," *Fragiles Lumières de la terre*, p. 206; Ricard, p. 87; Saint-Pierre, p. 81; Robidoux, pp. 228-229; Warwick, pp. 144-149; Donald Cameron, "Gabrielle Roy: A Bird in the Prison Window," in *Conversations with Canadian Novelists* (Toronto: Macmillan of Canada, 1973), pp. 136, 139-141; Socken, pp. 345-350; Paul Socken, "The Influence of Physical and Social Environment on Character in the Novels of Gabrielle Roy," *DAI*, 28 (December 1977), 3490A (University of Toronto); Jeannette Urbas, "Gabrielle Roy et l'acte de créer," *Journal of Canadian Fic-*

tion, 1, IV (1972), 51-54.

[31] Roy, *La Montagne secrète,* pp. 93, 148, 131. See also Roy, "Jeux du romancier et des lecteurs," p. 263; Gagné, *Visages de Gabrielle Roy,* pp. 142, 215-218; Saint-Pierre, p. 69; Grenier-Francoeur, pp. 394-405; Warwick, pp. 144-149; Michel-Lucien Gaulin, "Le Thème du bonheur dans l'oeuvre de Gabrielle Roy," Thesis Université de Montréal 1961, pp. 145-157.

[32] Roy, *La Montagne secrète,* p. 221. See also pp. 24-25, 64-65, 77, 83-84, 93-94, 100, 105, 167-168, 180-182, 186, 213; Roy, *Alexandre Chenevert,* p. 255; Roy, "Les Terres nouvelles de Jean-Paul Lemieux," p. 43; Saint-Pierre, pp. 114, 117, 123-125; Gaulin, pp. 145-157; Grenier-Francoeur, pp. 389-391, 394-405; Socken, "Art and the Artist in Gabrielle Roy's Works," pp. 345-350. D.G. Jones notes that in his final self-portrait, Pierre wears the horns of a primitive divinity, a symbol of god-like power. See D.G. Jones, *Butterfly on Rock: A Study of Themes and Images in Canadian Literature* (Toronto: University of Toronto Press, 1971), pp. 26, 183. Gaston Bachelard writes of the ultra-sensitivity of the poet to the universe and, therefore, of the cosmos created by the word. See Gaston Bachelard, *La Poétique de l'espace,* Bibliothèque de philosophie contemporaine (Paris: Presses Universitaires de France, 1978), pp. 161-167; Gaston Bachelard, *La Poétique de la rêverie,* Bibliothèque de philosophie contemporaine (Paris: Presses Universitaires de France, 1974), pp. 157-163. With this aesthetic ideal of recreation and the pride of rivaling God, Pierre's views, once again, resemble those of nineteenth-century French poets.

[33] Roy, *La Montagne secrète,* pp. 103-104, 123. See also pp. 83-84, 108-109; Saint-Pierre, pp. 120-121.

[34] Roy, *La Montagne secrète,* p. 124. See also pp. 46, 75, 77, 78, 95-96, 99-100, 106, 114-115, 149, 203-204.

[35] Personal interview with Gabrielle Roy, 29 June 1980; Roy, *La Montagne secrète,* pp. 55, 189, 190, 215-218. See also Saint-Pierre, pp. 82-87; Gaulin, pp. 145-147.

[36] Roy, "*Terre des Hommes:* Le Thème raconté," p. 204; Roy, "Jeux du romancier et des lecteurs," p. 270; Roy, *La Montagne secrète,* pp. 112, 222. The first quotation is also cited both in French and as Mathew Arnold's original English statement, "emotion recollected in tranquility," in Roy, "Jeux du romancier et des lecteurs," p. 270. In this work see also pp. 265, 266, 269, 271, 272. See also Roy, *La Montagne secrète,* pp. 15-17, 19-21, 28, 39, 113, 132, 135, 207; Roy, *Alexandre Chenevert,* pp. 143, 249-255; Roy, *Rue Deschambault,* p. 245; Gabrielle Roy, "Témoignage," in *Le Roman canadien-français: Evolution-témoignage-bibliographie,* eds. Paul Wyczynski, Bernard Julien, Jean Ménard et Réjean Robidoux,

Archives des lettres canadiennes, Tome III (Montréal: Fides, 1977), pp. 303-304; Roy, "Entretiens," 6 août 1969, 8 juillet 1969, 11 septembre 1970, 29 juillet 1969, as quoted in Gagné, *Visages de Gabrielle Roy,* pp. 178-182.   In this last work, see also pp. 183-189, 192-202.   Personal interview with Gabrielle Roy, 29 June 1980; Gaulin, pp. 151-157.

[37] Roy, *La Montagne secrète,* pp. 180, 221, 200.   See also pp. 19-20, 24-25, 56-59, 64-65, 75, 77, 83-84, 94, 101-109, 112, 172-175, 179, 190; Roy, "Jeux du romancier et des lecteurs," p. 264; Roy, "*Terre des Hommes:* Le Thème raconté," p. 201; Ricard, pp. 29, 108-111; Robidoux, pp. 230-232; Socken, "Art and the Artist," pp. 345-350; Bachelard, *La Poétique de l'espace,* pp. 4-14.

[38] Roy, *La Montagne secrète,* pp. 199, 104.   See also pp. 100, 147, 172-175, 179, 211-212, 217, 218; Gagné, *Visages de Gabrielle Roy,* pp. 175-176, 219-221; Cameron, p. 144; Saint-Pierre, pp. 78-87, 111-114; Robidoux, pp. 225-227; Bachelard, *La Poétique de l'espace,* pp. 15-16; Jacques Scherer, *Le "Livre" de Mallarmé: Premières Recherches sur des documents inédits* (Paris: Gallimard, 1957); Paula Gilbert Lewis, *The Aesthetics of Stéphane Mallarmé in Relation to His Public* (New Jersey: Fairleigh Dickinson University Press; London: Associated University Presses, 1976).

[39] Roy, *La Montagne secrète,* p. 222.   See also pp. 203-205; Urbas, pp. 52-53.

[40] Roy, "Le Pays de *Bonheur d'occasion,*" pp. 121-122.   It is noteworthy that the conclusion of the French edition of *La Montagne secrète,* as quoted above, uses an exclamation point, thereby suggesting the possibility of hope.   In the English-language edition, the novel concludes with a question mark, thus indicating somewhat less optimism.   See Gabrielle Roy, *The Hidden Mountain,* trans. Harry Binsse, New Canadian Library, No. 109 (1962; rpt. Toronto: McClelland and Stewart Limited, 1975), p. 186.

CHAPTER IX

Religious Faith

Given Gabrielle Roy's birth and upbringing as a French-speaking, Catholic Manitoban and her literary desires to depict humanity in general, but understandably reflected in the context of francophone Canadian society, it is surprising that religion does not play a greater role in her aesthetic universe. A few religious figures are scattered throughout, and religious questions are raised, but such concerns are not usually related to the spiritual realm *per se* but rather to the life of people on this earth. Roy herself maintained that she had retained the Catholic dogma that she had learned as a child, although she had informally broken her ties with the Church in 1937. In her later years she managed to reconcile her adult beliefs with those of her childhood and returned to her own personal form of a Christian religion. This evolution of her religious thoughts was the result of three sources of inspiration: the ecumenical movement founded by Pope John XXIII; the death of Roy's sister, Anna, in 1963; and, most importantly, a 1947 meeting with and the reading of the works of Teilhard de Chardin.[1]

When one becomes familiar with the personal vision of the world as formulated by this twentiety-century theologian, one can clearly distinguish the particular facets of his thoughts that deeply influenced Gabrielle Roy. For Teilhard de Chardin the history of the world can be analyzed through the stages of development of life, thought, and a sense of human unity. It is this third stage that is in the process of marching toward a unique circle or *foyer* of perfection. The force that pushes one toward this progress is love, a call to union in both spirit and body and a means to conquer both oneself and the universe. It is, for Teilhard de Chardin, woman who will effect this personal conquest for everyone. The power of love, and especially of the spirit, is essential in this modern world in order to combat the existence of absurdity and human solitude.

There exists, therefore, in every individual, the need for some absolute, here translated as the progression toward this third critical point of humanity in history: the goal of a harmonized collectivity of soul and conscience. It is this ideal of human unity toward which one must strive and in which one must believe, for the true sense of the Earth is to be revealed as the existence of a part of each individual in all others.[2]

In a 1965 interview, Gabrielle Roy spoke of this influence of Teilhard de Chardin's optimistic theory upon her own beliefs. In doing so, she underscored the fundamental duality of ideal humanism and tragic realism that characterizes her religious faith, as well as her entire vision of humanity and the world:

> "Oui. J'espère, en effet, de toute mon âme que ce qu'il [Teilhard de Chardin] a entrevu et tenté de nous faire voir est vrai—surtout la perfectibilité de l'homme—car ce serait la réponse, il me semble, à nos interrogations les plus angoissées. Quelquefois encore, cependant, devant la malignité humaine et les misères de notre condition, je suis reprise de doute et me demande si nous progressons vraiment vers quelque chose de meilleur. . . . Puis l'espoir me revient. Car, de quoi s'agit-il, au fond? sinon de faire confiance à la création, à son but profond? Et qui pourrait, en fin de compte, ne pas faire confiance à la création!"[3]

It has been shown that Roy's works are both characterized and dominated by the presence of women. These female characters usually fulfill the roles either of mothers or maternal schoolteachers, both surrounded by children. It is noteworthy that very few of these women choose the childless life of a nun. Interestingly, it is two young Royan women who demonstrate an early propensity for this calling, with their preference for the mystical world and their desires for martyrdom. Not at all understood but admired by her mother, Yvonne Lacasse leans toward a life of religion as a means of escape from reality. Christine's sister, Odette, decides to enter a convent, thereby evoking an emotional but proud and understanding reaction on the part of her mother who sadly observes that her daughter is abandoning both her youth and her freedom. The only adult nun in this literary world is Maman's childhood friend, Odile, now Soeur Etienne-du-Sauveur, whose life is described as being in total solitude, having no story to be told, and retaining an affection for the outside world. It may be presumptuous to base an interpretation on the existence of only three personnages, but it does seem as though the chosen life of a nun, in Gabrielle Roy's fiction, is not a preferred role for a woman.[4]

Four out of the five clergymen created by Roy are much more positively drawn, although they resemble the typically divided character more than a spiritual advisor. The most fully developed priest figure in this literary world and the one who most clearly exhibits the internationalism and ecumenism preached by Teilhard de Chardin is le Capucin de Toutes-Aides of *La Petite Poule d'eau,* published three years after Roy's meeting with the French theologian. This delightful individual, seen as a simple priest and ironically compared by a Protestant woman to John Knox, does play the role of a serious confessor and God's representative upon this earth. He is also a dissatisfied man, constantly dreaming of new goals to improve the Church and to better the lives of the faithful. It is this last characteristic that forms the initial link between this priest and the human world in which he lives. A clever politician and business man, whether it be to obtain church bells or to sell furs at a high price in Toronto on behalf of the Métis in his region, le Capucin de Toutes-Aides enjoys the temporary feeling of being wealthy with all of these furs, loves being the strongest on Earth as is God in heaven, and, therefore, fearing his own ambition, checks with God in order to justify his more worldly actions.[5]

All of the priest's actions, however, are justifiable, for he maintains that his three loves are beauty, God, and humanity. He especially adores God and humanity while travelling on the road, for le Capucin de Toutes-Aides is a nomadic priest, a man who thrives on vagabondage and feels freer to love as he moves further North. Like all Royan creatures, however, he also tires of such a life and needs to sense the stability of the protective home and the human qualities of security and warmth, reflected in a maternal woman like Luzina Tousignant. This priest is basically a sociable human being, open to, interested in, and understanding of others. Despite his designated role in the Catholic Church, he is even sensitive to the problems of women and their numerous pregnancies:

> Même au confessionnal, ce n'était pas le mauvais côté de la nature humaine qui ressortait à ses yeux. Il y saisissait bien souvent la bonne volonté des âmes. Quelquefois, en plein coeur, il recevait

la révélation de cette droiture profonde des âmes. Il regardait alors au-delà de sa pénitente d'un oeil plein de mélancolie; et ce qu'il contemplait, c'était l'inépuisable somme de bonté dans le monde, la tragique, parfaite bonne volonté de tant d'humains et qui n'arrivait quand même pas à changer le monde.[6]

Father Eugène of *La Rivière sans repos* is similarly oriented toward the world, as he brings the marvels of nature, in the form of a successful garden, to the harsh Eskimo region. His Protestant counterpart, Reverend Hugh Paterson, likewise preaches charity and love among all people, on a road toward progress. The Pastor even more closely resembles the Capuchin, however, in his nomadic existence throughout the northern-most areas of Canada, while both men can be linked to the character of le Père le Bonniec of *La Montagne secrète* who travels as a missionary in the North and, as with the Capuchin's love for music, greatly appreciates art.[7]

This fourth clergyman, however, is not always certain of the role, either religious or lay, that he should be playing in life. He thus reminds one of the only truly spiritual and, at times, antipathetical religious figure in Roy's works: l'Abbé Marchand of *Alexandre Chenevert*. Preferring God to humanity and taking the divinity's part against that of mortal beings, this priest views life as insignificant in comparison with eternity. The sole Royan religious person to be depicted as being devoid of human emotions and indulgence and as being the police of God, Marchand's ironically pathetic presence at the bedside of dying people like Chenevert powerfully adds to an already existing atmosphere of novelistic absurdity. Significantly, how-ever, this rapport between religion and the absurdity of life is limited to one work of fiction. In other works, it will be religion and, rather, the tragedy of life that will be linked.[8]

All these individuals who have obeyed the calling of a religious vocation speak on behalf of the Church, traditionally a powerful force in Quebec, but relatively unimportant in the Royan world. It is, logically, the Catholic Church that is the most prevalent in these works, although it is placed in rela-tion to the Anglican, Presbyterian, and Greek Orthodox Church-es. The modern-day, urban Church has already been seen as a commercial, impersonal business in which holidays are pack-aged and sold, and the figure of Christ is electrified. Three years prior to this negative depiction in *Alexandre Chenevert,*

Roy had similarly described the current Church as a frenetic circus, the inspiration for medieval-type pilgrimages during which religious objects are bought and sold.[9]

Preaching a love for honest joys, this Church also advocates female resignation to multiple pregnancies as a religious obligation. In this sense, Roy viewed the Church as anti-feminist. It is partially for this reason that few of her female characters, with the infrequent exception of Maman, turn to this organized institution for aid. During a visit to her local chapel, Martha even blames the Ukrainian saints for her present state of solitude. This chapel has, moreover, significantly fallen into ruin. It has symbolically returned to the natural countryside, for it is in the midst of nature—as in the little country chapel that enlarges onto the surrounding landscape in *Cet Eté qui chantait*— that the true Church, the truly holy place, is to be found.[10]

If the roles of Royan nuns, priests, and the Church can be interpreted as being both positive and negative, the role of religion itself can be similarly treated. The power of religion, for example, is seen as inspiring a fanaticism among the Ruthenean immigrants who consider themselves to be a chosen people. Elsewhere religion, specifically in the sight of sacred images, produces a flood of painful memories for Florentine. Before and after the seduction-rape scene, one notes a deep sense of guilt for the young woman and for Jean, both born and raised as Catholics. Religion, however, can also be useful or, more precisely, used: Florentine prays to the Virgin Mary and even promises to go to mass daily if only she can triumph over Jean.[11]

But usually for most Royan characters, religion is a simple, even child-like concept, reflecting the deep faith and piety of French-speaking Quebecers and Canadians, as well as Roy's belief in a Christianity of love, as described by Teilhard de Chardin. It is, moreover, a personal and natural concept whereby Martha can envision immortality and eternity in the wind, and Martine can experience a renewed sense of baptism in a country river. The ideal religion, therefore, is once again revealed in the tiny country chapel, penetrated by the immensity of the outside, and during a mass conducted by people, attended by neighboring animals, and accompanied by the music of nature. The people receive communion; the countryside is reborn after a powerful storm; and the animals continue to observe their human companions:

> On dirait qu'à nos bêtes domestiques est venu pour nous aujour-
> d'hui un sentiment d'adoration. Ou peut-être une humble, une
> confuse jalousie. Qu'est-ce qu'ils connaissent de plus que nous?
> Ont vu aujourd'hui? Reçu? Et qui laisse pour un moment sur
> leur visage cette beauté?[12]

It is clearly suggested in this passage that what these creatures of nature have experienced is the vague presence of some
spiritual being, of God. If the predominant concept of religion
in the Royan literary universe is a positive, natural one, then
the related vision of God is similarly personal, natural, optimistic,
and humanistic. For many of Gabrielle Roy's characters, the
image of God is that of goodness and love. It is an obscure
notion born out of solitude and usually experienced in a natural
surrounding. Alexandre Chenevert feels the presence of God
while alone at Lac Vert:

> La solitude parut absence. . . . Pourtant, au centre de cette ab-
> sence, il y avait comme un regard qui ne perdait aucun geste,
> aucune pensée d'Alexandre Chenevert. Etait-ce Dieu qui, par
> cette nuit profonde, au fond des savanes, avait encore repéré
> Alexandre? . . . Dieu régnait ici dans son caractère le plus ambigu.

Chenevert begins to sense an aura of peace; he finally sleeps.
God has become his companion, his personal friend. Similarly,
Martha, envisioning God as an image or dream stemming from
a state of solitude, speaks to the divinity in nature. Cordorai
discovers his own vision of God in the perfection of solitary
nature, in the splendid mountain, and, finally, Martine leans
closer to a supreme being, as she bathes in the refreshing water.
For all of these gentle beings, a personal, vague faith and hope
for the future have been born.[13]

For some characters, the simplicity of their vision of God
stems, more precisely, from the same child-like image of the
divinity that they held in their youth. Rose-Anna Lacasse, for
example, can only think of God as the very old white-bearded
man who was part of her childhood. It is a similarly simple,
innocent picture of heaven that Yvonne paints for the dying
Daniel. With this interpretation of God in Roy's first work
of fiction, however, comes a related attitude, on the part of
certain characters, that raises serious questions about the relationship between a supreme being and humanity. The funda-

mental reason that Rose-Anna cannot envision God in a more mature manner is that, since her youth, she has rarely prayed to the divinity directly and has preferred to rely upon the intercession of saints. She believes that God is too busy, too tired to pay much attention to mortal beings. Martha, too, may speak to God, but, questioning this nature, she feels that this being does not listen to the living. At the end of her life, therefore, she prefers to confide her soul to the wind rather than to a supreme being who, as believes Chenevert, remains untouched by the love and piety of humanity.[14]

This old man with a white beard, this Jehovah or God of Jansenism, therefore, can be an angry God, punishing humanity for excessive pride with the shipwreck of the Titanic and instilling in people a fear of the divine. This God is the creator and giver of justice and, like l'Abbé Marchand, a law enforcer who will not permit any personal judgment by mortals. But people do interpret and judge God, for it is only in this manner that they can form their own personal vision of a divinity. They can then proceed to live upon the earth and ultimately face death.[15]

It is these human concerns that are the most profoundly discussed in *Alexandre Chenevert,* with its presentation of a tragic vision of God in a rapport with humanity. The bank teller's relationship with a supreme being is stressed on two major occasions: during his vacation at Lac Vert and during his last months in the hospital. Faithful to his paranoid nature, Chenevert had always believed that God was dissatisfied with him. It is only after his arrival at Lac Vert and significantly during sleep that he senses a new forgetfulness and freedom: "Il fut délivré de Dieu et des hommes. Alexandre n'avait plus à répondre du péché originel, non plus que de ces armes d'aujourd'hui. . . ." The insignificant martyr, scapegoat, and modern Jesus Christ is temporarily released from his designated role in life. Later during his stay in this earthly paradise devoid of sin, Chenevert, still maintaining a preference for humanity, decides upon a magnanimous truce with God:

> Dieu presque toujours lui tenait compagnie ces jours-ci. C'était comme s'il eût pardonné à Alexandre toutes les fautes commises depuis le commencement des siècles.
> Mieux encore:
> Alexandre éprouva que lui-même . . . pouvait enfin pardonner

> à Dieu la souffrance jetée si libéralement aux quatre coins du monde.
> Une légèreté parfaite dilatait son âme.[16]

There is no doubt that a dangerous attitude of pride accompanies Alexandre's act of mutual pardon, but such an attitude must be seen against the backdrop of this pathetic individual's belief that both he and humanity suffer greatly alone, without dignity, and without any understanding by a supreme being. It is this particular belief that haunts him while in the hospital and pits him, the defender of people, against l'Abbé Marchand, the defender of God. Confessing to a priest, "le moins fait pour le comprendre," and feeling even more vulnerable and guilty in his prone position, Chenevert whispers that God does not love him. When Marchand argues that if this were so, Christ would not have suffered and died for humanity, Alexandre's true beliefs are crystallized:

> Hélas! parce qu'il était Dieu justement, la passion du Christ n'avait pas ému complètement Alexandre. N'y avait-il pas eu des milliers d'hommes qui avaient souffert autant sinon plus que le Christ, pour des motifs dérisoires. . . ? Et combien d'hommes, s'ils avaient eu la possibilité comme Jésus de racheter les autres par leur mort, n'eussent pas longtemps hésité. Mourir sans profit pour personne, là était la véritable passion. Mais c'était une pensée qu'il fallait cacher à tous . . . de peur de scandaliser. Alexandre fut perdu de crainte à l'idée que Dieu le punirait d'une telle liberté de pensée à son égard.

A guilt-ridden Catholic, Chenevert sincerely tries to believe that God, in an unimaginable state of solitude, truly desires this confession of love. He fearfully repeats the words of the priest but silently retains his sympathies for humanity.[17]

Ironically, it is the priest who experiences a partial conversion as a result of having known Chenevert. He becomes, at least, somewhat more humble and more sensitive to the agony of humanity. As for the bank teller, all he can do is to ask for deliverance in death from the supreme being whom he sees as the cause of his torment. Chenevert dies with a facial expression that reveals his immense human tenderness for others. Even after death, he is not fully abandoned to God, for first, masses are said in his honor, and then, as Roy clearly states, "ailleurs que dans les églises," his name remains alive in the memories of people. Alexandre Chenevert may have, like Christ, suffered and died both because of and on behalf of humanity, but his role in life was a purely human one.[18]

Considering the serious questions concerning God and humanity that are raised especially in *Alexandre Chenevert,* one must place Gabrielle Roy's characters in a position of defending and speaking on behalf of humanity, while only partially accepting God. In the Royan world, it is realistically and tragically difficult to reconcile the human and the divine. Religion and abandonment to God, therefore, are rarely totally successful solutions to the problems of the world. In Roy's hope for the truths enumerated in the theories of Teilhard de Chardin and in her own humanistic and natural literary vision of religion and God, however, she still retained her sense of optimism and idealism for humanity and for the universe. Any movement toward progress must thus find its source in and be activated by the capabilities and faith of human beings, united in their own form of spiritual humanism.

NOTES

[1] Personal interview with Gabrielle Roy, 29 June 1980; Gabrielle Roy, *"Terre des Hommes:* Le Thème raconté," *Fragiles Lumières de la terre: Ecrits divers 1942-1970,* Collection Prose Entière (Montréal: Les Editions Quinze, 1978), pp. 207-208, 210-222, 232; Marc Gagné, *Visages de Gabrielle Roy* (Montréal: Librairie Beauchemin Limitée, 1973), pp. 14, 83-84, 90-91, 225-232, including personal interviews with Roy on this subject.

[2] Jules Carles, *Teilhard de Chardin,* SUP "Philosophes" (Paris: Presses Universitaires de France, 1971), pp. 48-63, 106-108, 110-111. See also pp. 5-20, 24-48, 73-74, 83-88, 92-95, 100-102, 115-117, 123, 128.

[3] Gabrielle Roy, le 2 septembre 1965, as quoted in Gérard Bessette, *Une Littérature en ébullition* (Montréal: Editions du Jour, 1968), p. 306.

[4] Gabrielle Roy, *Bonheur d'occasion* (1945; rpt. Montréal: Librairie

Beauchemin Limitée, 1973), pp. 82, 316-317; Gabrielle Roy, *Rue Deschambault* (1955; rpt. Montréal: Librairie Beauchemin Limitée, 1974), pp. 26, 49-50, 69, 72-73, 128-131. Gabrielle Roy's own sister, Bernadette, became a nun, Soeur Léon de la Croix. See Marie-Anna A. Roy, *Le Miroir du passé,* Collection Littérature d'Amérique (Montréal: Editions Québec/Amérique, 1979), pp. 79-83, 151-154, 244-252.

[5] Gabrielle Roy, *La Petite Poule d'eau* (1950; rpt. Montréal: Librairie Beauchemin Limitée, 1970), pp. 174-180, 187-200, 207-210, 214-226, 230, 239, 248, 253-254. See also John Hind-Smith, *Three Voices: The Lives of Margaret Laurence, Gabrielle Roy, and Frederick Philip Grove* (Toronto: Clarke Irwin, 1975), pp. 96-97.

[6] Roy, *La Petite Poule d'eau,* pp. 241-242. See also pp. 172, 184, 185, 211, 227, 231, 236, 237, 240, 243, 245, 263, 269-272.

[7] Gabrielle Roy, *La Rivière sans repos* (Montréal: Librairie Beauchemin Limitée, 1971), pp. 21, 23-24, 82, 301; Gabrielle Roy, *La Montagne secrète* (1961; rpt. Montréal: Librairie Beauchemin Limitée, 1974), pp. 129-130.

[8] Gabrielle Roy, *Alexandre Chenevert* (1954; rpt. Montréal: Beauchemin, 1973), pp. 320-322, 324, 351, 378-379, 381-382. Prior to his meeting with Marchand, Chenevert viewed Dr. Hudon in the role of a priest, almost as God. See p. 171. Roy herself stated that the bank teller's pride was evident at the end of the novel because he thought that he was superior to the priest. L'Abbé Marchand's attitude, however, is similar: that of a sense of superiority over others. Personal interview with Gabrielle Roy, 29 June 1980. See also Gagné, pp. 59-61, 233 where Marchand is likened to Paneloux of Camus's *La Peste.*

[9] Roy, *La Petite Poule d'eau,* pp. 187-201; Roy, *Alexandre Chenevert,* pp. 264, 270, 303-305; Roy, "Sainte-Anne-la-Palud," *Fragiles Lumières de la terre,* pp. 123-130. This last work was originally published in 1951.

[10] Roy, *Bonheur d'occasion,* pp. 172-176, 289-290; Roy, *La Petite Poule d'eau,* pp. 105, 199, 244-245, 253-256, 260, 269; Roy, *Rue Deschambault,* pp. 130-131; Gabrielle Roy, *Un Jardin au bout du monde* (Montréal: Librairie Beauchemin Limitée, 1975), pp. 175-180; Gabrielle Roy, *Cet Eté qui chantait* (Québec-Montréal: Les Editions Françaises, 1972), pp. 135-141; Personal interview with Gabrielle Roy, 29 June 1980; Alice Parizeau, "Gabrielle Roy, grande romancière canadienne," *Châtelaine,* 7, No. 4 (avril 1966), 120.

[11] Roy, *Rue Deschambault,* pp. 119, 148-149, 156; Roy, *Bonheur d'occasion,* pp. 125-126, 177, 179, 184.

[12] Roy, *Cet Eté qui chantait,* p. 141. See also pp. 135-140, 155-160; Roy, *Un Jardin au bout du monde,* pp. 33, 38-41, 214-217; Roy, *Bonheur*

d'occasion, p. 263; Roy, *La Petite Poule d'eau,* pp. 187, 198-199; Roy, *Alexandre Chenevert,* p. 231; Roy, *La Montagne secrète,* p. 129; Gagné, p. 58; Monique Genuist, *La Création romanesque chez Gabrielle Roy* Montréal: Le Cercle du Livre de France, 1966), pp. 21, 147-152.

[13] Roy, *Alexandre Chenevert,* p. 204. See also pp. 207-208, 211, 215, 220, 222, 235-237, 241, 246, 286, 369-370; Roy, *Un Jardin au bout du monde,* pp. 172, 175-180; Roy, *La Montagne secrète,* pp. 100-105, 108, 123, 129, 221; Roy, *Cet Eté qui chantait,* pp. 155-160, 175; Roy, *La Petite Poule d'eau,* pp. 190-193, 254-256, 260; Gagné, pp. 58, 247-257; André Brochu, "Gabrielle Roy," Notes from course on author, Université de Montréal, Printemps 1978, taken by one of his students.

[14] Roy, *Bonheur d'occasion,* pp. 88-90, 319-320; Roy, *Un Jardin au bout du monde,* pp. 172, 175-180, 199, 214-217, Roy, *Alexandre Chenevert,* pp. 378-379.

[15] Roy, *Rue Deschambault,* pp. 94, 96, 109, 156; Roy, *Alexandre Chenevert,* pp. 320-322. See also Michel-Lucien Gaulin, "Le Thème du bonheur dans l'oeuvre de Gabrielle Roy," Thesis Université de Montréal 1961, pp. 94-109; Soeur Marie du Rédempteur, "Le Thème de la solitude dans l'oeuvre de Gabrielle Roy," Thesis Université de Montréal 1963, pp. 99-101.

[16] Roy, *Alexandre Chenevert,* pp. 209, 246. See also pp. 59, 249.

[17] Roy, *Alexandre Chenevert,* pp. 323, 327. See also pp. 294, 318, 326, 328-330, 351; Personal interview with Gabrielle Roy, 29 June 1980; Jack Warwick, *L'Appel du nord dans la littérature canadienne-française,* trans. Jean Simard, Collection Constantes (Montréal: Editions Hurtubise HMH, 1972), pp. 210-212.

[18] Roy, *Alexandre Chenevert,* p. 384. See also pp. 380, 382; Gagné, p. 249.

CHAPTER X

Literary Visions of the Future

In her beautiful essay devoted to the 1967 Montreal World's Fair, Gabrielle Roy writes of the influence upon her of Saint-Exupéry from whose novel, *Terre des hommes,* this universal exhibition drew its title and its ideology. She describes this poet-pilot, a part of humanity, as contemplating during the mysterious night "les fragiles lumières de la terre" and as searching for and discovering "en elles des raisons d'espérer." It is these words, "fragiles lumières de la terre," that were chosen by François Ricard as the title of a compilation of Roy's earlier writings, for, as Roy herself states, they constitute a "fil d'Ariane" throughout her works and underscore in her essays her own outlook "à la fois tremblant et espérant." In 1980 the author again reiterated that, both in her fiction and reality, there are always lights, the dawn, and the possibility of *recommencement* for everyone, but that these lights are inevitably fragile and, even as in *Cet Eté qui chantait,* temporary. What is important, however, is that, as for Alexandre Chenevert and Lac Vert, these rays of hope exist.[1]

What these words essentially emphasize is the constant duality between tragic realism and faith that is present in Roy's literary vision, as well as in her vision of and hope for humanity and the world. Marc Gagné applies such a distinction to Roy's various works, to her essays as opposed to her fiction. He sees, especially, an attitude of faith in God, progress, and humanity throughout her essays and articles of journalism, while in her works of fiction, he distinguishes primarily "l'observatrice impitoyable d'une certaine société mais pitoyable aux hommes qui la composent." François Ricard, in his analysis of *Cet Eté qui chantait,* states that "innocence et bonheur reposent ici sur un fond de détresse." It is a "détresse vaincue, certes, dépassée par l'espérance, mais jamais au point de se taire complètement ni de cesser de menacer, conférant ainsi à la vision heureuse un accent de gravité. . . ." It is, in fact, in this gentle ode to nature that the narrator hears around her and within the human heart the voices of "peur et bonheur, effroi et confiance. . . ."[2]

In *La Petite Poule d'eau,* another hymn to the beauty of life, the narrator speaks of the sorrow of the world, filled with joy and love, for, as the author admits: "Sans doute l'espoir et le désespoir se côtoient dans mes livres comme ils se côtoient dans ma vie." One cannot ignore any aspect of the world, for it is this fusion of happiness and tragedy that constitutes reality and that causes one to adore life: "Ne nier ni la beauté du monde ni l'énigme de la douleur, tout n'est-il pas là, en effet, pour un coeur franc et sincère? Et n'est-ce pas l'attitude exacte qui convient à celui qui écrit comme à celui qui lit?"[3]

It has been seen that, maintaining that she simply wrote about what she saw, Gabrielle Roy remained a realistic observer of everything around her. As such, she has often created texts that are characterized by melancholy and pessimism and has frequently raised in her works of fiction serious, distressful, and tragic questions about the nature of God, humanity, the world, and, therefore, progress. The portrait of humanity, as depicted by Roy, is of the fragile, weak, and ignorant "déshérités que nous sommes" who "s'en désolent et lancent leur cri d'impatience et de détresse." It is a portrait of people as a mere grain or dust of existence, as lost children who often find it difficult and painful to follow life but who continue to ask "nos pauvres questions humaines."[4]

Royan humanity is disinherited essentially because people now live far from their primitive source and, therefore, have lost the fundamental pleasures of life. Existing in a state of solitude and exile, they do try to plant flowers in their world, but such acts are still performed within an often claustrophobic cage. The cry of distress uttered by these people is, in addition, a desperate call for communication, for relationships are often impersonal, silent, and lacking in overt expressions of love. Existences are too frequently parallel, separate, or pathetic mistakes.[5]

It has been emphasized that the most dominant trait of the majority of Roy's characters is dissatisfaction. They are essentially malcontents who, as changeable and unstable as the wind, are constantly searching, constantly being driven by their impossible goals, and constantly haunted by their "désirs tragiques de perfection. . . ." Obeying calls emanating from within themselves, these characters—who find even the act of existing to be a problem or an enigma—must be seen, in this sense, as the instruments of their own suffering and torment. They are truly tragic figures, with the painful lucidity of both their own situation and others around them.[6]

Humanity as portrayed in Roy's fiction, however, is not solely responsible for its tragic condition. Some of the blame must also be placed upon a certain determinism or fate that stems from both heredity and exterior circumstances. This determinism is a Royan variant of French Naturalism, as well as of original sin, and, as such, it encircles humanity, these "Ames en peine," within a recurring cycle of suffering and pity where even the possibility of *recommencement* becomes a rebirth within this same pathetic state. Royan characters, therefore, struggling against both themselves and the outside world, are forever being placed on guard against the hope for too much happiness and freedom, for ideals do exist but are distant from the real, daily world.[7]

The world against which Roy's characters struggle is, at times, seen as a cold, sorrowful place in which societies are unjust, and an atmosphere of pessimism and fatalism reigns. It is a world that, like humanity, desperately worries about its future: "D'où viendrait la clarté qui guiderait le monde?" In certain texts this exterior world is clearly tainted with tragedy, while in *Alexandre Chenevert* in particular, it is more precisely clouded by absurdity. Gabrielle Roy herself disavowed any acceptance of a philosophy of the absurd, as formulated by Albert Camus. She felt, that if there were no unknown and unforeseen mysteries, then life and the world would be boring and dull, and absurdity would triumph. Roy may have rejected the use of the specific word, "absurd," but one cannot deny that the tone of several of her works, and especially of her novels, and the revolt of many of her characters against their existences and the outside world, are remarkably similar to those of Camus's writings.[8]

Given the above elements that constitute a literary vision that is tragic, it is not surprising that in her essays, Roy held an ambivalent attitude toward the notion of progress. Seen as having its source either in an individual's or in humanity's dissatisfaction and often leading to sorrow, progress consists of a vital forward movement, soon opposed by periods of stagnation or even by a reverse motion. It resembles a person who "marche avec peine dans la tempête; il avance de deux pas et recule d'un pas; il ne sait plus très bien s'il accomplit quelque progrès au milieu des rafales qui le poussent et le retiennent. Tour à tour l'espoir luit, puis s'éteint." Progress can, in addition, bring with it a dangerous sense of egotism and, most importantly, the sacrifice of simple, natural goodness and happiness in favor of a gain in modernism. The Royan concept of progress, therefore, is typically ambiguous and antithetical.[9]

Corresponding to the negative aspects of a dualistic concept of progress are, thus, positive characteristics that stem from Roy's initial optimism and faith in the progress of humanity and the world, as first evidenced in her early journalistic writings. The naïveté of this early confidence may have waned, but Roy's hope for the future slowly matured into what can be called humanistic realism/idealism from which she developed her own desired definitions of progress. It is, or at least should be, a moral advancement, a movement toward perfection and fulfillment in love, and, in general, "la lente montée continue des êtres vers une meilleure humanité." The stages of this elevation of humanity, now on the true path of progress, must begin when each individual becomes content with oneself and with life: "Quand on aime la vie, c'est alors qu'elle-même nous aime le plus, comme par un prodige d'entente." The first of Gabrielle Roy's hopes and goals, therefore, is the attainment of self-discovery and of unity and reconciliation with one's own being.[10]

An individual cannot, however, live alone in this world, despite any persistent desires for solitude. A conflicting and yet equally important need of people, therefore, is to be found in an effort toward solidarity with others. Even in her essays, Roy was fully aware that such an attempt toward collective unity may be difficult, may still be a dream, but it is the responsibility of humanity to strive toward goals of universal friendship, of "l'interdépendance humaine . . . à tous, par tous et pour tous":

> Nous savons que nous sommes conviés d'abord à parcourir un rude et long chemin vers un but obscur qu'on appelle salut, progrès, évolution, universalité ou fraternité.
> Une tâche âpre, c'est vrai, mais exaltante, nous appelle . . . vers une vision unique . . . la grande paroisse universelle.[11]

This possible interpretation of Roy's hopes and goals as

dreams reminds one of the world and the characters that she has created in *La Petite Poule d'eau*.   Life as described in these stories is that of security and freedom, human exchange, love, tenderness, and hope.   It is a world inhabited both by Luzina, who inspires optimism in others and sincerely believes in the goodness of human nature, and by the Capuchin, who is certain that people have been created to love one another and to achieve a state of perfect concord.   *La Petite Poule d'eau* has been seen, in fact, as a depiction of life before the fall.   In 1956 Gabrielle Roy wrote that this work was inspired by her hope at that time for a new beginning, if even distant, for humanity.   In 1973 she admitted that it was a "dream-like sort of story . . . life such as it might have been, or could have been, or could be."   It is this last thought, however, that then underscored Roy's continued optimism and faith for humanity and the world.   In 1980 she stated that she had once believed *La Petite Poule d'eau* to be merely a dream, but that she was no longer so sure.   Her humanistic idealism remained intact.[12]

To give additional credibility to the firmness of Roy's optimistic convictions and faith, one can easily turn to her other writings throughout which can be seen these same positive elements.   If Roy could define her ultimate goal as an image on the beautiful horizon of "le cercle enfin uni des hommes," she was referring to her desires of friendship and solidarity that are also espoused by Emmanuel, Alexandre, and Reverend Paterson and that are partially achieved during an enchanted summer.   Her characters all strive, in addition, for the ideal world of "le pays de l'amour" in which the love for oneself and the love and tenderness for others can overcome the often tragic state of human existence.   Such warmth for others leads to mutual understanding, especially of the human suffering and fragility that unite everyone into a common bond.   Only then can true communication commence.   It is this profound need to vanquish one's solitude by standing on a common shore, by trying "à travers la vie à tâcher de nous rencontrer" that is the most immediate goal of all of Gabrielle Roy's characters and the author's most deeply desired hope for humanity.[13]

A world of solidarity, friendship, love, tenderness, understanding, and communication is one in which people are aware of and concerned about others.   It is an ideal place where "en donnant et non pas en recevant . . . on acquiert la clarté qui innonde le coeur."   It may be a distant goal, a potential rather than a reality, but, as Gabrielle Roy optimistically notes: "Terre des Hommes *arrive* chaque fois peut-être que nous parvenons à nous mettre à la place des autres." Human reconciliation is at least partially accessible.[14]

If *La Petite Poule d'eau* depicts a world in which human unity can be attained, it also offers to Roy's readers the image of another important goal, that of true communion between humanity and the universe. Royan characters do often struggle against their environment, but there are times, as in *La Montagne secrète* and *Cet Eté qui chantait,* when a certain harmony is sensed, when "une sorte de résonance intérieure avec l'univers" or "une mystérieuse et secrète entente" is reached. Speaking to people both poetically and musically, the earth presents its symbol of reconciliation with humanity, as Paul Socken aptly notes, in the rainbow: "Alors apparaît un arc-en-ciel tendu de part en part de l'étang comme un pont suspendu. Puis une portion croule, et le pont s'arrête à mi-chemin du ciel, un peu comme le pont d'Avignon à mi-chemin du Rhone." Such communion remains an ideal, still to be perfected.[15]

This perfection or purification of oneself, humanity, and the world constitutes an additional Royan goal for the future. Using her persistent preference for cycles or circularity, Roy envisions this future destiny as resembling a primitive past of child-like innocence and peace. Added to this collective dawn or *recommencement* in nature, however, will be all of the experience that humanity has gained during its ascent toward the ideal. This new world, bathed in an atmosphere of tenderness, therefore, will be filled not with naïveté but with a sort of realistic innocence and simplicity.[16]

In this newly reborn world, as described in her essays, Roy still naïvely believes that individuals will joyfully accept their responsibilities, with "la sensation d'accomplir une tâche qui nourrissait le monde, enrichissait l'amitié. . . ." Happy to complete this designated task with care and love and to aid in "le spectacle ordonné de chaque être humain à sa place," each person, now with the dignity of being a unique creator, will, like the writer-artist, make this world more agreable: "A chacun de travailler dans sa sphère; c'était ainsi que le monde se portait bien."[17]

Given Gabrielle Roy's insistence that an ideal world of human and natural reconciliation is possible—despite its distance, its difficulty and pain in attaining, its fragility, and, perhaps, even its temporary nature—one can assuredly state that her faith surpasses, if even only slightly, her tragic vision. It is for this reason that Marc Gagné has accurately characterized all of her works as remaining open at their termination, inviting her next work to begin and offering her characters another chance in the future. Roy herself fully agreed with such an interpretation of her fiction, for she continued to insist that there would always be a ray of hope on the horizon, always the opportunity for a new beginning, always a new day before humanity.[18]

In a 1965 interview, Gabrielle Roy stated that she had always been interested in humanity, in "ce qui touche le plus grand nombre possible d'êtres humains." Fifteen years later in another interview, this same notion was more precisely defined as including not only the contradictory yet complementary problems, preoccupations, and concerns of her diverse characters, but also those of the broadest possible spectrum of readers for her works. In her later years, Roy had, in fact, become increasingly desirous of affecting as many people as possible through a fictional world that revealed her universal literary vision of humanity. She could thus fulfill her greatest goal: to be classified no longer as a *Québécoise*, French-Canadian, or Canadian writer, but to belong to world literature.[19]

NOTES

[1]Gabrielle Roy, "*Terre des Hommes:* Le Thème raconté" and "Présentation," *Fragiles Lumières de la terre: Ecrits divers 1942-1970,* Collection Prose Entière (Montréal: Les Editions Quinze, 1978), pp. 212, 9; Personal interview with Gabrielle Roy, 29 June 1980. In this same interview, Roy also spoke humorously of how people have consistently confused the wording of this title. They have said to her, for example: "Oh, que j'aime le titre de votre nouvelle oeuvre, *Petites Lumières de la terre,*" or "*Fragiles Lueurs de la terre, Fragiles Lumières du monde, Lumières pauvres de la terre,*" and the like. In a 1979 interview, Roy also referred to her

belief in the temporary nature of joy. See Gilles Dorion et Maurice Emond, "Dossier Gabrielle Roy: Questionnaire," *Québec Français*, No. 36 (décembre 1979), p. 33.

[2] Marc Gagné, *Visages de Gabrielle Roy* (Montréal: Librairie Beauchemin Limitée, 1973), pp. 19-20; François Ricard, *Gabrielle Roy*, Ecrivains canadiens d'aujourd'hui, No. 11 (Montréal: Editions Fides, 1975), p. 145; Gabrielle Roy, *Cet Eté qui chantait* (Québec-Montréal: Les Editions Françaises, 1972), p. 76. See also Paul Socken, " 'Le Pays de l'amour' in the Works of Gabrielle Roy," *Revue de l'Université d'Ottawa*, 46, No. 3 (juillet-septembre 1976), 323.

[3] Dorion et Emond, p. 33; Gabrielle Roy, "Jeux du romancier et des lecteurs," L'Alliance Française, Montréal, 1er décembre 1955, as quoted in Gagné, p. 269. See also Gabrielle Roy, *La Petite Poule d'eau* (1950; rpt. Montréal: Librairie Beauchemin Limitée, 1970), p. 243; Personal interview with Gabrielle Roy, 29 June 1980. In the Alliance Française lecture and in the 1980 interview, Roy mentioned the influences of André Gide and Albert Camus on the development of her dualistic vision. See also Gabrielle Roy, "Le Pays de *Bonheur d'occasion*," in *Morceaux*, ed. Robert Guy Scully (Montréal: Les Editions du Noroît, 1978), p. 120; Gabrielle Roy, *La Montagne secrète* (1961; rpt. Montréal: Librairie Beauchemin Limitée, 1974), p. 207; Paul Socken, "Use of Language in *Bonheur d'occasion*: A Case in Point," *Essays on Canadian Writing*, No. 11 (Summer 1978), p. 71; Donald Cameron, "Gabrielle Roy: A Bird in the Prison Window," in *Conversations with Canadian Novelists* (Toronto: Macmillan of Canada, 1973), pp. 130-131.

[4] Dorion et Emond, p. 34; Roy, *Cet Eté qui chantait*, p. 203. In the second work, see also pp. 93, 174, 198, 202. See also Gabrielle Roy, *Bonheur d'occasion* (1945; rpt. Montréal: Librairie Beauchemin Limitée, 1973), p. 287; Gabrielle Roy, *Un Jardin au bout du monde* (Montréal: Librairie Beauchemin Limitée, 1975), p. 61; Socken, " 'Le Pays de l'amour' in the Works of Gabrielle Roy," pp. 317-318.

[5] Gabrielle Roy, *Alexandre Chenevert* (1954; rpt. Montréal: Beauchemin, 1973), pp. 151, 167-168; Gabrielle Roy, *Rue Deschambault* (1955; rpt. Montréal: Librairie Beauchemin Limitée, 1974), p. 179; Gabrielle Roy, "Les Terres nouvelles de Jean-Paul Lemieux," *Vie des Arts*, No. 29 (hiver 1962-1963), p. 43; Roy, *Cet Eté qui chantait*, p. 93; Roland-M. Charland et Jean-Noël Samson, *Gabrielle Roy*, Dossiers de documentation sur la littérature canadienne-française (Montréal: Fides, 1972), p. 18; François Ricard, "Gabrielle Roy ou l'impossible choix," *Critère*, No. 10 (janvier 1974), pp. 97-102; P.-E. Roy, "Gabrielle Roy ou la difficulté de s'ajuster à la réalité," *Lectures*, N S, 2, No. 3 (novembre 1964), 57-58.

[6] Gabrielle Roy, *La Route d'Altamont*, Collection L'Arbre, No. 10

(Montréal: Editions HMH, 1966), p. 199. See also pp. 142, 146; Roy, *Bonheur d'occasion*, pp. 243, 266; Roy, "La Camargue," *Fragiles Lumières de la terre*, pp. 132, 135; Roy, *Rue Deschambault*, p. 179; Roy, *Cet Eté qui chantait*, pp. 74, 202-203; Roy, *Un Jardin au bout du monde*, pp. 177-178; Gagné, pp. 78-79, 201-202, 244; P.-E. Roy, pp. 57-58.

[7] Roy, "Ames en peine," *Cet Eté qui chantait*, pp. 65-76. See also Gagné, pp. 150-151; André Brochu, "Gabrielle Roy," Notes from course on author, Université de Montréal, Printemps 1978, taken by one of his students; Socken, " 'Le Pays de l'amour' in the Works of Gabrielle Roy," p. 323; Michel-Lucien Gaulin, "Le Thème du bonheur dans l'oeuvre de Gabrielle Roy," Thesis Université de Montréal, 1961, pp. 21-30.

[8] Roy, *Bonheur d'occasion*, p. 285; Personal interview with Gabrielle Roy, 29 June 1980. In the first work, see also pp. 281, 345. In the interview, Roy also stated that she felt that people were creating their own hell in this world. See also Roy, *La Petite Poule d'eau*, pp. 242-242; Roy, *Alexandre Chenevert*, p. 30; Gaulin, pp. 30-36; P.-E. Roy, pp. 59-61; Jack Warwick, *L'Appel du nord dans la littérature canadienne-française*, trans. Jean Simard, Collection Constantes (Montréal: Editions Hurtubise HMH, 1972), pp. 212-213.

[9] Roy, "*Terre des Hommes:* Le Thème raconté," p. 230. See also pp. 216, 227; Roy, *Rue Deschambault*, p. 64; Roy, *La Petite Poule d'eau*, pp. 124-125, 143-145; Roy, *Cet Eté qui chantait*, p. 94; Gagné, pp. 12-13, 82-83, 90-92; Jacques Blais, "L'Unité organique de *Bonheur d'occasion*," *Etudes Françaises*, 6, No. 1 (février 1970), 44-49. It should be noted, however, that the resulting movement of progress, although slow, is a forward one.

[10] Dorion et Emond, p. 35; Roy, *La Route d'Altamont*, p. 232. See also Roy, *La Petite Poule d'eau*, pp. 33, 83; Roy, "*Terre des Hommes:* Le Thème raconté," pp. 226-228; Gagné, pp. 36-39, 43-44; Blais, pp. 45, 46, 49. François Ricard calls this aspect of Roy's beliefs "hopeful realism." See Ricard, "Le Cercle enfin uni des hommes: Hommage à Gabrielle Roy pour sa trentième année de création littéraire," *Liberté*, 18, No. 1, année 1976, numéro 103 (janvier-février 1976), 60-63.

[11] Roy, "*Terre des Hommes:* Le Thème raconté," pp. 209, 212. See also pp. 205, 211, 215, 218.

[12] Cameron, pp. 131-132; Roy, "Mémoire et création: Préface de *La Petite Poule d'eau*," *Fragiles Lumières de la terre*, pp. 196-197; Personal interview with Gabrielle Roy, 29 June 1980. See also Roy, *La Petite Poule d'eau*, pp. 31-33, 93-94, 132, 183, 184, 254-255, 270; Ricard, *Gabrielle Roy*, pp. 66-74.

[13] Gabrielle Roy, "Mon Héritage du Manitoba," *Mosaic*, 3iii (1970), p. 79; Roy, *La Route d'Altamont*, pp. 143, 57. See also Roy, *Bonheur*

d'occasion, pp. 266, 281; Gabrielle Roy, *"Bonheur d'occasion* aujour-d'hui," *Le Bulletin des Agriculteurs,* 44, No. 1 (janvier 1948), 23; Roy, *Alexandre Chenevert,* pp. 18-19, 68, 181-183, 354; Roy, *Rue Descham-bault,* pp. 179, 217; Roy, "Jeux du romancier et des lecteurs," p. 272; Roy, "Le Manitoba," *"Terre des Hommes:* Le Thème raconté," *Fragiles Lumières de la terre,* pp. 120, 227-228, 230-231; Gabrielle Roy, *La Rivière sans repos* (Montréal: Librairie Beauchemin Limitée, 1971), pp. 226-227; Roy, *Cet Eté qui chantait,* pp. 60-61, 198; Roy, *Un Jardin au bout du monde,* pp. 31, 172; Roy, "Le Pays de *Bonheur d'occasion,"* p. 116; Dorion et Emond, pp. 33-35; Cameron, p. 131; Ricard, Note, *Fragiles Lumières de la terre,* by Roy, pp. 11-12; Gagné, pp. 44, 83, 254-257; Ricard, *Gabrielle Roy,* pp. 8, 128-131, 151-153; Gaulin, pp. 21-24, 159-164; Ricard, "Le Cercle enfin uni des hommes," pp. 60-63, 78; Socken, " 'Le Pays de l'amour' in the Works of Gabrielle Roy," pp. 309-323; Paul Socken, "Art and the Artist in Gabrielle Roy's Works," *Revue de l'Uni-versité d'Ottawa,* 45 (1975), 347, 349-350.

[14]Gabrielle Roy, "Plus que le pain," *Le Bulletin des Agriculteurs,* 38, No. 2 (février 1942), 35; Roy, *"Terres des Hommes:* Le Thème ra-conté," p. 233. In the second work, see also p. 231. See also Roy, *Rue Deschambault,* pp. 26, 169; P.-E. Roy, pp. 59-61; Socken, " 'Le Pays de l'amour' in the Works of Gabrielle Roy," pp. 317-323.

[15]Roy, *La Montagne Secrète,* p. 180; Roy, *Cet Eté qui chantait,* pp. 51, 140. In the second work, see also p. 203. See also Roy, *La Petite Poule d'eau,* pp. 254-255; Personal interview with Gabrielle Roy, 29 June 1980; Socken, " 'Le Pays de l'amour' in the Works of Gabrielle Roy," pp. 309-315; Ricard, *Gabrielle Roy,* pp. 142-150.

[16]Roy, "Les Hutterites," "Le Manitoba," *"Terre des Hommes:* Le Thème raconté," *Fragiles Lumières de la terre,* pp. 29, 118, 209; Roy, *Alexandre Chenevert,* p. 221; Roy, *Rue Deschambault,* p. 293; Cameron, p. 131; Ricard, "Le Cercle enfin uni des hommes," pp. 60-63; Socken, " 'Le Pays de l'amour' in the Works of Gabrielle Roy," pp. 309-315.

[17]Roy, "Les Pêcheurs de Gaspésie: Une Voile dans la nuit," *"Terre des Hommes:* Le Thème raconté," *Fragiles Lumières de la terre,* pp. 91, 206; Roy, *La Petite Poule d'eau,* p. 171. In this last work, see also p. 83. Such an ideal world also resembles that desired by Stéphane Mallarmé.

[18]Gagné, pp. 259-261; Personal interview with Gabrielle Roy, 29 June 1980.

[19]Gabrielle Roy, le 2 septembre 1965, as quoted in Gérard Bessette, *Une Littérature en ébullition* (Montréal: Editions du Jour, 1968), p. 308; Personal interview with Gabrielle Roy, 29 June 1980.

BIBLIOGRAPHY

Allard, Jacques. "Le Chemin qui mène à *La Petite Poule d'eau.*" *Cahiers de Sainte-Marie,* No. 1 (mai 1966), pp. 57-69.

Atwood, Margaret. *Survival: A Thematic Guide to Canadian Literature.* Toronto: House of Anansi Press Limited, 1972.

Auerbach, Erich. *Mimesis: The Representation of Reality in Western Literature.* Trans. Willard R. Trask. Princeton: Princeton University Press, 1953.

Babby, Ellen R. "Alexandre Chenevert: Prisoner of Language." *Modern Language Studies,* 12, No. 2 (Spring 1982), 22-30.

-------. "The Language of Spectacle and the Spectacle of Language in Selected Texts of Gabrielle Roy." *DAI,* 41 (1981), 4708A (Yale University).

-------. "The Narrator as Persona in Selected First Person Narratives of Gabrielle Roy." *Littérature québécoise* Section, Northeast Modern Language Association Convention, North Dartmouth, Massachusetts. 21 March 1980.

Bachelard, Gaston. *La Poétique de l'espace.* Bibliothèque de philosophie contemporaine. Paris: Presses Universitaires de France, 1978.

-------. *La Poétique de la rêverie.* Bibliothèque de philosophie contemporaine. Paris: Presses Universitaires de France, 1974.

Beaudoin, Réjean. "Gabrielle Roy: L'Approche de l'oeuvre." *Liberté,* 20, No. 3, année 1978, numéro 117 (mai-juin 1978), 89-91.

Belleau, André. *Le Romancier fictif: Essai sur la représentation de l'écrivain dans le roman québécois.* Silléry, Québec: Les Presses de l'Université du Québec, 1980.

Bertrand, M. "*La Montagne secrète* et l'esthétique de Gabrielle Roy." Thesis. Université de Montréal 1965.

Bessette, Gérard. *De Québec à Saint-Boniface: Récits et nouvelles du Canada français.* Toronto: Macmillan of Canada, 1968.

-------. "French Canadian Society as Seen by Contemporary Novelists." *Queen's Quarterly,* No. 2 (1962), pp. 177-197.

-------, L. Geslin, et C. Parent. *Histoire de la littérature canadienne française par les textes.* Montréal: Centre Éducatif et Culturel, 1968.

-------. *Une Littérature en ébullition.* Montréal: Editions du Jour, 1968.

------. *Trois Romanciers québécois.* Montréal: Editions du Jour, 1973.

Blais, Jacques. "L'Unité organique de *Bonheur d'occasion.*" *Etudes Françaises,* 6, No. 1 (février 1970), 25-50.

Bouffard, Odoric. "Le Canadien-français entre deux mondes." *Culture,* 28, No. 4 (décembre 1967), 347-356.

Bourbonnais, Nicole. "La Symbolique de l'espace dans les récits de Gabrielle Roy." *Voix et Images,* 7, No. 2 (hiver 1982), 367-384.

Bournebeuf, Roland. "Formes littéraires et réalités sociales dans le roman québécois." *Livres et Auteurs Québécois* (1970), pp. 265-269.

Brochu, André. "Gabrielle Roy." Notes from course on author, Université de Montréal. Printemps 1978, taken by one of his students.

------. "La Littérature québécoise, d'hier à demain." *Liberté,* 19, No. 3, année 1977, numéro 111 (mai-juin 1977), 37-40.

------. "La Structure sémantique de *Bonheur d'occasion.*" *Revue des Sciences Humaines,* 45, No. 173 (janvier-mars 1979), 37-47.

------. "Thèmes et structures de *Bonheur d'occasion.*" In *L'Instance critique.* Montréal: Leméac, 1974, pp. 206-246.

Brown, Alan. "Gabrielle Roy and the Temporary Provincial." *The Tamarack Review,* No. 1 (Autumn 1956), pp. 61-70.

Bureau, Jean-Joseph. "Le Complexe de la maternité chez Luzina dans *La Petite Poule d'eau* de Gabrielle Roy." Thesis. Université de Montréal 1961.

Cameron, Donald. "Gabrielle Roy: A Bird in the Prison Window." In *Conversations with Canadian Novelists.* Toronto: Macmillan of Canada, 1973, pp. 128-145.

Carles, Jules. *Teilhard de Chardin.* SUP "Philosophes." Paris: Presses Universitaires de France, 1971.

Chadbourne, Richard M. "The Journey in Gabrielle Roy's Novels." In *Travel, Quest, and Pilgrimage as a Literary Theme: Studies in Honor of Reino Virtanen.* Eds. Frans C. Amelinckx and Joyce N. Megay. Imprint Series, Monograph Publishing on Demand. Lincoln, Nebraska: Society of Spanish and Spanish-American Studies, 1978, pp. 251-260.

Charland, Roland-M. et Jean-Noël Samson. *Gabrielle Roy.* Dossier de documentation sur la littérature canadienne-française. Montréal: Fides, 1972.

Chateaubriand, François-René de. *Atala/René.* Paris: Garnier-Flammarion, 1964.

Chevalier, Jean et Alain Gheerbrant. *Dictionnaire des symboles: Mythes, rêves, coutumes, gestes, formes, figures, couleurs, nombres.* Paris: Robert Laffont/Editions Jupiter, 1982.

Collet, Paulette. *L'Hiver dans le roman canadien-français.* Québec: Les Presses de l'Université Laval, 1965.

Cotnam, Jacques. "Cultural Nationalism and Its Literary Expression in French-Canadian Fiction." In *The Cry of Home: Cultural Nationalism and the Modern Writer.* Ed. H. Ernest Lewald. Knoxville: The University of Tennessee Press, 1972, pp. 268-298.

Dagognet, François. *Gaston Bachelard.* SUP "Philosophes." Paris: Presses Universitaires de France, 1972.

Desrochers, Jean Paul. "La Famille dans l'oeuvre de Gabrielle Roy." Thesis. Université Laval 1965.

Dorion, Gilles et Maurice Emond. "Dossier Gabrielle Roy: Questionnaire. *Québec Francais,* No. 36 (décembre 1979), pp. 33-36.

Dumont, Fernand et Jean-Charles Falardeau, eds. *Littérature et société canadiennes-françaises.* Québec: Les Presses de l'Université Laval, 1964.

Falardeau, Jean-Charles. *Imaginaire social et littéraire.* Montréal: Editions Hurtubise HMH, 1974.

------. *Notre Société et son roman.* Montréal: Editions Hurtubise HMH, 1972.

Ferron, Jacques. *Au fond de mon arrière-cuisine.* Montréal: Editions du Jour, 1973.

Gagné, Marc. "*La Rivière sans repos* de Gabrielle Roy: Etude mythocritique incluant 'Voyage en Ungava' (extraits) par Gabrielle Roy." *Revue de l'Université d'Ottawa,* 46, No. 1 (janvier-mars 1976), 83-107.

------. "*La Rivière sans repos* de Gabrielle Roy: Etude mythocritique incluant 'Voyage en Ungava' (extraits) par Gabrielle Roy (suite)." *Revue de l'Université d'Ottawa,* 46, No. 2 (avril-juin 1976), 180-199.

------. "*La Rivière sans repos* de Gabrielle Roy: Etude mythocritique incluant 'Voyage en Ungava' (extraits) par Gabrielle Roy (suite)." *Revue de l'Université d'Ottawa,* 46, No. 3 (juillet-septembre 1976), 364-390.

------. *Visages de Gabrielle Roy.* Montréal: Librairie Beauchemin Limitée, 1973.

Gaulin, Michel-Lucien. "Le Monde romanesque de Roger Lemelin et Gabrielle Roy." In *Le Roman canadien-français: Evolution-témoignage-bibliographie.* Eds. Paul Wyczynski, Bernard Julien, Jean Ménard et Réjean Robidoux. Archives des lettres canadiennes, Tome III. Montréal: Fides, 1977, pp. 133-151.

------. "*La Rivière sans repos* de Gabrielle Roy." *Livres et Auteurs Québécois* (1970), pp. 27-28.

------. "Le Théme du bonheur dans l'oeuvre de Gabrielle Roy." Thesis. Université de Montréal 1961.

Genuist, Monique. *La Création romanesque chez Gabrielle Roy.* Montréal: Le Cercle du Livre de France, 1966.

Green, Mary Jean. "Gabrielle Roy and Germaine Guèvremont: Quebec's Daughters Face a Changing World." *Journal of Women's Studies in Literature*, 1, No. 3 (Fall 1979), 243-257.

Greenspan, Arthur. "A propos de *L'Arrache-coeur:* Interview avec Mireille Dansereau." *The French Review,* 53, No. 6 (May 1980), 865-871.

Grenier-Francoeur, Marie. "Etude de la structure anaphorique dans *La Montagne secrète* de Gabrielle Roy." *Voix et Images,* 1, No. 3 (avril 1976), 387-405.

Grosskurth, Phyllis. *Gabrielle Roy.* Canadian Writers and Their Works. Toronto: Forum House, 1972.

-------. "Gabrielle Roy and the Silken Noose." *Canadian Literature,* 42 (1969), 6-13.

Hayne, David. "Les Grandes Options de la littérature canadienne-française." *Etudes Françaises* (février 1965), pp. 68-69.

Hébert, François. "De quelques avatars de Dieu." *Etudes Françaises,* 9, No. 4 (novembre 1973), 345-349.

-------. "Gabrielle Roy: *Ces Enfants de ma vie.*" *Liberté,* 20, No. 1, année 1978, numéro 115 (janvier-février 1978), 102-105.

Hind-Smith, John. *Three Voices: The Lives of Margaret Laurence, Gabrielle Roy, and Frederick Philip Grove.* Toronto: Clarke Irwin, 1975.

Hughes, Terrence. *Gabrielle Roy et Margaret Laurence: Deux Chemins, une recherche.* Collection Soleil. Saint-Boniface, Manitoba: Editions du Blé, 1983.

Imbert, Patrick. "*Rue Deschambault* ou l'ouverture au monde." *Les Lettres Québécoises,* No. 5 (février 1977), pp. 32-33.

Jones, D. G. *Butterfly on Rock: A Study of Themes and Images in Canadian Literature.* Toronto: University of Toronto Press, 1971.

Jones, Grahame C. "*Alexandre Chenevert* et *Kamouraska:* Une Lecture australienne." *Voix et Images,* 7, No. 2 (hiver 1982), 329-341.

Kushner, Eva. "Dossier Gabrielle Roy: De la représentation à la vision du monde." *Québec Français,* No. 36 (décembre 1979), pp. 38-40.

Laflèche, Guy. "Les Bonheurs d'occasion du roman québécois." *Voix et Images,* 3, No. 1 (septembre 1977), 96-115.

La Follette, James E. Jr. "Le Parler franco-canadien dans *Bonheur d'occasion.*" Thesis. Université Laval 1949.

La Rocque, Gilbert. "Marie-Anna A. Roy: Les Dernières Ecritures." *Québec/Amérique: Magazine d'information,* 2, No. 3 (1980), 38-39.

Le Grand, Albert. "Gabrielle Roy ou l'être partagé." *Etudes Françaises,* 1ere année, No. 2 (juin 1965), pp. 39-65.

Lemire, Maurice. "*Bonheur d'occasion* ou le salut par la guerre." *Recher-*

ches Sociographiques, 10 (1969), 23-35.

Le Moyne, Jean. "La Femme dans la civilisation canadienne-française." In *Convergences.* Montréal: Editions HMH, 1969, pp. 69-100.

------. "La Littérature canadienne-française et la femme." In *Convergences.* Montréal: Editions HMH, 1969, pp. 101-108.

Le Vasseur, Joseph-Marie. "Gabrielle Roy, peintre de la famille canadienne-française," Thesis. Université de Montréal 1960.

Lewis, Paula Gilbert. *The Aesthetics of Stéphane Mallarmé in Relation to His Public.* Cranbury, New Jersey: Fairleigh Dickinson University Press; London: Associated University Presses, 1976.

------. "The Feminine World of Gabrielle Roy's *Bonheur d'occasion.*" George Washington University, Washington, D.C. 6 August 1980.

------. "Feminism and Traditionalism in the Early Short Stories of Gabrielle Roy." Quebec Women's Studies Section, Association for Canadian Studies in the United States, East Lansing, Michigan, 23 October 1981.

------. "The Fragility of Childhood: Gabrielle Roy's *Ces Enfants de ma vie.*" *The American Review of Canadian Studies,* 9, No. 2 (Autumn 1979), 148-153.

------. "Gabrielle Roy and Emile Zola: French Naturalism in Quebec." *Modern Language Studies,* 11, No. 3 (Fall 1981), 44-50.

------. "The Incessant Call of the Open Road: Gabrielle Roy's Incorrigible Nomads." *The French Review,* 53, No. 6 (May 1980), 816-825.

------. "Language, The Writer-Artist, and The Work of Art: The Aesthetics of Gabrielle Roy." In *The French Experience in North America/Etre français dans l'Amérique du Nord.* Acts of an International Conference at the University of Maine at Orono. Forthcoming.

------. "The Last of the Great Storytellers: A Visit with Gabrielle Roy." *The French Review,* 55, No. 2 (December 1981), 207-215.

------. "Montreal and Paris in the Novels of Gabrielle Roy." French-Canadian Literature in Canada and the United States Section, Rocky Mountain Modern Language Association Convention, Denver, 18 October 1980.

------. "The Resignation of Old Age, Sickness, and Death in the Fiction of Gabrielle Roy." *The American Review of Canadian Studies,* 11, No. 2 (Autumn 1981), 49-66.

------. "Response: Pathological Images in the Quebec Novel." Literary Perspectives Section, Fifth Biennial Conference of the Association for Canadian Studies in the United States, Washington, D. C. 29 September 1979.

------. "*Street of Riches* and *The Road Past Altamont:* The Feminine World of Gabrielle Roy." *Journal of Women's Studies in Literature,*

1, No. 2 (Spring 1979), 133-141.

------. "The Themes of Memory and Death in Gabrielle Roy's *La Route d'Altamont.*" *Modern Fiction Studies*, 22, No. 3 (Autumn 1976), 457-466. Excerpts rpt. in *Contemporary Literary Criticism*. Vol. X. Detroit: Gale Research Co., 1979.

------. "Tragic and Humanistic Visions of the Future: The Fictional World of Gabrielle Roy." *Québec Studies*, 1, No. 1 (June 1983), 234-245.

------. "Trois Générations de femmes: Le Reflet mère/fille dans quelques nouvelles de Gabrielle Roy." L'Héritage français en Amérique Section. American Association of Teachers of French, Lille, France, 27 June 1983. *Voix et Images*. Forthcoming.

------. "Unsuccessful Couples, Shameful Sex, and Infrequent Love in the Fictional World of Gabrielle Roy." *Antigonish Review*, 12, No. 48 (Winter 1982), 49-55.

Lombard, Bertrand. *"La Route d'Altamont."* *La Revue de l'Université Laval*, 21, No. 2 (octobre 1966), 196-198.

Mailhot, Laurent. *La Littérature québécoise.* Que Sais-Je?, No. 1579. Paris: Presses Universitaires de France, 1974.

Maillet, Antonine (Soeur Marie-Grégoire). "La Femme et l'enfant dans l'oeuvre de Gabrielle Roy." Thesis. Université Saint-Joseph de Memramcook 1959.

Major, Jean-Louis. "Mémoire, création/clichés: *Fragiles Lumières de la terre* de Gabrielle Roy et *Une Mémoire déchirée* de Thérèse Renaud." *Lettres Québécoises*, No. 12 (novembre 1978), pp. 34-36.

Mallarmé, Stéphane. *Oeuvres complètes.* Bibliothèque de la Pléiade. Paris: Editions Gallimard, 1945.

Marcotte, Gilles. *Les Bonnes Rencontres: Chroniques littéraires.* Collection Reconnaissances. Montréal: Editions Hurtubise HMH, 1971.

------. "En relisant *Bonheur d'occasion.*" *L'Action Nationale*, 35, No. 3 (mars 1950), 197-206.

------. *Une Littérature qui se fait.* Montréal: Editions HMH, 1968.

------. *Présence de la critique.* Montréal: Editions HMH, 1966.

Marie du Rédempteur, Soeur (Pierrette Seers). "Le Thème de la solitude dans l'oeuvre de Gabrielle Roy." Thesis. Université de Montréal 1963.

McPherson, H. "Prodigies of God and Man." *Canadian Literature*, No. 15 (Winter 1963), pp. 74-76.

Merzisen, Yves. "L'Inspiration romanesque de Gabrielle Roy." *DAI*, 35 (1974), 3755A-3756A (British Columbia).

Morissette, Robert. "Interview avec Gabrielle Roy." In "La Vie ouvrière urbaine dans le roman canadien-français contemporain." Thesis. Université de Montréal 1970, pp. 164-168.

Moss, Jane Byers. "Pathological Images in the Quebec Novel." *The Ameri-*

can Review of Canadian Studies, 10, No. 1 (Spring 1980), 39-47.

Murphy, John J. "The Louvre and Ungava." *Renascence: A Critical Journal of Letters,* 16, No. 1 (Fall 1963), 53-56.

------. "Visit with Gabrielle Roy." *Thought: Review of Culture and Ideas,* 38, No. 150 (Autumn 1963), 447-455.

Novelli, Novella. "Concomitances et coïncidences dans *Bonheur d'occasion." Voix et Images,* 7, No. 1 (automne 1981), 131-146.

O'Donnell, Kathleen. "Gabrielle Roy's Portrait of the Artist." *La Revue de l'Université d'Ottawa,* 49, No. 1 (janvier-mars 1974), 70-77.

Paradis, Suzanne. *Femme fictive, femme réelle: Le Personnage féminin dans le roman féminin canadien-français, 1884-1966.* Québec: Editions Garneau, 1966.

Parizeau, Alice. "Gabrielle Roy, grande romancière canadienne." *Châtelaine,* 7, No. 4 (avril 1966), 44, 118, 120-123, 137, 140.

Pascal, Gabrielle. "La Condition féminine dans l'oeuvre de Gabrielle Roy." *Voix et Images,* 5, No. 1 (automne 1979), 143-163.

------. "La Femme dans l'oeuvre de Gabrielle Roy." *Revue de l'Université d'Ottawa,* 50, No. 1 (janvier-mars 1980), 55-61.

Poulin, Gabrielle. "Une Merveilleuse Histoire d'amour: *Ces Enfants de ma vie* de Gabrielle Roy." *Les Lettres Québécoises,* No. 8 (novembre 1977), pp. 5-9.

Racine, Claude. *L'Anticléricalisme dans le roman québécois: 1940-1965.* Collection Littérature: Les Cahiers du Québec. Montréal: Editions Hurtubise HMH, 1972.

Reid, Malcolm. *The Shouting Signpainters: A Literary and Political Account of Quebec Revolutionary Nationalism.* New York: Monthly Review Press, 1972.

Ricard, François. "Le Cercle enfin uni des hommes: Hommage à Gabrielle Roy pour sa trentième année de création littéraire." *Liberté,* 18, No. 1, année 1976, numéro 103 (janvier-février 1976), 59-78.

------. *Gabrielle Roy.* Ecrivains canadiens d'aujourd'hui, No. 11. Montréal: Editions Fides, 1975.

------. "Gabrielle Roy ou l'impossible choix." *Critère,* No. 10 (janvier 1974), pp. 97-102.

Ringuet. "Conversation avec Gabrielle Roy." *La Revue Populaire,* 44e année, No. 10 (octobre 1951), p. 4.

Robidoux, Réjean et A. Renaud. *Le Roman canadien-français du vingtième siècle.* Ottawa: Editions de l'Université d'Ottawa, 1966.

------. "Le Roman et la recherche du sens de la vie: Vocation: Ecrivain." In *Mélanges de civilisation canadienne-française offerts au professeur Paul Wyczynski.* Ed. Pierre Savard. Cahiers du Centre de Recherche en civilisation canadienne-française, No. 10. Ottawa: Editions de l'Université d'Ottawa, 1977, pp. 225-235.

Roy, Gabrielle. *Alexandre Chenevert.* 1954; rpt. Montréal: Beauchemin, 1973.

------. "A Okko." *La Revue Moderne,* 22, No. 12 (avril 1941), 8, 9, 41, 42.

------. "Après trois cents ans." *Le Bulletin des Agriculteurs,* 37, No. 9 (septembre 1941), 9, 37-39.

------. "L'Arbre." *Cahiers de l'Académie canadienne-française,* No. 13 (1970), pp. 5-27.

------. "Avantage pour." *La Revue Moderne,* 20, No. 6 (octobre 1940), 5-6, 26.

------. "L'Avenue Palestine." *Le Bulletin des Agriculteurs,* 39, No. 2 (février 1943), 7, 32-33.

------. *Bonheur d'occasion.* 1945; rpt. Montréal: Librairie Beauchemin Limitée, 1973.

------. "*Bonheur d'occasion* aujourd'hui." *Le Bulletin des Agriculteurs,* 44, No. 1 (janvier 1948), 6-7, 20-23.

------. "Bonne à marier." *La Revue Moderne,* 20, No. 2 (juin 1940), 13, 40-42.

------. "La Camargue." *Amérique Française* (mai-juin 1952), pp. 8-18.

------. *The Cashier.* Trans. Harry Binsse. Introd. W. C. Lougheed. 1963; rpt. New Canadian Library, No. 40. Toronto: McClelland and Stewart Limited, 1970.

------. "Cendrillon '40." *La Revue Moderne,* 21, No. 10 (février 1940), 8, 9, 41, 42.

------. *Ces Enfants de ma vie.* Montréal: Editions Internationales Alain Stanké Ltée, 1977.

------. *Cet Eté qui chantait.* Québec-Montréal: Les Editions Françaises, 1972.

------. *Children of My Heart.* Trans. Alan Brown. Toronto: McClelland and Stewart Limited, 1979.

------. "Comment j'ai reçu le Fémina." *Le Devoir,* 15 décembre 1956, pp. 2, 7.

------. "La Conversion des O'Connor." *La Revue Moderne,* 21, No. 5 (septembre 1939), 4-5, 32-33.

------. *Courte-Queue.* Images, François Olivier. Montréal: Editions Internationales Alain Stanké Ltée, 1979.

------. "Dead-leaves." *Maclean's,* 1 June 1947, pp. 20, 37-38, 40, 42.

------. "De Prague à Good Soil." *Le Bulletin des Agriculteurs,* 39, No. 3 (mars 1943), 8, 46-48.

------. *De quoi t'ennuies-tu, Eveline?* Montréal: Editions du Sentier, 1982.

------. "La Dernière Pêche." *La Revue Moderne,* 22, No. 7 (novembre

1940), 8, 9, 38.

------. "De turbulents chercheurs de paix." *Le Bulletin des Agriculteurs,* 38, No. 12 (décembre 1942), 10, 39-40.

------. "Les Deux Saint-Laurent." *Le Bulletin des Agriculteurs,* 37, No. 6 (juin 1941), 8, 9, 37, 40.

------. "Du port aux banques." *Le Bulletin des Agriculteurs,* 37, No. 8 (août 1941), 11, 32-33.

------. "Ely! Ely! Ely!," *Liberté,* 21, No. 3, année 1979, numéro 123 (mai-juin 1979), 13-26.

------. "Embobeliné." *La Revue Moderne,* 23, No. 6 (octobre 1941), 7, 8, 28, 30, 33, 34.

------. *Enchanted Summer.* Trans. Joyce Marshall. Toronto: McClelland and Stewart Limited, 1976.

------. "Est-Ouest." *Le Bulletin des Agriculteurs,* 37, No. 7 (juillet 1941), 9, 25-28.

------. "Femmes de dur labeur." *Le Bulletin des Agriculteurs,* 39, No. 1 (janvier 1943), 10, 25.

------. "Feuilles mortes." *La Revue de Paris,* 56ᵉ année, No. 1 (janvier 1948), pp. 46-55.

------. *Fragiles Lumières de la terre: Ecrits divers 1942-1970.* Collection Prose Entière. Montréal: Les Editions Quinze, 1978.

------. (Aline Lubac). "La Fuite de Sally." *Le Bulletin des Agriculteurs,* 27, No. 1 (janvier 1941), 9, 39-40.

------. *Garden in the Wind.* Trans. Alan Brown. 1977: rpt. Toronto: McClelland and Stewart Limited, 1979.

------. "Le Gardien de l'horizon." *Liberté: Nos Ecrivains par nous-mêmes,* 25, No. 1, numéro 145 (février 1983), 71-72.

------. "Gérard le pirate." *La Revue Moderne,* 22, No. 1 (mai 1940), 5, 37-39.

------. "La Grande Berthe." *Le Bulletin des Agriculteurs,* 39, No. 6 (juin 1943), 4-9, 39-49.

------. "La Grande Voyageuse." *La Revue Moderne,* 24, No. 1 (mai 1942), 12, 13, 27-30.

------. *The Hidden Mountain.* Trans. Harry Binsse. Introd. Malcolm Ross. 1962; rpt. New Canadian Library, No. 109. Toronto: McClelland and Stewart Limited, 1975.

------. "Une Histoire d'amour." *La Revue Moderne,* 21, No. 11 (mars 1940), 8, 9, 36-38.

------. "Introduction: Le Thème raconté/The Theme Unfolded." In *Terre des Hommes/Man and His World.* Montréal and Toronto: La Compagnie canadienne de l'Exposition universelle de 1967/Canadian Corporation for the 1967 World Exhibition, 1967, pp. 21-60.

------. *Un Jardin au bout du monde.* Montréal: Librairie Beauchemin Limitée, 1975.

------. "Jeux du romancier et des lecteurs." L'Alliance Française, Montréal. 1ᵉʳ décembre 1955. In Gagné, Marc. *Visages de Gabrielle Roy.* Montréal: Librairie Beauchemin Limitée, 1973, pp. 263-272.

------. (Aline Lubac). "Le Joli Miracle." *Le Bulletin des Agriculteurs,* 26, No. 12 (décembre 1940), 8, 29-30.

------. "La Justice en Danaca et ailleurs." In *Les Oeuvres libres.* Paris: Librairie Arthème Fayard, N S, No. 23 (1948), pp. 163-180.

------. Letter to author. 27 March 1980.

------. "Le Long, Long Voyage." *Le Bulletin des Agriculteurs,* 41, No. 5 (mai 1945), 8-9, 51-52.

------. "La Lune des moissons." *La Revue Moderne,* 29, No. 5 (septembre 1947), 12, 13, 76-80.

------. "Ma Cousine économe." *Le Magazine Maclean,* 3, No. 8 (août 1963), 26, 41-46.

------. "Le Manitoba." *Le Magazine Maclean,* 2, No. 7 (juillet 1962), 18-21, 32-38.

------. "Le Monde à l'envers." *La Revue Moderne,* 21, No. 6 (octobre 1939), 6, 34.

------. "Mon Héritage du Manitoba." *Mosaic,* 3iii (1970), 69-79.

------. *La Montagne secrète.* 1961; rpt. Montréal: Librairie Beauchemin Limitée, 1974.

------. "Un Noël en route." *La Revue Moderne,* 22, No. 8 (décembre 1940), 8, 32-34.

------. "Le Pays de *Bonheur d'occasion.*" In *Morceaux du grand Montréal.* Ed. Robert Guy Scully. Montréal: Les Editions du Noroît, 1978, pp. 113-122.

------. "La Pension de vieillesse." *Le Bulletin des Agriculteurs,* 39, No. 11 (novembre 1943), 8, 32, 33, 36.

------. Personal interview. 29 June 1980.

------. *La Petite Poule d'eau.* 1950; rpt. Montréal: Librairie Beauchemin Limitée, 1970.

------. "Les Petits Pas de Caroline." *Le Bulletin des Agriculteurs,* 26, No. 10 (octobre 1940), 11, 45-49.

------. "Peuples du Canada." *Le Bulletin des Agriculteurs,* 38, No. 11 (novembre 1942), 8, 30-32.

------. "Pitié pour les institutrices." *Le Bulletin des Agriculteurs,* 38, No. 3 (mars 1942), 7, 45-46.

------. "Plus que le pain." *Le Bulletin des Agriculteurs,* 38, No. 2 (février 1942), 9, 33-35.

------. "Préface." In Roy, Gabrielle. *La Petite Poule d'eau.* Toronto:

Clarke, Irwin and Col., 1956.

------. "Préface de *René Richard.*" In Ricard, François. *Gabrielle Roy.* Ecrivains canadiens d'aujourd'hui, No. 11. Montréal: Editions Fides, 1975, pp. 171-174.

------. "Réponse de Mademoiselle Gabrielle Roy." In *Société Royale du Canada, section française,* No. 5 (1947-1948), pp. 35-48.

------. *La Rivière sans repos.* Montréal: Librairie Beauchemin Limitée, 1971.

------. *The Road Past Altamont.* Trans. Joyce Marshall. Introd. Joyce Marshall. 1966; rpt. New Canadian Library, No. 129. Toronto: McClelland and Stewart Limited, 1976.

------. "Le Roi de coeur." *La Revue Moderne,* 21, No. 12 (avril 1940), 6, 7, 33-39.

------. *La Route d'Altamont.* Collection L'Arbre, No. 10. Montréal: Editions HMH, 1966.

------. *Rue Deschambault.* 1955; rpt. Montréal: Librairie Beauchemin Limitée, 1974.

------. "Sainte-Anne-la-Palud." *La Nouvelle Revue canadienne,* 1, No. 2 (avril-mai 1951), 12-18.

------. "Sécurité." *La Revue Moderne,* 29, No. 11 (mars 1948), 12, 13, 66, 68, 69.

------. "Security." *Maclean's,* 15 September 1947, pp. 20-21, 36-39.

------. "Sister Finance." *Maclean's Magazine,* 15 December 1962, pp. 35, 38-44.

------. "Six Pilules par jour." *La Revue Moderne,* 23, No. 3 (juillet 1941), 17, 18, 32-34.

------. "La Sonate à l'aurore." *La Revue Moderne,* 22, No. 11 (mars 1941), 9, 10, 35-37.

------. "La Source au désert." *Le Bulletin des Agriculteurs,* 42, No. 10 (octobre 1946), 10-11, 30-47.

------. "La Source au désert." *Le Bulletin des Agriculteurs,* 42, No. 11 (novembre 1946), 13, 42-49.

------. "Souvenirs du Manitoba." *La Revue de Paris,* 62e année, No. 2 (février 1955), pp. 77-83.

------. *Street of Riches.* Trans. Henry Binsse. Introd. Brandon Conron. New Canadian Library, No. 56. Toronto: McClelland and Stewart Limited, 1967.

------. "Témoignage." In *Le Roman canadien-français: Evolution-témoignage-bibliographie.* Eds. Paul Wyczynski, Bernard Julien, Jean Ménard et Réjean Robidoux. Archives des lettres canadiennes. Tome III. Montréal: Fides, 1977, pp. 302-306.

------. "Les Terres nouvelles de Jean-Paul Lemieux." *Vie des Arts,* No. 29

(hiver 1962-1963), pp. 39-43.

———. *The Tin Flute.* Trans. Hannah Josephson. New York: Reynal and Hitchcock, 1947; Trans. Alan Brown. New Canadian Library, No. 5 Toronto: McClelland and Stewart, 1980.

———. "Ukraine." *Le Bulletin des Agriculteurs,* 39, No. 4 (avril 1943), 8, 43-45.

———. *Ma Vache Bossie.* Montréal: Les Editions Leméac, Inc. 1976.

———. "Un Vagabond frappe à notre porte." *Amérique Française* (janvier 1946), pp. 29-51.

———. "La Vallée Houdou." *Amérique Française* (février 1945), pp. 4-10.

———. "Une Voile dans la nuit." *Le Bulletin des Agriculteurs,* 40, No. 5 (mai 1944), 9, 49, 53.

———. "Voyage en Ungava." In Gagné, Marc. "*La Rivière sans repos* de Gabrielle Roy: Etude mythocritique." *Revue de l'Université d'Ottawa,* 46, No. 3 (juillet-septembre 1976), 369-383.

———. *Where Nests the Water Hen.* Trans. Harry L. Binsse. Introd. Gordon Roper. New Canadian Library, No. 25. Toronto: McClelland and Stewart Limited, 1970.

———. *Windflower.* Trans. Joyce Marshall. Introd. Lorraine McMullen, 1970; rpt. New Canadian Library, No. 120. Toronto: McClelland and Stewart Limited, 1975.

Roy, Marie-Anna A. *Le Miroir du passé.* Collection Littérature d'Amérique. Montréal: Editions Québec/Amérique, 1979.

Roy, P.-E. "Gabrielle Roy ou la difficulté de s'ajuster à la réalité." *Lectures,* N S 2, No. 3 (novembre 1964), 55-61.

Sainte-Marie-Eleuthère, Soeur. *La Mère dans le roman canadien-français.* Québec: Les Presses de l'Université Laval, 1964.

Saint-Pierre, Annette. *Gabrielle Roy: Sous le signe du rêve.* Saint-Boniface, Manitoba: Editions du Blé, 1975.

Savoie, Guy. "Le Réalisme du cadre spatio-temporel de *Bonheur d'occasion.*" Thesis. Université Laval 1972.

Scherer, Jacques. *Le "Livre" de Mallarmé: Premières Recherches sur des documents inédits.* Préface Henri Mondor. Paris: Gallimard, 1957.

Shek, Ben. "L'Espace et la description symbolique dans les romans 'montréalais' de Gabrielle Roy." *Liberté,* 13i (1971), 78-96.

Sirois, Antoine. "Costume, maquillage et bijoux dans *Bonheur d'occasion.*" *Présence Francophone,* No. 18 (printemps 1979), pp. 159-163.

———. *Montréal dans le roman canadien.* Montréal: Marcel Didier, 1968.

Socken, Paul. "Art and the Artist in Gabrielle Roy's Works." *Revue de l'Université d'Ottawa,* 45 (1975), 344-350.

———. *Concordance de* Bonheur d'occasion *de Gabrielle Roy.* Waterloo, Ontario: University of Waterloo Press, 1982.

------. *Gabrielle Roy: An Annotated Bibliography.* Downsview, Ontario: ECW Press, 1979.

------. "Gabrielle Roy as Journalist." *Canadian Modern Language Review,* 30, No. 2 (January 1974), 96-100.

------. "L'Harmonie dans l'oeuvre de Gabrielle Roy." *Travaux de Linguistique et de Littérature* (Université de Strasbourg), 15, No. 2 (1977), 275-292.

------. "The Influence of Physical and Social Environment on Character in the Novels of Gabrielle Roy." *DAI,* 38 (December 1977), 3489A-3490A (University of Toronto).

------. " 'Le Pays de l'amour' in the Works of Gabrielle Roy." *Revue de l'Université d'Ottawa,* 46, No. 3 (juillet-septembre 1976), 309-323.

------. "Use of Language in *Bonheur d'occasion:* A Case in Point." *Essays on Canadian Writing,* No. 11 (Summer 1978), pp. 66-71.

Soumade, F. "*La Montagne secrète.*" *La Revue de l'Université Laval,* 16, No. 5 (janvier 1962), 449-451.

Srabian de Fabry, Anne. "A la recherche de l'ironie perdue chez Gabrielle Roy et Flaubert." *Présence Francophone,* 11 (1975), 89-104.

Sutherland, Ronald. *The New Hero: Essays in Comparative Quebec/Canadian Literature.* Toronto: Macmillan of Canada, 1977.

------. *Second Image: Comparative Studies in Quebec/Canadian Literature.* Don Mills, Ontario: New Press, 1971.

Sylvestre, Guy. "*Alexandre Chenevert.*" *Nouvelle Revue canadienne,* 3, No. 3 (avril-mai 1956), 155-156.

------. "Aspects de notre roman." *L'Action Universitaire,* 14, No. 1 (octobre 1947), 18-34.

------. "Réflexions sur notre roman." *Culture,* 12, No. 3 (septembre 1951), 227-246.

Thério, Adrien. "Le Portrait du père dans *Rue Deschambault* de Gabrielle Roy." *Livres et Auteurs Québécois* (1969), pp. 237-243.

Urbas, Jeannette. "Equations and Flutes." *Journal of Canadian Fiction,* 1, ii (1972), 69-73.

------. "Gabrielle Roy et l'acte de créer." *Journal of Canadian Fiction,* 1, iv (1972), 51-54.

Vachon, Georges-André. "L'Espace politique et social dans le roman québécois." *Recherches Sociographiques,* 7, No. 3 (septembre-décembre 1966), 261-273.

------. "Une Tradition à inventer." In *Littérature canadienne-française.* Montréal: Presses de l'Université de Montréal, 1969.

Vanasse, A. "Vers une solitude désespérante." *L'Action Nationale,* 55, No. 7 (mars 1966), 844-851.

Vuong-Riddick, Thuong. "Aspects du monde de Gabrielle Roy: *La Rivière sans repos* (1970), *Cet Eté qui chantait* (1972), *Un Jardin au bout du monde* (1975)." *Les Lettres Québécoises,* No. 7 (août-septembre 1977), pp. 47-50.

Warwick, Jack. *L'Appel du nord dans la littérature canadienne-française.* Trans. Jean Simard. Collection Constantes. Montréal: Editions Hurtubise HMH, 1972.

Whitfield, Agnès. "*Alexandre Chenevert:* Cercle vicieux et évasions manquées." *Voix et Images du Pays,* 8 (1974), 107-125.

Wyczynski, Paul, Bernard, Julien, Jean Ménard et Réjean Robidoux, eds. *Le Roman canadien-français: Evolution-témoignage-bibliographie.* Archives des lettres canadiennes. Tome III. Montréal: Fides, 1977.